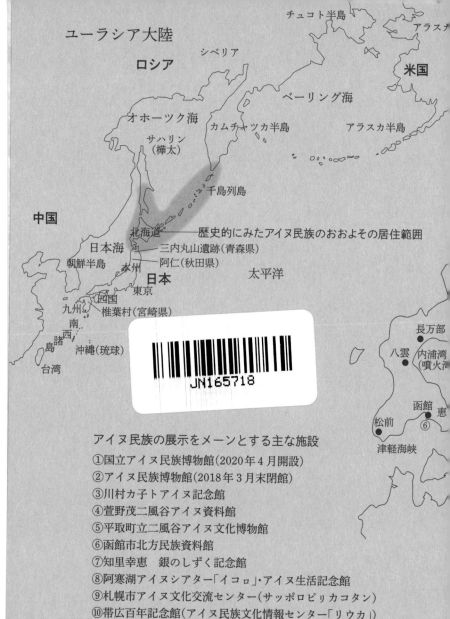

ルウンペ（木綿衣）＝
加藤シヅエさん製作、
協力：津田命子さん
ruunpe (a cotton garment with narrow strips of appliqué) handmade by Ms. Katō Shizue=Thanks to cooperation of Tsuda Nobuko-Fuci

アットゥシ（樹皮衣）＝
太田栄子さん製作、
協力：津田命子さん
attus (a garment made of elm-*Ulmus laciniata*-bark) handmade by Ōta Eiko=Thanks to cooperation of Tsuda Nobuko-Fuci

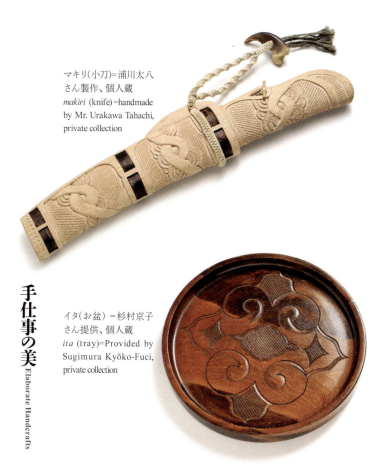

マキリ(小刀)＝浦川太八
さん製作、個人蔵
makiri (knife)=handmade
by Mr. Urakawa Tahachi,
private collection

イタ(お盆)＝杉村京子
さん提供、個人蔵
ita (tray)=Provided by
Sugimura Kyōko-Fuci,
private collection

手仕事の美 Elaborate Handcrafts

彫刻● Wood Carving

儀式に使う祭具イクパスイや、山行に必需品のマキリ（小刀）の柄や鞘、お盆などに精巧な文様が施された。イクパスイにはクマや舟などを立体的に彫ることもある。近年は、伝統にとらわれない自由な発想のアート作品も多く生み出されている。
Characteristic elaborate patterns have been carved on handles and sheaths of knives, trays, and *ikupasuy*, utensils for religious rites. Sometimes miniature bears or boats are sculpted on *ikupasuy*. Nowadays, Ainu wood carvers also create modern artworks.

芸能・口承 Performing Arts and Oral Tradition

舞台芸術 ● Theatrical art

阿寒湖アイヌシアター「イコロ」で、2019年3月からアイヌ民族の古式舞踊や現代舞踏とコンピューターグラフィックス（CG）映像を組み合わせた創作舞台「阿寒ユーカラ『ロストカムイ』」の上演が始まった。近代に入って絶滅したオオカミへのアイヌ民族の畏敬の念や世界観を伝える。

A creative performance *Akan Yukar 'Lost Kamuy'* started in March 2019 at the Akanko Ainu Theater 'Ikor' beside Lake Akan. The Ainu people have regarded the wolf as a *kamuy* (god, deity). However, wolves were made extinct in the modern period in Japan, including Hokkaido. Combining Ainu traditional dance, contemporary dance, and computer graphic image, this program shows how deeply the Ainu have revered wolves.

サロルンチカプリムセ
(鶴の踊り)白老
＝旧アイヌ民族博物館
所蔵資料
sarorun-cicap-rimse
(Dancing of Cranes) in
Shiraoi=Collection of
former Ainu Museum.

踊り　● Dancing

イオマンテ(霊送り儀礼)のような大きな儀式では神々に感謝を表し、喜んでもらうための踊りがつきものだった。ツルの踊りなど生き物の動きを模したものや弓の舞い、剣の舞いといった生業・儀礼に根ざしたもの、複数の女性が一人の男性を奪い合う余興的なものなど多彩なレパートリーがある。

Dancing is indispensable at important rituals such as the *iomante*, the so-called 'bear festival,' to express gratitude to the gods. Like the dance of the crane, some imitate wild animals. Ainu also have dances based on livelihood/rituals, such as, for example, dances with bows and dances with swords. Some performances add to the fun of banquet, such as the dance in which several women scramble for a sexy man.

姉妹デュオ「カピウ&アパッポ」(2011年、釧路ジス・イズでのコンサート。右が郷右近富貴子さん、左が床絵美さん) =©2016 office+studio T.P.S
Sister Duo "Kapiw & Apappo" (Kushiro Concert at a cafe "This Is" in 2011. Gōukon Fukiko (right) and Toko Emi)©2016 office+studio T.P.S

ムックリの演奏、白老=旧アイヌ民族博物館所蔵資料
Performance of *mukkur* in Shiraoi =Collection of former Ainu Museum

歌と楽器演奏 ● Singing and instrumental music

多くの踊りに歌はつきもので、単独で聞かせることもあった。特徴的なスタイルに、女性が漆器シントコの蓋(ふた)を囲んで手を付いてリズムを取りながら輪唱していくウポポがある。楽器にはムックリと呼ばれるネマガリダケ(チシマザサ)を素材にした口琴や五弦琴のトンコリがある。

Dancing is normally accompanied by singing. Some songs are also independently sung. In one characteristic genre of Ainu songs called *upopo*, singing in a circular canon, several women sit around the round lid of a *sintoko* (a large lacquer ware) and sing while tapping the lid in staggered rhythm. Ainu play the *mukkur*, a mouth harp made of bamboo grass *(Sasa kurilensis)* and a stringed instrument from Sakhalin having five strings called the *tonkori*.

西川北洋筆「明治初期アイヌ風俗絵図」
＝函館市中央図書館蔵
Meijishoki Ainu Fūzoku Ezu (Picture of Ainu Customs at the beginning of the Meiji period) painted by Nishikawa Hokuyō=Collection of Hakodate Main Library

芸能・口承 Performing Arts and Oral Tradition

語り ● Oral tradition

英雄叙事詩、神謡、散文説話など各ジャンルでたくさんの口承が伝えられ、家庭内や集まり、儀式などで披露された。英雄叙事詩は超人的な少年の冒険談、武勇伝が主で、神謡は神々が自身の経験や教訓、失敗談を一人称で語るという特徴がある。

Ainu people have handed down numerous oral traditions through the genres of heroic epics, tales of gods, stories narrated in prose style and so on. Tales have been narrated within the family, at meetings, and during rituals. Topics of heroic epics are mainly the adventures and battles of a superhuman boy. Tales of gods contain the experience, lessons, and failures of the gods in stories told in the first-person.

信仰 Spiritual Life

カムイ（神さま） ● *kamuy* (gods, deity, spiritual beings)

カムイは「自然神」と「人文神（人格神）」に二分される。自然神はさまざまで、野生動物や鳥、貝、大地、湖、樹木、雷をはじめとする自然現象、火、疱瘡（天然痘）などがカムイとみなされている。

Gods can be classified into "gods of nature" and "personified gods." There are various kinds of "gods of nature" such as wild animals, birds, shells, land, lakes, trees, natural phenomena like thunder, fire, smallpox and so on.

アイヌ、日本人、その世界

〈凡例〉

一、アイヌ語には日本語にない発音があるため、伝承者や言語学者が表記を工夫してきた。本書では普及しているカタカナ小文字表記（アコロイタク方式）を使っている。実際の発音は北海道新聞のインターネットサイト「アイヌ語発音講座紹介：どうしん電子版（北海道新聞）」で視聴、習得できる。

一、引用文ないし引用に準じた文中の（　）内は原文に元々あったもの、［　］内は本書の筆者（小坂洋右）が新たに加えた補足説明である。

一、引用文の一部は、本書の著者（小坂洋右）が現代文に直したりして、読みやすさを優先した。伝承されてきた物語は紙幅の関係で要約している。原典に当たれるよう、いずれも注に出典を付した。

一、引用文中の中略は「……」で表記している。

一、なお、英語版は日本語版の内容をやや絞り込んだダイジェスト版で、海外の人に分かりやすいように構成も一部変えている。

はじめに

古来、誕生は死を必要とした。

この地上も人間も、まだつくられていなかった遠い昔、天上界の重い位(くらい)の神さまたちが集まり、下界に有能な神々を送り込んで国土や動物、植物をつくることにした。国土がだんだん広くなるにつれて見通しがきかない所が出てくると、神々はフクロウ神が夜の見張りをする高い丘の上に丈夫な木をつくった。

そのチキサニ[ハルニレの木]はうら若く美しい姫神だったがゆえに、雷神に思いを寄せられる。姫神は火だるまになって、その美しい姿は永遠に地上から消え去った。が、その火の中から赤ん坊が誕生する。それが「人間くさい神さま[半神半人]」を意味するアイヌラックルだった。(注1)

火と木と死が生命を授け、それが人間の始祖となった——これがアイヌ民族の神話のあらましである。

一方、現存する日本最古の歴史書「古事記」では、オホゲツヒメからさまざまなおいしい食べ物を

3

供されたスサノオが、ヒメがそれを自身の口や鼻、尻から出しているのを覗き見て知り、汚いものを食べさせたと腹を立てて殺してしまう。殺されたヒメの体から生まれ出たのがカイコであり、稲であり、アワ、小豆、麦、大豆だった。カミムスヒ（神）はそれらの種を集めて人々の食べ物とした。

古事記のこの一節は、たとえて言えば、乱造や猥雑さと渾然一体となった「豊かさ」をいったん断ち切ることで、秩序立った「栽培」に変えるという行為にほかならない。

では、圧倒的な力を持ちながら、気まぐれで、理不尽な雷が木を焼き払いつつ生命を授けるアイヌ民族の神話的世界はどう読み解けるだろうか。

雷がもたらす山火事によって森は一時、焼け野原になり、死と静謐に支配される。だが、歳月によって森は必ず蘇る。長い目で見ると、雷は森林の交替と再生を促すのだ。これは「循環」という自然の摂理ともみなせる。

こうした始原にまつわる物語を比較するだけでも、どうも狩猟採集に生きてきたアイヌ民族と農耕社会を生きてきた日本人（和人）には、発想のうえで違いがあるような気がしてくる。となると、日本列島、特にアイヌ民族の故地であり、次第に和人との接触、移住をみた「北海道」の歴史はこうした二つの世界観のせめぎ合いと捉えることができるかもしれない。

一般に、狩猟採集社会は平等や分配に重きを置き、個人の能力や異才を認める側面が強いとされ、農耕社会、特に稲作民は計画的で集団主義。協調を大事にし、その分、異分子を許さない土壌があるとされる。が、果たしてアイヌ民族の社会、和人の社会もそれぞれ、そうした特質を持ってきたのだろうか。

ひとつだけ先取りして言えば、狩猟は命を奪う残酷な行為のように見えて、狩猟民は実際のところ、個々の命を大切に扱い、自分たちが土地や自然環境とつながっていることを日常的に意識しながら生きている。それは伝統的なアイヌ民族の生き方にも当てはまる。

本書の狙いは、狩猟採集・漁撈、そして交易に生きてきたアイヌ民族の精神世界や伝承に分け入りつつ、縄文時代という狩猟採集社会から弥生時代以降、農耕社会に転じて久しい和人との違いを浮き彫りにしていくところにある。その対比を通して、自然と人のかかわりは本来、どうあるべきか、私たちは何を失い、それをどうやって取り戻すべきなのか、その道筋が見えてくるはずである。また、生き方や社会の違いもあって、両者の「出会い」には歴史的に不幸な戦いや差別がつきまとったが、その根底に何があったのか、見つめ直すことで新たな関係づくりも提起したい。

本題に入る前に、アイヌ民族の特徴をかいつまんで挙げておく。

第一に、アイヌ民族は北海道を中心とする日本列島北部から樺太(サハリン)南部、千島列島全域、カムチャツカ半島南部に至る範囲に暮らしてきた先住民族である。狩猟採集に加えて、サケ・マスの漁撈や毛皮などの交易も盛んに行ってきた。第二に、畏怖される強い存在であるヒグマが北海道などには生息している。アイヌ民族にとって、クマは尊敬に値する強い神さまで、儀式において丁重にもてなす一方で、生活のために闘い、倒す相手でもあった。畏れを抱かせる生き物がいることが、その精神文化に多大な影響を与え、文化に複雑さと深みをもたらしてきたと私は考えている。

第三にはたくさんの口承伝承が音声資料や筆録で残されていて、それを通じて世界観をうかがい知ることができる。第四には、強力な国家をすでに千三百年前に樹立した和人と隣り合わせに生き

てきたことだ。のち、一七一一年にロシア帝国が千島列島に進出すると、北部千島、中部千島に暮らすアイヌ民族はロシアの支配下に置かれ、その結果、アイヌ民族は、日本とロシアの両大国から同化政策によって言葉や文化を奪われていくことになる。苦難続きの中で、それでも独自の文化は維持されてきた。ただし、いまは狩猟で生きる人はほとんどいなくなり、和人と変わらない現代的生活を送っている。章を追って明らかにしていくが、現代においても、文化を受け継ぎ、伝統的な精神を持っている人は数多くいる。

例えば、古い布を組み合わせてシマフクロウなどをあしらい、物語世界を表現している宇梶静江さんは「人間だけが偉いわけではない。自然を汚して私たちは生きてはいけない。そのことをアイヌの人たちはよく知っている。朝夕、私は心の中でこう話しかけています。『川の神さまありがとう』『土の神さまありがとう』『空の神さまありがとう』と……」などと語る。

北海道の自然環境についても、最小限のことを知っておいてもらいたい。冬にはたくさんの雪が降り、北部や東部の寒さの厳しい地域では気温が氷点下二〇度から三〇度にも下がる。こうした気候のもと、ヒグマのほかキツネやシカ、タヌキ、野ウサギ、シマフクロウやタンチョウ、オオワシがすみ、海にはアザラシやクジラ、シャチ、トドや、まれにラッコの姿が見られる。

北海道の人類史で人の大規模な交替の痕跡が認められないことから、アイヌ民族のルーツを大きな流れでみれば、一万五千年前から約二三〇〇年前にかけて一万年の長きにわたって持続した縄文人にまでさかのぼるに違いない。生き物の魂が再生し、命が循環するという考えを持つ点、集団間の組織的な戦闘によって権力を集中、拡大しようとする社会的志向がなかった点で、アイヌ民族

6

の精神文化や社会構造には縄文文化と共通する部分がある。狩猟採集民が培ってきた生き方、ものの見方、言い換えれば「自然哲学」は私たちに複眼的な視点を与えてくれるばかりか、行きづまった現代社会に持続的で調和的な方向づけをするためのヒントを与えてくれるのではなかろうか。

本書は、アイヌ民族と日本人の精神世界の違いに分け入り、双方の関係史などを記録や証言、口承伝承をもとに俯瞰する第一部「人々は聴き　大地は見てきた」と、北海道を中心に国内外の各地を巡り、現代を生きるアイヌ民族との出会いをルポルタージュ風にまとめた第二部「世界は変わった　でも、生きていく」の二部構成で展開する。

アイヌ、日本人、その世界＊目次

はじめに——3

第一部　人々は聴き　大地は見てきた——13

一章　日本昔話はなぜ「野生」を拒むのか——14
　猿の婿殿(むこどの)を殺してハッピーエンド——14
　カッコウの神さまと結婚するアイヌ民話——16
　獲ったクマには祈りを捧げる——18
　稲作民と狩猟民　精神文化のせめぎ合い——20

二章　命を奪うがゆえに
　いたずらしたキツネに謝る父親——24
　魂は肉体から離れて生きられる——28
　「私は死んで息子を探し出せました」——30
　和人には生き返らせる力がない——32

命を奪う重み伝える物語——36

三章　命を奪われるがゆえに

クマの生態を熟知し、冬眠中に穴猟——42

襲って来たクマの性格を判定——45

犠牲者は「メスグマに愛された」——48

魂の世界で人は野生動物と添い遂げられる

獲物になりきって狩りをするハンター——51

ある日、家の裏にクマの巣穴が——53

人間がクマとシャチの間を取り持つ——55

育てたクマの霊を神々の世界に帰す日——57

——61

四章　日本人はいつから「狩猟民の心」を失ったのか

秋田の阿仁にマタギを訪ねる——66

巻き狩りでクマを獲る猟師集団——66

かつては日本人にも野生動物との婚姻譚——71

日本列島の古い形を残すのは「アイヌ民話」——74

和人の蝦夷地支配、アイヌ民族との衝突——77

松浦武四郎が告発した悲劇の女性たち——79

一二歳の少年までも強制労働に——84

開拓使を辞めた良心の役人たち——86

五章　知里幸恵「神謡集」という贈り物

「神はいつまで私たちを苦しめるのでしょうか」——90

友人の死　悲惨すぎる人生——92

「北海道は、先祖の自由の大地でした」——98

抵抗感を持ちつつ、橋渡し役に——99

いつか和人と肩を並べる日がくる——103

「結婚不可」の残酷な宣告——106

第二部　世界は変わった　でも、生きていく

一章　「喪失」の時代の先住民族社会

知里幸恵　銀のしずく記念館の誕生——112
あえて稲作を受け入れなかった可能性——114
「代わりに失うものがあるかもしれない」——116
「縄文」は一万年の持続社会——120
先住民族が「クニ」を造らなかった理由(わけ)——123
人間、土地、動物——互いの切ってはならない関係——126
北米にも共通の物語——131

二章　未来をつかむための闘い

目の前で逮捕された父親——138
「取り締まりは餓死者を出しかねない」——140
サケを迎える儀式、一〇〇年ぶりの復活——142
「祖先と同じに捕りたいだけなんだ」——145
遺骨はいまだ大学の保管庫に——150
二〇一七年、ドイツからの遺骨返還——153
先行国に水を開けられる先住民族政策——155
「あの人たちは見捨てないから」——158

三章 アイヌ文化への再評価

福島原発事故からの逃避行────165
アイヌ芸能が魅力的に映る時代────167
危機言語「アイヌ語」の復活は?────170
シラッチセ──狩猟を肌で感じられる場所────174
生き物と人間の信じ難い「助け合い」────179
「あなたには三億人の同胞がいる」────183

あとがき────188
年表：アイヌ民族をめぐる主な出来事────194
註────198
参考文献────223

第一部 **人々は聴き　大地は見てきた**

一章　日本昔話はなぜ「野生」を拒むのか

猿の婿殿を殺してハッピーエンド

日本昔話を代表する「鶴の恩返し」は、日本人の優しさと、哀しい社会の掟が相混じり合ったお話だ。

おじいさんが、罠にかかって苦しむ鶴を助けてやるところから話は始まる。その後、美しい娘がおじいさん、おばあさんを訪ねて来る。娘が「私は機を織りますが、決してのぞかないでください」と戒めたのに、おじいさんは部屋をのぞいてしまい、びっくり仰天。あの日助けた鶴が、自分の羽根を抜いては機を織っているではないか。「姿を見られてしまっては、もうこの家に居続けるわけにはいきません」。娘は「ご恩は一生忘れません」と感謝しつつ、鶴の姿に戻って飛び去っていく──。

日本人で「なぜ鶴はおじいさん、おばあさんのもとを去らなくてはいけないの？」と問いただす人はほとんどいないだろう。そこから、日本人の感覚の中には「正体を見破られた野生動物は、われわれ人間とは一緒に暮らせない」という前提があることが分かる。それはなぜか──。

日本昔話が生まれた里山は、お百姓さんたちが肩を寄せ合い、田んぼや畑を耕して暮らす村落だった。農耕民にとっては、割り当てられた自分の農地こそが命である。となると、おのずと「自分の持ち場」と「その外側」で線引きをせざるを得ない。よそ者に入り込んでもらっては困るという発想が生まれてくる。

とはいっても、里山に暮らしていれば野生動物との接触は避けられない。動物たちは周縁に居着き、得てして作物をちょうだいするために里に下りてくるからだ。そうなればなおさら、頑として生活圏を守らなくてはならないという意識が強まる。作物や農地を荒らす生き物と、農業で生きる自分たちは「共存できない」のだ。

「鶴の恩返し」からうかがえる里山集落の人々の自然観は、そんなふうにひもとける。だから、正体を見られた鶴がおじいさんたちのもとを去っていく結末を、子どもたちも、読み聞かせた親の側も、ごく自然な展開として受け入れてきたとも言える。

日本昔話の「猿の婿入り」はもっとすごい。相手が猿とはいえ、自分の婿さまを殺してしまうのだから。

話はこうだ。ある日、おじいさんが畑仕事をしていると猿が出てきた。「手伝ってくれ。娘を一人嫁にやるから」と頼むと手伝ってくれた。おじいさんが「猿の嫁になってくれないか」と手を上げる。娘に懇願すると、三番目の娘が「なら、銀のかんざしと水がめをください」と手を上げる。娘は迎えに来た猿に水がめを背負わせ、大きな堤のふちでかんざしを水中に落とし、「拾ってください」と促して、

15　一章　日本昔話はなぜ「野生」を拒むのか

拾おうとした途端、猿を後ろから押して水に落とす。水がめに水がたまって猿は溺れ死に、娘は家に帰って親子仲良く暮らした——という筋書きだ。

こと動物との結婚に関して言えば、「野生」を最後は排除して終わる展開が日本昔話ではほとんどで、日本昔話の研究者は「動物婚は殺されて終わる場合が圧倒的だが、動物嫁は殺されることはなく、正体を見られたので自分から去る、または、正体を知った人間が追いだすという終わり方をしている」と結論づけている。

カッコウの神さまと結婚するアイヌ民話

では、狩猟を伝統としてきたアイヌ民族の物語はどうなのか。

その一つ、「カッコウの妻になった娘」は、盗賊に襲われた一家の父親が、生後間もない娘をひしにくくりつけ、見守ってくれるよう神々に頼んで妻とともに殺されてしまう場面から始まる。娘はカッコウの神さまに命を救われ、その妹として育てられ、ついには結婚してその妻になる。

ところが、神さまがずっと人間と一緒にいるわけにはいかず、ある日、カッコウ神である夫は「六年間、自分を偲んで暮らせば人間の若者が訪ねてくるから、結婚して最初に生まれる男の子は私の息子と思って、二人目、三人目の子はその若者の子として育ててくれ。そのうち、お前は死ぬだろうから、そうしたらお前の魂を私は受け取って、すばらしい夫婦、本当の夫婦生活を神の国で送ることになるだろう」と言い残して神々の世界に帰って行く。娘が言いつけを守ると、カッコウ神の言づ

第一部　人々は聴き　大地は見てきた　16

て通りのことが実現していく——というストーリーだ。

日本昔話の「鶴の恩返し」では、おじいさん、つまり人間の側が掟を破ったことによって娘（鶴）が人間界を去らなくてはならなくなる。一方、アイヌ民族の「カッコウの妻になった娘」の物語は、人間の娘がカッコウ神の言いつけを信じ、実行することで、最後はカッコウ神と神々の世界で再び結ばれて本当の結婚をする展開になっている。鶴が人間の元を去らなくてはならない日本昔話とは対照的に、アイヌ民族の物語では「異種」の壁を越え、神としての野生の生き物と人間が最後の最後に結婚を成就する。

ここから、農耕民の物語世界と狩猟民の物語世界、言葉を変えれば互いの世界観、精神文化が根本において異なっていることが分かってもらえるだろう。

アイヌ民族の伝承にはクマの神さまと結婚するお話もある。

母親と二人で暮らしていた娘がクマ神に見初められ、男の子と女の子を産み落とす。ところが、ある日、クマ神が「私には神々の国に妻となるはずの女がいるのだ。一緒になる気がしないできたが、親父が一緒になれという。だから従うが、そのうちりっぱな男がやって来るから、お前はその男と結婚して人間の子孫をつくってくれ」と切り出す。クマ神は続けて「私はカムイモシリ〔神々の国〕ではどうやっても子供ができず、妻が子供を欲しがるだろうから、そのうちに〔お前との間にできた〕私の息子をカムイモシリに連れて行く。そうすれば親父も妻も喜んで、その母親であるおまえに敬意を払うだろうから、おまえがまだ年取らないうちにカムイモシリに連れて行く。そこで、本

当の結婚、真の結婚生活をすることにしよう」と言い残し、実際そのようになっていくという筋だ。[注5]

　人間の娘が、一方はカッコウ神と、もう一方はクマ神と結婚する二つの伝承からは、狩猟に生きてきたアイヌ民族にとって、野生動物との結婚は、物語のうえではごく自然に受け入れられるものだと分かる。だが、物語から見えてくることはその一点にとどまらない。クマ神の物語を子どもに焦点を当てて捉え直すと、娘とクマ神の間に生まれた二人の子どものうち、男の子は神々の世界で、女の子は人間の世界でと、互いに別々の世界で暮らしていく将来が読み取れる。きょうだいが二つの世界に生きることで、神々の世界と人間の世界に最初に二人の子をもうけた女性は、人間界で人間の男性との間に子どもを増やし、その後、神々の世界でさらにクマ神と子どもを作るであろうから、母親である女性もまた両方の世界を仲介することになる。その結果、二つの世界のつながりはいっそう強固なものとなる。

　そう見ていくと、物語の骨子は、人間界と神々（野生の生き物）の世界をつなぐところにあるようにも思えてくる。別な言い方をすれば、神々と人間、人間と野生動物がお互いの緊密さを物語を通じて再確認しているのである。野生動物との間に一線を引くどころか、距離をできる限り縮めようとする姿勢がそこから読み取れる。頑として人間界の領域を守り続け、野生との境界を決して見失うことがない日本昔話との違いが、ここにきてますます鮮明になってくる。

獲ったクマには祈りを捧げる

第一部　人々は聴き　大地は見てきた　18

ここまではあくまで「お話」のなかの世界だった。だが、アイヌ民族が、実生活においても、同じまなざしを持って野生動物と向き合ってきたことを古老は教えてくれる。

その一人が、三六回ものクマ撃ち体験をつぶさに一つ一つ記憶にとどめ、エカシとしての尊敬を得ていた道東・白糠の根本与三郎エカシだ(注6)。エカシによれば、クマはカムイ〔神さま〕であり、獲った時には敬意と拝礼を欠かしてはならないのだという。

であれば、獲った数を人と比べたり、自慢したりするものではない。「和人〔日本人〕のなかには一人で五〇頭も獲ったと言っている人がいるけど、我々はコタン〔アイヌ集落〕で自分たちが分け合って食べるために獲るわけだから、昔はコタン全体で年に二頭か三頭。それしか獲らない」。獲れた時には火をおこし、メンバーのリーダー格が火の神さまを通じてヒグマの神に「よーく自分たちに授かって呉れた。これから里に下げてから大勢の村人と一緒になって、必ず盛大に天国〔神の国〕に送るから、今しばらく待っていてください」と祈りを捧げ、狩りを応援してくれたさまざまな神々にもお礼を伝えてほしいと火の神さまに依頼するという(注8)。

白糠の自宅で狩猟の経験談を語る根本与三郎エカシ
(撮影:小坂洋右)

このエピソードから、アイヌ民族は、たとえ狩りの対象となる野生動物に対しても、親近感や敬愛の情を抱いてきたことが分かる。それどころか、根本エカシの言葉からは、崇拝や信仰とも言うべき意識が伝わってくる。

「はじめに」でも述べたように、アイヌ民族はこんに

ち、狩猟だけで生きる人がほとんどいなくなり、日常の暮らしぶりは和人と変わらない。ただし、そのことは、世代を重ねるなかで培われてきた狩猟民的な発想が完全に消し去られたことを意味するわけではない。現代を生きるアイヌの人たちと話をしていても、自然・動植物への親近感や命を尊ぶ気持ち、環境破壊への憤りが読み取れることが多々ある。それはすなわち、狩猟採集という伝統的な生業に培われてきた心のありようが、一世代や二世代で消滅するものではないことを示している。

稲作民と狩猟民　精神文化のせめぎ合い

さて、農耕民の精神と狩猟民の精神の違いに話を戻そう。双方の物語を比較することで、互いの心象風景に相当の隔たりがあることが見て取れた。

とはいえ、長大な人類史をひもとけば、弥生時代が始まる二三〇〇年前まで、日本列島は全体が縄文文化、つまり狩猟・採集・漁撈をベースとした暮らし一色に染まっていた（地図1）。誰もが野生動物や川魚、海の魚、山菜、ドングリなどの木の実、貝をとって暮らしていたということだ。驚くべきことに、そうした時代は一万年も継続した。だから、狩猟採集という生き方やそこから生まれた物の見方、考え方は、原日本人の基層を成すと考えて間違いない。

日本列島で片や農耕社会、片や狩猟社会へと大きく袂を分かったのが、弥生時代の始まりであり、それが二三〇〇年前という時期だった（表1参照）。

自然人類学者、埴原和郎の二重構造モデル（二重構造説）(注9)によれば、稲作技術を身につけた人々が

中国大陸から九州北部や中国地方に渡来して稲作が始まり、縄文時代は終わりを告げた。以来、千年の間に少なく見積もって九万四千人、最大で一五〇万人にも及ぶ渡来人が移住し、在来の旧縄文系の人々と混血しながら稲作文化を日本列島に浸透させていったとされる（地図2）。

一〇万人から一五〇万人もの渡来人と言えば、それはそれは大きなインパクトだったと容易に察しがつく。ただ、重要なのは、在来の縄文人と渡来人がすっぽり入れ替わったり、縄文人が滅ぼされたわけではないということだ。文化史で説明すれば、狩猟民の心を持っていた集団や社会が、稲作に転じたことで農耕民のそれに次第に置き換わっていったと言えるだろう。

それでも、稲作の広がりは本州の北端までで、津軽海峡を渡ることはなかった。日本列島のうち、北海道だけは弥生時代以降も縄文時代と変わらない狩猟採集に小規模な作物栽培が加わる暮らしが続いたのである。その後、北方から渡来した海洋民族オホーツク文化人（オホーツク人）の影響も受けつつ、一二、三世紀から津軽海峡を隔てて南側の稲作農耕文化圏と北側の狩猟採集文化圏の境界が、じわじわと崩れていく。和人が北海道の南端に少しずつ足がかりをつくり、北海道全域から、さらには樺太、南千島へと影響力を強めていくからだ。決定的な農耕・稲作の波が産業化、工業化とともに押し寄せたのは、今から一五〇年前（地図3）。明治政府による北海道の編入からだった。政府は和人の農民を大量に移住させるとともに、大資本と結んで炭鉱業や製鉄業、造船業、製紙業などを次々興（おこ）していく。先住のアイヌ民族に対しては、生業や文化・言葉を奪い、農業に駆り立てる同化政策を推し進めた。

不幸な時代は長きにわたった。今なお完全に解消されたとは言い難いなか、アイヌ民族の復権と真の共生を進めるためには、先述したような生業の違い、自然観の違いに気づき、その根っこにある精神文化を理解することが欠かせない。本書の目的の一端もまた、そこにある。

時代	日本の年代	北海道の年代	
500BCE	縄文時代（15000年前〜2300年前）		
紀元	弥生時代 (2300年前〜 紀元3世紀)	続縄文時代 (2300年前〜7世紀)	
500CE	古墳時代 (3〜7世紀)		オホーツク文化期 (5〜10世紀)
	奈良時代(710年〜)	擦文時代 (7〜13世紀)	
1000CE	平安時代 (794年〜)		
	鎌倉時代 (1185年〜)		
1500CE	室町時代 (1338年〜)	アイヌ文化期 (13世紀〜)	
	江戸時代 (1603年〜)		
	近現代(1868年〜)		

表1　日本（北海道を除く）と北海道の時代区分

読み手に、アイヌ民族の伝統文化や世界観を知ってもらうこと。それは「精神的に満ち足りた生き方とは何か」について思い巡らすことにもなるはずだ。

ということで、次章以降、アイヌ民族の自然観や世界観を、エピソードや物語をつてに伝えていく。しばし、お付き合い願いたい。

23　一章　日本昔話はなぜ「野生」を拒むのか

二章　命を奪うがゆえに

いたずらしたキツネに謝る父親

山中で炭焼きをしていたアイヌ民族の父子がある日、木を伐りに行くと、前日、使ったあと、きちんとしまってあったはずのノコギリやマサカリがばらばらに散らばっている。見ると、雪の上にキツネの足跡が点々とついており、マサカリの柄にはキツネの歯形もついていた。誰がどうみても、キツネの仕業である。

こういう場合、たいていの人はキツネにいまいましさを感じ、気性の激しい人ならば「あの野郎」ぐらいの罵声を発するかもしれない。

ところが、父親にはそんな発想は、はなからなかったようだ。まだ少年期の息子の前で枯れ枝を集めて火を焚き、その火のそばにあぐらをかいて座り、おもむろに神々に礼拝を始めたのである。

「アイヌネヤッカ　カムイネヤッカ　ウレシパネマヌプ……」

アイヌ〔人間〕である私は、子供を育てるため、お金というものを欲しいがために、こうして

静かな山、山のふところ深くはいりこんで立木を伐り、山に住んでおられる諸々の神のお住居や庭を荒らしていることは、本当に心苦しいことであります。

けれども神も人間も同じことで、私にも大勢の子供がいます。その子供たちに食べ物を食べさせて、ひもじい思いをさせないためには、静かな山へ来て働かなければなりません。神よ、そのことをお考えくださって、どうぞアイヌの行為をお許し下さい。(注1)。

キツネの悪さに怒るどころか、自分たちが神々である野生動物の暮らす領域に入って活動していることを「お許しください」と謝り、神々に寛大な計らいを希う。これがその時、父親が取った行動だった。

これは実話である。日高・平取町二風谷のアイヌ文化伝承者、萱野茂エカシ（一九二六～二〇〇六年）が回想記『おれの二風谷』に、自身の幼少期の体験として書き残している。時は戦時中である。キツネは「足の軽い神さま」を意味するケマコシネカムイなどの呼び名で神々の座の一角を占めている。だからそもそも軽々しくは扱えないが、神々に敬意を表するばかりでなく、むしろ「山に入っている自分たちをお許しください」と神々に寛容な対応を求めたのが父親の拝礼だったのである。そこから「自然を畏れ、その前にかしこまる」というアイヌ民族の基本的態度が読み取れる。

二章　命を奪うがゆえに

「山に入る」という神々の領域への立ち入りだけでも「済まない」という気持ちを抱くのであれば、クマを獲る、シカを獲るとなれば、なおさらであろうことは想像がつく。それは、命を直接的に奪う行為だからだ。しかも、クマのことをアイヌ民族は尊敬すべき神と見なしてきたのである。では、狩猟という行為は、どのように受け止められてきたのだろうか。まず、前章で触れた根本与三郎エカシの話に再度、耳を傾けてみよう。アイヌ民族が盛んにクマ猟を行っていた時代を知る最後の世代の一人だ。

「捕獲する動物は、自分の憂さ晴らしのための対象にしたり、苛め苦しめて快感を味わったり、捕獲頭数を競って地位や名誉を得るのではないし、人の社会への侵入者としての害獣として駆除するためのものでもなく、アイヌは、飽くまでも神が人に授けてくれた食材、食料としてみんなで食べ、僅かずつでも分け合って、食事できることに感謝する対象物であるということを、礼木（れいき）［宅四郎］叔父から教えられた。

だから、必要以外には、むやみに獲るものではないし、死に当たっては、可能な限り苦しまずに、安楽且つ、確実に死を迎えるように、心臓や頭を狙い、必ず止（とど）めを撃つことにしている。従って、神様から授かった肉を売ってぜんこ（金銭）にしようという考え方は昔のアイヌには一切なく、俺も礼木叔父も肉を売ったことはない」

ここで読み取れるのは、自然の恵みとそれを与えてくれる神々への感謝の念であり、恩恵を平等に分け合うという狩猟民に共通する特質である。

雪に覆われた山に猟に入る姉崎等さん（渡部さゆりさん提供）

クマ撃ちが盛んだった時代を生きたもう一人、千歳の姉崎等エカシ[注2]もこんな談話を残している。

「私はやっぱり一つの命をもらって恩恵をいただいたという感謝の気持ちはあったですよ。クマでなくても小さな動物でもそうです。小さな動物にはイナウ[木幣][注3]〔木を削ってつくる祭具、神々への供物〕を作るというようなことはしなかったですが、米粒をあげて祭ってやることはしました。……ハンターは、動物の命を取るんですから、嬉しいことはないんですよ。リスのような小動物だと、助けてくれといわんばかりに手を合わせて拝むようにするんです。

それでもハンターは銃を向けて落として、ものの命を取ってきて自分たちの生活を潤しているんだから、感謝の気持ちは持たなければならない。クマを招待するにしても人間と同じで、うわべだけの招待だったらクマも嬉しくはないですよ。心のよい人の家に招待されたいという話があるの

27　二章　命を奪うがゆえに

は、人間の心を正しく運べよ、とアイヌは考えたからだと思います」(注4)

単独で約四〇頭、仲間と約二〇頭ものクマを獲ってきた経験者の談だけに、姉崎エカシの話は何とも分かりやすく、説得力がある。

魂は肉体から離れて生きられる

だが、一つだけ、引っかかる言葉がある。「うわべだけの招待だったらクマも嬉しくはないですよ」というひと言だ。姉崎さんはクマを殺しているのである。なのに、「招待する」というのはいかなる意味で言っているのか。

実は、アイヌ民族は伝統的にこう考えてきた。神々（カムイ）はふだんは神々の国（カムイモシリ）に住んでいて、時に人間界（アイヌモシリ）に降りてくるのだが、その時、肉と毛皮をお土産に身につけてくる。カムイは「この人こそ、自分が招かれるのにふさわしい人物だ」と見込んだ男性の矢や弾を自ら受け取ってその家の客人となる。

つまり、獲られた側からすれば「招かれる」ことになるし、獲った（矢を受け取ってもらえた）側からすれば「自分を認めてくださったカムイを招く」ことになる。そして、獲った人は、カムイに認めてもらったわけだから、カムイへの感謝を表すために、宴を催し、神々への祈り（カムイノミ）を捧げ、人間界のお土産をたくさん持たせて神々の国に帰ってもらう。

すなわち、アイヌ民族にとって、クマを狩ることは、自分が狩猟の技にいかに長け、クマを倒せるほど強いかを見せつける場ではなく、人間とクマ（カムイ）の互いのつながりを再確認する行為には

第一部　人々は聴き　大地は見てきた　28

かならないのである。

ただ、ここでむしろ不思議さが増した人もいるだろう。「殺されたのに、なぜクマは神々の国に帰ることができるのか」と。そこがまさに狩猟民の狩猟民たるゆえんの発想なのだ。彼らは、魂（霊）と肉体は別ものと考えている。魂はあくまで肉体をお土産として身につけてくるのであって、肉体を残し置いても魂は魂として生き残っている。

だから、アイヌ民族の伝承には、死後、自分の両耳の間に座って、死んだ自分の体や霊を送る儀式、人間の場合、自分自身のお葬式の様子を見ている場面が出てくる。

例えば、「気がつくと、山ほどの大きさの熊〔自分〕の屍が長々と伸びていて、我輩〔の魂〕はその耳の間に座っていた。噂に高いウラシペッの首長が、二人の若者を従えて我輩に拝礼していた」といった具合に……。

魂と肉体を別々のものと考えていて、分離できるという発想があるからこそ、こうした情景描写がなされ、アイヌ民族の間では何の違和感もなく受け止められてきたのである。

実生活でも、山でクマを獲ったものの、夕暮れ時などで条件が悪く、猟小屋や集落（コタン）に下ろせない時には、翌日戻って来るまでクマの霊が一人で寂しくないようにと、木を削って「話し相手の神〔ネウサラカムイ〕」を作り、その場に置いていくことも行われた。こうした配慮もまた、霊が肉体から離れて「死後」も存在するということでは、人間も同じだ。

肉体と霊（魂）が分離できるという自然観の現れだ。

かつては、人が亡くなった時には、あの世でも生前と同じ生活を送れるよう、生活道具や、時に家

29　二章　命を奪うがゆえに

も持たせてやることを忘れなかった。あの世はこの世と正反対で、壊された道具や、焼かれた家が、りっぱに使える形で再生すると考えられているから、わざと壊したり、焼いたりして本人の元に送り届けた。また、持ち主が健在でも、祭具や道具が使い古されて、役割を終えたと判断されると、イワクテという送りの儀式を通してその魂が神々の国に帰された。こうした習慣からは、道具などの「物」もまた魂を宿しているという発想がうかがえる。

「私は死んで息子を探し出せました」

口承伝承にも、こうした魂の分離という発想が明確に読み取れるものがある。

「山姥にさらわれた石狩人の物語」は、石狩の村長が、妻に子どもができないので、同じ集落の女性を第二夫人として迎えたところ、男の子が生まれ、三人でかわいがりながら育てる場面から始まる。だが、ある日、実の母である第二夫人がその子をおぶって山にオオウバユリの球根〔鱗茎〕を採りに行き、子どもを寝かせて掘っているうち、子どもが神隠しに遭ったように居なくなっていることに気づく。気が触れたようになって村に戻った女性は、食べ物も喉に通らないでとうとう死んでしまう。

この女性を主人公にするお話ならば、主人公が亡くなったこの場面で物語が終わるのがふつうだ。しかし、アイヌ伝承はここからが新たな展開の始まりとなる。

山姥にさらわれた男の子は、晴れた日には巨大な風倒木のおばあさんの上で、雨の日や夜はその下で泣き暮らしているうちに、体じゅうにキノコが生えてきた。ある日、死者の装束に身を固めた

女性の姿が目に留まる。女性は自分に近づくと、「お前は私の息子だ」と告げる。
「死んでみて、私は初めてお前のいるところが分かったので、早速ここまでやって来たのです。そ の気があるのなら、お父さんの元に帰ることができますよ」と、霊になった母親は息子に手順を教 え、男の子は教わった通り、母親がやって来た道をたどることで父親と再会し、跡継ぎとしてりっ ぱな狩人に育つ。そして「お前たちが子どもを持っても」決して山の中で 外であろうと畑の中で あろうと 幼い赤子や幼い子供を（ただで）お前たちが寝かせることはしてはならんぞ」と教訓を残 してこの世を去る。ここまできて物語は完結するのである。
物語で見逃せないのは、愛する子どもを見失った母親が、食事を摂らないことで死に、死んだこ とで魂が自由になって子どもの居場所を突き止めることができたという点だ。魂と肉体が別である ということはもとより、魂こそは自由に動き回れて、世界を広く見渡すことができるという含みが この物語にはある。
山菜の採集や漁撈、交易も生きる糧ではあったけれども、かつては頻繁に狩猟に出ていたアイヌ 民族の日常は、命を奪うことを宿命づけられてきた。そんななかで霊（魂）と肉体は別々に存在でき、 死んだ後も霊は残るばかりでなく、魂は神々の国に帰り、人間はあの世で同じような暮らしを続け るという世界観を身につけるに至った。そういう世界観は当然、伝承にも反映される。そうして、農 耕に生きる人々からみれば、やや荒唐無稽と思われるストーリーが生まれ、語られてきたのだ。

和人には生き返らせる力がない

もしも、魂と肉体が一体のものであるという感覚で生きていればどうなるか。死んだら、あるいは生き物を殺したらそれですべてが終わりであり、生命の循環はそこで断ち切られ、あの世での新たな生活や生き物の再訪は見込めない。

もっとも、それは悪いことばかりではない。日本昔話の「猿の婿入り」が、娘が猿を殺してめでたしめでたしとなるのは、猿が霊もろともその場で死んでしまうからであり、そうでなければ、悪霊の化け猿になっておじいさんの一家が猿に苦しめられる後日談が語られることになる。霊の再訪があり得ない前提こそが、「猿の婿入り」を成り立たせる根幹であり、その根底には霊が肉体もろとも死んでしまうという発想があるのである。

人の霊に関しては、日本語に怨霊（死霊、生き霊）や御霊という言葉があるように、和人社会にも霊が恨みを持ち続けて人にたたるとか、そうした霊でも鎮めれば一転、平穏を保つ側に回るとして、霊の存在が強く信じられていた時期はあった。ただ、それも一一八五年の壇ノ浦の戦いで平家が滅ぼされた源平の合戦や、南北朝の内乱期、足利尊氏への恨みを抱いたまま一三三九年に病没した後醍醐天皇の辺りまでで、戦国時代を境に怨霊への畏れは一気に弱まって今に至るとされている。

実はアイヌ民族は、和人の生き物観に魂の分離、霊の解放がないことを読み取っていた節がある。それを如実に表す物語が、主人公であるアオバトの神さまがアイヌの国から和人の国を目指して飛

び立つ「アオバトが小さくなったわけ」である。

アオバトの神は旅の途上、アイヌの人格神サマユンクルから「和人というものは紙の御幣〔アイヌ民族が木で作るイナウと対比している〕で神さまを祀るものですよ」と諭され、自分の客人になるよう勧められるが、その助言を振り払って和人の国にたどり着く。そして、矢を受け取り、和人の殿様の客人となるが、サマユンクルが言ったことは本当で、どうにも生き返ることができない。そして、「土とともに腐り、地とともに腐り、腐ったにおいが神さまたちを脅かし、私〔アオバトの神〕の風下を通るのを恐れて私の風上を通るようになった。そのうち、うじがわいて腐ったあげくに小さなアオバトとなって私は生き返った」という結末を迎える。

和人の風習に従っては、本来、生き返ることができるものも復活はかなわないというこの物語からは「和人は、生き物を再生する力を持っていない」というアイヌ民族の認識が見て取れる。物語にのっとれば、和人のやり方では、死んだ肉体に宿っていた魂は肉体とともに腐っていくだけなのだ。それはひるがえって、和人は魂を肉体から解き放つことができない、和人の自然観はそもそも魂と肉体の分離を前提としていないということになる。

これは「稲作農耕」と「狩猟採集」という生業の違いに根ざした、自然観の違いを反映したものであり、アイヌの側は和人との相違を明確に意識していたということにもなる。

ただし、現在の本州以南に魂の分離という発想を持っている人々がまったくいないわけではな

クマの巻き狩り前の神社参拝のため山に入る秋田県阿仁のマタギ衆（撮影：小坂洋右）

い。私が知る限り、その一集団は秋田や山形、新潟、長野など東北・中部の山々で狩猟をしてきたマタギ衆であり、もう一方は九州の山間部で狩猟にも従事しながら暮らす人々である。

今は半農半猟で暮らすが、マタギにとって獲物は山の神からの授かりものであって、動物そのものを神とは考えていない点でアイヌ民族とは異なる世界観に生きている。ただ、獲ったクマの毛皮を脱がせた後、頭の側を尻側に、尻の側を頭側にと反対向きで亡骸に被せるケボカイ（解体）の儀式は、魂が自身の肉体に戻ることを諦めさせて、まっすぐ山の神のもとに帰らせるためだと、マタギの古老は語る。とすると、「魂の分離」という発想に限って言えば、マタギとアイヌ民族の生命観には共通点があるとみなせる。

九州の山間部で狩りをしてきた人々もまた、山の神に授かったシカやイノシシを、吊した状態で一晩置いて、山の神に霊を持っていってもらってから解体を始める。その点で、同じく魂の分離を意識していることが読み取れる。[注12]

アイヌ民族の世界観に基づけば、この人間界にも神々の世界にもたくさんの霊がいて、二つの世界を行き来している。クマは、人間界に肉や毛皮を授けた後、霊だけは人間が執り行う儀式を通してお土産を持たされ、神々の世界に帰っていく。その霊送りのうちでも村を挙げて行う盛大な儀式が「クマ祭り」として知られてきた「イオマンテ［イヨマンテ］」であり、山中、仕留めた現場ないし狩小屋で行われる仲間内の儀式が「ホプニレ」ないし「オプニレ」、「オプニカ」である。イオマンテ

狩猟文化は九州の山間部にも今なお息づいている＝宮崎県・椎葉民俗芸能博物館（撮影：小坂洋右）

の対象はクマに限らない。コタン（集落）の守り神という意味でコタンコロカムイと呼ばれてきたシマフクロウやキツネ、ワシ、オオカミなどの霊も同様に送られてきた。

サケを司る神、シカを司る神がそれぞれ人間界に下ろし与えてくれるサケやシカもまた、死後、魂は神々の国に戻って行く。アイヌ民族の伝承のなかには、魂を元の神さまたちに送り返すための作法を人間が怠ったり、誤ったりしたことで、神々が腹を立ててサケやシカを人間界に下ろさなくなり、その結果、人間が飢えに苦しんだ、それを見かねた別の神が、それぞれを司る神に取り

入ってサケやシカを復活させたという物語もある。「だから、人間の側が作法を守らなくてはならない。作法を守ればサケもシカもまた戻ってきて自分たちも、ほかの生き物たちも飢えることがないのだよ」という教訓譚である。

環境の悪化を、もしかしたら自分たち人間の側に責任があるのではないかと考える姿勢からは、循環的、持続的な発想とともに、自然の変化を前にして、謙虚さをもって、へりくだってそれに向き合うアイヌ民族の姿勢もまた読み取れる。冒頭で、雷神とチキサニ姫（ハルニレの女神）から半神半人のアイヌラックルが生まれた創世神話を紹介したが、アイヌラックルは魔神たちをやっつけて人間界を守り、狩りの仕方や食べられる山菜などをアイヌ（人間たち）に伝授したあと、今度は神の力を乱用するなど人間たちが堕落していく姿に落胆してアイヌモシリ（狭義では北海道、広義では人間界）を去ったと伝えられている。アイヌ民族がそういう構図で世界の成り立ちを伝承してきたことからも、自分たち人間の側が至らないことで大事な存在をみすみす失ってしまうという見方、まずは自分の胸に手を当てて、自分の側に何か失態や悪かった点はないだろうかと自省する態度がうかがえる。

そうした生き方を貫いてきた人々は、命を粗末にすれば、どれほど恐ろしい結果が待っているのかを示す物語もまた伝えてきた。

命を奪う重み伝える物語

命を無為に奪うことがどれほど重い科(とが)に値するのか、それを伝えるアイヌ伝承が「トピウの卵(注14)」

である。

どこから来たために、たった一人でこの大きな家にいる女で私はあるのか。

ある日、薪を取りたくなった。突然、そう思ったので、薪を取りに山へ行った。

世間ではシントコと呼ばれるものがあった。

蓋を取ってのぞいてみると、トピウという鳥がいて、飛び立った。

その後に卵が二つあった。

そこでそれを手に取って握り潰してぐちゃぐちゃにした。

するとあの鳥が私の上を飛び回りながら落とす涙が夏の雨のように降り注いだ。

羽ばたきの音が、二つの言葉、三つの言葉になって私に聞こえた。

このように。

「この女め。たった一人で暮らしているので、さみしい思いをしているのを哀れんで、それゆえにかけがえのない私の子どもたちを、私はお前を見守っていたものなので、お前の話し相手になるといいと思ってしたことであったのに、お前は殺してしまったのか。

これからお前のしたことのバチが当たって、このようになるぞ。

自分のしたことを歌にして、冬六年、夏六年歌い続け、あごが膝にくっつくだろう。手は尻の肉にくっつくだろう。

そうして、火にくべるものもなくなってしまう。お前は転がって行って鉢だのシントコだの

何であろうがくわえて出してきて火にくべる。そうしているうちに、火にくべてしまって、シントコも鉢も燃やしてしまうと、その次に座っている場所がくぼんで、はまってしまうせいで罰が当たったのだと歌い続けたあげく、お前は首だけ出して、これこういうことをしたせいで罰が当たったのだとお前の上に土が崩れ落ちて死んでしまうのだぞ」

と、羽ばたきの音が聞こえてきたのだった。

しかし、鳥ふぜいの言った言葉が、おそろしいものかと思いながら、薪を取って背負って下りて来た。歌を歌いたいとも思わずに下りてきたのだ。家の入り口に入って大きな荷物を背中から下ろして投げ出すと、そのとたんに歌を歌いたくなってどうしようもなく、それから歌を歌い、高く声を上げ、低く声を落とし、そして小さな卵二つをつぶしたことを言いながら歌を歌った。

そうしていると、外を通る人がそれを耳にして、家に入ってきて、「本当にそんな馬鹿なことをしたのか」と言いながら、二回も三回も私を殴(なぐ)りつけて置き去りにしていった。あらゆるものを食べて、もはや食べ尽くすのも時間の問題になった。すると、私のあごが膝にくっついた。手は尻の肉にくっついた。火にくべるものもなくなった。

そこでごろごろ転がって行って、シントコだのをくわえてきては火にくべた。そこにくぼんできて、そのうちに指折り数えてみると、もはや夏六年、冬六年になるだろうと思う頃、座っていたところがくぼんで、ついにもはや首だけを突き出している

ありさまだったが、私に罰が当たった様子はこういうことなのだと言いながら、今はもう私の上に土が崩れ落ちてきた。

これからは女たちよ、決してこのようなことをするなよと言いながら、私は土に埋まって行ったのだ。

卵を二個、握り潰したことが、これほどのバチとして自身に返ってくるものなのか——。このことと一つとっても、アイヌ民族のこの伝承は、一度聞いたら二度と忘れられないほどの強烈なインパクトを持って命の重みを訴えてくる。

このトピウという名の鳥が実際、どの鳥を指すのか、物語を受け継ぎながらも一九九三年に亡くなった千歳の語り部、白沢（しらさわ）ナベさん自身知らず、知里真志保（ちりましほ）博士の『分類アイヌ語辞典 動物篇』にも記載がない。鳥の存在そのものも謎めいているが、なぜ女性が一人暮らしなのか、なぜ突然、薪を採りに行きたくなるのか。アイヌ民族の暮らしや歴史に即した物語世界の解説がなければ、不可解さが残る展開だ。

物語を採録した言語学者の中川裕（ひろし）によると、一人暮らしの描写から始まるアイヌ伝承は少なからずあり、盗賊団に襲われて村人が皆殺しに遭ったか、流行病によって村が全滅してしまったことが、理由として考えられるという。結果として、たった一人、赤ん坊が生きて残されたところから、ドラマが始まるのである。

このトピウの物語では、家の中に宝物（シントコなど）が残されているので、中川は流行病による村

の全滅が想定されるとみている。

赤ん坊が一人残されながらも何とか生きてこられたのは、神さまが陰ながら見守り、支えてきたからで、これは第一章の「カッコウの妻になった娘」の物語を思い出してもらえれば、「そうか」と分かってもらえるだろう。だから、「突然、薪を採りに行きたくなった」というのも、実はこの女性を守り育てていたトピウの神がそのように仕向けたのであって、まさか女性が卵を握りつぶす行動に出るとは思わずに、語り合う相手を寄こしてあげようとの善意でしたことであった。それが図らずも裏切られ、トピウの神は自分の子どもの命が奪われたことへの嘆きと、女性が自分を裏切り、命を軽んじたことへのショックからこの地上に涙の雨を降らせたのである。

この女性が天涯孤独の状況で生を受け、一人っきりで何の常識も習慣も教えられずに育ったことを勘案すれば、私自身は個人的にはこの女性に対して同情の念を禁じ得ない。肉親や村の隣人たちを失っただけでも耐えがたい苦しみなはずなのに、さらに自身にも七転八倒の苦しみが与えられるこの女性の生涯は、あまりに薄幸である。しかも、あごが膝にくっつき、手が尻にくっつくさまは、ヒナがまだ卵の中にいる時の姿勢を連想させ、その格好で土に埋もれていくという死に方も非常に残酷な「仕返し」のように見て取れる。

中川は、この物語の解題で、こう指摘している。

「かつてアイヌの人々は狩猟民族であり、動物の命を自分の手で直接奪って生活の糧とするのがなりわいであった。しかし、だからこそ自分の生命が他者の生命によって生かされているのだという、実感に基づいた思想を築き上げてきたのであり、この話に出てくるような無益な殺生(せっしょう)というも

第一部　人々は聴き　大地は見てきた　　40

のを、強く戒めたのである。

この物語の主人公はトピウの神が自らに与えてくれたものの意味を探ろうともせずに、また、自分の腹を満たして生き長らえるためという必要性もなく、意味なく生命を抹消した。それこそアイヌの最も忌むべきことであった」(注16)

こう言うことができるだろう。狩猟採集を中心に生きてきたアイヌ民族は命を奪う暮らしのなかで、肉体と魂（霊）が分離でき、魂は肉体の死後も生き続けるという発想を得るに至った。神々である野生の生き物は人間に獲られた後、儀式を行ってもらえれば神々の元へと帰ることができる。カムイから人間のもとに遣わされるサケヤシカもまた、きちんと作法を守って命を奪えば、神々の元へと戻り、再び人間界に姿を現すことができる。だが、無駄に命を奪う行為は許されず、それには自身の悲惨な結末が待っている。

狩猟社会の伝統において、命を奪うことで生活そのものを成り立たせてきたなかで培われてきたのが、こうした自然哲学であったのだ。

三章　命を奪われるがゆえに

クマの生態を熟知し、冬眠中に穴猟

　命を奪う行為だが、狩猟で生きる人々のなかにどのような発想を生み出し、それがどのような自然観に至るかを前章でみてきた。中でも重要なポイントは、アイヌ民族にとって、狩りとは、自分の技や強さを見せつける場ではなく、獲る側（人間）と獲られる側（カムイ）が互いのつながりを再確認する場だということだった。それはすなわち、カムイに自分の矢や弾を受け取ってもらえるように、カムイを迎えるにふさわしい人間として振る舞い、自身を磨かなくてはならないことを意味する。
　アイヌ民族は一二月から一月にかけての冬ごもり直後や春先のまだ穴で冬眠している時期に数人のグループで穴グマ猟を行ってきた。穴グマ猟の時期が終わると、明治以前だと毒矢による弓猟のほか、仕掛け弓（クアリ、クワリないしアマッポ）が使われた。クマやシカの通るケモノ道に糸を張っておき、触れると自動的に毒矢が発射される仕組みである。だが、毒矢を使う猟は明治政府に禁じられ、重要な食糧源で、毒矢や追い落とし、川・海への追い込み、罠（わな）で獲っていたシカは狩猟免許の制限や生息数の激減で猟が困難になっていく。近年、シカが急増し、ヒグマも人里への出没が増えた

第一部　人々は聴き　大地は見てきた　42

ことから、ハンターの出動が要請されるようになったものの、明治以降、狩猟者が和人から遠ざけられてきたアイヌ民族の狩猟者はこの間、大きく数を減らし、今は担い手の多くが和人という現実がある。

戦後、穴グマ猟を数多く経験してきた根本与三郎エカシたちのスタイルはこうだった（注1）。一〇月、一一月にまず、以前、冬眠に使われてきた穴を見て回る「初期のカムイチセノンカラ〔クマの家の見回り〕」に出る。出かける前や山で寝泊まりする際には、火の神と狩猟を司るニヤシコロカムイ（注2）への祈りを怠らない。

それぞれの穴にクマがその年、入るか入らないかは、以前使った敷き草がそのまま放置されているかどうかで、まず判断する。敷き草が放置されたままになっていれば、その穴は放棄されたと見なし、そうでない穴について、今度は入るか否か、入るならいつ冬眠に入るかの判断をしていく。「冬眠が近い」との判断には、足跡探しが物を言う。穴ごもりが間近になるにつれて、雪に記された足跡に、穴に出入りした時につく土がわずかに混じるようになるからだ。足跡を消すためだろう。クマは大雪が降るのを察知して、その直前に急いで穴に入ることが多い。とはいえ、クマが入った穴の入り口には呼吸による霜柱ができるから、入っているかどうかは判別できる。

穴に入ったからといってクマはすぐに眠りに就くわけではない。一〇日ぐらいの間は、時に外に出て日向ぼっこをしたり、食べ物の残りを探し歩いたりすることもあるから、この期間はまだ様子見である。本格的に穴ごもりに入り、巣穴から出てこなくなるのは二週間から二〇日ほどたってからという。

その時期になると、数人で出かけて行き、巣穴の少し前にリュックや上着、首に巻いてきた手ぬ

ぐいを置くか枝に掛けるかする。それは準備が整わない前にクマが出てきた時にまっ先にそこに向かわせるための誘導物だ。その後、付近からアオダモなど、しなりのある木を長さ三メートルぐらいに切ってきて、出ようとするクマの止め木として穴の前に立て、クマが顔を覗かせるのを待つ。時にクマはものすごいうなり声を上げる。その凄みを根本エカシはこう表現した。

「鳥肌が立つっていうでしょ。ああいう感じですよ。一回聞いただけで体の毛が立つくらいの迫力がありますよ」。なかなか出てこない時には、メンバーの一人が穴の前にあぐらをかいて「早く出てきて客の座に授かれ。お前を必ず神の国に送ってやるから、俺らに授かれ」とクマに向けてカムイノミ（神々への祈り）をするという。

地域差はあるだろうが、猟にはさまざまな決まりごとがあった。出猟前は女性との交わりは慎む、山に入ったら猟仲間を名前で呼ばない、名前を呼ばれても返事をしない、亡くなった人のことやクマが嫌いなヘビやワシのことは口にしない――。道東・鶴居の八重九郎エカシは、仲間と手分けしてクマの足跡を見つけた時には日常で使われる「カムイ」「キムンカムイ」などの呼称は使わずに「パセ・チロンノプ・カムイ（位の重い狐の神）が歩いた跡がある」と言い換えるとし、山言葉（隠語）があったことが知れる。ちなみにパセは「位の重い」の意味で、チロンノプ、チロンヌプだけだと一般にはキツネを指す。

また、同じ道東の弟子屈・屈斜路コタンで生まれ育った弟子豊治エカシ（一九二三〜一九九四年）は、クマはカムイなので寝ているところを撃つのは失礼だから、声を掛けて目を覚まさせてから撃つものだとし、姉崎等エカシは相手が興奮している状態では撃たず、いくらすぐ目の前にいてもクマの

心が鎮まるのを待ってから引き金を引いていた。どんな手段を取っても討ち取ればいいというものではなく、やはり神さまとしての扱いをしたうえで弾を受け取ってもらうというのが基本なのだ。

襲って来たクマの性格を判定

狩猟する側が命を奪おうとすれば、相手も抵抗する。狩る側にとっては、反対に自分の方が命を奪われる結果になりかねないリスクを常に負う。

日常的な観察を通じてクマの習性を熟知していたアイヌ民族であっても、ヒグマに突如襲われたり、追っていたクマの逆襲に遭って命を落とす、ケガをさせられるといった事例が全くなかったわけではない。その場合、どう受け止めるのか。

白老（しらおい）の指導者で、イソンクル（狩猟に長けた人）と認められていた宮本イカシマトク・エカシ（注6）（一八七六〜一九五八年）の談によると、地域ではかつて、出猟中にヒグマに殺された場合、クマから好かれて神の国にもらわれていったと信じられたという。（注7）人に手を掛けたクマをとらえた場合は、体を詳しく調べて、悪心を起こして襲ったものか、単に出来心で殺したのか、あるいは自衛のためにやむなく襲いかかったのかを吟味した。

長い狩猟の経験から、男たちはクマの相貌から凶暴なのか、それとも、もともとは臆病で優しい個体なのか、見極めることができたとされる。そして、優しいクマと判断された場合は、普通のクマの霊を送る時より少ない数のイナウを捧げて、神々の国に送り返し、神々に詫びを入れさせた。一

方、悪相が現れていれば、イナウは捧げず、皮に頭をつけて剝ぎ、西の方向に向けて腐れ木の上に被せ、肉は切り刻んで腐った木や根株の上に放置した。この手立てによって、復活できなくなると考えられていた。

故意にコタン（集落）を襲って来たような性悪グマの場合は、あごを外して便所の陰に捨て、皮を剝いで腐れ木の上に掛けて腐るに任せたという。北海道南部、長万部でもクマの性格や加害の程度で対応を変え、性根が悪いクマの場合、やはり復活させないために、鼻先を下向きにして土に埋めていた。

古老の証言からは、人を殺めたとしても、心を改める機会を与え、復活の余地を残すことに重きを置いた地域があったことがうかがえる。十勝地方の音更ではイナウなしで体を細かく切り刻むものの、場を立ち去るに当たって「改心すれば必ずりっぱな心の良いクマに生まれ変わって再びアイヌたちから神として祭りをしてもらい、親元の国に送り返されるぞ」と言い聞かせた。道南の八雲では、背中側の皮を残したまま腹側の皮を剝いで、皮を裏返しにするようにしたうえで、殺された人の下に埋葬しながらも、「このように醜い体にして懲らしめてやるから、心を改めて生まれ変わって善良なクマになるように」と言い含めたという。

また、人がケガだけで生還した場合は、傷が治れば、そのことに感謝しつつイナウを捧げてクマの霊を神々の国に帰していたようだ。

古老の証言を元に各地の対応をまとめた犬飼哲夫と門崎允昭は、アイヌ民族は①人喰いグマを魔が取り憑いた悪神とみなし、自分たちの力で、できるだけ懲らしめ、神とは扱わない②クマの本性

は常に良き神とみなし、過失を改めれば正しい神になり得る余地も与えている③極めて凶悪なクマは永久に出現を望まない④どこまでもクマを狩猟の相手として善良に柔軟にしておきたい態度がうかがえる——と結論づけている(注8)。

旭川育ちで、小学三年生の時、父親をクマの事故で亡くした砂沢クラ・フチ（一八九七〜一九九〇年）の体験は、そうしたクマへの対処法が現実に、どう適用されていたかを教えてくれる。

クラ・フチの地域では、人を殺めたクマもそうやって葬られた。ところが、その後、おじたちが別のクマを獲ってよく観察すると、そのクマには歯も爪もない。それであの人殺しグマが生まれ変わって現れたのではないかと泣きっ面で帰宅した。それでもその晩、おじの一人の夢枕にクマが立って「人を殺したのは悪かった。もう決してしないから許してくれ。イナウを作って神の国へ送ってくれたら、おまえを見守り、いつも猟があるようにする」と言ったのでそのクマの霊を神の国に送ったというのである(注9)。

たとえ自分たちを襲ってきた相手であっても、アイヌ民族がその真意、その性格、反省の度合いを見極めたうえで対応を決めていた傍証といってもいい事例であろう。つまり、立ち位置をまずは相手の側に置いたうえで対応を決めていたのである。

とはいえ、アイヌ民族にとってクマはカムイ（神さま）である。であれば、襲われてけがをした、しかも自分を傷つけた相手が神さまである——という二重のショックを本人や猟の仲間は受けること

になる。そうしたショックを何とかして緩和しなくては、心安らかにはいられない。そうした場面で、葛藤を幾分かでも和らげるためにアイヌ民族が力を借りたのが伝承、平たくいえばお話の世界だったように思える。

例えば「人を見そめて下界に落ちたメスグマを改心させたサッポロの人」(注10)の物語がそうだ。

犠牲者は「メスグマに愛された」

物語の語り手はサッポロに住む若者である。彼が和人との交易のためにサッポロ川を下っていくと、今まで見過ごしていたところに家があるのに気づく。訪ねたところ、家の外は荒れていて、祀られているヒグマなどの頭骨は古びており、家の主（あるじ）は猟に優れた人物なのだろうが最近は久しく狩りには出ていないことが推察できた。戸口に現れた年配女性もやつれていて、生活に難儀していることが読み取れる。衰弱しきって病人にしか見えないその家の主（あるじ）が涙ながらに語った半生は次のようだった。

自分は元は釧路〔クスル〕の出身で、母親、妻とともにこの地に住み着き、娘を授かったのだが、ある日、山猟に出ると、毛並みがピカピカ光っているメスグマが飛びかかってきて自分をいたぶり、仰向けにして上に覆（おお）い被（かぶ）さり、自分の顔を見つめた。かろうじて手だけは動いたので、小刀を引き抜くと、メスグマの開いた口に手を入れて、その舌を切り取った。メスグマはひどく暴れ回り、自分にはといえば、自力では動けなかったが、ほどなく探し出を散々な目に遭わせたのち、息絶えた。自分はといえば、自力では動けなかったが、ほどなく探し出された。それで、メスグマの頭を切り離して山から下ろすよう指示し、家の自分の枕元に置いた。当

第一部　人々は聴き　大地は見てきた　48

初は誰かが自分を嫉妬して呪ったのではないかと思った。というのも、妻がつくったものを食べようとすると、傷の痛みがひときわ全身を駆けめぐったからだ。それで妻は必要な時以外は外にいるようになり、妻がたきぎを集め、娘が水汲みをして、やっとのことで生きてきたのだ……。

ここから、事の背景を察したサッポロの若者が解決に乗り出す。

主人の話を聞いて、激しい憤怒の情を俺は抱いた。まんじりともしないで、翌朝、まだ暗いうちから主人の枕元を眺めて見たら、もうすっかり古くなったクマの頭骨があったので、俺はヒグマの神さまの長に文句をつけた。

「あの年配の婦人は、大変な苦労をして子の面倒を見ている。息子は妻も持ち、娘をも持っている。神さまともあろうものが、その事実を見ないで、見知らぬふりをしているのか」

それからそのメスグマの頭骨へも抗議した。

「妻もある男がいったい何でまた、あのようなことになるのか。その後、ずっと老婦人は苦労し、実にかわいそうである。夢にでもお前が反省したりしないならば、俺はお前の父親や母親に訴えるものを」

果たしてその翌日に俺は夢を見たのであったが、そこに現れたのはヒグマの衣裳である黒い小袖を着たヒグマの長の神さまであった。

「サッポロ川の川上に住まわれる人、人の中の長、人間の若者よ。そなたが来てくれたおかげ

で、人間の話す言葉を初めて神さまたちが耳にしたものだから、知らないできたことが分かった。わしのろくでなしの娘、あの尻腐れ者が、クスルから逃れてやってきた若者と一緒になりたくてしたことだ。そうはいっても若者を殺して魂を取ることは難しく、当然ながら神から罰を受けるものだから、魂を取りたくても取れず、それこそ一計を案じて『この若者がどうにかしてケガが完治するまで見守りましょう』とわしに言ったものだから、それとしておいたのだ。娘は本心では、主人と一緒になりたくてやっているわけだが、妻が炊事をし、主人に食事をさせようとすると嫉妬し、それによってより一層、主人の具合を悪くしている。今回のことはわしの娘が望んでやったことだから、湿った国にわしが追放してもいいのだが、娘はなかなか手強く、わしだけで十分に納得させることはできそうにない。どうかわしに代わって、そなたが十分に言い含め、伝えてくだされや。このわしをかわいそうに思ってそうしてくれたなら、わしはそなたを豊かにさせようぞ。

この家の主人のけがは、娘がやったことなので、娘自身が何とかして命だけでも取り留めるように配慮しよう。主人には正妻がいるのだから、妻が家の主人に食事を作っても決してこれからは主人の具合が悪くなるようなことはなく、水汲み女にでも、飯盛り女にでも召使いでもいいから、人間の国土であの家の主人と一緒にいるようにと、わしは娘を説得するからな。なお重ねてそなたがそのようにしてくれたならば、けっこうなことであるぞ」。話をしてくれるのを夢に見せられた。

俺は何度も感謝して重厚な拝礼をした。メスグマの頭骨に向かって、俺は徹底して文句を

言ったのであったが、やはり元は位の重い神の仲間だからと思い、削りかけ製の包みの中へ俺はその頭骨を入れてやった。

俺はさらにこの家に泊まったのであったが、今度はあまりにも美しい娘が夢の中に立って、「私の至らないところから家の主人に迷惑をかけました。かつてはこの家の主婦が料理をして主人が食事をしようとするとそれに私は腹を立てていたのですが、あなたが言ってくださる言葉を私は肝に銘じました。不自由な体ではあっても何とか主人が歩くこともでき、起きあがることもでき食事もできるようになるよう、私は見守っていきます。あれ以来、嫉妬することもなくなりました。あなたに感謝をいたします。今のあなたが幸せな以上にあなたを幸せにしながら暮らすつもりでございます」と言うのを俺は見た。

その後、あの寝床に就いていた家の主人は、あんなに話をすることも不自由で言葉に力もなかったものが、声も力強く大きくなり、俺に話をし、幾度も語りかけてきた……。

魂の世界で人は野生動物と添い遂げられる

物語の筋書きからは、野生の生き物が人間に惚れ込むことがあり、魂と肉体が別々なものとしてある以上、魂の世界では夫婦になることができるという狩猟民としての発想が読み取れる。ただし、同時に、夫婦になるために無理やり魂を奪う行為は神の一族であっても許されないことも示される。霊の世界でクマと人間が一緒になることは可能だが、筋の通らないやり方をしては神々が同意してくれないようだ。(注11)

51　三章　命を奪われるがゆえに

しかも、メスグマの愛情たるや、相手を傷つけ、苦しませずにはおかないほどの狂おしいものがある。看病したいといいながら、逆に容体を悪化させているのは倒錯的とも言える。神々の中でも位の高い父グマはそんな状況や娘の謀りを知って激怒するが、サッポロの若者の協力を得て娘グマを改心させつつも、娘の想いをむげにはできず、主人のそばに置いて下働きさせながら一緒に暮らさせるという妥協的な道を選ぶのである。

メスグマは人間界に下りて人の姿で奉仕することで、主人への思いを一定程度かなえつつ、恋慕の情が高ぶるあまり犯してしまった罪の償いをし、なおかつ解決に力を貸してくれた若者への恩を忘れず彼を見守る守護神としての役目も買って出る。クマの王であるその父親もまた、人間に対しすまないという気持ちを持ち続ける。一方、サッポロの若者は主人に代わってメスグマに復讐するわけではなく、あくまで神として敬い、神としての振る舞いをすべきことを論し、悟らせることで一度は不正常になったクマ（神）と人間（主人）の間を取り持つ。

先にも述べた通り、アイヌ民族はヒグマのいる山野を猟の領域としている以上、現実の上でも猟に出てクマの逆襲に遭ったり、運悪く何かの巡り合わせで殺されたり、けがをさせられることがあった。クマに襲われれば、現代の感覚であれば、凶暴なヤツだ、人喰いグマに違いないと呪い、怯えるが、クマに愛されたがゆえに命を取られそうになったという解釈もあり得るのだ。

そうみていけば、一時的には対立状態になったクマと人間が和解し、正常なつながりを取り戻すという「関係修復」が、この物語の根底にあることは明らかだろう。野生動物にけがをさせられたり、殺された人のことを「やられた」のではなく「愛された」と解釈するというその発想の転換だけでも、

家族や集落の人々の悲しみは和らぎ、不幸をある種の運命と納得させる方向に導くのだ。

獲物になりきって狩りをするハンター

だが、この物語が含むのは、果たしてこれだけだろうか。「愛された結果」と解釈することで心痛を和らげられるのは事実だとしても、解釈はあくまで解釈である。そこには「人と野生動物は情を通じ合えない」という前提が存在している。だが、「現実として」人と野生動物の間に横たわる異種の境界が揺らいで、一体化していく境地がないと、断定することはできるだろうか。

これは決して現実離れした発想ではない。姉崎等エカシは、自分が子どもの頃、こんなふうに言われたと語っている。「あんたクマを獲るんだったらクマになりなさい。イセポ コイキ（ウサギ猟）のときはイセポ（ウサギ）にならなかったらそんなもの獲れないんだって」。長じて実際に狩りを始めると、その教えが身をもって理解できた。「私は、クマを自分の師匠だと本気で思っています。なぜクマが師匠かというと、クマの足跡を見つけたときにクマを一生懸命追って歩く、そうやって追っていくうちに、山の歩き方やクマの行動などをすべて学んだからなのです」。

アイヌ民族出身の言語学者、知里真志保（一九〇九〜一九六一年）は、神謡（カムイユカラ）の「ユカラ」とは物語の語りだけを意味するのではなく、「ユカルは動物の鳴声――動物は神であるから、それは同時にまた神の歌声である――でもあった。しかも一方ではユカルには『真似る』という意味があり、その語原は恐らく yuk-kar で、『獲物をなす』『獲物のさまをなす』『獲物の真似をなす』『獲物になりきる』ということだったらしい」と述べている。ここでもまた「獲物をなす」、言い換えれば「獲物になりきる」

53 三章 命を奪われるがゆえに

いう行為が浮上してくる。知里真志保は、動物の鳴き声や動作の真似はかつては儀礼で演じられたものと推測しているが、姉崎エカシの言葉に従えば、実際の狩猟でも獲物の動きがまねられたと考えても、それほどの飛躍ではないだろう。

何カ月もの間、シベリアの狩猟民ユカギールのヘラジカ狩りなどに同行したデンマークの人類学者レーン・ウィラースレフは「ユカギールの狩人たちは獲物の動きをまね、ほとんど同化しながら、自身が獲物に変身してしまう一歩手前で『自我』をかろうじて保ち、引き金を引くのだ」と、狩る側の心理を描写している。その際、狩人にとって大事なことは、自分を魅力的に見せることだとも言う。

「狩猟者は、獲物にとって性的に魅力があるように見えなければならないし、友好的で無害に見えなければならない。……そのようにして、動物は狩猟者を邪霊や捕食者としてではなく、無害な恋人や同じ種の一員として認識するようになる。狩猟者は、獲物のアイデンティティを身にまとい、獲物の行動や感性に響き合うようにふるまって、獲物との間に『共感関係』を築いているのだと言うことができるだろう」(注15)

ウィラースレフが語るこの境地において、狩る者、狩られる者から異種の壁が取り払われるどころか、互いの関係は恋愛にも近くなる。

ウィラースレフはそれを補強する逸話も記している。ユカギールの男性たちは、猟にあまりに恵まれすぎると、「自分は動物の支配霊に愛されているのではないか」と心配し始めるのだという。愛されているかもしれないことに不安を覚えるのは、支配霊の子

第一部 人々は聴き 大地は見てきた 54

どもたちをこれほどたくさん受け取ったからには、支配霊は今度は自分の霊魂を寄こせと要求してくるかもしれないという懸念がわいてくるからで、死の予兆を感じ取った時点で猟を一時的に断ったり、狩りそのものをきっぱり辞めたりすることもあるというのだ。

狩りの対象をまねることが演技を超えて迫真性を帯び、互いの感情の交感まで至ることがあり得るのだとすれば、クマを愛することも、クマから愛されることも両方が成り立ちうるということになる。となれば、サッポロの若者の物語で「主人」を襲ったメスグマの恋愛感情も、やや倒錯したその表現の仕方も「現実としてあった」可能性が否定できなくなる。ただし、性的な魅力を醸し出すユカギールの狩りのようなありようがアイヌ民族に当てはまるのかどうかは、今の段階では定かなことは言えない。ここでは、伝承からは少なくとも「野生動物に襲われたのは愛された結果」との解釈は成り立つというところを押さえて、次に進もう。

ある日、家の裏にクマの巣穴が……

アイヌ伝承に、シャチ神とクマ神、そして人間という、日常での交わりがありえそうにない三者が、互いの関係を図らずしてこじらせてしまうものの、人間が間に入って何とか解決を図る複雑怪奇な物語がある。

「家の裏で熊神が巣を造って仔を産む」(注17)の語り手はウラシベッという人間の村を治める男性で、ある朝、家の裏手にクマの巣穴が出来ていることに気づいて驚き、家から弓矢を取って戻ったところ、飛び出してきたメスグマに追いかけられる。だが、足に自信があったこの男は攻撃をかわし、メス

グマを振り払い続けるうち、クマの方が疲れ死にしてしまう。男はメスグマを猟小屋に運んで、言葉をかけた。「なぜに、俺の何に腹を立てて、お前は俺を追いかけたのだ。お前が神であって、良い精神、良い考えの持ち主なのか、お前の言い分を俺が聞いて、成り行きによって丁寧に俺がお前を祀るか、粗末にするか分からないが、今夜の夢をじっくり聞き、それから送ってやるつもりだ」。そう伝えて男は寝た。

「祀るべきか、それともぞんざいに扱うか」。主人はなぜ迷い、思い悩んでいるのか。先ほどの「サッポロの人の物語」をすでに知っている読者にはある程度、察しがついていることだろう。そう、こういう場合は、自分、つまり人間の側からの解釈ではなく、相手方の動機が大事なのである。メッセージを相手が伝えてくるのが夢見で、夜、床に就いて夢に相手が現れるのを待つのである。

まさか眠るとは思わなかったのに、ほんとうにぐっすり眠り、いびきをかいて眠りこけてしまった。俺の枕元に黒い小袖だけを着た神の若い女性、しどく若い少女ほどの者が俺に背を向けていて、泣きに泣いて今にも泣き死にしそうにしていて、ようやく俺の方に向き直った。

「もしもし ウラシベツの村長(むらおさ)よ、人の長たるお方よ。言うのもお恥ずかしいのですが、もはや私が語らなければどうしようもないので、お話しいたします。私は山の東端に棲むクマ神の末娘で、沖の神〔シャチ〕の息子を夫にして仲良く暮らしておりました。やがて身ごもり出産間近になったちょうどその頃、人間のあなたが度胸でも足の速さでも何につけても人間を超えて

いるという評判が立っていることが本当に腹立たしくて、あなたを殺したくなったのです。我慢すればするほど殺したくなったから、あなたが眠っている隙を狙って殺そうとして、こっそり忍び寄ったところに、突然お腹が痛み出し、子どもを産みたくなりました。どうにもならなくなって、あなたの家の後ろに巣を造り、二匹の子を産んだのです。
でもやっぱりあなたを追いかけて、追いついて捕まえ、殺してやろうと思っていたら、ほんとにまぁ、私も足の速さが自慢なのになかなかあなたに追いつけない。出産直後のせいなのか、いろんな神罰が下ったものか、私は疲れて死んでしまいました。
本当に恥ずかしいことです。何神に操られてあんな罰当たりな行為をしたのか。今はもう本当に私は後悔し、自分自身を恨んでいるのです。今これから神の国でも神々が私を罰するでしょう。どうかどんなに私に腹を立てていても、私を憐れんで神の国の一員に私がなれるよう、神々に取りなしてください。その後で、私が落ち着いた時に、少しでも返礼するつもりですよ」
と神の若い女性が言ったように俺が思ったところでもう夜が明けて、それは夢なのであった。

人間がクマとシャチの間を取り持つ

本当に俺は驚いた。このようにも神の娘は話した。
「どんなにあなたが怒っていても、私の子どもたちを二匹とも育てて、丈夫に大きくしてから神の国へ送ってくださったならば、私の父母の元へ行けるのでございます」

本当に腹が立つ。なんだって山神〔熊神〕の娘が夫を得て妊娠しているとはいえ、俺を殺したくなるというのだ。しかし、今はもう後悔して俺に取りなしてくれと言うからまた憐れを覚えて、俺は山を下りて村人に指図した。

大勢の衆がクマ肉を背負って戻った。酒造りだの団子造りだのをしてさまざまなイナウを造って神の霊送りをやり終えた。二匹の子グマはあまりに幼いから俺が面倒を見て妻と二人で育てた。こうして毎日暮らしていたところ、ある晩また俺が眠ったら、夢枕に現れたあの神の若い女性は、前とは格段の差の美しさ。長い間泣いているものだから、もう今は目まで突き出しそうになっていて、言うには

「もしもし、人の長たるお方よ。なにゆえにあのような罰当たりな悪い行いを私はしたのでしょうか。私は、供えられたあのようなイナウやお酒やおいしい食べ物だのをたくさん持って、まっしぐらに父母の許へ行きました。私の兄たち、姉たち、みんながなぜあんなことをしたのかと私を大声で叱りましたが、ウラシベツの首長のその申し立てがまこと立派ゆえ、私は助けられてとても嬉しかったのです。けれど、沖の神は立腹して、持ち出した主張はこうでした。

『山の東端のお方の娘はあのように美しい女だから、まさかあんな恐ろしい、よからぬ気持ちを持っているとは思わなかったのに、まあ、あんな振る舞いをするとは。そんなことなら、たった今からわしの妻ではない。そのようなことをした者は一族もろとも人間の村を守ることはできないから、山の東端を司る神の子どもたちは一人残らずみな即刻、鳥もいなく、森も林もない国土、砂漠の国に行ってしまえ』と沖の神は激怒して、私の父や母、兄たちがみな言葉を尽く

して詫び謝っても私たちは即刻、この村から放逐され、今はもう一族すべてが人間の村を永久に追放されました。

あなたのところにいる私の子どもら二人は、沖の神の子どもでもあります。あの人は探して二人とも一刻も早くとりあげたいのです。どんなにあなたたち夫婦が私の子どもたちを可愛がっていても、沖の神の気持ちは私の手に余るものだから、明日になったら、幣場〔祭壇〕〔注18〕のところでわが子たちの頭を叩くだの、首を絞めるだのして殺してイナウや供物で天国へ魂送りすれば、沖の神は喜んで子どもたちを受け取って、天国で子どもたちは可愛がられて育てられるでしょう。遠いところからでも私は見守ることができるのです。

あなたが私を祀った供物やイナウのおかげで、とても立派な食事を持ってこの淋しい国へ行けるのをほんとうに感謝しているのです。わずかなお酒でもあなたが醸したなら、宴席の終わりにでも私を思い出したならば、堅いストゥイナウでなりとも、干した酒の搾り滓でなりとも私を祀ってくれるならば、本当にあなたに感謝していつまでもあなたに憑いてお守りいたします。子どもがないあなたたちが子どもを欲しがっていることも私はわかっているので、私の霊力によってあなたたちに子どもも授けてあげましょう」

その若い神の娘が俺に言い遺したように思ったところで目が覚めた。

夢で告げられた通り、ウラシベッの長は二頭の子グマを絞めて神々の国に送り返し、その後もクマ神一族の境遇に同情しつつ、ことあるごとに供物と祈りを捧げ続けた。じき、欲しかった子ども

59　三章　命を奪われるがゆえに

「このようなわけで、山の東端の神の末娘が俺を殺したくなって危うく殺されそうになったが、彼女が後悔してすぐまた俺の守り神になって運を良くしてくれたおかげで、今あるのがお前たちなのだから、いつまでも、鳥もいなく、森も林もない国土にいる山の神をお前たちは祀るのだぞ」

も授かり、今まで以上の運を得て大首長になり、死を前にして子どもたちに次のように言い残す。

物語は、話のこの結末を待たずして、誰しも、襲って来たクマが性悪でないことを納得させられる展開である。

物語の精妙なところは、全体を通して、メスグマは自分の意志で首長を殺そうとしたわけではなく、何者かに操られた結果、殺したくてたまらなくなったように読み取れる点である。聞き手は、操っている者がいるとすればその正体は誰か、それがいつ明かされるのか、とはらはら期待しつつ話に聞き入るに違いないが、正体は最後まで明かされない。

黒幕の正体が明かされれば、誰が何の目的でそんな悪行をさせたのかが白日のもとにさらされる一方で、それではクマ族とシャチ族、その間に立つ人間の緊迫した関係が一気に崩れて緊張感が失われてしまう。意図されているのは、全体を通して、メスグマが本当に悪いわけではなく、むしろある意味で被害者なのかもしれない、メスグマもまた同情を受けるに足るということを聞き手に強く認識させるところにあるような気がしてくる。

物語には、魂（霊）と肉体は別であるというアイヌ民族の生命観もまた如実に表れている。例えば、人間が命を奪うことでメスグマの子どもたちの魂を解き放ち、シャチ神の元に届ける場面である。

シャチはいかに強い神さまだとしても、肉体に閉じ込められた霊を自分自身の手で自由にすることはできず、人間界から神々の国に引き取るためにはそこに人間が介在して霊を解放することが必要なようだ。

育てたクマの霊を神々の世界に帰す日

これは、子グマを二歳ぐらいまで飼った上で、その霊を神々の国に送り返すイオマンテ(クマシマフクロウなどの霊送り)の儀式に根拠、ないし正当性を与える物語とも受け取れる。こうした「飼いグマ儀礼」は、アイヌ民族のほかにはサハリン(樺太)と大陸アムール河流域の先住民族の間でしか知られていない。地域は限定されているが、これは狩猟民の世界観が最も精緻に表わされている儀式形態だともされている。

アイヌ民族の場合、子グマはたいてい春先の穴グマ猟で得て、集落に連れ帰る。そして、家族同様に、女性がお乳をあげたり、食べ物を口移しで与えたりして大事に育て上げ、冬場に各地のコタンから人々を招いて霊を送り返すことになる。人間に送り出されて神々の国に戻った霊はほかの神々に、人間たちがどれほど自分を大切にしてくれたか、そしてたくさんのお土産を持たせてくれたかを語り示す。それによって、ほかの神々も人間の集落にいけば温かいもてなしを受けると知って、積極的に神々の国を出立し、人間の国に向かうようになるのである。

これは「観念」のレベルにとどまる話ではない。旭川の杉村京子フチは、母親のキナラブック・フチが子グマを抱いている写真を見せながら、一九七七年二月一八日に旭川で行われたイオマンテ

で、自分が育てた子グマ「キサラ」の最期を見届けた時を『ああ、よかった。[矢を]受け取ってくれた』と思ってね、うれしさがこみ上げてきた。涙が出たよ」と振り返ったのである。

この話を聞き、さらに自分自身でも一九八〇年代から九〇年代にかけて白老で行われた二回のイオマンテに参加して、アイヌ民族がそうした世界観を実体として

子グマを抱く杉村キナラブック・フチ（左）（杉村京子さん提供）

持ってきたことを私は確信した。アイヌ民族の伝統社会では、カムイモシリは実体として存在してきたし、イオマンテによってカムイはカムイモシリに実際に帰っていたのである。

話をメスグマとシャチの物語に戻そう。展開において、ヒグマとシャチの幸せな結婚生活が「襲撃事件」を機に一転、修復不能なほどの確執に変わる点を見逃すわけにはいかない。

そこから終盤への展開については、こう読み解くこともできるのではなかろうか。人間の長が、シャチとヒグマの間に生まれた子どもたちの霊を儀礼を通してシャチの元に返すことで、シャチがクマ一族に抱く怒りは、解けないまでも少なくとも和らぎはする。人間には感謝の念を抱き、ヒグマ側にとっては懸案の一つが解決をみる。それはメスグマの霊が「わが子たちを天国へ魂送りすれば、沖の神は喜んで子どもたちを受け取って、子どもたちは可愛がられて育てられるでしょう。遠いところからでも私は見守ることができるのです」と語っていることからも明らかだ。二人の子の霊を解放することによって、母親であるメスグマもまた、自分が遠いところに追放された後であっても子どもたちを見守ることができるという含みもある。

人間はシャチとクマの橋渡し役を演じて不幸な関係の修復に努め、その結果、シャチにもクマにも恩を売る。つまりありがたがられる存在になる。さらに言えば、クマの一族はアイヌ語で「ニタイサクモシリ　チカプサクモシリ」と呼ばれる木もなく鳥もいない砂漠のような国土(注24)に追放されるが、彼らの境遇を不憫(ふびん)に思う人間が祈りとともにさまざまな供物を祭壇に捧げてくれるからであって、この点でも人間は温情をもってヒグマたちの生存に欠くべからざる役割を果たすことになる。

ただ、それは一方通行の「施し」ではなく、メスグマも人間の守り神となって暮らしを見守り、首長の一家を繁栄させる約束をし、それを実際に果たしていることもまた語られる。クマ族によって恩恵を受け、互恵の関係が成り立つのである。

このようなクマ族の側もまた、クマ族の一家を語ったうえで男性は「このような訳(わけ)で　山の東端の神（熊神）の末娘が俺を殺し

たくなって、危うく殺されそうになったが、すぐまた彼女が後悔して　すぐまた俺の守り神になって運をよくしてくれたおかげで今あるのがお前たちなのだから　いつまでも鳥無き森無き国にいる山の神をお前たちは祀るのだぞ」と自分の子どもたちに言い聞かせる。この遺言によって、人間が一代限りでなく、子々孫々までクマの一族を助け、同時にクマの側からも子孫たちが見守られ、栄えていく未来が暗示される。

　結論を言えば、「人間がクマに襲われる」という状況を発端にしながら、入り組んだ利害衝突の修復が自然な形で巧みに行われ、人とクマにおいては、かえってお互いが助け合いの関係にあることを示されるのがこの物語なのだ。それは神さまであるクマに襲われるという不正常な関係を修復し、正常化することにほかならず、解釈による「世界の再構築」とみることもできる。

　アイヌ民族が、現実の暮らしや生業でも、物語の上でも、このように精緻（せいち）な世界像や関係性を築いてきたことが、ここにきて鮮明に見えてきた。アイヌ民族にとって、動植物や自然現象、物など、身の回りや山野の、実にさまざまなものがカムイ（神さま）であることを考えると、日々の暮らしの基調には、カムイたちに囲まれ、見守られている感覚があったものと想像できる。もちろんいい神ばかりではないし、時に神さまが注意を怠り、魔物につけ入る隙を与えたり、災害や事故が起きたりもするから、神さまに抗議したり、悪魔払いをすることだってある。一方で、狩りや山菜採りから無事に戻り、家族や集落に平穏な日々が続けば、そのことをカムイたちに感謝することも忘れなかった。

　次章では、縄文時代の狩猟採集社会から米づくり主体の農耕社会へとシフトした本州以南の人々

の精神文化の変化を探り、アイヌ民族との関係史にも踏み込んでいきたい。

四章　日本人はいつから「狩猟民の心」を失ったのか

秋田の阿仁にマタギを訪ねる

春先の締まった雪がザッザッと踏み音を立てる。緩い勾配の杉の木立を少し登ると「大山神」と墨書きされた鳥居と神社が迫ってきた。

秋田県阿仁地区比立内。阿仁は「マタギ〔猟師〕の里」と呼ばれる土地柄で、ほかに打当、根子といったマタギ集落が点在する。ウサギやヤマドリ、タヌキなども獲ってきたが、春は何といっても集団でのクマ猟の季節だ。

集団猟に際して、これから山に入るという時に必ずしないといけない儀礼が、山の神を祀った神社での拝礼である。二〇一七年四月十五日午前七時。五十代から八十代まで十三人のマタギ衆が集まった。

巻き狩りでクマを獲る猟師集団

先に述べたように、肉体と魂の分離という生き物観を持っている点で、マタギとアイヌ民族は共

クマの集団猟を前に山の神を祀った神社に参拝する阿仁のマタギ衆（撮影：小坂洋右）

通の精神文化を持っている。だが、アイヌ民族はクマ自体を神（カムイ）と見なすのに対し、マタギは山の神からの授かり物と考えている点で全く同じではない。単独での忍び猟も行うが、マタギといえば何といっても集団での巻き狩りである。一方、いくつかの文献に当たった限り、アイヌ民族がクマの巻き狩りをしたとする記録は見当たらない。

クマは追われると上手（かみて）に向かって逃げる習性がある。だから、勢子（せこ）たちが声を張り上げながらクマを追い上げ、上手で待ち構える撃ち手が仕留めるというのがマタギの巻き狩りの基本だ。言葉で言えば簡単だが、地形とクマの動きを先読みし、互いの連係を保ちつつ予定された場所に追い詰めるには、相当の熟練がいる。

齢（よわい）七〇歳。マタギ衆を統率する鈴木英雄さんが言うには、マタギも今は人数を減らし、

マタギを統率する鈴木英雄さんに案内された猟場（撮影：小坂洋右）

生きる基本は半農半猟。つまり農業抜きで暮らしは成り立たなくなった。それでも猟の伝統は現代に脈々と引き継がれている。反対にアイヌ民族のクマ撃ちが近年、数を極端に減らしたのは、個人や小グループで狩猟を行っていたがゆえに、直接の後継者が現れなければ途絶えざるを得ない側面があるようにも思える。

集団猟への同行はかなわなかったが、鈴木さんは個別に猟場（クラ）の一つに案内してくれた。雪に覆われた急峻な山肌に、幾筋もの沢が刻まれ、下から見上げても緊迫感がよぎる。そこはクマが好んで居着く場所で、過去に何度も猟運に恵まれたと言う。

阿仁から車で南に下ること三時間。山形県との県境、湯沢市（ゆざわし）には、山間（やまあい）で単独の忍び猟を続けてきた湯ノ岱（ゆのたい）マタギがいる。その一人、菅詔悦（すがしょうえつ）さんの狩猟スタイルは、十二月下

旬ごろ、クマの足跡やドングリなどの食べ跡を観察して歩き、そろそろ穴をつけて穴の前でじっと待つ。現れたクマとはしばし、にらめっこになる。七三歳になる今も猟に出て、クマと対峙すると言いつつ、こんな言葉が口を突いて出た。
「若いころはただ獲っていたんです。でも、四一歳ごろからクマの気持ちが分かるようになって、撃てないときが出てきた。嫌な予感がしたり、おまえには獲られないぞって相手が殺気で勝っていたりするときがあるんです。以後、今までにそんなことが一〇回ぐらいはありましたね。そんな時は『次は勝負だぞ』と約束して、ゆっくりその場を離れるんです」
クマの気持ちが分かって、クマを相手に約束を交わす。だから、撃つときもあれば、撃たないときもある――。おそらく、菅さんの前にも同じ心境に至った人がいたはずだし、そういう人はマタギだけでなく、アイヌ民族にも同じくいたに違いない。そんな思いを抱きながらマタギの里、秋田を後にした。

マタギは江戸時代には文献に登場し、阿仁には、さかのぼって平家の落人説もあるというから、興りは相当古いのかもしれない。ただ、本州、九州、四国の全体を見渡しても、狩猟で生きる人びとは、ごく少数派であり続けた。和人の主たる生業は長らく農耕であり、農耕文化が支配的だったと言ってまちがいない。

第二章で「アオバトが小さくなったわけ」という物語を例に、和人に祀られたのでは生き返ることができない、和人には生き返らせる力がないのだとアイヌ民族がみなしていた事例を紹介した。

69　四章　日本人はいつから「狩猟民の心」を失ったのか

そこから、「アイヌ民族は和人には魂の分離という発想がないと考えていた節がある」と推察した。これは、この物語が成立した時期に、和人の精神文化とアイヌ民族のそれとが、ある種の断絶を感じさせるまでに違いを際立たせていたことを示す。

例えば、先に紹介した日本昔話の「猿の婿入り」は、おじいさんが猿に手伝ってくれないか、耕してくれたら娘を嫁にやると約束するものの、嫁いでゆく娘が巧みな計略で猿を殺してしまう物語だった。猿を殺した結果、「娘はおじいさんの元に戻って家族仲良く暮らしましたとさ」と、めでたしめでたしで結ばれる。だが、猿の立場に身を置けばどうだろう。人間はこれほどまでに身勝手なのか──ということになりはしまいか。自分は人間の求めに応じて手伝いをしてあげた、娘をやるという約束だって、おじいさんの方から提案してきたのではなかったか。なのに、嫁にはやらないというならまだしも、なぜ、俺が殺されなくてはならないのか──。

「猿の婿入り」は、どう読んでも、人と猿の関係が対等ではない。人間の側は野生動物に対しては騙してもかまわないという前提がない限り、成り立たない展開である。

もちろん、日本昔話のなかには生き物を大事にしたり、助けたりする話はいくつもあって、日本人（和人）の自然に対する姿勢は敵対的ということはなく、むしろたいていは優しいまなざしで自然界を見つめていることは否定できない。ただ、「猿の婿入り」のような「結婚」や「同居」が絡み始めると、話は違ってくる。鶴の恩返しのように罠にはまった鶴を助けることはしても、やはり同居はさせられないというところに話は落ち着くのだ。

かつては日本人にも野生動物との婚姻譚

前述のように、渡来人の大量移住に伴って稲作農耕文化が大陸（中国）から入ってくる前、二千三百年前までの日本列島は、あまねく縄文人が狩猟採集・漁撈によって生きていた。

シカやイルカの頭骨がきれいに並べられた縄文の遺構からは野生動物への信仰が明確に読み取れ、道具など「物に宿る魂」を送っていたと見られる遺構も見つかっている。生き物ばかりか物にも魂が宿り、それが分離可能で、その魂をどこかへ安住させる「送り儀礼」があったと想像される点でアイヌ文化と共通点が少なくない。生産力を拡大する技術革新や道具の発達を目指すよりも、儀礼や呪術に使う道具づくりにせっせと励んでいたことが遺物の変遷からうかがえ、そこからも自然や生き物、物との関係性を重視した精神文化が浮かび上がる。

縄文文化は一万年もの長きにわたって列島の隅々に根を下ろしていたから、自然と向き合って暮らすその「心のありよう」は深いところに刻み込まれていたはずである。であれば、農耕文化が支配的になった弥生時代以降も、なおしばらくの間は狩猟採集時代に培われた口承や信仰、儀礼が残存し、一人一人の心の中で農耕文化と拮抗していたと考える方が自然である。だが、現代に受け継がれた日本昔話が「野生」を最後は拒む筋立てになっていることは、縄文の狩猟採集的な自然観が稲作農耕的な自然観に、じわじわと取って代わられたことを意味する。

しかし、民俗学の先学たちは、本州以南の各地に残された伝承に分け入ることで、その輪郭をつかん長い時間の経過が横たわるがゆえに、和人が縄文的発想を失っていった過程は明確ではない。

でいた。そうして得られた知見では、野生動物との距離が近い伝説は農耕社会に変わったあとでも、かなり遅くまで残っていたようだ。

例えば、もとは竹田出雲が著した浄瑠璃で、江戸時代、盛んに歌舞伎で上演された演目に「芦屋道満大内鑑」がある。

時は平安期、朱雀帝の時代。白い虹が太陽を貫くという異変が天に起こり、天文学〔陰陽〕の大家に、安倍安名、蘆屋道満という二人の高弟のいずれに跡を継がせるかを決めないままに亡くなっていたことが判明する。安倍安名と恋仲にあり、夫婦の約束を交わしていた賀茂保憲の養女、榊は隠されていた秘伝書を安名に渡そうと試みるが、伯父の岩倉治部に盗まれてしまい、その責めを負って自害する。榊も秘伝書を失った安名は発狂して信太の森をさまよううち、秘伝書を奪った岩倉治部の手下、石川悪右衛門に追い詰められたキツネを助けることになる。が、自身もけがを負わされ、ついには榊の後を追って自害を考える。と、その安名の前に榊と生き写しの女性が現れたではないか。それは榊の実の妹、葛の葉であった。葛の葉は安名を献身的に介抱し、二人はついには夫婦となって童子〔子ども〕をもうける。

ところがだ。童子が五歳になった年に「葛の葉」を自ら名乗る女性がよそから安名を訪ねて来る。見れば、今まで一緒に暮らしていた葛の葉もいる。あろうことか、二人の葛の葉が自分の前にいるのである。すると、母は童子に「自分はあの時、父に助けられた白ギツネです。恩返しに介抱するうち、夫婦になり、お前までもうけた。本物の葛の葉が現れた以上、自分は居られない」と伝え、障子

に「恋しくば尋ね来てみよ　いづみ〔和泉の国〕なる信太の森のうらみ葛のは」という和歌をしたためて森に帰って行く。

童子があまりに母を恋しがるので、安名は童子を抱えて森へと向かい、「たったひと言、童子にことばを交わしてくれ。この子はかわいくないのか」と呼び続ける。安名は「いかなる怪しい形であっても厭わない。せめてこの子の知恵がつくまで、育ててくれよ」と願うが、白ギツネは本性に返って茂みに消えて行く……。

結局は「野生」との別れが話の結末ではある。だが、以前紹介した「鶴の恩返し」などと比べると、「野生」との距離がより近いことだけは言えるだろう。それが如実に現れているのは、葛の葉がキツネの化身であると分かってなお、安名が一緒に暮らしたいと願う場面であり、童子が半分は人間、半分はキツネの子としてその後も生き続けることである。

日本の古代文化を探究した民俗学者の折口信夫(一八八七～一九五三年)は、妻の姿をした者が同時に二人現れて、夫が迷うという型の話は、平安末期につくられた今昔物語にもあるとし、「芦屋道満大内鑑」の祖型は少なくとも平安期までさかのぼれるようだとする。そのうえで、奈良時代以前の伝説を集めた日本霊異記の中に、子どもをもうけた妻がキツネだったと正体がばれて、夫の頼みに応えて夜だけは訪ねてくる物語があることを紹介している。この話は正体がばれて「野生」の世界に戻って行くという鶴の恩返しと展開は似ているが、人間とキツネの間に子どもができ、しかも正体がばれてなお、逢い引きを繰り返すという点で、動物との婚姻が十分に成立していると言え

そうである。

稲作農耕の定着とともに狩猟採集の自然観が薄まり、「野生」との間に距離感が生じると、かつては人から敬われつつも、狩られる対象であったシカやイノシシは、農作物を喰い荒らす害獣と見なされ、一転、駆除や駆逐の対象となる。そして、それが伝承や芸能にも反映されてゆく。

折口信夫は、古くは日本の芸能にシカの謝る所作を持ったものがあった、それは万葉集を見てもわかるとしている。奈良・平安時代（八〜一二世紀）に、動物との婚姻譚が語られている一方で、万葉集が編まれていく七世紀から八世紀にかけての時代にはすでに農作物を食べる野生動物が「人間の仇」と見なされるようになっていたのだとすれば、この辺りは、二つの文化的要素が拮抗する混濁の時代と言っていいかもしれない。

日本列島の古い形を残すのは「アイヌ民話」

民俗学で折口信夫と双璧を成す柳田國男（一八七五〜一九六二年）もまた、若くて美しい娘が水の神（ヘビ）に娶られる物語が、時代を経るに従って恐ろしいこと、不安なこととと感じられるようになってゆく流れを筋書きの変遷から解き明かしている。

名主・荘屋という類のある旧家の娘のところへ、夜深く人知れず通うて来る若者があるというのは、中世最も普通だった婚姻の方式である。……そのうちにおいおいと娘は身もちになった様子が見える。子の父は誰かと母が尋ねると、このあたりの人とは思われぬ上品な青年であ

るが、まだ名も家も語らないというので不審する。……それでは試みに苧環の糸の端を、そっとその衣裳に附けておいてみよと、教えるところまでは古今ともに同じで、それから後が物語の形は分岐している。

この上品な青年というのが、実はヘビの化身であり水の神である。古くは八世紀初めに成立したとされる『古事記』中巻、崇神天皇の項の「三輪山伝説」に原型とも取れる話があって、姫のもとに名も知らぬ美青年が通って来て身ごもり、糸を頼りに若者の後をたどると三輪山の神の社っていたというのがそのあらましである。のちには後段にいくつものバリエーションが生まれたもの、中世以来、水の神が針の鉄気の毒にあたって命を落とす展開が多いというのが、柳田國男の見いだした結論である。中世以前は「是」とされ、受け入れられていた水の神と人間の娘の結婚が、それ以後は、ヘビを殺すことで断ち切る形に変わっていったということになる。

ただ、すでに娘のお腹の中にはヘビとの間にできた赤ちゃんがいる。それも「始末」しなければ家系の中にヘビの血が入り、子孫はヘビを祖先に持つものとなる。

さて、どうするか。中世以降の人々が考え出した話の結末はこうである。

「人が糸に附いてはるばると跡を追うて来たとも知らず、岩屋の奥では唸き声が聞え、またひそひそと問答の声がする。それだからあのようにたって止めたのに、由ない人間の娘などに恋をするから、こうした悲しい目に遭うのだと一方がいうと、いやいや身はたとえ針の毒に傷つけられて死のうとも、種は人間に残して来た。思いおくことは少しもないと一方が答える。……大蛇の母は死ん

で行く子の答を聴いて、いやいや人間という者はなかなか賢い。もしも五月の菖蒲と蓬の葉を煎じて、それで行水を使わせたとしたらどうする。あるいは九月節供の菊を酒に入れて女に飲ませたら、胎内の子が皆下りてしまうではないか……。それを立聴きしていた母もしくは乳母が、すっかり聴いて帰ってその通りにしたというのが、多くの昔話の結末になっている」

この筋立てでは、結婚を拒む状況に加えて、ヘビの血縁もまた完璧に断ち切っている。

狩猟採集から稲作農耕へと暮らしぶりが一変した本州以南の人々の内面は、単純には解きほぐせないほど輻輳した変化を経てきたに違いない。ただ、流れとしては、狩猟採集に基づく自然観を喪失していく方向で一貫していたと思われる。

アイヌ伝承も含め、日本列島全域の伝承を比較研究した稲田浩二は、列島全体を俯瞰する目で次のように洞察した。

「日本の本州、四国、九州も古い時代はアイヌ族の地および日本列島の南西諸島と同様の昔話を伝承していたが、その後本州、四国、九州の伝承のみが独自な発展を遂げ、結果的に日本列島の両端の地域に古態が残ることになったのではないか。本州、四国、九州に残る伝承は後世の変容が著しく、一方で両端の地域のものはより古風な伝承に属していると考えられる」

そのうえで、「それらの伝承の変容の時期と起源を考えると、採集狩猟生活ののち農耕が始まった流れから、本州、四国、九州の伝承は水田稲作の始まった農耕牧畜時代に入ってその構成が変質したのではないか。一方アイヌ族と南西諸島の伝承は、採集狩猟時代——水田稲作のはじまらない縄文時代以前——の構成を留めていると考えられる」と結論づけている。

当然のことながら、それは、アイヌ民族や南西諸島の人々が今に伝えている物語の数々が、そっくりそのまま過去にさかのぼり、場合によっては縄文時代にまでたどれるということを意味するわけではない。そもそも北海道ではシンボリックな生き物が、縄文時代においてヘビやイノシシであるとすれば、続縄文時代にはヒグマや海のほ乳類に交替している。一三世紀に始まるアイヌ文化期になると、ヘビはカムイの座は占めるものの、ヒグマ、シャチ、シマフクロウが存在感をひときわ放っているように見える。となれば、物語のラインナップや題材も、「主役格」の交替に伴って変わっていったと考える方が自然である。ただし、北海道では狩猟採集民としての暮らしぶりが一貫して続いてきている以上、生き物と親和性の強い世界観はいつの時代にもあったはずであり、物語の根底を流れる自然観や「野生」との距離感は連綿と受け継がれてきたのではないかと想像できる。

和人の蝦夷地支配、アイヌ民族との衝突

だが、話には続きがある。稲作農耕の始まりから千年以上の歳月を経ると、ついに和人が本州から北海道（蝦夷地）に本格進出し始める。稲作農耕の導入にのっとれば、それはかつて「縄文人」としての一体性を源流に持ちつつも、いつしか断絶を生じた二つの文化圏の「あらためての出合い」だったとみなすこともできよう。

ただし、稲作農耕の導入によって社会も個人の心持ちも様変わりしていた和人と、狩猟文化を守り続けてきたアイヌ民族の出会いは次第に緊張から衝突に行きつき、箱館（函館）近くで和人の鍛冶屋がアイヌの若者を小刀（マキリ）で刺し殺したことを発端に、一四五七年、アイヌ民族最初の大規

模な決起、コシャマインの戦いが勃発する。アイヌ民族側は和人の館を次々落としていったが、最後は形勢が逆転し、敗北に終わる。

「出会い」は端からいびつで、不幸に彩られていたのである。

和人との接触が進んだことは、一方で交易の隆盛ももたらした。小刀などの刀剣類や斧、鍋、漆器などを得る代わりに、ヒグマの毛皮やクマの胆（胆嚢）、アザラシなど海獣の皮、鷲の羽、生け捕られた鷹狩り用の鷹などが、より頻繁に本州に送り出されるようになった。それは生活のために必要最小限をはるかに超える数の野生動物を獲ることを意味した。

これまで見てきた通り、アイヌ民族は生き物（カムイ）そのものが肉や毛皮といった土産物をもたらすために目の前に現れたり、シカやサケを司る神が自分たちに授けてくれると考えているから、獲物に恵まれること自体は本来、葛藤を生まない。ただ、大量に獲って、そのほとんどを交易に回すことには、何らかの心理的なあつれきがあった可能性がある。時代はずっと下るが、前章で紹介した八重九郎エカシは、毛皮が頭の部分を欠いていると商品価値が半減するにもかかわらず、アイヌの伝統にのっとってクマの頭皮をつけたまま霊を神々の国に送り帰し、毛皮商から見ればむざむざ価値を下げて毛皮を手放していた。つまり、お金を稼ぐことより、伝統とカムイの方を重んじていたのである。それは、さかのぼって、毛皮の「大量商品化」が始まった時代にも、何らかの葛藤があったことを想像させる。

江戸時代に入ると、松前藩が幕府からアイヌ民族との独占的交易権を得て、米が穫れない蝦夷地

でどう稼ぐかに腐心する。藩にとって、直接の支配地（和人地）は北海道南部の一角に過ぎず、その先には依然、アイヌ民族の大地（モシリ）が広がっていた。松前藩は当初、直轄地以外を細分化して家臣にそれぞれの地で交易できる権利を分け与えた。主に米を干鮭（乾燥させたサケ）と交換したが、次第にアイヌの側に不当なレートが課されていく。その後、場所請負制度のもと、家臣たちから経営を任せられた商人が実質的な権限を握ると、肥料を取るためのニシン漁が主流となり、各地の漁場（ぎょば）（場所）で、商人配下の支配人や番屋詰めの和人たちがアイヌ民族を連行し、酷使する事態を招いた。

その間、一六六九年のシャクシャインの戦い、一七八九年のクナシリ・メナシの戦いと、アイヌ民族はコシャマインの戦いののちも大きく二度にわたって立ち上がった。(注12)おおざっぱに言えば、シャクシャインの戦いの背景にはサケの交易で和人の側から不当な交換率を課されたことへの不満に加え、和人の砂金掘り、鷹師、猟師が蝦夷地で野放図に活動を始めたことがあり、クナシリ・メナシの戦いには漁場労働でアイヌ民族が酷使、虐待されたことが要因として大きかったが、いずれも松前藩によって鎮められ、幕府の蝦夷地直轄期を挟みつつも、和人によるアイヌ支配は弛む（ゆる）ことがなかった。

松浦武四郎が告発した悲劇の女性たち

商人によるニシン漁、サケ・マス漁が盛んになるとともに、山間部に暮らしていた人々までもが漁場のある海岸部に強制的に連行されたり、生まれ育ったコタン（集落）から遠く離れた漁場に連行

されることが頻繁に行われるようになる。

悲惨を極めたひとつが、北海道東部のシャリ（斜里）場所だったことを、幕府お雇いなどの身分で蝦夷地を六度にわたって探査した幕末の探検家、松浦武四郎（一八一八～一八八八年）が書き残している。うちウナベツでは、腰が二重になるばかりに曲がった老人や、血色が悪く杖をついてやっと歩けるような病気の者が、子どもたちとともに潮だまりでカレイなどの魚やホッキ貝を採っており、武四郎が尋ねると「舎利・網走両所にては、女は最早一六七歳にもなり、夫を持べき時に至れば遣られて昼夜の差別なく責遣われ、其年盛を百里外の離島にて過す事故、終に生涯無妻にて暮す者多く……」などと、その窮状を訴えた。[注13]

場所を請け負う商人の包囲網を逃れ、自身の才覚で自立的に交易を行った「自分稼ぎ」や、苛烈な支配を嫌って個人や集団でほかの場所に逃げ延びた人々など、松前藩や幕府の圧政に絡め取られず、したたかに生きたアイヌもいなかったわけではない。[注14] 津々浦々、蝦夷地全体が収奪や酷使に覆われていたという見方はできないものの、多くの人々が言われなき支配と困窮にあえぎ、苦しめられていたことは否定できない。

強制的連行の日常化に伴い、コタンに残る者は老人、幼児、病人や運上屋（会所）で雑用に駆り出される女性のみという地域が生まれ、和人との接触による天然痘や梅毒、麻疹などの流行、男性未婚者の増加、和人出稼ぎ人にはらまされた女性への堕胎強要による出生率の低下で人口は一気に減っていく。一八〇七年（文化四年）に約二万六千人を数えたアイヌ人口は、半世紀後の一八五四年

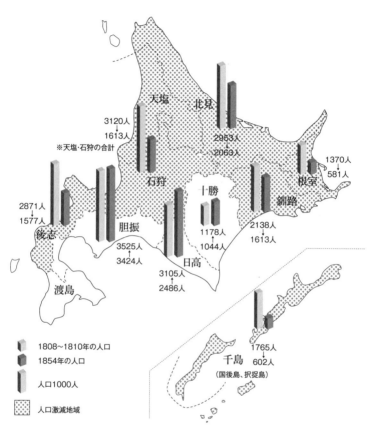

表2　19世紀前半のアイヌ人口の変化（『地図でみるアイヌの歴史』を元に作成）

（安政元年）には約一万八千人へと三割も減少したと見積もられている（表2参照）。

そんななかでも恨みつらみ、悔しさの最たるものは、一族の女性がよそ者である和人の性的欲求を満たすために連れて行かれ、妾同然の扱いをされたことであろう。松浦武四郎の『近世蝦夷人物誌（アイヌ人物誌）』には、相手が人の妻であろうと、結婚前だろうと、おかまいなしに、場所の番人らがコタンから女性を連れ去って我が物にしていた逸話が繰り返し書かれている。蝦夷地の現実をあまりにあけすけに告発したせいだろう、一八五七年（安政四年）ごろに執筆を終えて出版願いを出したものの、箱館奉行が難色を示し、世に出るまでに五五年の歳月を待たなければならなかった「発禁の書」である。

武四郎の記述でとりわけ涙を誘うのは、悲惨な境遇の末にひっそりと身を寄せ合って暮らした三人の女性の話である。

石狩川をさかのぼって旭川に至る手前のイチャン〔深川市一已〕の老女ヤヱコヱレは二人の娘が結婚し、五人の孫にも恵まれて幸せに暮らしてきた。ところが、番人の虎松という男が長女のペラトルカを横取りしようと夫を遠方の漁場に行ってしまう。次に長女を自分の漁場に連れて行ってしまう。孫たちも漁や山仕事へと駆り出され、本来、大家族に囲まれて天寿を全うできたはずなのに、天涯孤独になってしまったのである。あちちから魚を一匹、二匹もらい受けて生き長らえていたが、ついに家を捨て、鍋一つ、マサカリ一丁を持って山に入る。

これだけでも悲話の極みである。だが、話には続きがある。

下流にはカバタ〔樺戸、月形町〕という集落があって、そこではイリモという二九歳の女性を妻にしていた。ところが、ここでも番人がヤエレシカレに関係を迫り、ほどなくイリモを遙か遠く小樽の漁場に送ってヤエレシカレを思うままにしていたため、ヤエレシカレの体にもじき移る。すると番人は一椀の米も一服の薬も与えることなく彼女を見捨てたのである。鼻が落ち、体が爛れ腐ったヤエレシカレは川に身を投げようとしたところを止められ、連れられた先が老女ヤエコエレの元だった。

こうして二人が山中で暮らしているところへ、今度は七一歳になる老女ヒシルエが下流の雨竜からやって来た。ヤエコエレ同様、彼女にも息子が二人いたが、夫婦共々運上屋に連れて行かれ、自分は暮らしに行き詰まって野草の根などを口にしながら食いつないできたというのである。

松浦武四郎（三重県松阪市松浦武四郎記念館所蔵）

新たに加わったヒシルエに、二人はここで死んで霊となってあの支配人や番人たちに恨みを晴らすのだと語り、ヒシルエも同様の思いを告げた。

武四郎が三人を訪ねた時は、フキの茎で作った小屋に三人揃って居たが、ヤエシカレは体が半ば腐乱して臭気を放ち、我慢できないほどだったと記している。武四郎は米やタバコ、針を与えて去り、この話が

83　四章　日本人はいつから「狩猟民の心」を失ったのか

時の箱館奉行、堀織部正〔堀利煕〕の耳に届くと、ヤヱコヱレの次女が呼び出されて玄米などを与えられ、親元に戻って養うよう取り計られた。

一二歳の少年までも強制労働に

武四郎が一八五八年（安政五年）の探査を元に著した『左留日誌』には、日高地方、沙流川流域の各コタンのアイヌ家庭が、働き盛りの青年夫婦を中心に軒並み和人の「雇（下働き）」に取られていることが記されている。しかも連れられた先は海岸線に沿って東におよそ三五〇キロも離れたアッケシ（厚岸）の漁場である。

武四郎の記録では、父親六〇歳、母親五一歳、長男が一四歳、その嫁が一〇歳、次男が一二歳、三男が一〇歳、その妹が七歳、四男が五歳という八人一家は、父親、母親、そして一二歳の次男トッカラムまでが雇に取られている。

残された方も子どもばかりの暮らしで、窮状は察するに余りあるが、一二歳で漁場に連れて行かれたトッカラムもまた、平常心でいられなかったことは想像に難くない。

追い詰められた少年は、自分の指を切り落とせばけが人として家に帰してもらえるだろうと考えて左手の人差し指を自ら切って落としたが、それでも帰してもらえず、フグの胆汁を体に塗りつけたところ、全身真っ黄色になり、その体を見た和人の親方がついに彼を病気とみなして帰郷を許したという。

とてもありえそうにないこのエピソードは、決して作り話ではない。子孫によって今に至るまで語り継がれている一族をめぐる実話である。(注15)

当時75歳だった貝沢トロシノさんのアイヌ民謡を録音する萱野茂さん
（1966年撮影。『妻は借りもの』から転載）

留意しないといけないのは、このような出来事は決して、歴史の彼方(かなた)の昔語りではないということである。というのも、トッカラムの孫は、参議院議員として国会で初めてアイヌ語で質問をした萱野(かやの)茂エカシなのだ。二〇〇六年に七九歳で亡くなるまで、古老から伝承を聞き取ってまとめ、アイヌ民具を集めて萱野茂二風谷アイヌ資料館の開設につなげ、アイヌ語辞典の刊行まで成し遂げた功績は、今も多くの人の記憶に刻まれている。

萱野エカシの家系一つとっても、江戸時代と現代は決して途切れてもいなければ、遠すぎて実体を失った過去でもない。

武四郎の『近世蝦夷人物誌』には杉村キナラブック・フチの母方の祖父も登場する。トック(徳富)(新十津川町)コタンの指導的地位にあったトミハセ(トミパセ)(注16)で、親思いの心根の良い人物として描かれている。それだけではない。言い表せないほど

の苦悩をそれぞれ背負いつつ、身を寄せ合って暮らした先の逸話のうち、最初に山に入った老女ヤエコエレの郷里イチャンは、キナラブック・フチの父方のコタンで、自身の生まれ故郷でもあった。ただ、フチは一八八八年（明治二一年）の生まれで、幼い頃に雨竜に移っているから、ヤエコエレと直接の面識はないと思われる。

開拓使を辞めた良心の役人たち

続く封建時代から近代日本への移行をめぐっては、北海道がいつ、どのような形で日本に編入されたのかという、重要な問題がある。最後の幕府を築いた徳川家康は松前藩にアイヌ民族との交易を認める黒印状(こくいんじょう)を与えたが、歴史学者の海保嶺夫(かいほみねお)はこの黒印状の意味するところは「えぞ地〔北海道〕は日本の外にあり、松前藩はアイヌ民族と対等の立場にあることを示した」としている。（注17）だとすれば、松前藩と江戸幕府によって、北海道の実質的な支配が進められたのは確かだとしても、北海道の領土化はしていないということが言える。

一七九二年（寛政四年）に、開国を求めるロシア初の公式使節アダム・ラクスマンが保護した漂流民の大黒屋光太夫(だいこくや こうだゆう)を乗せて根室に現れ、幕府の沙汰を待ちつつ八カ月もの間、居続けたが、その時、幕府の老中松平定信(まつだいら さだのぶ)は自身の手記『魯西亜人取扱手留(ロシアじんとりあつかいてどめ)』でラクスマンの思惑を「日本の地ではないので、追い払われないことを知っているからネムロで知らせを待つというのだ」と分析している。これは定信、すなわち幕府が、根室も含めた蝦夷地を「日本の領地内ではない」とする明確な地理的概念を持っていたことを表している。

江戸幕府とロシア帝国が一八五五年に交わした日露修好通商条約（日露通好条約）で、両国が択捉島とウルップ島の間に国境を引いたことで、国際的な形式では北海道も含めて択捉島以西が日本に領有されたという見方もできなくはない。だが、国境画定の過程で居住者であり、先住民族でもあるアイヌの人々が意思を問われる場面はなく、「住民は自決権を有し、その意思が尊重されるべきだ」とする規範に照らせば有効性には疑問符が付く。

蝦夷地を北海道と改称し、国郡制を敷いた一八六九年（明治二年）八月一五日が事実上の併合とみられるが、例えば、小・中学生向け副読本『アイヌ民族：歴史と現在――未来を共に生きるために〈改訂版〉』（二〇〇八年三月初版、公益財団法人アイヌ文化振興・研究推進機構発行）はこの経緯を「一八六九年に日本政府は、この島を『北海道』と呼ぶように決め、アイヌの人たちにことわりなく、一方的に日本の一部にしました」と記している。この記述に照らせば、蝦夷地（北海道）の併合を、検証抜きで既成事実のように語ってはならないことが分かる。

とはいえ、明治に入ると、日本政府が北海道の土地をアイヌ民族から取り上げ、国有地や商業資本向け、和人の移民向けに分割していったのも事実である。

そんななか、江戸時代から近代、明治維新期への橋渡しをしつつ、苦衷を抱えていたのも松浦武四郎だった。武四郎が著した蝦夷地の報告は、各地の地理・産物を詳らかにすると同時に、松前藩が始めた場所請負制度が、いかにアイヌ民族に困窮と苦難をもたらしているかの「告発」でもあった。蝦夷地に通じた第一人者とみなされた武四郎は、明治政府から開拓使の重責、開拓判官に任命される。ただし、受諾に当たって、武四郎が出した条件があった。それは、念願としてきた「悪徳商

人の排除と場所請負制度の廃止」だった。ところが、請願は実現をみるどころか、商人の妨害工作まで耳に入ってくる。諸悪の根源とみなしたこの制度が、名前を変えただけで温存されると見て取るや、武四郎は辞表を出して開拓使を去った。任命からわずか半年後だった。

武四郎だけでない。開拓大判官の松本十郎は、漁撈を続けたいという願いを無視して、開拓使が樺太アイヌをサハリンから宗谷経由で北海道内陸部の対雁（江別市）に騙して連れて来た強制移住政策に抗議して職を辞した。北海道大学の前身である札幌農学校を卒業後、開拓使に入庁し、分県後、札幌県に勤務した内村鑑三もアイヌ民族への川ザケ漁復活案が却下されるのと相前後して役所を去った。キリスト教思想

内村鑑三

松本十郎（『松本十郎頌徳碑の栞』から転載）

家、非戦論者として世に出るのはそれからだ。

優秀な人材が、強権的で、聞く耳を持たない政府、政権に絶望し、良心の呵責を覚えて相次ぎ職を辞していった開拓使。そこからはアイヌ民族の境遇改善という明るい兆しは見いだせない。事実、明治政府はおかまいなしに苛烈な政策を次々打ち出していく。

その到達点が、一八九九年（明治三二年）制定の北海道旧土人保護法であった。北海道を日本の領土に一括編入し、土地を国有化し、商人、企業、和人入植者に貸与、売買したのち、最後の最後に地

味の悪いわずかな土地の分与を条件にアイヌ民族に農耕を強いた——。これがこの法律の本質である。川でサケを捕ることを禁じ、シカ猟も一部規制から全面禁止へと時を追って厳格にし、本来の生業では立ちゆかなくされていたから、多くのアイヌの人々は泣く泣く慣れない農業に活路を見いだすほかなかった。だが、それも大方はうまくいかなかった。のちに問題が顕在化する教育格差、経済格差は、この時代に「政策によって生み出された」ものなのだ。

五章　知里幸恵「神謡集」という贈り物

「神はいつまで私たちを苦しめるのでしょうか」

言葉や文化を奪うとは、何と残酷な政策であろう。そんな信じがたいことまでもが、明治以降には行われるようになった。

江戸時代がけっして良かったわけではない。松前藩は日本語の読み書きをあえて教えないことでアイヌ民族を劣等な地位に押しとどめて支配関係を強める方針で臨んだし、一時的に蝦夷地を直轄にした幕府といえば髪型や服装、名前だけを和風化しようと試みて、たいがいは無視されたり、反発を受けたりした。それに対し、明治政府は同化の姿勢で一貫し、その徹底ぶりも際立った。アイヌ民族から母語を奪い、伝統文化もアイデンティティーも失わせる——。その圧力は「日本国家の構成員として「同化」する」というよりも「アイヌ民族の排除」(注1)だったと指摘する専門家もいるほどのすさまじさで個々の家庭、個人に浸透していった。

学校でも役所の手続きでもアイヌ語は使えない。一歩、家の外に出れば、万事が日本語でなくては成り立たない環境がつくられ、家庭内でも時代が下るにつれて、子どもたちが日本語で生きてい

くように仕向けるほかない風潮が生まれてゆく。特に北海道旧土人保護法（一八九九年）、旧土人児童教育規程（一九〇一年、北海道庁令）が定められた一九〇〇年（明治三三年）ごろを境にその空気が強まり、一九二〇年代末には「現在においてはほとんどアイヌ語を用いる者はなく、青年らはおおかた知らない」との調査結果がまとめられるほどに至った。親や祖父母は子どもたちの前ではアイヌ語を使わなくなり、アイヌ語の物語は語られる機会がめっきり減った。

自分たちの未来が見通せなくなるにつれて、民族のなかから苦悩を自らの筆でつづる人物が現れるのも、しごく当然といってよかった。

　　過去幾千年の歴史を
　　顧（かえり）みる時
　　国は滅び
　　また興（おこ）り
　　またほろびる。
　　神は何故（なにゆえ）に
　　敗残（はいざん）の何時（いつ）まで
　　苦しめ給うのでしょうか！
　　何故に
　　何時まで。

91　五章　知里幸恵「神謡集」という贈り物

神をうらみ
神に反抗して
人を呪うほど
私たちの心は荒みきっているのです。
かつての大民族が
今わづか一万五、六千の
少数になって
北海の島の
ところどころに存在しているのです。(注3)

この一文をしたためたのは知里幸恵。「銀の滴降る降るまわりに、金の滴降る降るまわりに」のフレーズで有名な『アイヌ神謡集』を著したその人である。

友人の死　悲惨すぎる人生

知里幸恵は北海道旧土人保護法の制定から四年後の一九〇三年、登別に生まれ、六歳の時、キリスト教伝道のため旭川に派遣された伯母の金成マツと三人で暮らし始めた。祖母も伯母も口承が達者で、家ではアイヌ語が話されていた。祖母のモナシノウクと三人で暮辺倒だから、幸恵は自ずとアイヌ語と日本語のバイリンガルに育った。一方、学校では日本語一

伯母の金成マツ（右）と並んで写真に収まる知里幸恵
知里幸恵　銀のしずく記念館寄託［佐々木豊氏］収蔵品、知里森舎提供）

転機は十五歳の時だった。その記憶力や言葉の才能が、マツらを訪ねてきたアイヌ語学の言語学者金田一京助を驚かせ、一九歳の誕生日を前に、促されて上京。東京・本郷の金田一宅で短い生涯の最後の四カ月間を『アイヌ神謡集』出版のために注ぎ込むことになる。

世の動きに聡かった十代の才媛は、ほかの誰よりも同胞の将来を暗雲立ちこめたものと捉えていた。心臓に病気を抱え、無理ができない身でありながら、伝承をアイヌ語と日本語の対訳にしていく作業に精魂使い果たすまで没入したのは、そうした予見に駆り立てられ、いま残さなければ言葉も物語も消滅してしまうという切迫感に突き動かされたからだった。

ところが、金田一邸で神謡集を推敲していたそのさなかにも、心をかき乱す出来事が相次ぎ起こる。その一つが、旭川時代の親友、やす子の死だった。

貧困家庭に育ったやす子は一〇代で女郎屋に売られ、体を壊し、腰から下半分が腐ったようになって実家に帰って来た。だが、彼女から東京の金田一宅に届いた手紙には、まだ借金が残っているので、治っても雇い主のもとに戻らなければならない、いったい自分は早く治ってほしいと祈るべきか、それとも治らないようにと祈るべきかとつづられていた。その手紙の後を追うように届いたのが、彼女の訃報だった。身も心もずたずたに傷つけられた末のやす子の死は、幸恵の心をもまた打ちのめした。

やす子の死の衝撃を幸恵は日記にこうつづった。

運命に逆らおう、自然の力に抵抗しようと思うのは罪ぢゃないか。おのれただ人ではないか。小さい、いと小さい人の力が絶大無限の神の力にさからおうとするのはあまりに愚かな事ではないか。何故神は我々に苦しみをあたえ給うのか。試練！　試練!!　胸に燃ゆる烈火の焔をやききたえ、泉とほとばしる熱血の涙に我身を洗う。そうしてみがきあげられた何物かは、最も立派なものでなければならぬ。

私たちアイヌも今は試練の時代にあるのだ。神の定めたもうた、それは最も正しい道を私たちは通過しつつあるのだ。捷路などしなくともよい。なまじっか自分の力をたのんで捷路などすれば、真っさかさまに谷底へ落っこちたりしなければならぬ。

ああ、ああ何という大きな試練ぞ！　一人一人、これこそは我宝と思うものをとりあげられてしまう。

旭川のやす子さんがとうとう死んだと云う。人生の暗い裏通りを無やみやたらに引張り廻され、引摺(ひきず)りまわされた揚句(あげく)の果(はて)は何なのだ！　生を得ればまたおそろしい魔の抱擁(ほうよう)のうちへ戻らねばならぬ。

死よ我を迎えよ。彼女はそう願ったのだ。然うして望みどおり彼女は病に死した。何うして(ど)これを涙なしにきく事が出来ようぞ。心の平静を保つことに努めつとめて来た私もとうとうの平静をかきみだしてしまった。(注5)

親友の死に衝撃を受けたのが一九二二年六月二九日の日記だった。それから二週間後、七月一二

日の日記には、幸恵がまた別の出来事に心を傷つけられたことが分かる。

〔アイヌ神謡集の編集者〕岡村千秋さまが『私が東京へ出て、黙っていれば其の儘アイヌであることを知られずに済むものを、アイヌだと名乗って女学世界などに寄稿すれば、世間の人に見さげられるようで、私がそれを好まぬかも知れぬ』と云う懸念を持って居られるという。そう思っていただくのは私には不思議だ。私はアイヌだ。何処までもアイヌだ。何処にシサム〔和人〕のようなところがある?! たとえ、自分でシサムですと口で言い得るにしても、私は依然アイヌではないか。つまらない、そんな口先でばかりシサムになったって何になる。シサムになれば何だ。アイヌだから、それで人間ではないという事もない。同じ人ではないか。私はアイヌであったことを喜ぶ。私がもしかシサムであったら、もっと湿いの無い人間であったかも知れない。アイヌだの、他の哀れな人々だのの存在をすら知らない人であったかも知れない。私はアイヌだから、他の哀れな人々だのの存在をすら知らない人であったかも知れない。私はアイヌだ。神の試練の鞭を、愛の鞭を受けている。それは感謝すべき事である。(注6)。

文面から察するに、岡村が「アイヌであることを隠していれば世間から見下げられることもないのに、なぜあえて名乗るのだ」と、幸恵の行為をたしなめるようなことを口に出したのだろう。それは幸恵を思いやってのアドバイスだったかもしれない。だが、憤りに近い反発心を覚えるほどに、この時期、幸恵のアイヌとしての自己認識は高まっていたようだ。

「私はアイヌであったことを喜ぶ。私がもしかシサムであったら、もっと湿いの無い人間であった

「かも知れない」という一文は、アイヌ民族の心を持つ方を自分が選ぶと宣言しているように読める。日記のなかだからだろうが、裏を返せば、「和人は心にうるおいがない」とストレートに言っているのと同じである。それは「自分たちは差別されている側であるがゆえに、そうした立場の人たちの心情が理解できる」ということだけではないはずだ。そうであれば、「うるおい」という言葉はもとより使わないはずである。もっと積極的、肯定的な意味合いで、アイヌ民族の精神の本質に対する幸恵自身の共鳴がこの文脈からは感じ取れる。

あくまで私見ではあるが、アイヌ民族にとっての喪失の近世、近代と同時に、幸恵は和人の側の喪失も見て取っていたのかもしれない。口承を演じ、それに耳を傾け、興が乗れば踊り、歌う。さらには野や山にさまざまな神々の姿を見い出して、自分たちがその守護、恵みによって生かされていることを常に意識して暮らす。それは、今は失われつつあるかもしれないが、アイヌ民族本来の生き方である。しかし、和人はそうした習慣や感性をとうの昔になくし、物語を自ら覚え語ることも、興に任せて踊り歌うことも忘れてしまっているのではないか。

野山で授かりものがあれば、それを分かち合って生きる。そうした伝統的生活こそが「うるおい」なのだとすれば、それもまたアイヌ民族の古来からの生き方だ。そうした伝統的生活こそが「うるおい」なのだとすれば、それもまたアイヌ民族の古来からの生き方だ。分け合いもない。弱い者に共感せず、優越感に浸って差別を差別とも思わない。幸恵が発した「シサムであったら、もっと湿いの無い人間であったかも知れない」という言葉は、もしかしたらそれぐらい重い問いの発露だったのかもしれないと思うのだ。

もう一つ、幸恵の日記から読み取れることがある。それは、編集者の岡村千秋をはじめ、師と仰ぐ

金田一京助に対しても例外なく、和人には絶対に自分たちの境遇、思いは分からないという途絶感を幸恵が感じていたことである。金田一も岡村も、ともに幸恵の協力者であり、一定程度、理解者だったことはまちがいない。だが、異郷で最も近いところにいた和人からも、幸恵はある種の疎外感を感じさせられていたようなのだ。

神謡集の完成を心待ちにして全身全霊を捧げつつも、自身の体を蝕む病魔、同胞の死と、相次ぎ不幸が降りかかってくる。幸恵の心は動揺し、希望と絶望の間を行きつ戻りつした。が、次第に自分はアイヌであるという意識を強め、民族が築いてきた文化の豊かさ、その価値に目を開かされていったというのも確かである。それがこの間の幸恵ではなかったか。

「北海道は、先祖の自由の大地でした」

こうした複雑な胸の内を知れば、幸恵が唯一、完成品として世に遺した『アイヌ神謡集』も違った視点で読み解くことができる。

本編はアイヌ語、日本語の併記だが、序文のみ、幸恵自身が日本語だけで書いている。その序文に、彼女の胸中にあった複雑な思いが凝縮されている。

その昔この広い北海道は、私たちの先祖の自由の天地でありました。天真爛漫(てんしんらんまん)な稚児(ちご)の様(よう)に、美しい大自然に抱擁(ほうよう)されてのんびりと楽しく生活していた彼等(かれら)は、真に自然の寵児(ちょうじ)、なんという幸福な人たちであったでしょう。

第一部　人々は聴き　大地は見てきた　98

冬の陸には林野をおおう深雪を蹴って、大地を凍らす寒気を物ともせず山又山をふみ越えて熊を狩り、夏の海には涼風泳ぐみどりの波、白い鷗の歌を友に木の葉の様な小舟を浮べてひねもす魚を漁り、花咲く春は軟らかな陽の光を浴びて、永久に囀ずる小鳥と共に歌い暮らして蕗とり蓬摘み、紅葉の秋は野分に穂揃うすすきをわけて、宵まで鮭とる篝も消え、谷間に友呼ぶ鹿の音を外に、円かな月に夢を結ぶ。嗚呼なんという楽しい生活でしょう。平和の境、それも今は昔、夢は破れて幾十年、この地は急速な変転をなし、山野は村に、村は町にと次々々に開けてゆく。

「その昔」の北海道が自由の天地だったと表現して、その時代を生きた自分の祖先たちは「なんという幸福な人たちだったでしょう」と幸せを過去形で表現するその書き出しからすでに、いま、自分たちは不幸のさなかにあり、自由も奪われたのだという訴えがストレートに伝わってくる。
生業とする狩猟採集・漁撈が何の制約もなくできたかつての暮らしぶりを、まるで目の前で繰り広げられているかのように生き生きと描き出すことで、理想的な暮らしとは正反対の現在の苦境が、よりいっそう強く浮かび上がる効果を生み出している。

抵抗感を持ちつつ、橋渡し役に

ただ、なぜ序文は日本語だけで書かれたのか。バイリンガルだった幸恵の言語能力からすれば、アイヌ語と両方で書かれてもおかしくないのに、それをしなかったのはなぜなのか――という疑問

がわいてこないわけではない。

その答えの一端は、序文の後段にある。そこで幸恵は「多くの方に読んでいただく事が出来ますならば、私は、私たちの同族祖先と共にほんとうに無限の喜び、無上の幸福に存じます」との投げかけをしているのだ。つまり、想定されている主たる「読み手」は和人なのだということが、ここから分かる。

「日本の社会で公（おおやけ）に出版される本だから、手に取る大多数であろう和人を読み手に想定したのだろう──」と、そんなふうに果たして単純に言ってしまえるだろうか。当時、幸恵のみならず、アイヌ民族がさらされていた絶対的な同化圧力や政府の強権、和人の権威的態度を勘案すれば、幸恵自身も、抗い難いその渦中（かちゅう）に自分の身の置きどころを作らなくてはならなかったということがまず想像できるのである。

そう考えると、引用した「序」の書き出しの最後の一文、「この地は急速な変転をなし、山野は村に、村は町にと次第々々に開けてゆく」に「誰がそうしているのか」という主語が明示されていない理由も見えてくる。幸恵がそこに「変転し」「開けてゆく」と自動詞を使ったのは、その行為者である「誰か」をあえてぼかさざるを得なかったということなのだ。つまり、和人や入植者、政府を糾弾（きゅうだん）する空気がそこで醸し出されるのを避けたかったということであろう。この一文からだけでも、自らも含めて同胞が追い込まれた悲惨な状況を嘆きつつ、その元凶には直接触れられない、それどころか、その元凶である側の人たちに「私たちのことを知ってもらえれば、それは喜びです」と自分の側から接近を図らなくてはならないというジレンマが透けて見える。

幸恵が『神謡集』を脱稿した大正期と言えば、道都、札幌の中心部にあった四つのコタン（集落）すべてが消滅してすでに四〇年が経過していた。札幌のアイヌは、石狩川の支流である琴似川水系にコタンをつくって、遡上してくるサケを重要な食糧源として暮らしてきたが、開拓使は一八七八年（明治一一年）、支流でのサケ漁を全面禁止にした。食い詰めたコタンの人たちは、一部は石狩川の河口に、一部は幸恵が伯母らと暮らすことになる石狩川のはるか上流、旭川に移住する。コタンの消滅と相前後して周辺には札幌駅や北海道大学、琴似駅、大通公園がつくられた。それはまさに地域からアイヌという「主役」がいなくなる一方、新たな主役と公言するのは恐れ憚られる和人が山野を切り拓き、市街地を築いていく状況にほかならなかった。

序文から和人に対する複雑な感情と同胞の境遇への苦衷が読み取れる『アイヌ神謡集』。では、本編はどうなのだろうか。

アイヌ民族にとって神々は大きく二つに分けられる。一つは人格神であり、もう一つは自然神で、自然神には野生動物や鳥、貝などのほか、雷や火、山、天然痘といった自然現象も含まれる。必ずしも善なる存在ではなく、神々のなかには悪意あるものや悪戯なものもいる。そうした神々を主人公に、祖先が伝えてきた数々の物語から幸恵が『神謡集』に選んで収めたのは一三編。これまで見てきたように、根底には狩猟民としての発想があることから、農耕民にはそもそも、アイヌ伝承の本質は理解しにくいはずである。なのに、まず見て取れるのは、幸恵が選んだ物語はいずれも和人に限らず、万人に受け入れられやすい筋書きのものばかりだということである。

キツネが悪心を起こして人格神のオキキリムイら三人が乗った舟を暴風に巻き込むものの、逆に自分が殺されてしまう話。ウサギの兄が面白がって人間のワナをしているうちに自分がワナにかかってしまい、助けを呼んでくれと弟ウサギを仲間のもとへ遣わしたが、弟の方は途中で自分の役目を忘れてしまうという兄弟の物語。人間の村を襲って来た谷地の魔神をオキキリムイが退治する痛快譚。カエルが刀の鞘彫りをしていたオキキリムイに悪戯を仕掛けようとして殺される物語もある。

これらの物語に共通するのは、ひと言で言えば、悪者は退治され、悪戯や悪心は自分自身に返ってくるという「因果応報」である。だからこそ、元来、勧善懲悪の展開を好んできた和人の感性にも響くところがある。ほかにも、水が干上がって苦しんでいた沼貝の神さまが、自分を踏みつけにしたサマユンクルの妹の粟畑を枯らし、自分を助けてくれたオキキリムイの妹の畑には豊作をもたらしたという物語がある。これもまた、良いことをすれば、自分も幸せになるんだよという、応報譚と読める。

そうした物語を選んだ背景には、キリスト教という幸恵の信仰の影響もなかったわけではないだろう。ただ、それをある程度、勘案しても、物語の選択には、社会で圧倒的な優位性を持っていた和人にも受け入れられやすいようにしたいという意識が働いていたように思えて仕方ない。もちろん、そこには自分たちの伝承世界を和人にこそ知ってもらいたい、という前向きな役割認識もあったに違いないが……。

いつか和人と肩を並べる日がくる……

ただし、幸恵の胸中が、和人への橋渡し的な役割を自認するだけでは収まっていなかったことが、序文の後段に出てくる一文からうかがい知れる。

　その昔、幸福な私たちの先祖は、自分のこの郷土が末にこうした惨めなありさまに変わろうなどとは、露ほども想像し得なかったのであります。

　時は絶えず流れる、世は限りなく進展してゆく。激しい競争場裡に敗残の醜をさらしている今の私たちの中からも、いつかは、二人三人でも強いものが出て来たら、進みゆく世と歩をならべる日も、やがては来ましょう。それはほんとうに私たちの切なる望み、明暮祈っている事で御座(ござ)います。

　いまは同胞みなが辛酸をなめさせられているけれども、いつか、たとえ数人でも一目置かれる人物が出てくれば、状況が好転し、尊厳を取り戻せる日がくることだろう。見返してやりたいというような復讐心ではなく、むしろ「希望」に近い期待心が、「いつかは、二人三人でも強いものが出て来たら、進みゆく世と歩をならべる日も、やがては来ましょう」という一文には込められている。
　思えば、一三編のなかで最も知られた第一話「梟(ふくろう)の神の自ら歌った謡」にも、同じような切望が織り込まれているのかもしれない。いまは貧乏人になりさがっているけれども決して卑しくはない家

系の男の子をシマフクロウ神が助けて銀の滴や金の滴を降らせるというのが第一話の展開である。心根のよい貧乏人が金持ちを見返し、立場が逆転するという、話の骨格だけをみれば日本昔話でも語られてきた組み立てではある。だが、貧乏な子どもが幸せになる展開に、幸恵が苦難のさなかにあるアイヌ民族の未来を重ね合わせようとしたと捉えるのは、果たしてうがちすぎだろうか。

もっと言えば、『神謡集』に幸恵が、サケが産卵のために遡ってきたのを、川を汚して引き返させた「悪者」が退治される物語を二編収録している。類似する話をあえて複数入れたのは、その筋書きに強い思い入れがあったと考えるべきであろう。うち一編の悪者は「小男」で、もう一編では「悪魔の子」だが、序文の「この地は急速な変転をなし、山野は村に、村は町にと次々々に開けてゆく」という一節や、サケ漁を禁じてアイヌ集落を消滅や困窮に追い込んだ政府の政策と併せて想像を巡らせると、ここにもまた、開発の名のもとに自然を改変しながら、法令の遵守を求めてアイヌからサケを奪った和人に対する抵抗感がどこか潜り込んでいると考えたくもなる。

一方で、こうも思わないではいられない。幸恵が選び出した神謡一三編に共通する「良いことをすれば報われる」という応報観は、話としては分かりやすいけれども、幸恵の胸中には「私たちの祖先、同胞は世に恥じることのない正しい生き方をしてきたはずなのに、いまは貶められ、差別的な扱いに甘んじているではないか。それはなぜなのか。正しい生き方をしても報われない自分たちは、何ゆえにこれほどの苦難の道を歩まなくてはならないのか」という疑念が悲しみとともによぎっていたのではなかったか。

明らかに幸恵はジレンマのなかに生きていた。ジレンマに苛（さいな）まれつつ、『神謡集』の前文を日本語

で書きつづり、分かりやすくも含蓄のある口承伝承を選んで、アイヌ語から日本語へ、日本語からアイヌ語へと行きつ戻りつしながら、いまだ誰も作り上げたことのない文章世界を世に送り出そうと呻吟(しんぎん)を重ねていたのである。

つまり幸恵は、和人が自分たちアイヌ民族にどんな仕打ちをしてきたかという抵抗感を拭い去れないままに、和人への橋渡しという役割を自らに課した。加えて伝承が途絶えてしまう前に同胞のためにも伝え残しておかなくてはならないという使命感にもとらわれていた。さらには、自身が信仰していたキリスト教精神との折り合いもつける必要があった。幸恵にとっては、そのいずれも重たく、心の内で拮抗していたはずである。

しかし、幸恵本人が「これは自分が担わなければならない活動だ」と悟っていた以上に、本当に幸恵をおいては、ほかの誰にもできないはずの事業だった。幸恵は、アイヌ語も口承も失われていく時代を生きながら、自身は同居する伯母や祖母のお陰でアイヌ語にも口承にも通じ、なおかつ日本語も堪能だった。さらに文才・詩情を併せ持ち、ローマ字表記も会得していた。当時、カタカナの小文字を使うアイヌ語表記法はまだ編み出されておらず、自分なりの解釈をもとにローマ字で音を書き取るほかなかった。列挙したこの五つの条件をすべて備え、なおかつ前人未踏の難関に挑む気概と使命感を持つ人物でなければ到底、日本語対訳付きの出版はおぼつかない。その奇跡的な一点に、知里幸恵という少女が生を受け、函館の英国聖公会アイヌ学校でローマ字表記を習得した伯母の金成マツと一緒に暮らすという巡り合わせが起きたのである。

そんな諸条件に恵まれていたとはいっても、成し遂げようとしていた事業へのひたむきさ、その思いの切実さ、そして民族同胞への誠実さを思う時、幸恵が、一個の人間が抱え込むにはあまりに重たいものを背負い込んで歯を食いしばって机に向かっていたと想像せずにはいられない。なぜ、いたいけな少女がこれほどまでに苦しまなくてはならなかったのか――それを思う時、言葉を奪い、差別を繰り返し、集団としての存続を脅かしてきた政府や行政、和人の罪深さをやはり見すごすことはできない。

「結婚不可」の残酷な宣告

『アイヌ神謡集』でもう一つ見て取れるのは、婚姻譚が一つもないことである。

その手の物語が神謡にないわけではない。天界を統率する神（雷神）から求婚の手紙を受け取ったワシ神の首長の娘が嫁入り支度を調えて天界へと向かう「雷神に求婚されるワシ神の物語」とか、汚らしいおじいさんに姿を変えてやって来た国造りの神を迎え入れて結婚した「国造りの神にかかわれたシマフクロウ神の娘の話」、若い雷神に見初められて結婚したカエルの首領の妹の話などが実際語り伝えられてきた。結婚の後日談まで広げれば、さらわれた夫を火の女神が海の怪物から取り戻すお話や、シマフクロウである自分の夫をかどわかした水の神の娘に戦いを挑み、最後は三人で暮らすことを了承するクモの長の娘の話などがある。

だが、『神謡集』には、結婚にかかわる物語は一つも採録されていない。このことに気づいた時、私は幸恵への同情を抑えることができなくなった。いや、それは考えすぎかもしれない。たまたま

そうなっただけかもしれない。実は幸恵には、結婚を誓った相手がいたのである。旭川の北、名寄に住むアイヌ民族の青年、村井宗太郎（曾太郎）である。ともに結婚を誓いながら、しかし、幸恵自身は自分の体が病弱なことから、一緒になることに一抹のためらいを感じてもいたようだ。村井の家が農家であることから、娘の体を気遣った幸恵の母親ナミが結婚に反対の意向を示したことも、状況をいっそう複雑にしていた。

耐え難い苦しみと、それがうそだったかのような平静を交互に繰り返す心臓の狭窄症は、上京後、目に見えて悪化してきた。亡くなる十日ほど前、一九二二年の九月七日には、心臓の状態を診察した医師から「結婚不可」の宣告が下された。この時代であれば、「出産には耐えられない」という意味合いであろうが、この言葉が幸恵から結婚の望みを奪い、どん底に突き落としたことは想像に難くない。その絶望の淵から気力を振り絞って、幸恵は次のような手紙を両親に書き送った。

　静かにさえしていれば長もちしますって。診断書には、結婚不可ということが書いてありました。何卒安心下さいませ。
　私は自分のからだの弱いことは誰よりも一番よく知っていました。それでも、やはり私は人間でした。また此のからだで結婚する資格のないこともよく知っていました。人のからだをめぐる血潮と同じ血汐が、いたんだ、不完全な心臓を流れ出づるままに、やはり、人の子が持つであろう、いろいろな空想や理想を胸にゑがき、家庭生活に対する憧憬に似たものを持っていました。本当に、肉の弱いように私の心も弱いのでした。自分には不可能と信じつつ、それでもそ

107　五章　知里幸恵「神謡集」という贈り物

うなんですから……。充分にそれを覚悟していながら、それでも最後の宣告を受けた時は苦しうございました。いくら修養しよう、心ぢゃならない、とふだんひきしめていた心。ずっと前から予期していた事ながらつぶれる様な苦涙の湧くのを何うする事も出来なかった私をお笑い下さいますな。ほんとうに馬鹿なのです、私は……

この手紙を書きながら、幸恵はいったいどれほどの涙をこぼしたか。
「安心ください。静かにさえしていれば長もちしますって」と両親を気遣う表現には、言葉とは裏腹の悲しみの極致を感じずにいられない。「ほんとうに馬鹿なのです、私は」と自身を責めるひと言には、いつか下される宣告に、どこにもやり場がないことをとうに悟っていた早熟の少女の、それでも心が理性に従ってくれない苦悩が痛いほど込められている。
「結婚不可」という最終宣告。しかし、幸恵は同じ手紙に、この苦しみの中から自分の使命はやはり一つしかないとの結論に至ったこともまた書き添えた。

それは、愛する同胞が過去幾千年の間に残しつたえた、文芸を書残すことです。この仕事は私にとってもっともふさわしい尊い事業であるのですから。過去二十年間の病苦、罪業に対する悔悟の苦悩、それらのすべての物は、神が私にあたえ給うた愛の鞭であったのでしょう。それらのすべての経験が、私をして、きたえられ、洗練されたものにし、また、自己の使命はまったく一つしかないと云うことを自覚せしめたのですから……。

私の今の心持は、非常に涙ぐましい程平和で御座います。にくみもうらみもなく、ただ感謝にみちています。私のすべての気持をかきあらわすことはとても出来ません。ただ、此の事で、名寄の村井が何んな事を感ずるかと云うことが、私の胸を打ちます。しかし、何卒彼が本当に私をよりよくより高く愛する為に、お互いの幸をかんがえ、理解ある判決を此の事にあたえる様に、と念じています。

本当に罪深い私でした。何卒おゆるし下さいませ。(注9)

両親への手紙をしたためてから一一日のちの一九二二年九月一八日、幸恵は夕食前、ようやく『アイヌ神謡集』の校正を終えた。仕事を終えた高揚感はあったものの、食卓を囲んだ金田一京助は疲れの色を見て取り、「無理をされたので、顔色が少し悪いようです」と気遣った。幸恵は「少し風邪のようです」と答え、京助の息子、春彦に向かって翌日、一緒に根津神社のお祭りに行くことを約束し、春彦を喜ばせた。

その後、午後八時半ごろに心臓が急に痛み出し、幸恵は倒れ伏した。京助が呼んだ近所の医者が注射を勧めると、「それは最後の手段だそうですね。私はまだしたくはありません」と断ったが、京助が大学の知り合いの医者を手配しているうちに、心臓麻痺を起こした。医師が幸恵の死を告げたのはこの日の午後一一時だった。

幸恵はあれほど念願した自分の本を手にすることなく一九歳で召された。『アイヌ神謡集』の出版

は、その翌年の一九二三年（大正一二年）だった。

第二部

世界は変わった　でも、生きていく

一章 「喪失」の時代の先住民族社会

知里幸恵 銀のしずく記念館の誕生

知里幸恵が、生まれ故郷の登別で新たな「命の灯」をともしたのは、二〇一〇年九月一九日。この日、姪の知里（横山）むつみさん、作家の津島佑子さん、小野有五・北大名誉教授ら、多くの人たちの熱意で「知里幸恵 銀のしずく記念館」がオープンした。

幸恵が心臓の発作で還らぬ人となったのは一九二二年九月一八日だから、実に八八年の歳月が流れている。それでも人々は、アイヌ文化の伝承という役割を強烈に自覚しながら燃え尽きた、幸恵の一九年の生涯をついぞ忘れることはなかったのだ。加えて言えば、彼女が最後の最後まで推敲し続けた数々の神謡を後世に伝えていくことがいかに大事か、世代を超えてその認識が受け継がれてきたのである。

記念館建設に向けた思いをむつみさんはこう語った。

「幸恵自身、偏見に苦しみました。それでも日記に次のように書き残しました。『私はアイヌだ。……私はアイヌであったことを喜ぶ。私がもしかシサム（和人）であったら、もっと湿いの無い人間

夫の横山孝雄さんと知里幸恵像を囲む姪の知里むつみさん（撮影：小坂洋右）

であったかも知れない……』。幸恵はあの厳しい時代にアイヌ民族として生きる『アイヌ宣言』をしました。だからこそ、今に伝える意義があるのです」

むつみさんも特に小学時代はひどい差別を受けて、自分がアイヌ民族であることをことさらに意識するようになったという。差別体験は幸恵とも重なる。ただ、「[幸恵は幼いころ、]母方の祖母モナシノウクからユーカラなどを教わり、アイヌ文化の基礎を会得しました。これに対し、私はアイヌ語を学ぶ機会がありませんでした」と、育った環境は大きく異なっていた。

戦後間もない一九四八年に生まれたむつみさんの成長期、家の中でアイヌ語を使うことをためらわせる同調圧力は変わっていなかった。社会のなかに、子どもには日本語だけ覚えさせればいい、その方が和人と

変わらない暮らしをしていくためにいいのだ、と思わせる空気が依然強かったのだ。幸恵と同じく、むつみさんも人生の最後を病気に苦しめられた。初代館長として記念館の運営に多忙を極めるなかで、がんが判明したのである。宣告を受けたことは親しい人たちには隠さなかった。札幌から何度かお見舞いに訪ねるなかで、むつみさんの体調とともに気になっていたのは、記念館の先行きだった。市立や北海道立といった公立ではなく、NPO法人「知里森舎(しんしゃ)」が運営している。それだけに、将来にわたって存続していけるのか、そこを確かめておきたかった。

やや酷な質問だとは思いながらも、切り出した私に、むつみさんは揺るぎない口調で答えた。「もちろん楽ではないです。でも、入館料と友の会会員の年会費で何とか続けていける道筋はついていますよ。だから、心配なさらなくても大丈夫です」と。記念館を創設するだけでも大変なのに、それだけでない。館が存続していける手立ても、この人はしっかりと整えていたのだ。そして、開館六年後の二〇一六年九月に永い眠りに就いた。

あえて稲作を受け入れなかった可能性

札幌から登別までは約一三〇キロ。そこから伊達を経て、噴火湾(内浦湾)をぐるりと回り、さらに二〇〇キロの行程を行くと、函館市や松前町などが所在する北海道の南の端に到達する。

むつみさんの訃報に沈んだ翌二〇一七年の五月、私は函館の中心市街地からさらに約四〇キロ、車で小一時間の距離にある恵山岬(えさん)に立った。足もとには本州側で縄文文化が弥生文化に取って代わられたちょうどその時期、北海道で言う「続縄文時代」の始まりを告げる代表遺跡「恵山貝塚」が眠っ

ている。

津軽海峡を望む北海道の南端まで足を運んだのは、本州以南で縄文時代が終わり、本州側と北海道側がそれぞれ暮らし方の異なる道を歩み始めて以降の二三〇〇年に及ぶ時間を肌で感じたいという思いがあったからだ。

地球が最も冷え込んで海面が一三〇メートルも低くなった氷河期にも、津軽海峡は海峡として存在していた。つまり、一万年をさかのぼる以前にもここには海があり、北海道と本州は隔てられていたのだ。津軽海峡はそれほどの深さを持っているのである。

一方、北海道とサハリン（樺太）、サハリンとユーラシア大陸を現在、ぶっ切りにしている二つの海峡は氷河期には陸つづきで、二万五千年～三万年前には先人が北からのルートで大陸から北海道へと足を踏み入れた。「旧石器」と呼ばれる時代のことである。

北海道の南端にたどり着いた人々の目には、海峡を隔てて本州北端の陸地が見えた。向こう岸に何があるのか、行って見てみたい、最初はそんな衝動に突き動かされたのかもしれない。縄文時代に入った一万五千年～一万二千年前以降、人々は舟で対岸に渡り、そこから再び戻って来るだけの技術を身につけた。

縄文も時代が進むと、両岸の交流はどんどん活発になり、一万年前ごろには津軽海峡文化圏と呼ばれるほどの一体性が、海峡を挟んで両側に築かれる。

それから数千年という長い時間が過ぎた。そして今から二千三百年ほど前、「稲作の伝播」（注3）という日本列島を大きく揺るがす出来事が起きる。大陸（中国）からの渡来人によって、まず列島南部にも

一章　「喪失」の時代の先住民族社会

たらされた新しい文化、新たな生き方は、ほどなく本州の北端まで拡大し、対岸の北海道に移植しようと思えばできなくはない状況になった。だが、稲作の浸透は本州の北端までで、ついぞ北海道へは上陸しなかった。そして、その時期を境に津軽海峡の両側は二つの文化圏に袂を分かったのだ。以来、二千年以上にわたって、別々の文化が両岸で時を刻むことになる。

「代わりに失うものがあるかもしれない」

今日は五月らしい爽やかな天気だ。空は晴れ渡り、海峡の波はいくぶん輝いて見える。晴天のせいか、その先の下北半島はむしろ霞んでいた。

私は近年、弥生時代の初期、北海道の側に暮らしていた縄文人は、あえて稲作をしない道を選んだのかもしれないと考えるようになった。

本州側で稲作が始まってからも両岸の交流が続いていたことは、考古学によって裏づけられている。対岸で稲作が始まったことを北海道側の人々が見聞きしていなかったはずはない。おそらくは米の味も知っていたであろう。米作りに取り組んでみようという意気盛んな挑戦者が出てきてもおかしくない状況である。しかし、米作りが試みられた遺構は北海道側では見つかっていない。

挑戦した結果、根づかなかった——。つまり、従来のように「北海道の気候は寒冷だから稲作に適さず、狩猟採集が続いたのだろう」というのも大筋のシナリオとしては外れてはいないかもしれない。だが、一度重なる品種改良を経たとはいえ、いま、北海道ではかなり北部の地域まで田んぼが広がり、稲作が普通に行われている。となれば、当時、絶対に米が作れないというものでもなかったので

続縄文時代初期の代表遺跡、恵山貝塚（撮影：小坂洋右）

はないのか。

　実は緊密な共通文化圏を形成しながら、縄文時代からすでに両岸を分けていた顕著な要素があった。それは食生活の違いである。

　非常に分かりやすい例が虫歯の比率だ。本州の縄文人は虫歯の比率が一〇パーセント前後に達するのに対し、北海道の縄文人は二パーセントと極端に低い(注5)。その一番の原因は、縄文期の本州ではドングリやクリ、トチといったでんぷん質の木の実が多く食べられていたのに対し、北海道ではタンパク源となるサケやタラなどの魚、ホタテやホッキといった貝類、シカをはじめとする陸獣、イルカやクジラ、アザラシといった海獣が多く食べられていたからだとみられている(注6)。

　北海道の南端から広大な噴火湾を巡って室蘭に至る一帯は、魚類や貝類、山菜が豊饒(ほうじょう)で、人々

は続縄文時代に入ってからも、大型のヒラメなど海の魚を捕る技術をさらに洗練させながら、食糧に困らない暮らしを続けたようである。

本州の側を見れば、二千三百年前を境にドングリやトチの実が米に変わった。だが、北海道の側では何も魚や肉、貝を米に置き換える必要はなかったのではなかったか。ひと言でいえば、文字通り「足りていた」のである。

いや、食べ物のことだけではなかったかもしれない。村落の中に、農耕を取り入れて暮らし方が一変すれば代わりに失うものがあるかもしれないと畏れた人物がいたかもしれない。それは森や海、山、野生動物との深いつながりであったり、自然への畏敬や神への祈り、それに伴う祭りや儀礼、多様な口承であったりするのだ。

本州でも、近年の研究で、弥生文化の浸透が同心円状に均質的に進んでいったわけではないことが分かってきている。例えば、近畿地方の南部ではむしろ、農耕社会の到来に伴う権力の集中や社会の階層化に抵抗するかのような動きがあったとみられているのだ。

それを指摘するのは、考古学者の寺前直人である。「中国文明に起源をもつ権力集約型の社会統合は、巨視的にみれば紀元前一〇〇〇年紀以降、東アジア世界を席巻していったことは、その後の日本列島における社会変遷をみても間違いなかろう。そのようななかで、大阪湾沿岸地域を中心とする近畿南部社会は、文明の波が強まる初期金属器段階をむかえても、それまでの社会秩序を維持させることに一時的に成功した。文明に抗う社会装置、すなわち西方世界とは異なる青銅器や石製短剣をはじめとする石器を重用して……その独自の文化は、競争力の高い制度や『適切な』最新技術

第二部　世界は変わった　でも、生きていく　118

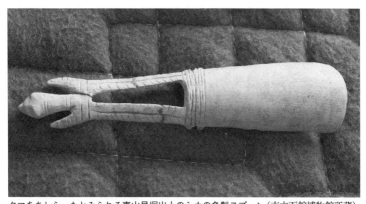

クマをあしらったとみられる恵山貝塚出土のシカの角製スプーン（市立函館博物館所蔵）

の運用を拒み、石器の生産や流通といった伝統的なネットワークにつらなる関係者の既得権益を守るために「文明に抗うための社会的装置を」重視し続けたのである」

また、東北北部の津軽平野では、自然災害が相次いだ弥生中期に水田が放棄され、人々が狩猟採集生活に戻った可能性が指摘されている。少なくともこの時代、続縄文文化の担い手を北海道から受け入れ、弥生文化に融合させることなく互いに雑居する状態にあったことが、遺跡の状況から読み取れるのである。(注8)

こうしたいくつかの点を考え合わせれば、北海道側の縄文人があえて稲作を選び取らなかったという可能性も、簡単には切って捨てられない。この見方に立てば、北海道の南端に竪穴住居を築き、続縄文時代前期の恵山文化を担った人々は、弥生文化の防波堤になったと言って言えなくもない。

加えて、恵山文化には土器の取っ手がクマだったり、骨製スプーンの持ち手にやはりクマや海獣があしらわれ

119　一章　「喪失」の時代の先住民族社会

ていたりするという特徴がある。この時期、北海道側の人間が、依然、自然と深く結びついていた証拠であり、もっと踏み込めば、本州側の農耕化に触発され、狩猟採集漁撈に基づく自分たちの自然観をより強く意識した現れとみていいかもしれない。

「縄文」は一万年の持続社会

続縄文文化を担った人々の思考に迫るためには、先行する縄文期の評価が欠かせない。その特徴は何といっても一万年も続くことのできた持続性にある。その持続性は何によってもたらされたのか。

一つに、戦争がごく少ない平和的な社会だったことが人骨の痕跡から推測されている。米国の経済学者サミュエル・ボウルズは受傷人骨、つまり陥没させられたり、へし折られたり、武器による打撃を受けたとみられる約五千体の人骨の分析を通じて先史時代の狩猟採集社会における戦争による死亡率を平均一四パーセントと算定しているが、縄文人の分析結果は調べられた二千五百八十二体のうち、暴力によるとみられる受傷例は二三体しかなく、比率は〇・九パーセント、大人に限定しても一・八パーセントとごく低かった。(注9)

本州以南では、弥生時代に米作りが始まってからわずか五五〇年後に巨大な墳墓を作る古墳時代に移行し、農耕が富の蓄積を促し、格差と権力者を生み出したことが明らかにされている。縄文社会にも、権力者や格差が富の蓄積がゼロだったわけではない。例えば、今から約三〇〇〇年前、縄文後期、北海道恵庭市のカリンバ3遺跡では、死者に装身具や副葬品が添えられた墓群と副葬品のない墓群が明

集落の規模が巨大なことで注目された青森県の三内丸山遺跡（撮影：小坂洋右）

瞭で、社会格差の存在を想像させる。だが、それが「権力者の誕生」といえるほどの格差だった可能性については否定的な見方があるうえ、縄文晩期になると副葬品がなくなっていき、他の遺跡にも格差の存在を示す遺構は見つからない。このことから、縄文社会は格差の拡大を抑制する何らかの仕組みを持っていたのではないかと見る向きもあるのだ。(注10)

縄文期の大規模遺跡として有名なのが、青森の三内丸山遺跡である。それまでの縄文時代の常識をひっくり返したインパクトは、集落規模の大きさであり、住居跡の多さだった。暮らしやすかった約六〇〇〇年前の温暖期でも縄文人の人口が日本列島全体で三〇万人前後と見積もられているなかで、最盛期の三内丸山には五百人もの住民がいたとの見方がある。五五〇〇年～四〇〇〇年前の一五〇〇年間に、約四〇ヘクタールの広大な範囲にわたって一〇棟を超す大

型の竪穴住居と七八〇軒にもおよぶ住居がつくられたと推定されているのだ。そんな三内丸山遺跡に関しても、考古学者の小山修三が「三内丸山の発掘は、富が特定の人またはグループにいったん集中したあと、宴会や祭祀の形で還元するという社会がすでに縄文時代にあったことを明らかにした」とし、縄文社会に「貧しくなる」ための儀式があったのではないかと提起しているのである。

〔三内丸山遺跡の〕盛り土にはヒスイ製品のように高価なものが容赦なく捨てられている。捧げ物の価値に見合った御利益があるわけだ。また、大量の完形の土器を故意に破壊したように見えるのは、アメリカ北西海岸諸族のポトラッチを思わせる。リーダーたちが財力を競う大がかりな祭りがあったと思われる。(注11)

集落がそこまで大きくなっても、縄文人が権力を集中し、人々を統治するクニ造りの方向を志向しなかったことがここ三内丸山遺跡からも知れる。労力をクニ造りに費やすのではなく、儀礼や信仰に注ぎ込んでいたようなのだ。

環境考古学者の安田喜憲はこう書いている。

〔縄文の〕文明原理は、平等主義に立脚した社会制度を有していたということである。たしかに縄文時代中期以降は、階級差を匂(にお)わせるものも存在するが、エジプトやメソポタミアのよう

に、巨大な王は出現しなかった。墓においても、その副葬品に大差はなく、階級社会の装置を文明原理に取り入れない、何らかの独自の平等主義に立脚した社会制度があったものとみなされる。生産物が貯蓄しやすく、このために容易に貧富の差や階級差が生まれやすい穀物農業を受容することを回避する文明の装置と制度系を有していた。

……こうした文明原理を永続的に維持するために、縄文土器や土偶を大量に生産する知的・芸術的行為やストーンサークルの構築あるいは巨木の祭などの宗教的祭祀といった、日々の生業活動とは異質の直接生産には結びつかない文明の装置・制度系をきわだたせて発展させた。(注12)

縄文人は王を出現させず、クニを造ることはなかった。だが、代わりに得ていたものがあったというのだ。それは平等主義に基づく社会や文化の持続性であり、手間と時間を惜しまずに生み出されたエネルギッシュな造形や精緻な儀礼・信仰の場だったのである。

先住民族が「クニ」を造らなかった理由（わけ）

そうなると、クニを造らないことの意味を、さらにポジティブに捉える必要があるような気がしてくる。より強い表現を使えば、クニを造らないことに価値を見いだしていたのではないか、世界はあえてクニを造らなかった人々と、クニ造りに突き進んでいった人々に二分されてきたのではないか——という問いである。

探せば、クニを造らないことに積極的な意味を見いだした文化人類学者も見つかる。その代表格

が、南米パラグアイの先住民族アチェ族などのフィールド調査を元に『国家に抗する社会』を著したフランス人、ピエール・クラストルだった。

クニができなかった地域、集団は「富が蓄積できず、王のような権力者が出現できなかった」とされてきた。それに対し、「先住民族社会だって、その気になりさえすれば富の蓄積ができないわけではない。なのにあえて蓄財を拒んできた。集団を束ねる首長だって戴きはするが、むしろその首長が権力を持てないように、うまくコントロールする仕組みを持ってきた」というのがクラストルの見方である。できるのにあえてそうしないできた——そこに先住民族社会の一つの原理と知恵があるというのである。

クラストルが強調するのは、先住民族の集落の長になることは、権力への近道ともいえる蓄財にはつながらないということである。長たる者にはむしろ、気前のよさと集落の同胞を助ける資質が求められており、実際にその暮らしぶりはむしろ貧困の部類に入るほどだった。クラストルはさらに、富を有しないばかりか、首長は権威や権力も持たされていないと説く。

では、その役割は何か。

それは「平和をもたらすこと」であり、「自分の財物について物惜しみせず、村人を助けること」である。とりわけ、平和を維持するためには「弁舌に巧みであること」が必要とされる(注13)。クラストル自身の言葉を借りれば、「首長は裁可を下す判事というよりは妥協点を探る調停者なのだ」(注14)。

クラストルはこうも書く。

首長は社会に仕えるのであり、権力の真の場としての社会そのものとして首長に対して権威を行使するのだ。だからこそ首長がこの関係を自らの利益のために逆転し、社会を自分のために奉仕させ、権力と名付けられたものを部族に対して行使することは不可能なのだ。未開社会は、首長が専制主に転化するのを許容しない。(注15)

首長が権力と財力を欠くが故に「王」は出現しないし、クニは生まれない。そこにはクニを造ろうとする動機は出て来ようがない。

クラストルは、「富の蓄積」を避ける仕組みを社会経済的側面からも考察した。先住民族社会は、食べ物を探し、確保するのに精いっぱいで、余剰を生み出す能力がないともされてきた。だが、クラストルが観察で明らかにしたのは、望みさえすれば物質的な財の生産を増加させるのに必要な時間を持っているにもかかわらず、それをしない社会風土だった。余った時間は、さらなる労働にではなく、祈りや儀礼、創造に惜しげもなく注ぐ――。ここまでくると、まさに考古学者が明らかにしてきた縄文社会のありようと重なる部分があることに気がつく。

これまで述べてきた通り、持続を旨とし、クニを造らないできたのが日本列島全土に暮らしていた縄文人であり、クニ造りに向かったのがその後の本州、九州、四国の弥生人であった。クニを造らない発想は、日本列島の大部分が弥生文化にのみ込まれた後も、北海道でだけは確固として息づき続け、アイヌ民族の精神文化にも流れ込んだものと考えられる。

だが、前述の通り、一三世紀にアイヌ文化が形成されたのち、和人が次第に北海道のアイヌ民族

を圧迫し、南端部に拠点を置いてじわじわと侵食を始める。明治期に入ると、おびただしい数の移住者が本州以南から北海道全域に入植し、アイヌ民族への差別が激しさを増し、言葉や文化を奪う同化政策の嵐が吹き荒れる。同化の対象は言葉や文化にとどまらず、狩猟採集という生業そのものを封じ、農業に仕向けていく農民化政策の形も取った。この間、あまりに激しく変化していく北海道の人間、社会、自然や風景に思いを巡らすと、能動的、主体的にその道を選び取ったのかどうかは別にして、稲作文化を受け入れなかった恵山貝塚の担い手、二三〇〇年前の続縄文人が歩んだ道を、果たして前向きに評価すべきか、逡巡せざるを得なくなる。それでも当時、暮らしを「変えなかった」ことの意義、本州以南と一線を画したことの意味は、もっと注目され、深く掘り下げる必要があると思うのだ。

人間、土地、動物——互いの切ってはならない関係

明治維新後、大量の和人の移民が押し寄せ、苦境が続くなかでも、アイヌのエカシたちは祈りを忘れないでいた。

アコローモシリー　ヤユンークルモシリー　モシリーノシキーワー　チエリキンテー
アコロイシカラー　イシカラホントモー　ソラプチーウンペ　クネワ……

「私たちの大地　(この)陸の人々の大地[北海道]　大地の中ほどを　遡る　私たちの石狩川　(そ

の）石狩川の中流域の空知（という地方）に暮らすものが私でして……」

祈りの主は砂沢友太郎エカシ。幼くして父親をクマに襲われて亡くした砂沢クラさんの夫である。招かれた先の大雪山の層雲峡で一九六四年に行ったカムイノミ（神々への祈り）の中で、砂沢エカシは「現在では和人〔シサム〕というものが　そこに集落を作り……様々な仕事というもの（をして）それで生計を立てて暮らしているのです」と、変わりゆく北海道の様子も神々に報告した。

砂沢エカシは北海道の中央部、現在の雨竜町にかつてあった伏古コタンに生まれ育ち、そのころ芦別市に居を構えていたが、伝わっているところによれば、父祖の地は小樽で、祖先は和人に追われて石狩川を遡り、空知川流域の歌志内付近に移り住んだ。ところが、和人が炭鉱を拓いたためにそこにも居られなくなり、今度は空知川を下ってソラチプト（滝川市）に暮らし始めたが、そこにもまた鉄道敷設の労働力として囚人たちが入って来たため、再度の移住を余儀なくされた。その先が砂沢エカシが生まれた伏古コタンだったという。

砂沢エカシが祈りの言葉を遺した一九六〇年代と言えば、一八六九年（明治二年）の北海道併合、開拓使設置から一〇〇年が経過し、高度成長による観光ブームにあやかって、北海道内では木彫りのヒグマが人気のお土産として買われ、アイヌ民族の工芸家が潤った時代でもあった。だが、そうした恩恵に与ったのは一部の人たちで、それも永続的ではなかった。一方で、その一〇〇年は、アイヌの人たちが、さまざまな産業分野に次々進出してくる和人に追われ追われて、住居を転々とせざるを得ない立場に置かれた時代でもあったことが、砂沢エカシの祖先の遍歴から浮かび上がる。

127　一章「喪失」の時代の先住民族社会

狩猟や採集に生きてきた人々が故地から引きはがされるということは、何を意味するのか。狩猟採集という生業を棄てさせられることが、暮らしばかりでなく心のうちにどれほど深刻な影響をもたらすのか。

コタン（集落）は暮らしの単位であったばかりでなく、さまざまな儀式、祭りの中核でもあった。そのコタンごとに、あるいは流域の複数のコタンから人を集めて行われてきた祭礼が、次々と灯を消していく。家々の外につくられた祭壇（ヌサ）ではそれぞれの地域に根ざした神々が祀られ、周辺には、何かの危険が迫っている時など、カムイが人間に知らせてくれるチノミシリ（私たちが祈るところ）があり、狩りや山菜採りを行うそれぞれのイウォロ（猟場）があった。サケの産卵床であるイチャンや網をかける漁場オヤウシ、水の湧くメム（泉）、通行が困難な断崖絶壁ウェンシリ（ウェイシリ）、山菜が豊富なハルシナイ……それぞれのコタンの住民に共有された地名は、その土地固有の地形、獲物や山菜が豊富な場所、聖地、気をつけなくてはいけない難所を教えてくれていたのだ。

だから、二風谷ダム建設をめぐって自身の土地が強制収用された時、萱野茂エカシがまず北海道収用委員会に訴えたのは地名と暮らしの結びつきだった。

ダム地域内の七二の地名を全部列挙したあと、萱野エカシは続けた。

「なぜ、このようにアイヌが自分たちが生活している範囲に丁寧に名前をつけたかと言えば、狩猟民族であったからであります。たとえば、狩りに山へ行き、シカをとり、あるいはクマをとった場合、それらの肉を一人で背負って帰ることができないときに、家族や村人に肉を取りに山へ行かせます。そのときに、どの沢のどの台地に肉を置いてきたかをはっきり教えなければ、肉のあると

ろへ家族や村人は行くことができないのであります。そのような理由から、アイヌたちは自分たちの行動範囲に、まるで自分のたなごころを指すかのように名前をつけ、それを若者たちへ教え、その地名を覚えることが狩猟民族の心得の第一歩であったのであります」

萱野エカシは松浦武四郎が残した地名と自身が知っている地名の数を対照しながら、道内全域にはおよそ四万八〇〇〇個所のアイヌ語地名があるはずだと示した。

住民間で共有される地名だけでない。「この岩のそばで獲物を授かった」「あの倒木を利用してあの日、野宿した」「あの沢で危ない目に遭った」などと、それぞれの個人としての日々の体験が共有された地名に追加され、集落と土地、個人と土地が明確なイメージや関係づけによって緊密なネットワークを築いていく。だから、故地を離れるということは、そうした一切のものから断ち切られ、無縁と化すことを意味したのである。

さらに、同化への圧力は、故地を追われる、追われないにかかわらず、地域や家庭で最も重要な「祈り」をも変質させ、時に喪失させた。例えば、一九二〇年（大正九年）生まれで、幼少期を日高各地で過ごし、一九五〇年に十勝の上士幌町糠平に移り住んだ渕瀬一雄さんは一九三九年（昭和一四年）ごろ、一九歳で初めてクマを獲った時、自分の親は神に誓って「神々の世界にクマの霊を送り」返していたけれども、自身はアイヌが猟をするとき、どのように神に祈るかは知らないことを悟った。それで「年寄りのまたぎ〔猟師〕が十人ほど集り、これからの世代はシサンプリ〔シサムプリ、和人の流儀〕になるからと『宇宙に向かって誓った』」のだという。

この「宇宙」とはいったい何を意味するのか。渕瀬さんは続けて「私たちの神というのは天照

大御神だから宇宙に誓ったのだ。誓いをしないと『逆さたたり』があるからだ」と説明している。クマを獲った時にはお祈りをしないと良くないことが起きるということは知っていたものの、どう祈るのかが分からない——。そういう事情なのだろうが、カムイノミ（神々への祈り）さえも和人式でやろうとする人たちが出てくるまでに、祈りの本質が変わりつつあったことがこの話から分かる。

アイヌ民族は、おのおのの家の中の炉縁で火の神を通じて神々に祈りを届け、家の外ではイナウが並ぶヌサで、やはり神々に祈ってきた。今でももちろん家の外にヌサを持ち、日ごろから祈りを欠かさない人たちはいる。が、世代間の変化、空気の違いを読み取り、ヌサを納めて日常的なカムイノミを自分の世代で終わりにする家庭もあった。

例えば、一九三〇年に静内（現・新ひだか町）で生まれた内海縣一エカシは、戦後間もない一九四七〜四八年ごろ、家に男手がないことからカムイノミに来てもらっていた近所のエカシが、相当の年配になった時点で自宅のヌサを納めたことを記録している。また、一九一六年、旭川生まれで杉村京子フチと親しかった熊田ハツエ・フチも、自身が二三、四歳だった一九四〇年ごろ、隣に暮らす門野ナンケアイヌ・エカシに家族でお願いして自宅のヌサを納めてもらったと伝えている。

そこに苦渋がなかったはずがない。だが、それは、きちんとした手順を踏まないでヌサが失われたり、祈る人がいないまま放置されることの方を畏れた決断でもあったのだ。内海エカシは「充分に満足なカムイノミをこれからも続けていくことが難しいのなら、将来的に粗末になる前に、自らの手でヌサを『納めて』しまおうと判断したのだと思う」と、ヌサを納めた近所の長老の思いを代弁している。

そこには多くの人が狩猟採集という生き方を捨てざるを得なかった暮らしの変化、それに伴う自然やカムイとの距離感も働いていたことは疑い得ない。山に入ること、野生動物を獲ること、神々の前に畏まり、感謝し、祈りを捧げることは不可分であり、本来、切り離すことができない性質のものなのだ。

アイヌ民族の精神文化の根底に何があるのか。ここにきて、あらためて問い直すことができるだろう。

これまで、人間の女性がカッコウ神やクマ神の妻になったり、人間の男性が自分を突然襲ってきたメスグマとの関係修復ばかりか、シャチ族の夫との仲介に一肌脱いだりする物語をみてきた。こうした伝承や祈り、あるいは儀礼は、人と動物、人と自然現象、動物同士が織りなす複雑な関係性をコタンの人々に常に確認させる効能を果たしてきたに違いない。言い方を変えれば、語られ、祈られ、祀られることで、動物神や鳥神、物神、果ては災害をもたらす神や病気の神までが、話し手や聞き手にとって特別な存在として位置づけられてきたのである。

北米にも共通の物語

私にとって、そうした「土地と人間」「自然と人間」の根源的な関係性を考えるきっかけを与えられたフィールドは一九八四年夏、二三歳の時のアラスカだった。私を後部座席に乗せた二人乗りの軽飛行機は、「低気圧の墓場」と言われるベーリング海に面したアラスカ半島の上空を飛び、人間の

土地から遠く離れた砂浜にがたがたと機体を揺すらせながら着陸した。ピストン輸送で北海道大学、明治大学の研究者六人を運び終えると、ブッシュパイロットは五週間後の迎えの日を確認して空に消えていった。

目の前には、寒さゆえに木がほとんど生えない無人のツンドラ地帯が広がっていた。およそ四二〇〇年前にこの地にたどり着いた数家族やその子孫たちが土を掘り込み、肩を寄せ合って暮らした竪穴住居跡が半分土に埋まり、草に覆われながら点在している。その小さな小さな「人間の土地」は、人跡が絶えて六〇〇年の歳月が過ぎていた。

それだけの時間があれば、「人間の土地」は「野生の土地」に還っている。グリズリー（ヒグマ）が現れ、数頭のカリブー（野生トナカイ）が列を成して通過し、ヤマアラシやオコジョ、キツネが頻繁に姿を見せる。夜にはオオカミの遠吠えが聞こえ、海にはアザラシがぽっかりと顔を浮かび上がらせ、貝は無尽蔵に採れ、サケが回遊し、潮が満ちてくるタイミングでカレイが手づかみできた。発掘作業の合間に、私たちはガンコウランの実を摘み、コゴミを見つけ、貝を剥いで、船員向けのビスケットをかじりながら半自給の暮らしを一カ月余り続けた。

アラスカの広大な大地を飛べば、この現代に至っても、人間の土地がほんのひと握りしかないことが一目瞭然、見て取れる。上空から見下ろせば、私たちが寝起きする三張のテントは「人間の土地」というよりも「人間の孤島」であり「人間の点」に過ぎないはずだった。六〇〇年前がそうだったように、私たちが去れば、ここはあっという間に野生の土地に立ち返ることも実感としてつかめる。私たちは野生動物を狩ることはしなかったが、ここに暮らした狩猟採集の民がどのような環境でど

第二部　世界は変わった　でも、生きていく　132

発掘調査を行ったアラスカのホット・スプリング遺跡（撮影：小坂洋右）

アラスカの遺跡地帯で目の前に現れたヤマアラシ（撮影：小坂洋右）

驚かされたのは、北米の先住民族の間にも、アイヌ民族と同じクマと人間の結婚譚があることだった。

ある秋の日、木イチゴを摘みに森に入った娘が、クマの糞を踏んで、滑って転んでしまう。近くにいて娘の悪態を聞いたクマは怒り、娘を森の奥のクマの村へ連れて行く。

のような生き物や植物をとりながら暮らしたのか、想像することはそう難しくはなかった。イメージが膨らんでくると、その延長上で自分たちが生きている気がしてならないのだった。

アラスカの上空を飛ぶと分かる。人間がどれほど都市でわが物顔をしていても、この地球上にその居住地はごく限られた一部分に過ぎず、圧倒的大部分はいまだ人を寄せつけない無人地であることに。われわれは地上を支配しているどころか、常に「野生」に取り囲まれ、弱く、孤立した存在なのだ。だからこそ、周囲の自然と、あるいは人間同士、集落間で折り合いをつけていかなくては消え入りかねないのだ。

クマの世界で生きてゆかねばならなくなった娘は、次第に、あれほど自分と違って見えたクマの姿に親しみを抱き始め、やがて若者のクマと結婚する。そして二度の出産を経験し、幸福な暮らしを営むうちに、かつて人間の娘がこの村に連れて来られた悲しい話も忘れていった。

が、ある日、聞き覚えのある犬の吠え声が近づいてきて、この幸福な家族に終わりが来る。それは娘の兄の犬で、行方不明になった妹を捜しに、村人たちと共に森の奥までやって来たのだ。クマの村では集会が開かれ、人間との争いを避けるために、この家族を村から出さなければならないと決める。一家は山の岩穴に逃げ込んだ。だが、もう助からないと知ったクマの夫はその晩、妻に告げる。

「私はもうすぐ死ぬだろう。おまえは人間の村に戻って、二つの世界をつなぐために、クマのクラン（家系）をつくるのだ」

そして朝になり、夫は岩穴の外へ出ていって、「死者の歌」を歌いながら殺されていった。娘は人間の村に戻ったが、子どもたちは生まれ育った村が忘れられず、クマの世界へと帰っていった。やがて娘は再び結婚をして、人間の子どもを産み、その子孫がクマの家系になっていった。(注23)

これはクリンギットインディアンが語り継いできた物語である。ここまで読み進めてきた読者にはもうおわかりだろう。これはクマの一族と人間の一族が緊密につながっていることを確認する物

語である。つまり、北米の伝承とアイヌ民族の伝承の双方に、一人の人間の女性を介して人間とクマが今は「親類」になっているという互いの関係性の始原を伝える物語が共通して受け継がれているのだ。

北海道から遙か何千キロもの距離を隔てた北米大陸で、類似の物語が語り継がれていることは、どう説明がつくのだろう。「伝播」という要素について確かなことは言えないが、いずれにしても、狩猟採集という共通の生き方、生命観が土台としてなければ、もとより世代を超えて語り続けられることはないはずだ。

実は、人類史的な時間軸で見れば、地球の広大な地域が「つい先ごろ」まで狩猟採集や漁撈で暮らしていたり、今なおその生活が根づいている領域なのである。ユーラシア大陸ではシベリアからカンジナビア半島北部にかけて、米大陸では北米、中米、南米の大部分、さらには東南アジアやアフリカの一部地域にまで及ぶ。厳密に言えば、北欧・ロシアのサーミ民族やアラスカの対岸、チュコト半島のチュクチ民族など、トナカイ飼育民として括られる人々もいないわけではない。だが、トナカイ飼育の興りは弥生時代の始まりと数百年しか違わない約三千年前とされ、牧畜業として大規模化するのは二百年ほど前と決して古くはない。(注24)この人たちにも狩猟採集で暮らしていた時代が長きにわたってあったのである。

北米と中米、南米を「大部分」と言ったのにはわけがある。この一帯では、いまの地図でメキシコを中心とするメソアメリカ文明と、高山帯のアンデス文明という農耕を基盤とする二つの文明が古くに勃興したからだ。とはいえ、南北アメリカ大陸全体を見渡せば、圧倒的大部分を狩猟採集や漁

第二部　世界は変わった　でも、生きていく　136

撈に依存する人々が占めてきた。特に北米では先住民族のほとんどが農耕文明とは無縁の生き方を続けてきた。となると、新大陸では農耕社会の方が例外的で、孤島を成していたという見方も成り立つ。

地球規模の視野に立てば、生業で色分けされた二三〇〇年前の世界地図の境界（ボーダー）の一線は日本列島の津軽海峡に引かれており、その南側では日本列島から中国大陸、さらにはアジアの南方にかけて稲作農耕地帯が広がり、その北側、北海道から樺太、シベリア、カムチャツカ半島、米大陸をほぼ覆い尽くす形で狩猟採集漁撈（一部は牧畜）地帯が広がっていたのである。

数百万年におよぶ人類史のなかで、一部地域で農耕や牧畜が始まったのはおよそ一万年前とされている。だとすれば、人類史の九九パーセント以上は狩猟採集生活だったとも言える。だが、その人類史の長大な縦軸のなかでは直近の、しかも「短期間」の間に農業革命があり、産業革命が起き、そして今や情報革命の時代に突入し、社会はあまりにも大きく変質した。その過程で各地の先住民族が次々、国家に征服され、その支配に甘んじた。人々は故地やコミュニティーから引きはがされて孤と化し、自然とのつながりも見失われた。と同時に、各国で是正が困難なほどの社会格差が進行した。そんな状況下、現代社会が失ったものを映し出す「鏡」となるものは何か――。その一つが先住民族の社会であることは間違いないだろう。世界の大きな部分が、人類史でいえば「つい先ごろ」まで、クニを持たない小規模なコミュニティーを持続させる選択をしてきたことに、もっと目が向けられるべきなのだ。

二章　未来をつかむための闘い

目の前で逮捕された父親

先住民族社会のありようだが、現代が失ったものを映し出す鏡だとしても、自身が奪われ、喪失したものを取り返さなくては正常な関係は築けない。アイヌ民族の復権がどこまで進んで、どこが停滞しているのか、そこも見ておく必要がある。

わたしが小学校に入る前、父の身の上に、いや私たち一家に大変なできごとがおこりました。ある日、長いぴかぴかの刀をさげた巡査（警官）が、わが家の板戸を開けて入ってきました。巡査が、『清太郎、行くか』と父に向かって言うと、父は、平ぐものように板の間にひれ伏して『はい、行きます』と答えるのです。静かに上げた父の顔の両眼から、大粒の涙がぼろっぼろっと落ちました。子供のわたしは、そのとき片目の父の両眼から涙がこぼれるのを見て、あれっ、目玉のないほうの眼からも涙が出たぞ、と思いました。

父は、鮭の密漁のかどで逮捕されたのです。毎夜毎夜獲ってきて、わたしたち兄弟や近所の

厳冬の1月、産卵のため最後の力を振り絞って千歳川上流にたどり着いたサケ（撮影：小坂洋右）

お婆さんたちに、さらに神々にも食べさせていた鮭はそのころ獲ってはいけない魚でした。(注1)

こうつづったのは、第一部でも登場した日高・平取町二風谷の伝承者、萱野茂エカシである。父親が逮捕されたのは「一九三三年（昭和八年）のことであったか」(注2)と記している。

萱野エカシはこうも書いている。

百二十年前の記録によると、山の斜面が一枚の茶色のじゅうたんが動いたかと思われるシカの大群。川では、川水が盛り上がるほどサケがそ上してきたと記されています。

そこへ、和人が雪崩のように移住、一方的に法律なるものを押し付け、アイヌが木を切れば盗伐したと逮捕、主食であるサケを捕れば密漁したと引っ張って行き、私の父も引っ張られた一人でした。(注3)

民族初の国会議員にもなった重鎮は「わたしたちアイヌは、アイヌ・モシリを『日本国』に売った

覚えも貸した覚えもないというのが共通の認識なのです」とも訴えた。そんな悔しい思いがあるからこそ、「一方的に法律なるものを押し付け」という言葉が出てくる。

父親だけでない。先にみたように、江戸末期に生まれた萱野エカシの祖父もまた、支配する側に苦しめられた。一二歳の少年でありながら、遠く三五〇キロも離れた厚岸の漁場に連れて行かれ、酷使されたのだから……。祖父やもっと先代にさかのぼって、どれほど多くの苦難が一族を見舞ったのか。なのに、「近代」という開けたはずの時代に入ってなお、密漁だ、規制違反だと親たちも苦しめられ続けなくてはならなかった。いや、近代こそ、政府の政策や法律による一律、網羅的で逃れようのない圧力が隅々まで加えられた、もっとたちの悪い時代だったのかもしれない。

「取り締まりは餓死者を出しかねない」

水産資源の保護を理由に、明治政府の開拓使が川でのサケマス漁の規制に乗り出したのは一八七六年(明治九年)。川の一部を横切るように杭を並べ、とどまるサケを捕る「テス網(テシ)漁」と「夜漁」が禁止された。「アイヌ民族を対象とする」とは書かれていない。だが、それがアイヌ民族の伝統漁法である以上、彼らが苦境に陥ることは明白だった。

規制を提案してきた東京出張所に対し、札幌の本庁は「過酷すぎる」と受け止め、「千歳郡の人々は山間部に暮らしており、川漁以外で暮らすことは困難」などと抵抗した。だが、開拓長官黒田清隆の意向で動く東京サイドは「全体の得失を考慮すれば少数者が被る影響は無視して構わない」「農業をさせればいいではないか」とごり押しし、実施させたのだった。「農業に仕向ける」「少数者は無視

する」というのはまさに同化政策の発想である。現地には実状を踏まえた温情を示す役人がいたものの、国の中央が偏狭な同化思想に立っていたことがこのやり取りから読み取れる。

さらに進んで全支流でのサケ・マス漁禁止が発布されたのは、わずか二年後の一八七八年だった。本流での引き網だけは認められたから、商業漁業や一定の資力がある和人入植者はサケ漁に参入できた一方、アイヌのサケ漁は石狩川でいえば千歳川や琴似川水系といった支流が主だったから、まさに生死に直結する厄災が突如、降りかかってきたことを意味した。現地の実情など何も分からない東京の役人は、殖産興業を人の命よりも優先したのだ。この措置が、札幌にあった四つのコタン消滅の一大要因にもなったことは先述の通りである。

開拓使を受け継いだ札幌県勧業課の役人として、一八八二年、全面禁漁後の千歳川流域の調査に派遣されたのが内村鑑三だった。調査の焦点は、どこまで厳密に密漁を取り締まるべきかにあったが、内村は勇気を持って密漁の黙認を提言する。

「もしこれ〔密漁〕を厳禁すればこの地のアイヌ民族を飢餓に陥れるのは必至である」。だから、監視は要しない。サケを常食としてきたアイヌ民族に対してはサケ漁を認めるのが唯一の飢餓対策であり、今後サケ漁を解禁する場合は上流の産卵地を保護しつつ、許可はその下流に出すべきだと内村は訴え（注6）。勧業課は実現に向けて動いたが、上層部は聞く耳を持たず、全面禁漁と密漁の取り締まりは続いていく。

一八八四年には、シカの不猟とサケの禁漁で十勝川筋のアイヌ民族が困窮しているとの訴えが札幌県に届いた。県から現地に派遣された栂野四男吉は、聞き取りをもとに「飢饉が最も酷だったの

は昨年冬末から今春、野草が生えるまでで、アイヌ民族の言によれば現に十数人の死者があった。ただし、餓死かどうかは定かではない。食糧不足の例を挙げれば、一度棄てたシカの骨を煮てその汁をすすり、サケやシカの皮切れも食べ尽くして、寒中、沼池に入って貝を探り、銀世界の中でヤドリギを求めてその緑の葉を食べたという」と報告した。(注7)

役人流の慎重な言い回しだが、このような状況下で死因が餓死以外だったと推測する方が難しい。一八八〇年代には自然産卵を促す種川（たねかわ）制度が道南・八雲の遊楽部（ゆうらっぷ）川や千歳川で導入され、千歳川では密漁の監視業務と産卵後のサケをさらい捕る役目を請け負うのと引き替えに、アイヌ民族にもそのサケが与えられた。が、こうした慣行はごく一部で短期間続いただけで、一八八八年から人工増殖が本格化すると廃（すた）れ、じき川でのサケ・マス漁は全面禁止と、さらに徹底されていく。

萱野エカシの父親清太郎さんの逮捕は、そうした一連の規制・取り締まりの延長線上にあったのだ。

サケを迎える伝統儀式、一〇〇年ぶりの復活

アイヌ民族にとって、サケがどれほど重要な食糧源だったか。それは「シペ、シェペ（本当の食べ物）」とか「カムイチェプ（神さまからいただいた魚）」と呼ばれていたことからも分かる。一九八〇年代に入って起きたのは、政府の禁漁政策で札幌市街地の四つのコタンが消滅して以来、途絶えていた「サケを迎える伝統儀式」を、市の中心部を流れる豊平川で復活させようとの取り組みだった。

札幌ではアシリチェプノミ（新しい魚への祈り）、地域によってはカムイチェプノミと呼び習わさ

サケの採捕許可を得て石狩川に網を掛け、アシリチェプノミの準備をする豊川重雄エカシ(「アシリチェプノミ　30年のあゆみ」より転載)

れる儀式がおよそ一〇〇年ぶりに復活したのは一九八二年。札幌市民の手で豊平川にサケを取り戻そうという「カムバックサーモン運動」が実を結び、最初のサケが戻った翌年だった。

復活の中核を担ったのは、今の北大農学部そばにあった札幌・コトニコタンにルーツを持つ豊川重雄エカシ(一九三一〜二〇一五年)と、アイヌ解放同盟の結城庄司代表(釧路出身、一九三八〜一九八三年)だった。豊川エカシらは復活から五年後、「儀式用のサケに限っては、川で捕ることを認める」との「特別採捕」を北海道庁に認めさせ、儀式は千歳や旭川、白老など各地に広がった。漁の経験がある豊川エカシは、いつの日かアイヌ民族に漁業権が返ってくることを願いつつ、「来てくれる人に一本ずつサケを持たせてやりたい」と、儀式前、石狩川河口に網を入れるのが慣例になった。

一九九三年の国際先住民年、土地や資源への集団伝統文化の復興や人権の擁護が推進された

葛野辰次郎エカシを祭司に豊平川河川敷で行われたアシㇼチェㇷ゚ノミ
=1993年9月15日(撮影:小坂洋右)

的利用権などを盛り込んだ二〇〇七年の国連先住民族権利宣言。二〇世紀から二一世紀にかけては、世界各国のいくつもの先住民族が、儀式用に限定されず、暮らしで食べる分のサケを捕る権利を獲得してきた。例えば、米国ワシントン州では一九七四年に地方裁判所のジョージ・ボルト判事が合衆国政府とアメリカ・インディアンが過去に結んだ条約を根拠に、先住民族には捕獲されるサケの五〇パーセントの権利があるとする判決を出した。

カナダでは一九八二年、憲法に先住権が明文化され、先祖伝来の生業活動を行う権利が認められた一方、その二年後に先住民族の長老が漁業法に反した伝統漁具を使って逮捕される事件が起き、裁判で「漁業法」と「先住権」のどちらが優先されるかが争われた。一九九〇年、連邦最高裁は資源保護が最優先されるものの、「先住民漁撈」は商業捕獲やスポーツフィッシングよりも優先順位が高いとし、長老の行為を「合法」とするスパロー判決を下した。現在、カナダでは自給用、知人への分配用、儀式用の捕獲がいずれも認められ、伝統的にサケを交易してきた民族に対しては民族間の交易も許されている。

「祖先と同じに捕りたいだけなんだ」

一方、日本国内では結城代表、豊川エカシがともに世を去る一方、三〇年経っても「儀式」と「伝統技術の継承」に限っての捕獲、それも特別採捕の許可申請と引き替えに認められるところから全く進まないできた。そこに二〇一八年八月、「紋別アイヌ協会の畠山敏会長が、特別採捕の申請を出さないで儀式用のサケを捕る決意をしたようだ。警察が申請を出すよう何度も説得に来ているらし

145 二章 未来をつかむための闘い

藻別川に丸木舟を下ろしてサケを捕ろうとする畠山敏エカシの前に立ちはだかって阻止する警察官＝2018年8月31日（撮影：小坂洋右）

い。このままだと密漁として逮捕されることもあり得る」との情報が仲間内を駆けめぐった。

儀式を二日後に控えた八月三一日午前三時。私は札幌から二五〇キロ離れたオホーツク海沿岸の漁業のまち紋別市に車を飛ばした。到着すると、バッコヤナギをくり抜いてつくった丸木舟を畠山エカシがまさにトラックに積み込むところだった。儀式の参加者らと一緒に藻別川の河口に行くと、コンクリートの護岸を一〇人前後の警察官が固めている。

「畠山さん、許可を取ってください」

警察官はその場を動かず、丸木舟を下ろさせない。

「許可？　何のためにするんだ」

畠山エカシが向こうを張って声を上

げた。

「北海道を売った覚えも、貸した覚えもないっていうのが平取から出た国会議員の萱野茂さんが言った言葉だ。あんた方が、どやどやと北海道に入ってきて、勝手に法律つくったんじゃないか。アイヌに聞いてつくったか。昔はここに一七、八軒のアイヌコタンがあったの。それを崩壊させたのが和人だって言うの。日本政府はアイヌを先住民族と認めた。おれは世界の先住民族の一人だ。世界で認められている自己決定権もある。それでやってるの。あなた方は世界の流れに逆行することをやっているんだ」

だが、警察は「われわれは儀式をやめてくれと言っているわけじゃないんです。許可を申請して法律にのっとってサケを捕ってくれと言っているだけなんです」と譲らない。

「あんた方がいう法律に触れるんなら、逮捕すればいいべや。我々の先祖は、若い男は連れられたら二度と帰って来られないところに強制収容されて働かされ、女は手込めにされて胎んだら堕ろす薬を強制的に飲まされたっていう。男によらず、女によらず奴隷のように扱われてきた。それは三代か四代前の話だ。そういうことを考えたら、和人に対して腹だたしいじゃないか。あなた方の先祖は土地も奪う、仕事も奪う、何もかも奪ってきただろう。われわれの祖先はここでサケを捕って暮らしてきた。それを再現して何が悪いの。一万円か、一万五千円もあれば魚は買えるよ。それもできる。だけど、市場から和人が捕った魚を買ってきて、アイヌの人たちに食べさせる、神さまに供える。和人か

ら買ってきたサケをよ、供物として神さまにあげる。それでどうなる。分からんべな、おれの気持ちは。法律法律って言うなら、国連の〔先住民族〕権利宣言が十何年も前に出て、つい先ごろは日本政府が国連人種差別撤廃委員会から「アイヌ民族に対して、土地や資源利用の権利を十分保障していない」との〕勧告まで受けて、なんで〔法律に反映〕しないのよ」

 警察は「許可を取ってくれ」の一点張りだ。一時間たち、二時間たっても状況は変わらない。舟を下ろせないまま、憤然とした表情で畠山エカシは河口を後にした。翌日の午前中にも、祭司を務める石井ポンペさん(むかわ町穂別出身)を伴って再度、河口に向かう。今度はロープを対岸に渡して網を仕掛ける計画だ。

 だが、ロープを対岸に投げようとする畠山エカシの前に今度も数人の警察官が立ちはだかってやはり阻止する。押し問答が続くなか、儀式で歌や踊りを演じるために札幌から到着した徳田昭子フチ(穂別出身)が畠山エカシの胸の内を推し量って口を開いた。

「私らからすれば、日本人が勝手に決めた法律なわけだ。北海道も、うちらから取ってしまったわけだし。うちらの家も土地もみんな奪って、さらに法律だからって言われても聞けんよっていうのが畠山さんの話なんだわ。その気持ち、私たちはよく分かる。でも、法律に照らし合わせてだめだっていうのもよく分かる。ただね、儀式の時ぐらいは、サケの儀式なんだから、サケを捕らせてくれてもいいんじゃないの。許可、許可っていうけど、昔は私たちに法律だとか、許可もらわないと捕れないのっていうのきな魚を捕って食べていたわけだ。それをなぜ、日本人の敷いたレールの上で、私たちアイヌがなんでここにが畠山さんの一番の疑問だと思うよ。日本人の許可もらわないと捕れないのっていうの

いないといけないのっていう話でしょ。あんたがたの先祖が勝手に北海道に入ってきたんだよ。あんたがたの先祖、もともと北海道かい。侵略してきたんだよ。うちらの海、うちらの川、うちらの大地だ、この北海道は」

警察も畠山エカシも、しばしその言葉に聞き入った。そのうち、言い合いを遠目に見ていたサケマス釣りの男性が、自分が海で釣り上げた魚を提供したいと申し出てきた。畠山エカシは感謝して受け取ると、自身で捕れなかったことを「残念だ」と言い残して河口を後にした。

徳田さんは「アイヌ半分、日本人半分の私としては日本の法律は守らなければと半分思っている。けど、そうじゃない畠山さんにとっては日本人が勝手に決めた法律という抵抗感があるんだろうし、税金も納めているわけだから、せめて儀式や先祖の供養に対しては捕るのを認めてくれてもいいんじゃないかっていう気持ちがあるんだと思うよ」と言う。

畠山エカシにとっては、七六歳という、自分の生き方を次世代に伝えおくべき年齢での行動だった。しかも、年一回の儀式は二〇回を数える。行動に移す移さないは別にして、同じ思いでいるエカシが他の地域にもいることをその後、知って、私は今回のことが北海道知事や国の役人に規則や法の改正を促すきっかけになるかもしれない、儀式用にとどまらず、自分たちが暮らす分だけでも捕れる時代が来るかもしれない、と淡い期待を感じないわけではなかった。

それは、そもそも論から言っても、論拠なき主張ではない。明治初期の一八七五年（明治八年）、河川を国の一元管理にしようとして混乱を招いたことから、政府は翌年、漁業管理を都道府県に委任するとともに、伝統的な権利関係にも配慮するよう求めた経緯があるのだ。湖沼河川は海面に準じ

る扱いを受けたことから、新潟県や山形県など本州の日本海側では人工増殖に寄与しつつ川でサケを捕る漁業協同組合や増殖組合が生まれ、こんにちに至るまで脈々と川漁を続けている。北海道の場合、開拓使がアイヌ民族に国の方針を当てはめず、伝統的な権利関係を問答無用で奪ったことが根っこの部分にあるわけで、なおかつ内村鑑三が禁漁策の撤回を役所内部から堂々と提言し、勧業課が実現すべく動いたことからも、こと伝統的にサケを捕ってきた先住民族アイヌに対しては、川でのサケ漁解禁はしごくまっとうな要請と言っていいのだ。

今からでも遅くない。要は、歴史的経緯の検証に基づくビジョンを、政府や北海道庁、北海道知事が持てるかどうかなのだ。つまり、アイヌ民族に対する川でのサケ漁業権の保障は、こうした歴史的アプローチからも、国際的な先住民族の権利アプローチからも、いずれからも導かれることになる。

世界を見渡せば先住民族の権利は拡大する方向で進んでいる。だから、国際世論の醸成や各国の先進事例という「外圧」が、変化の起爆剤になる可能性もある。いずれにしても、何が失われ、それをどう求めていくのか、各地のアイヌ民族の間で一定程度の共通認識が生まれれば、次なる動きにつながっていきやすい。

遺骨はいまだ大学の保管庫に

その意味でも、二〇一〇年代に入って道内各地のアイヌ民族が、研究者によって大学や博物館に持ち去られた祖先の遺骨を取り戻す動きを同時多発的に進めたことは先行事例になる。北大をはじ

北大から遺骨の返還を受けて浦河でアイヌ民族有志らが行った再埋葬＝2016年7月17日
（撮影：平田剛士）

め、東大や京大など全国一二大学と一三博物館施設が保管するアイヌ民族の遺骨は計約一七〇〇体にも及び、墓地から掘り出したものが大半だ。中でもコーカソイド（白人）に属するのか、モンゴロイドなのか、アイヌ民族の「人種」特定を主目的に複数の教授が精力的に各地のアイヌ墓地を掘り起こした北大は約千体と突出して多く保管している。

その北大をアイヌ民族有志が提訴する流れが決定的になったのは、二〇一二年二月一七日だった。前年、北大学長宛に祖先の遺骨の返還と謝罪を求めたものの反応がなく、学長と面談したいというその後の申し出も何度も先送りされたことに業を煮やした日高・浦河出身の小川隆吉エカシと城野口ユリさんらはこの日、厳しい寒さのなか、大学本部を直接訪ねた。だが、玄関先で留め置かれ、職員から「お答えはしませんが、ご意見はたまわ

りました」と、またもや先送りの返事しかもらえず、これ以上、交渉しても埒が明かないとの判断に至ったのだった。

　小川エカシら三人が北大を相手に遺骨返還訴訟を起こしたのはこの年の九月。謝罪はなかったものの、北大は二〇一六年三月、札幌地裁で和解に応じ、浦河・杵臼集落の一二体がこの年の七月に返還されて郷里の土に再埋葬された。だが、そこに、本来、最も喜ぶべきはずの城野口ユリさんの姿はなかった。無念の思いを抱えながら訴訟半ばで亡くなったのだ。

　浦河には、同じ日高地方の平取にルーツがある土橋芳美さんの姿もあった。

「あなたの祖先、平村ペンリウク・エカシ（一八三三〜一九〇三年）の遺骨は北大にあります。返還します」といったんは北大から確約を得たものの、その後、「遺骨は違う人のものでした」と前言を撤回され、受け取れないまま焦燥感に苛まれての参列だった。土橋さんは、ペンリウク・エカシの霊が自分に語りかけてくるような思いにとらわれ、それをそのまま字にした。それを出版したのが長編叙事詩『痛みのペンリウク　囚われのアイヌ人骨』だ。

　おまえは一二体の／遺骨の再埋葬に立ち会うために／浦河に行ったのう／杵臼コタンでの<ruby>先祖供養<rt></rt></ruby>イチャルパ／驚いたな／アイヌ語が響いておった／その昔／アイヌ語を覚えよと／役人たちが言ってきたとき／イギリス人の／バチラーが／「言葉を失ってはなりません」／と熱く語ってくれたことを思い出す／もう語る者もなくなっているかと／思っておったぞ／それが／高らかに／いい声の響きだ／帰ってきた霊に対して／今までさぞ辛かったろうと

／慰め／労り／今度こそ／故郷の大地に／静かに眠ってほしいと／語りかける／わしは／聞いておって／涙がとまらなかったぞ／生きている／われらアイヌの子孫が／生きて／アイヌ語を響かせておる／わしが死んで／一一三年がたつ／こうして／その昔／わしがしていたことを／する者がいるとはな／よくぞ／昔のイチャルパを／してくれたものよ

二〇一七年、ドイツからの遺骨返還

この間、海外からは、自主的な動きとしてアイヌ民族への遺骨返還が実現したり、その意向が示されたりしてきた。ドイツの学術団体「ベルリン人類学民族学先史学協会」は、一八八〇年の学術報告をもとに、団体が保管する遺骨一体が「札幌〔コトニコタン〕のアイヌ墓地から盗掘されたもの」と認定し、二〇一七年夏に日本に返還。オーストラリア政府も同国の先住民アボリジニの遺骨と交換で博物館が入手したアイヌ民族の遺骨を返還する決断をした。また、米カリフォルニア大学ロサンゼルス校（UCLA）付属のファウラー博物館からも、返還の可能性が示唆された。米国では一九九〇年に連

これらの動きは、それぞれの国の国内の取り組みも反映してのことだ。

浦河を皮切りに、他地域からも提訴が相次いだ。紋別アイヌ協会の畠山敏会長、十勝の浦幌アイヌ協会（差間正樹会長）と相次ぎ和解が成立し、それぞれ四体、七七体が返還される。その後、浦河にはさらに四体が返還され、二〇一八年六月には旭川アイヌ協議会（川村兼一会長）が遺骨三体と副葬品を取り戻した。(注12)

邦法である「アメリカ先住民墳墓保護返還法（NAGPRA）」が制定され、大学や博物館が国内の先住民族の遺骨を保管している場合は、帰属する部族を特定したうえで、返還を前提とした協議を進めることが義務づけられた。調査の結果、対象となる遺骨は国全体で一八万体を超え、二〇一五年末時点で約五万三千体が返還済みか、手続きが進んでいる状況だ。調査、輸送、再埋葬の費用は多くの場合、連邦政府が負担し、九四年以降、約四三〇〇万ドル（一ドル一一〇円で約四億七千万円）を超える予算が拠出されている。

　法制化はしていないものの、オーストラリア政府もアボリジニやトレス海峡諸島民の遺骨返還を各国に積極的に要請し、博物館協会や首都キャンベラの国立博物館が主導する形で数多くの帰還を実現している。ドイツもベルリン医科大がアフリカの旧植民地ナミビアの先住民族に返還した先例があった。

　対して日本はどうか。そもそもアイヌ墓地から遺骨を掘り出した北大などの研究者は、ほとんどのケースで集落名しか記録しておらず、それゆえ遺骨はそれが誰で、子孫が誰なのかが分からない形で大学に保管され続けてきた。にもかかわらず、二〇一四年六月に政府が示した遺骨返還の当初方針（ガイドライン）は、直系の子孫（祭祀承継者）(注13)が自ら自身の祖先の遺骨を引き取りたいと手を挙げた場合に限って返還に応じるというものだった。埋葬や供養を直接の子孫が自分の祖先に対して行う日本の民法に沿った形だが、元来「収集」の時点で個人名が記載されていないわけだから、「返してほしい」と申し出ようにも大半の子孫が断念せざるを得ない。

　アイヌ民族は伝統的に集落（コタン）の単位で埋葬や先祖供養を行ってきた、だから遺骨は集落に

第二部　世界は変わった　でも、生きていく　154

返してもらいたい——と、各地で先述のような返還訴訟が次々起こされてようやく、政府は集落や地域団体が受け皿になれるように二〇一八年一二月、ガイドラインを改正した。ただし、返還に向けた調査をはじめ諸経費に米国のような手厚い財政支援はない。返還、再埋葬、墓地・慰霊施設の維持管理には、コミュニティーの結束や人員の確保、継続的な資金力が必要で、健在な地域集団がある一方で、明治以降の同化政策のもと衰退したり、解体してしまった地域もある中では、依然、返還に二の足を踏む地域が多いと予想される。遺骨返還を本当の意味で実現する気があるのであれば、コミュニティーの再生・復興という原点に目を向けることが必要だが、今のところ、政府の動きからその視点はみえてこない。ということで、文部科学省の調査で把握された国内約一七〇〇体の遺骨の大半が、返還されないまま各大学に残り、二〇二〇年、国立アイヌ民族博物館の開設に併せて白老町に造られる慰霊施設に集約される見通しだ。

だが、アイヌ民族だけでない。世界各地の先住民族が、白老に集約的な慰霊施設が造られた経緯を知り、おびただしい数の遺骨が子孫や郷里に戻ることができないまま政府の管理下にある実態を目の前にした時、果たしてどのような思いを抱くだろうか。今から憂慮せざるを得ない。

先行国に水を開けられる先住民族政策

アイヌ民族の最大組織である北海道ウタリ協会（現・北海道アイヌ協会）が尊厳の回復と先住民族としての権利獲得を明確に掲げたのは、野村義一理事長時代の一九八四年。この年、協会が自ら策定し、総会で採択した「アイヌ民族に関する法律（案）」いわゆる「アイヌ新法案」を内外に提起した。

教育・文化対策、経済的自立の促進策や自立化基金の創設、民族政策を継続的に立案する中央審議機関・北海道審議機関の設置、国会・地方議会への民族代表の議席確保、国立研究施設の設置などを盛り込んだ。

野村理事長は「一番最初に挙げたのが人権問題です。……もしアイヌと和人との間に生活の格差があれば、その格差を埋め、対等にし、正常に社会に受けいれられるようにしなければならない。そうすれば、アイヌが自己卑下をすることもなくなってくるんではないでしょうか。そのために『アイヌ新法』を定める必要がある、と思うんです。……日常レベルで格差をなくしていく法律が必要なんです。それが『アイヌ新法』です」(注15)と意図するところを語った。

ところが、当時の横路孝弘北海道知事の諮問機関による討議で民族代表議席の構想が抜け落ち、舞台を国会に移して一九九七年に施行された時にはアイヌ文化振興法と名を変え、文化や言葉の復興のみに矮小化された法律になっていた。これには、すでにその職になかった野村前理事長をはじめ、アイヌ民族の多くが「後退している」(注16)と落胆を隠さなかった。その後、二〇年たってもアイヌ語の話者が大きくは増えていないことをみると、文化振興という眼目すら効力が限定的だったと言わざるを得ない。

一方で、一九九七年は、二風谷ダム裁判で、札幌地裁が公的機関としては初めてアイヌ民族を先住民族と認定し、個人の尊重と幸福追求権をうたった憲法一三条、少数民族の権利を掲げた国際人権規約（自由権規約）二七条を根拠に、アイヌ民族の文化享有権を認める画期的な判決を出した年でもあった。

二風谷ダム判決で勝訴の記者会見に臨む萱野茂エカシ（中央）と貝沢耕一さん（右）。
左は田中宏弁護士（萱野れい子さん提供）

沙流川をせき止めるダムは、まさにアイヌ民族が数多く暮らす平取町二風谷に造られた。「ダム建設用地にわれわれアイヌ民族が舟下ろしの儀式チプサンケを行ってきた場所や神々がいざというときに危急を知らせてくれる聖地チノミシリが含まれている。私たちが所有するその土地を強制収用したのは裁量権の乱用である」などとして萱野茂エカシと父、貝沢正さんの遺志を継いだ耕一さんが一九九三年に北海道収用委員会を訴えたもので、判決は、国の事業認定と強制収用を「違法」とし、事実上、萱野エカシたちの勝訴だった。

これはすなわち、アイヌ民族が伝統的に利用してきたり、儀式などを行ってきた場所を先住民族への配慮抜きで水没させたり、開発したりできないことを意味する。自身の伝統や文化を易々とは踏みにじられ

ないお墨付きをアイヌ民族は司法から得たことになるのだ。衆参両院が二〇〇八年、「アイヌ民族を先住民族とすることを求める決議」を可決したことで、その根拠はさらに強化されたとみていい。

だが、他国は先住民族としての「認定」からさらに進んで、実質的な権利を保障してきている。例えば、サーミ民族が伝統的にはトナカイ牧畜や漁撈で暮らしてきたノルウェーがそうだ。アルタダム建設という同じダム問題への抵抗運動が、ノルウェーでは政府の姿勢を大きく変える契機となり、ノルウェー国はノルウェー人とサーミ民族で構成されていると憲法に明記され、言語・文化振興や生活向上が国の責任とされるようになった。サーミ民族は、自分たちの政治組織「サーミ議会」まで持つに至り、政府がサーミの居住地域で政策を立案する際に諮問を受ける立場を与えられた。ノルウェーに限らず、先住民族が暮らす地域で、彼らが影響を受ける開発行為を決定するに当たって「事前の、自由な説明同意（インフォームド・コンセント）」を義務づけようとする動きが、「FPIC (Free, Prior and Informed Consent)」という略語とともに近年、国際社会に高まりつつある。

「あの人たちは見捨てないから」

日本国内では二〇一四年夏に、偏見や差別との闘いにいまだピリオドが打たれてはいないことを思い知らされる事件が起きた。札幌市議会の金子快之議員が「アイヌ民族なんて、いまはもういない」とツイッターで発信したのだ。金子市議は北海道新聞の取材に「同じ日本人なのに、少数民族という理由だけで優遇されるのはおかしい」と答え、アイヌ民族が存在しないと主張するばかりでなく、政策的な予算を投じることもまた問題だとの立場を打ち出した。

この時、発言の撤回を求める先陣を切った一人が、首都圏に暮らす古布絵作家の宇梶静江フチだった。浦河に生まれて二〇代で上京、一九七二年、三八歳の時に「同胞よ、手をつなごう」と新聞投稿を通じて首都圏のアイヌ民族に結束を呼びかけ、東京ウタリ会の創設につなげた。そしていま、関東圏では四つの団体が緩やかに連携しながらそれぞれの活動をするに至っている。その民族連帯の象徴でもある人が声を上げ、有識者や市民があとに続いたのだった。それでも金子市議はついぞ発言を撤回することはなかった。が、次の選挙で落選し、「札幌市民はヘイトスピーチを許さない」という姿勢が鮮明になった。

そもそも、これまで取り上げてきた江戸時代の漁場での強制労働、さらには明治以降の生業、文化、言葉、居住地、集落を奪う同化政策の過酷さ、残酷さを知ってなお、「アイヌ民族を優遇するのはおかしい」と言ってのけられる人が果たしているだろうか。だからこそ、歴史を学ぶことが大事なのだ。過去を知れば、現代のアイヌ政策はけっして「優遇」と呼べるような性格のものではないことに誰もが気づき、むしろ、その不十分さに愕然とするにちがいない。さらに言えば、いま、求められる政策は、賠償の発想と先住民族としての権利に基づき、教育や経済面の格差を是正するものであり、国が奪ってきたサケなどの資源や樹木の利用権などを保障しつつ、公正の実現を目指すものでなくてはならないと納得できるだろう。

ところが、政府が二〇一九年二月に国会に提出したアイヌ新法案「アイヌの人々の誇りが尊重される社会を実現するための施策の推進に関する法律案」は再び、その視点を欠いていた。それがゆ

えに、アイヌの多くの人たちが、今度も落胆させられることになった。法案は、アイヌ民族を「先住民族」と法律で初めて規定した点では評価できるものの、歴史認識も謝罪も賠償も欠いており、資源の利用権や遺骨の返還権など、国連の先住民族権利宣言に盛り込まれた先住民族としての権利（先住権[20]）に基づく施策が何一つ見当たらなかったのである。法的拘束力はないといっても、各国は国連宣言の主旨を国内政策に反映していく責務を負う。ましてや日本は国連総会で賛成票を投じた側だったのである。

植民地支配や同化政策を強いたという歴史認識なくしては、そもそも「先住民族」の認定はありえない。しかも、先住民族としての認定には、権利（先住権[21]）が表裏一体のものとして伴うことは、国際社会の共通理解になっている。だから、海外の有識者から間髪入れず「国際的にみると奇妙な法案」との厳しい指摘が投げかけられたのもうなずける。もう一つ見逃せない欠陥は、当事者であるアイヌ民族に事実上、自己決定権がない点だ。法案が明記する施策立案の主体は市町村であり、市町村がアイヌ政策推進の地域計画を立案して国に裁可を求め、国の認定が得られた事業には予算が付くというのが大枠である。法案は四月に成立したが、主体性、自己決定権がないばかりか、アイヌ民族が地域振興、観光振興の「看板」にされかねない危うさをはらんでいると言わざるを得ない。

法の成立と相前後して、アイヌ民族文化財団が、紋別アイヌ協会のカムイチェプノミへの助成を二一回目の二〇一九年度、初めて「不承認」とするなど、いくつかの団体への助成を打ち切ったことが判明した。それは、関係者の間に「復権の運動にかかわれば干されるのでは」「助成金を介した分断ではないのか」といったさらなる不安をかき立てることになった。

2002年の白糠ふるさと祭で神々に祈りを捧げる八重清次郎エカシ（大石義勝さん撮影）

各市町村に対しては、今後の法の運用、とりわけ地域計画の策定に当たって、アイヌ民族を主体として参加させ、意向を最大限、尊重していくことを望みたい。また、国や財団も「文化」の大枠を一方的に規定・限定したり、許認可権限を恣意的、排除的に行使することがあってはならない。文化は生き方や暮らしそのものであり、祈りや価値観、世界観までも含むものなのだ。

アイヌ民族を差別する側に立つ人にも、施策を立案する人にも、ぜひ知っておいてほしい事実がある。それは、とりわけ開拓期、和人が育てられなくなって残して行った子どもたちを引き取って育てたのがアイヌ民族だったということである。

「見捨てない」という心情は、「命を大事にする」という、彼らが生きるうえでの基本と一体のものであり、そうしたアイヌの

人たちの心根を和人たちは知っていたから、明治以降、入植の過酷さに耐えきれず子どもを置いて帰郷する場合には、入植したアイヌたちの知人に頼んだり、アイヌの家の前に置き去りにして行ったのである。この時代は、入植した和人たちにとっても苦難の時代であったのだ。

そうして引き取られ、育てられたアイヌに一人が、一九二四年に生後一週間でアイヌ女性に預けられ、「自分はアイヌ」と公言して釧路地方で生き、春採アイヌ古式舞踊釧路リムセ保存会の会長にも就いて、諸儀式で祭司を務めた八重清次郎エカシ(注22)だ。

　私の実父母は青森県の人で、どんな事情があったのかはわかりませんが、私達子供三人を他人にくれて自分達は青森県に帰りました。私は白糠町の磯トシと云う人（養母）にもらわれました。養母は毎日御飯をかんでは幼い私の口に入れて育ててくれたと言うことです。そのおかげで私は一人前に成長することができました。

　物のない頃ということで育ての親はどんなにか苦労したことでしょう。あるとき養母が私に『ミルク』を飲ませたいと町に買いにゆきましたところ商店の人にアイヌには売りませんと断られて泣きながら帰ってきたと話したことがありました。私はまさかと思い八歳の時養母と町に買い物に行きましたが矢張アイヌの人には売りませんと言われ、どうしてアイヌはこのような差別を受けなければならないのかと思いました。けれども私は良い育ての親にもらわれてしあわせ者でした。

　育ての親の愛情によって私も八歳になり白糠小学校にあがりましたが、この学校はアイヌば

第二部　世界は変わった　でも、生きていく　162

かりでした。生徒は八十人でした。私は一里半の道を歩いて通学しました。ウタリ〔アイヌ〕の子供達は良い人ばかりでした。けれども学校の帰りになると和人の子供達が待伏せして私をアイヌの子供と言っていじめたのです。
川にも投げ込まれ本もノートもつかえなくなり学校にも行けないこともありました。どうして私ばかりがこんなにいじめられるのかと養母に聞きました。養母はお前はアイヌの子供なのです。和人の子供に負けないで学校に行きなさいと言いました。それから私はアイヌであるんだと思い学校に行きましたがそれからもよくいじめられました。この悲しみは忘れることは出来ません。十二歳の時に養母が病気になりましたが、薬を買うお金もないので私が一年間五十円の約束で十勝に奉公に行きました。(注23)

育ての母親を助けたいという一二歳の男の子の決意もむなしく、トシさんはそれから一年もたたずに亡くなった。

命を救うということでは、別のエピソードも残されている。戦時中は、強圧的な炭鉱労働や鉱山労働から逃げ出した少なからぬ数の朝鮮人が「茅葺き屋根の家を頼れ」を半ば合い言葉にアイヌ家庭の戸を叩き、かくまわれた。とはいえ、そのまま置いていてはいつ発覚するとも限らない。家の主(あるじ)は山中に隠れ家を用意したり、炭俵の中に隠して大八車に乗せ、駅で切符まで買って列車に乗せていたというのだ。(注24)

そこまでとことん世話していたのか——と思わないでいられない話である。差別された側の人たちが、差別していた側の人たちも含めて隔てなく世話をしてきたことは、やはり稀有なことのように思える。繰り返しになるが、出自を問わず虐げられた人たちを救ってきたことは、このような実話を知ってなお、差別や偏見を平気で口に出せる人が、果たしているだろうか。こうしたことはアイヌ民族の生き方を知る上で、また、いわれなき差別を解消する意味で、もっと知られてもいい歴史だと思うのだ。

八重清次郎エカシの話ではもう一つ、言えることがある。それはアイヌ民族か否かの判別は、生まれ（血）の問題というより、「自分自身をアイヌと思っているか否か」というアイデンティティー（自己認識）の問題だということだ。両親が和人という清次郎エカシが、長じてその事情を知ってからもなお、「自分はアイヌだ」と言い続けたことが、それを端的に表している。だから「自分はアイヌである」というアイデンティティーを持つ人がいる限り、アイヌ民族がいなくなることはないし、事実、いなくなってはいないのだ。

清次郎エカシの場合はアイヌとして育てられたこともあっただろうが、和人からいじめられたことで、アイヌとしての自己、和人とは違う自分がより強く意識された部分もあったのではないだろうか。それは、知里幸恵が東京で、和人の家庭、和人社会にぽつんと混じって暮らす中で、次第に「自分はアイヌだ」という自意識を強めていったこととも共通する。そんななかで、二人にさらに共通するのは、アイヌであること、アイヌ文化を受け継いだことを肯定的に捉えるに至ったことだ。

三章 アイヌ文化への再評価

福島原発事故からの逃避行

エーエイ　エアウワ
エーエイ　エアウワ
ネンパク　ポ　エ・コロヤ？
レポ　エス　ク・コロネ
ネコン　エ・イキワ　エ・イペレ？
ク・イッカワ　ク・イペレ
ネコン　エ・イキワ　エ・イミレ？
エーエイ　エアウワ
ク・イッカワ　ク・イミレ

（あなたには何人の子どもがいるの？）
（三人いるよ）
（どうやって食べさせるの？）
（盗んで食べさせるよ）
（どうやって着せるの？）
（盗んで着せるよ）

釧路「ジス・イズ」で2011年8月に行われたカピウ＆アパッポの結成コンサート。右が郷右近富貴子さん、左が床絵美さん（©2016 office+studio T.P.S）

未曾有の大災害となった東日本大震災と東京電力福島第一原発事故から半年が近づきつつあった二〇一一年八月二一日、津波の被害を免れなかった釧路市内のジャズ喫茶「ジス・イズ」に、女性二人の伸びやかな声が響いた。

ライブコンサートを開いたのは、阿寒湖畔出身のアイヌ姉妹デュオ「カピウ＆アパッポ」。「エアウア」はアイヌ語でホオジロガモを指し、歌詞は二羽の母親が子育て上の大変さを吐露する内容だ。ただし、得てしてこの手の歌は、生き物に名を借りて人間社会の現実を訴えているものが多い。

奇しくも大震災の一〇日前に北海道新聞の編集委員として釧路に着任した私は、翌四月、妹のアパッポと郷右近富貴子さんが三人の子どもたちと参加する「親と子のアイヌ語学習」を湖畔の温泉街で取材していた。歌も、民族楽器のムックリも、人を感動させる演じ手としての才を受けた富貴子さんはそのころ、言葉も習得しようと子どもたちと一緒に頑

張っていたのだ。
姉妹にデビューの場を提供したジス・イズのマスター小林東さん（故人）もまだ元気な時期で、赴任以来、懇意にしてもらっていた。ただ、残念ながら、私はこの日のライブには行けずじまいだった。
このライブの熱気を知ることができたのは五年余りのちの二〇一七年春。二人を主役に据えたドキュメンタリー映画「kapiw と apappo ～アイヌの姉妹の物語」（佐藤隆之監督）が完成し、札幌のミニ映画館「シアターキノ」で上映された時だった。その時初めて、私は姉の床絵美さんが原発事故後、首都圏の自宅から、郷里の阿寒湖畔に暮らす富貴子さんらを頼って車で避難してきたことを知ったのだった。
映画はその逃避行から姉妹デビューまでを追っており、姉妹デュオの結成は、絵美さんが郷里で再び生活を築いていくためのよすがでもあったことが分かった。とすると、二人がホオジロガモの子育ての苦労を選んで歌った理由も分かるような気がしてくる。どんなことをしてでも子どもたちを安全なところで無事に育て上げる——そんな絵美さんの決意がそこに託されているように私は感じた。

アイヌ芸能が魅力的に映る時代

苦しみが幾世代にもわたって続いてきたアイヌ民族の歴史を思えば、歌うこと、伝承を語り合うことが、苦難を堪え忍ぶよすがとしても機能してきたに違いない。こうした伝統文化、さらには信

仰、世界観は、これからもこの大地（モシリ）で受け継がれていくのだろうか。歌や踊り、語りといった「演じるもの」に関しては、継承や創造の土壌はできつつあるのではないか――。ここ数年、私はそんな希望を抱くようになった。

それがまず「カピウ＆アパッポ」の映画上映の入り込みだった。初日の二〇一七年四月一日、札幌のシアターキノは満席。翌日、札幌のライブハウスでの二人のコンサートもチケットが取れない人気ぶりだった。

関心を集めているのはこのユニットだけでない。二〇一〇年に解散したパフォーマンス集団「アイヌレブルズ（Ainu Rebels）」もそうだったし、その代表を務めていた帯広出身の酒井美直（Mina）さんがその後、結成した二人組音楽ユニット「イメルア」も国際的な評価を得ている。女性ボーカルグループ「MAREWREW（マレウレウ）」は才気溢れる曲づくりと、輪唱（ウコウク）が生み出す無限性がまるで大地に抱かれたような感覚に誘う。ちなみに「カピウ＆アパッポ」の「盗んで食べさせる盗んで着させる」の歌は、マレウレウもレパートリーにしている。このほか、トンコリ奏者のOKI（オキ）さんはアイヌ民族の伝統的な曲想にダブ（ダブワイズ）やロック、レゲエの要素も合わせて独創的な世界をつくり出している。キダブアイヌバンド）」を率いて活動をしている「OKI DUB AINU BAND（オ

「アイヌ　ミート　ソマリアン」と題して、「kapiw と apappo」上映の前の月に札幌中心部のバーで行われたアイヌ民族若手の語りや歌、踊りの夕べもまた、予定の席数を超える人が列を成した。一〇人前後の出演者はその道で食べているプロではなく、学生や子育て世代が中心だ。なのに

れだけの人を集められることは驚き以外の何ものでもない。人いきれで息苦しいなか、英雄叙事詩の語りやウポポ（座り歌）、ヤイサマ（即興歌・抒情歌）などが次々披露され、ムックリ（口琴）の演奏が聴き手を魅了した。アイヌ民族の若い世代がここまで伝統舞踊や口承伝承を演じられるようになったこと自体が驚きだった。

考えてみると、一つには一九九七年に第一回が行われ、その後、毎年続いているアイヌ語弁論大会（イタカンロー）がある。子どもの部、大人の部の両方があり、大人の部は口承文芸部門と弁論部門に分かれている。弁論の部は、自分の考えをアイヌ語で伝えなくてはならないから、アイヌ語で作文ができるぐらいの習熟度が要る。口承の方は覚えるのも簡単ではないが、いかに心を込め、臨場感を醸し出すかも問われる。この二〇年の間、毎年、何人もが挑戦し、出来を競うなかで、どれだけの数の人がアイヌ語の習得に熱心に取り組んだことか。

弁論大会ばかりでない。二〇〇八年度から始まったアイヌ文化担い手（伝承者）育成事業の役割も大きい。アイヌ文化振興・研究推進機構から委託を受けたアイヌ民族博物館が、将来を担う若者たちを三年間預かり、伝統工芸やアイヌ語、芸能、儀礼などをみっちり教えてきた。

さらに札幌大学が二〇一〇年度からアイヌ子弟に対する奨学生制度を始めたことも育成につながっている。育て合うという意味を込めて「ウレシパ」と名付けられた奨学制度の受講生は、アイヌ文化を学ぶウレシパクラブに入会し、四年間、週二回の勉強会でアイヌ語や伝統舞踊を学んだり、学外で儀礼やイベントに参加したりと、さまざまな機会を通じて知識や経験を積んでいく。約二〇

人の学生の就学を資金面で支える企業の数も四〇社を超え、経済界を巻き込んだ持続的な仕組みが築かれている。

危機言語「アイヌ語」の復活は？

ただ、それでもアイヌ語は二〇〇九年、ユネスコ（国連教育科学文化機関）から消滅の危機にあり、その段階は極めて深刻なレベルにあると認定され、その後も全体状況はそれほど変わっていない。

「アイヌ語を日常的に使っている家庭は今はもうない」「話すことのできる人は十数人ほどしかいない」。そんな言われ方もされている。これほどまで危機的な状況に追い込まれたのは、明治以来、政府や教育機関の言葉の収奪がいかに徹底して行われてきたかを示すあかしである。ただ、「これから」に向けて大事なのは記録がしっかりなされていること、学ぶ場、機会が開かれてあること、そして習得のベクトルが少しでも上向きになっていることではないだろうか。

記録に関しては、アイヌ語の口承は何人もの伝承者の音声や筆録、日本語訳が相当の数、残されており、その気になれば、誰でも活用できる状況にある。弁論大会の開催や伝承の担い手育成事業、そして大学の奨学制度が一定程度の効果を上げているのをみれば、学ぶための制度や機会、つまり「文化伝承の舞台装置」をつくれば相当なことができるはずである。だから、そういう環境をどれだけ拡充させられるかで、アイヌ語を取り巻く「未来」が全然違ってくる。

海外に目を移せば、ニュージーランドの先住民族マオリは、危機的状況にあったマオリ語が一九八七年に英語と並ぶ公用語に定められ、幼稚園から大学に至るまでマオリ語による教育環境が

第二部　世界は変わった　でも、生きていく

整えられた。同時に、どうやって教えれば上達が早いのか、効果的な言語習得法「テ・アタアランギ法」が編み出され、幼少期に母語に浸るコーハンガ・レオ（言葉の巣）活動も通じて会話がある程度できる人が今や四人に一人の割合に達しているとされる。北海道内でも、現地で妻の真紀さんとともにマオリの言語習得法を学んできた関根健司さんが二風谷のアイヌ語教室でその手法の実践を二〇一四年から始めた。

もう一つ、重要なのが、アイヌ語による新聞の発行である。萱野茂エカシの息子志朗さんら有志によるアイヌ語ペンクラブが「アイヌタイムズ」を創刊したのが一九九七年。以後、年間三、四号を発行しながら二〇年余にわたる活動を続けている。また、志朗さんは二風谷でアイヌ語のミニFM局「ピパウシ」も運営している。

個別の活動の蓄積は欠かせない。が、将来に向けては、国や北海道、市町村がそれぞれに言語政策を立案し、言葉を学ぶための手法を体系化し、機会をさらに増やせるかどうかがカギを握る。もちろん国全体あるいは北海道内限定でも公用語や準公用語に指定できれば、もっと大きな前進が期待できる。岩手県遠野市のように、昔語りのふるさととして語り部を育て、口承が日常的にツーリストに語られるような場をつくることも一計である。

新たな神謡や説話を創作していく活動、すなわち言葉が創造性を持つことも欠かせない。それは言葉が生きているあかしでもあるからだ。

その点では、札幌在住の版画家結城幸司(ゆうじ)さんが「七五郎沢の狐(しちごろうさわのきつね)」という物語を作り、物語に共感し

結城幸司さんの原作・版画をアニメーション映画化した「七五郎沢の狐」のワンシーン
(©tane project/Koji Yuki)

た人たちがアニメーション映画化した動きが注目される。映画は全編アイヌ語で、日本語と英語の字幕がつけられている。そのこと一つとっても、「日本語だけが日常のことば」の日本社会にインパクトを与えるに十分だ。映画は二〇一五年の札幌国際短編映画祭の上映作品にも選ばれた。

　私〔母ギツネ〕は、先祖代々暮らしてきた沢が廃棄物で汚染されて生き物が消えたため、子ギツネのために餌探しの遠出を余儀なくされた。都会にさまよい出ると、人間の残飯をあさって肥え太ったネズミが「やせ衰えたその姿で、捕まえられるものなら捕まえてみるがいい。やがておまえたちは滅びる」と予言めいた挑発をしてきた。私は、人間に依存して太りすぎたネズミ

を捕まえることはできたものの、都会に順応することはできず、再び沢に戻った。しかし、そこにも居場所がなく、郷里を捨てるほかないと心に決めたのだった。

かつて人間が自然と調和していた時代、数多くの口承が生み落とされた時代、人と神、人と生き物は最後は互いの関係を修復することができた。だが、環境破壊が大規模化し、誰がどう手を下しているのかが見えなくなった現代社会では、物語は関係を再構築して終わることができない。物語の悲しい結末は、そういう時代の変化も暗示していると言えるかもしれない。

二〇一九年三月からは、明治政府が畜産業に脅威を与えるとして毒殺を奨励し、ついには絶滅に至ったオオカミに対するアイヌ民族の畏敬の念を表した創作劇「阿寒ユーカラ『ロストカムイ』」の公演が、阿寒湖温泉の阿寒湖アイヌシアター「イコロ」で始まった。オオカミの躍動をコンピュータグラフィックス（CG）でよみがえらせ、アイヌ古式舞踊や現代の舞踏を交えつつ、自然と人間の共存のあり方を問う内容。舞台監督を地元のアイヌ民族の木彫家、床州生さんが務め、クリエイティブディレクターの坂本大輔さんらが協力した。床さんは「和人の一線級の若手クリエイターと一緒に仕事をすることで、自分たちだけではできないものを創り出せた」と新しい方向性を示す。

生身の人間として生きる現代に、たとえ望ましくない状況がテーマであっても、その時代の特徴を反映した物語が生み出され、語られていくことは実に大事なことで、本来そうでなくてはならない。こういう現代だからこそ、伝統的な自然観、世界観に基づいた物語も、時代を織り込んで新たに創られる物語も、両方が語られるべきなのだ。

過酷な時代の連続によってアイヌ民族が失わせられたものは膨大で、その分、アイデンティティーや誇り、文化を取り戻すためには長大な時間と努力が必要となる。しかもそれは、政府や和人の支援や補償意識なしには、さらに遠い道のりにならざるを得ないということも認識されなければならない。

シラッチセ──狩猟を肌で感じられる場所

二〇一八年春には、二年後の国立アイヌ民族博物館設置に向けて、アイヌ民族が白老のポロト湖畔で運営してきたアイヌ民族博物館が閉鎖されることになった。博物館では、創設の一九八四年来、アイヌ民族の伝統にのっとって子グマを飼い、イオマンテ（霊送り儀礼）も行ってきた。かつてそこで学芸員として働いた私も、子グマの散歩をし、儀式にも参加して、エカシやフチ、職員らからさまざまなことを教わった。それだけに、飼われているヒグマの行方が気になった。野本正博館長は閉館の前の年、札幌来訪の折に、新設される国立博物館にはヒグマを飼う選択肢はないことを明かしたうえで、「人の手で育てられただけに野生に返すわけにはいかないし、かといって、人間の都合で、イオマンテを行って送ることもできないし……」と打ち明けてきた。その後、「イギリスに野生動物を引き取って、快適な環境で老後まで見届けてくれる施設がある。そこに送られることになったんだ」と教えられた。

その施設とは、英国中部のヨークシャー野生動物公園。移送計画は順調に進み、二〇一八年八月にオスのリク、カイ、アム、メスのハナコの四頭がいずれも健康な状態でイギリスに空路され、一・

第二部　世界は変わった　でも、生きていく　174

ヒグマの頭骨が祀られている本流のシラッチセのヌサ（撮影：小坂洋右）

六ヘクタールの広大な草地に放たれた。野本館長は自身の胸の内をそれ以上語らなかったが、それは野生動物を飼う伝統を持ってきたアイヌ民族としての最大限の意思表示のように感じられた。

背丈ほどもあるササをかき分けながら急勾配を上がると、突如、視界が開け、そびえ立つ崖の下にアイヌ民族のヌサ（祭壇）が現れた。

札幌の自宅から恵庭(えにわ)方面に車を走らせること小一時間。ここは通行止めの地点から漁川(いざりがわ)の河畔を少しさかのぼったところにある「本流のシラッチセ〔岩屋〕」だ。猟をするに当たって、家と山とを毎日往復するのでは効率が悪い。川沿いの、そそり立つ岩がやや手前に傾いて屋根のように覆い被さっている特異な地形を、

175　三章　アイヌ文化への再評価

カムイを祀り、狩猟の拠点としても使われてきた本流のシラッチセ（撮影：小坂康）

登山で言えばベースキャンプとして、この地域のアイヌ民族は狩猟に繰り出してきたのである。ここなら暴風雨や吹雪がしのげるし、川が近いから水が汲め、魚も捕れる。クマが獲れた場合、「起き上がらせる」という意味のホプニレないし、地域によってはオプニレ、オプニカと呼ばれる儀式を行って魂をカムイたちの世界に帰すが、獲ったその場で行うこともあれば、シラッチセやコタンまで運んで執り行うこともあった。また、地域によって狩りの拠点は岩屋ではなく、山中の木でこしらえた猟小屋だった。

本流のシラッチセでは向かって左手に炊事道具が固め置かれ、右手に祭壇があって、クマの頭骨とともに、たくさんのイナウが捧げられている。シラッチセは漁川沿いだけで少なくとも五カ所が確認されており、それほど遠くない時代までアイヌ民族の猟師が盛んに狩りをしていたことが分かる。

山の奥へ奥へと入り込む場合には、太い倒木の両側に松の枝などを葺いてつくる簡便な仮小屋で野宿する。「時によっては五分もあれば簡単にできる」と語るほど仮小屋作りがお手の物だったクマ撃ちの達人、姉崎等エカシ（千歳）は「山中で泊まることができるようになれば、猟で持って歩くものは銃などの猟具と塩ぐらいで、エゾライチョウなどを獲りながら食いつないで何日でも山にいられるようになる」と聞き書きに答えている。山猟ではとにかく身を軽くすることが肝心で、ほとんど身一つでクマやシカを追うわけだ。それは狩りをする人自身が「野生動物」に近づくこともまた意味していたはずである。

クマと何度も対峙し、何頭も獲ってきた姉崎エカシと釧路の隣、白糠町の根本与三郎エカシが相次ぎ亡くなったのは二〇一三年。それでクマを獲る人が全くいなくなったわけではないが、二人の語り部を亡くした今、かつての狩猟生活を肌で感じることができるのは、このようなシラッチセをおいてほかにない。春に本流のシラッチセを訪ね、風雪に倒れたイナウを元に戻し、短いお祈りを唱えて帰ってくるのが、私のここ数年の恒例になった。

同じ漁川沿いの盤尻のシラッチセでは、毎年夏前に千歳の伝承者野本久栄エカシが祭司を務め、和人の猟師も含めたゆかりの人たちでカムイノミ（神々への祈り）を行ってきた。

だが、あれは二〇一五年の四月だった。千歳市内の飲食店で野本エカシと待ち合わせし、互いの近況報告を交わしたあと、エカシが「これおまえに預けるから。これだけのイノンノイタク〔祝詞、祈りの言葉〕考えるの、けっこう苦労したんだぞ」と言いながら三枚の紙を差し出した。そこには野本エカシが毎年、シラッチセで唱えていた祈りの言葉がつづられていた。

それからほどなくだった。エカシの体調が悪化し、カムイノミの祭司を務められなくなったと人づてに耳に入ってきた。あの日、体調が悪いようには見えなかっただけに、なぜ急に症状が進んだのか、なぜ私に祈りの言葉を預けたのか、答えの出せない疑問が心の中に残ったが、むしろこのことで、自分はシラッチセから離れられなくなったのかもしれなかった。

参列した長老がめいめい、自分の言葉で祈るのが、アイヌ民族のカムイノミのイノンノイタクである。この日、シラッチセのヌサを前に、私はまず「これは野本久栄エカシのイノンノイタクです」と神々に断ったうえで、以前、預けられた祈りの言葉を捧げた。そのあとで、自分の言葉を短く継いで、拝礼した。

第二部　世界は変わった　でも、生きていく　　178

残雪がところどころ残るなか、上流に向かって少し歩くと、白いミズバショウの群落が目にまぶしい。冬眠から覚めたヒグマはフキノトウやアマニュウの葉を口にしてお尻の栓代わりにしていた止め糞を出し、湧き水の水藻やフキ、ザゼンソウ、ギョウジャニンニクを探し求めて、それを食べながら徐々に体力を回復するのだと、姉崎エカシや根本エカシは語っている。ヒグマがミズバショウを食べる姿も目撃されている。狩りをする人々が、どれほどじっくりクマの行動を観察し、生態を把握していたかが、そこからもうかがい知れる。

生き物と人間の信じ難い「助け合い」

父方の祖母がアイヌ民族で、北方四島の志発島に暮らしていたという石川美香穂さんと以前、このシラッチセを訪ねた時、不思議なことがあった。ヌサの数メートル前にタヌキが死んで横たわっていたのだ。

自然死している動物の遺骸を目にすること自体、まずない。地熱のあるところ、例えば、北海道東部、摩周湖と屈斜路湖の間にあるポンポン山などでは冬場、衰弱したエゾシカが暖を求めつつも最期を迎え、春先には死骸をいくつも目にすることがある。こうした特別な例を除けば、冬山も含めて山野をそれなりに歩いてきた自分でも、自然死との遭遇は数えるほどしかない。しかも、そのタヌキは、ヒグマの頭骨が祀られたヌサの目の前に、自分でそこを死地と選んだかのような格好で死んでいたのである。

タヌキのことをアイヌ民族はモユクと呼んでカムイと崇め、霊送りの儀礼も行ってきた。それは、

ないがしろにできない山の神(ヒグマ)のおじさん、ないしはきょうだいと見なされてきたこととも関係しているに違いない。地域によっては、クマのウッシウ(召使い)とも呼ばれていた。

根本エカシは「クマとタヌキは兄弟である。……タヌキへのカムイノミのとき、『欲を言う』。『お前はクマの先走りで、兄弟だから、今度はもっと大きいカムイ(クマのこと)を授けれ』と祈った」と述べている。そのようにしてタヌキに責任を持たせたうえで、頭をヌサの下の地面に置くと言うのである。まさに、そうした作法を知っていた誰かがクマの頭骨の前に安置したかのようにたタヌキがヌサの前に横たわっていたのだから、驚かないではいられなかったのだ。

同様のことが二〇一九年一月五日、新ひだか町静内の葛野次雄さん宅で、息子の大喜君を交えて行われた新年の伝統儀式アシリパノミに参加した朝にも起きた。タヌキが葛野家の敷地で自然死しているのが見つかったのだ。神々に一年の無事を祈る儀式のその日、まるでそこを死に場所と選んだかのように……。こんなことが重なって起きると、偶然とは思えなくなってくる。何か、私たちの目には見えていないものが作用しているのではなかろうか、と。

タヌキといえば、アイヌ民族の猟師が残したこんなエピソードがある。冬眠中のクマを撃ったら、タヌキがその冬眠穴から六匹もぞろぞろと出てきた――。つまり、クマとたくさんのタヌキが一つの穴の中で一緒に暮らしていたということである。

道東の糠平で後半生を過ごした渕瀬一雄さんは「タヌキは穴ごもりしているメスグマの穴の戸口まできて、黙って中にどんどん入って行き、生まれた仔グマと遊ぶ。乳を与えることもある。〔クマの〕乳飲み児は母グマにだっこされて寝ているが、一カ月すると四キロの重さになり、タヌキと遊

ぶことができるようになる。……タヌキにとっても暖かいクマの穴は有り難いものだ」と証言している。自然界で、タヌキがクマの子育てを手伝うというのは、種の壁を越えた助け合いであり、それを実際に自分の目で見て知っていたアイヌ民族が「おじと甥っ子、姪っ子」「きょうだい」の関係と見なしたということなのだろうか。

だとすれば、冬眠の穴から連れ帰った子グマをアイヌ民族の女性が自分のお乳をあげて育てるのも、奇異でも特別なことでもない気がしてくる。物語ではあるが、クマが自分の身を犠牲にして人間の命を救ったお話もある。悪者に殺されそうになった娘をクマが自分の背中におぶって海を渡り、体力を使い果たして自身は死ぬが、娘は実のおじいさんおばあさんと再会でき、そのクマの霊を丁寧に祀るという筋書きだ。

現実世界ではどうだろうか。クマが人を助けるなどということが、果たしてあり得るだろうか。実は、実話として記録されているエピソードがある。クマの巣穴に誤って落ちた人が母グマの手のひらを舐めさせてもらって生き延び、無事にコタンに戻れたという話だ。

クマの助けで生還した人は、釧路に近い標茶町虹別にあったシュワンコタンの川崎じいさんと呼ばれていた人で、証言したのは、近くの塘路コタンの重鎮、島太郎エカシの養子、直さんと結婚してシュワンコタンに一緒に住んだ一九二四年生まれの島マチエさんである。

ウサギの罠猟が得意で、コタンの人たちによくおすそ分けしていた川崎じいさんは、吹雪で道に迷い、クマが冬眠していた穴に落ちてしまった。クマが手を伸ばしてきたので、爪にかかってこれでおしまいだと覚悟を決めたが、相手に襲うそぶりはなく、何気なくという感じで手を伸ばしてく

る。もしかしたら、手のひらを舐めろということかもしれないと思って舐めてみると、すごく甘い。そのうち、おしっこがしたくなると、クマがそっちへ行けという所作をするので、そちらで用を足してきた。そうこうして一緒に過ごすうち、日差しも暖かくなって春らしくなってきた。すると、クマは入り口の方に行ってジェスチャーをする。川崎じいさんは、これは「出て行け」ということなんだな、と悟り、外界に出てついには自分の家があるコタンに戻ることができたという。(注8)

　北海道教育委員会が行った「アイヌ民俗文化財調査」の報告書に記載されている記録で、語り手も氏名を明らかにしているから作り話ではない。しかも、クマの冬眠穴で一緒に過ごす先のタヌキのエピソードなどを知ると、そういうことも起こっておかしくないと思えてくる。

　この手の出来事が全くの荒唐無稽でないことは、ツキノワグマを狩りの対象としてきた秋田・阿仁のマタギ（猟師）衆が、「クマは穴の中では人を襲わない」との先祖伝来の教えに従って、実際に穴にもぐり込んでクマの所在を確認してきたことからも知れる。二〇一七年に話を聞いた頭領（シカリ）経験者の松橋吉太郎さん（当時八四歳）も実際に穴にもぐって無事だった一人で、「おれたちは穴の中ではクマを撃たない。クマも穴の中では人間をかじらないと互いに約束がある。だから大丈夫なのさ」と語った。

　そもそも猟では弁当や獲物の臓物をカラスに分けて協力してもらい、クマがこもる穴の場所やオスかメスかを教えてもらうんだと姉崎エカシは語っているし、(注9)獲物の方向に導いてくれるとして小鳥のミソサザイはチャクチャクカムイ、トシリポクンカムイなどと呼ばれて崇められてきた。根本

エカシは「フーン、フーン」というニヤシコロカムイ［シマフクロウ］の鳴き声を聞けば、ヒグマがその方角にいると判断する」とし、弟子屈・屈斜路のアイヌはエゾフクロウの鳴き声でクマの穴の場所を見つけていた。

現代人は「種は種であって、種の間には越えがたい壁がある」という先入観にとらわれているがゆえに、野生の生き物との助け合いなど端からありえないと思いがちだ。かつて、私自身もそうだった。だが、今は、その見方は間違っているかもしれないと考え始めている。むしろ、それこそが現代人が失ってしまった感覚ではないのか、と思えるのだ。私たちが失った何か大事なものが、そこにあるかもしれないと想像し始めると、また違った世界が見えてくる。もしかしたら、現代を生きる私たちには、見えなくなったものがたくさんあるのかもしれない。むしろ私たちの世界の方が狭く、閉ざされたものかもしれないのだ。

「あなたには三億人の同胞がいる」

「自然を尊ぶ者は、自然を征服するものとは共存できないのではないですか」

シラッチセを案内した石川美香穂さんからメールが届いたのは、そんなことを考え始めた時期だった。彼女が二三歳の時以来、二〇年間の付き合いがある。だからこそその本心、重たい問いがそこにはつづられていた。

小坂さん、アイヌ民族にとって生きることの基本は、人徳のある人間になれということ、と

以前、教えていただきました。ずる賢い商人がアイヌを小馬鹿にした逸話はたくさん残っています。人格を基準にする彼らは、和人の本心をきっと簡単に見抜けた。そうはお考えになりませんか。闘っても、到底勝てないことを悟ったんだ、と思います。自然を尊ぶ者は自然を征服する者とは共存できない。アイヌのほとんどの人が矜恃を棄てたのは、アイヌ当人の心が、次第にユーカラの教訓を信じられなくなり、神々との取り引きをやめてしまったからじゃないのか。アイヌがアイヌをやめた。命だけが、まだ続いている。その子孫の私が、アイヌをそう受け取ってしまったら、アイヌは死んでしまうのでしょうか。

　かれらがいなくなった今、誰に尋ねたらいいのでしょう。その自然も、環境も、その人たちもいなくなって、何を手本としたらいいのでしょう。神々と正しく付き合い、悪心を持たなければ平穏に暮らせる、そう固く信じていたアイヌの人たちは結局、和人に騙されて衰退の一途をたどりました。弱い人たちだったと私は思っています。先住民の、自然を手本とした生活の規範は、人間の本質的な欲深さには対応できず、発展には限界がある、という気がしてなりません。

　あまりに重たい言葉に打ちのめされて、しばらくの間、何も手につかず、私は呆然と過ごした。だが、思い直し、何か返答しなくてはならない、と必死になって言葉を探し、ようやくメールで返事を出した。

第二部　世界は変わった　でも、生きていく　184

返事が遅れました。少なからぬ数のアイヌの人たちが神々との取り引きをやめたのだとしても、そうさせたのは外部の力であり、アイヌ自身が選び取ったわけではないことを、まずは忘れないで話を進めていきたいと思います。

あなた自身が何も受け取ることができないと言うのは、見誤りだと思います。あなたはすでに大事なものを受け取っているではないですか。「自然を尊ぶ者は自然を征服するものとは共存できない」とあなたが書く時、それはアイヌ民族の自然を尊ぶ思想に思いを寄せ、その価値観を共有しているからにほかなりません。

北米の先住民族チェロキー・ネイションで初の女性元首を務めたウィルマ・マンキラーさんがこう語っています。「先住民族のコミュニティーにはそれぞれの文化や言語、歴史、独自の生き方があり、その点で大きな多様性があります。しかし、違いはあるものの、地球上、各地の先住民族の間には自分たちの命は自然界の一部であり、自然とは切っても離せない関係にあるという共通の価値観があるのです」と。

世界各地の先住民族は何か大事なものを共通に持っている、だから先住民族は連携できる――というのがマンキラーさんの呼びかけでした。環境運動の面でも、マンキラーさんは先住民族の観点から活動を促してきました。「先住民族だけが、あらゆる生命とのつながりを理解しているわけではありません。異なる民族集団の何千人、何万人もの人たちが環境について深く思い巡らし、地球を守るために日々格闘しています。ただ、先住民族が違っているのは、口承伝承や儀礼を通じて『自分たちはこの大地に対して責任がある』と日常的に思い起こすことで恩

恵を得ていることです。生き方においてだけではなく、自身の心で、あるいは世界観によって大地と強くつながっているのです。自然環境の保護は知的な実践ではなく、神聖な義務なのです[注11]。

僕はマンキラーさんの考えに賛同します。最も大事なことは、大地や命あるもの、人のコミュニティとのつながりを認識し、自身の価値観を持つことなのです。それは自ずと自然保護の運動を促し、社会と環境の持続性を追究することに発展していきます。人も自然も共に弱く、すでに大きなダメージを受けてはいます。けれど、今なお存続している。

先住民族は世界全体にいったい何人ぐらいいるとお思いですか。二億五千万人から三億人と言われています。確かに民族単位で見れば、たった一人になってしまったヤーガン族のクリスティーナ・カルデロンさん[注12]のような人もいます。モンゴロイドの中で最も遠い南米の南端端パタゴニアに到達した人々の最後の一人とされている人ですが、先住民族というくくりで大集結すれば、それだけの数の仲間がいるのです。

その人たちがどのような社会の方向性を目指すのか、あるいはどのようなことを求めていくのか、先住民族の思いが結集した時、どれほどの影響力を持ち得るか、僕は想像することができます。ですから、絶望する理由はないのです。

「価値観」はすなわち、アイヌ民族の「人徳」に置き換えることができるでしょう。一方の「欲深さ」は「価値観を持たない生き方」と見なすことが可能です。僕は、「価値観」を失うことはブレーキをなくすのと同じだと考えています。もしも際限のない現代化を繰り返していけば、い

つか存亡の危機に直面するでしょう。ほとんどの人が、この社会の行き詰まりが表面化するまで、社会変革の必要性を感じないのでしょうか。崖っぷちに立たされるまで、先住民族の価値観に目を向けることはないのでしょうか。多くの人が欲深さを断ち切れないまま行けば、破滅的な方向に向かってひたすら疾走していくほかありません。

あとがき

本稿がほぼ完成した二〇一八年十一月、私は長年のお付き合いになる石原誠・イツ子夫妻の娘、真衣さんに真っ先に原稿を郵送した。その理由は、真衣さんが、十二歳の時に母親から教えられたアイヌのルーツ、アイデンティティーの問題を北大の大学院で突き詰め、その論考で博士号を取ったばかりだったからだ。博士論文には、祖母、母親がそれぞれどのような思いで自身の出自(しゅつじ)を受け止め、どのように生きることを選んだのか——が詳細に書かれていた。そんな関心と蓄積があるから、拙稿からも得るものがあるのではないかと考えたのだった。

真衣さんの祖母、一九二五年(大正一四年)生まれのツヤコさんは、両親ともにアイヌ民族だった。だが、ツヤコさんは和人と対等になるために懸命に働き、和人と結婚する。結果、アイヌ文化やアイヌ語とは無縁のまま生涯を終えた。当時、少なからぬアイヌの人たちが同様の道を歩んでいた。

一方、母親のイツ子さんは結婚前、アイヌ民族にかかわるさまざまな出来事を紹介する同人誌的な新聞「アヌタリアイヌ——われら人間」の刊行に携わった。しかし、漁業権や土地権の回復などを取り上げたことから公安に目を付けられ、三年ほどで廃刊を余儀なくされた。和人の誠さんと結婚したあとは、一時期、北海道ウタリ協会の刺しゅう教室に通ったものの、かえって伝統文化を何も身につけていないことを思い知らされ、以後、そうした活動から遠ざかってきた。

そういう環境で育った真衣さんは、成長とともに「アイヌでも和人でもない自分」を意識させられ、「日本社会に『アイヌ』か『和人』か、という枠組みしかないのはなぜなのか」という疑問にとらわれた。「そう悩んでいるのは自分一人だけではない」と気づくと、次第に「沈黙する人たち」の存在が大きくなり、研究のなかでは「サイレントアイヌ」という言葉を使うようになった――。

この本の原稿を送ると、真衣さんからほどなくメールが返ってきた。そこには私の原稿を俯瞰(ふかん)する、鋭い洞察が書かれてあった。

「自然とは混沌で、人類は混沌をおそれ、そこに分類体系と秩序をつくりだし、混沌に対応するために儀礼を施してきました。しかし、儀礼そのものが消失し、畏怖を抱かなくなり、科学とテクノロジーの発達により、人類は混沌に対峙する能力を失ってしまった」

その先に強烈なメッセージがしたためられてあった。

「アイヌでも、和人でもない、『透明人間』と自己を定義する私は、混沌そのものであり、人々の認識枠組みに引っかからない存在です。アイヌのルーツを持つ一個人としては、アイヌか和人か、あるいは先住民か非先住民か、狩猟民か農耕民かというポジションの、どこにも自分の置き場を見いだすことができません」

このひと言で、私は自分の原稿に、大きな視点が欠落していることを認識しないではいなかった。アイヌでも和人でもない「自分」を持つ人たちがいる。一般の人たちから、そうしたアイデンティティーが認知されていない以上、そういう人たちは自分から名乗らない、名乗れないという点で「サ

イレント」であり、他者からそのアイデンティティーが見えないという点では「透明人間」ということになる——。

真衣さんの指摘を受けて、私はあらためて思った。「現実には、自分はアイヌ民族であるという揺るぎない自己認識を持って生きている人の方がむしろ少ないのではないだろうか」と。であれば、「民族」という括りで、共通項をことさら強調したり、何かの規範を求めようとする行為は、実像と乖離（かいり）するリスクと背中合わせだとも言える。民族文化や精神世界と呼ぶものも、固定したイメージで捉えてはきっと認識を誤る。しかも、それは時代に応じて変化し、また変化することで生き続けるものでもあるのだ。

その後、真衣さんと直接、お話しする機会があった。

「分類できないものは『ないもの』にされているというのが、今の時代ですよね。『分からないものはない』という前提が現代社会にあるからです。でも、実際のところ、世界は分類できないものであふれているんじゃないでしょうか」。真衣さんは現代社会に対する認識をこうぶつけてきた。

その考えに納得しつつ、私は切り出した。「自分の見方は大丈夫なのか、これでいいのか、と思いながらこの原稿を書いてきた。それが正直なところです。それでも、何人ものアイヌの人たちと会い、話されたもの、書かれたものにも触れるうちに、アイヌ民族としての生き方、生きるうえでの核となるものが何かあるような気がしてきたというのも事実です」

真衣さんはうなずいた。「確かに私が会った人の中にも、アイヌ民族の世界観を引き継いで生きているんだなという人はいます。この原稿の延長線上で、これがいいことだからあなたはちゃんとし

たアイヌになりなさいと言われると困っちゃうけど、アイヌの人たちの世界観は近代化や原発などいろいろな問題に対するオルタナティブな考えになり得ると、私自身も思っています」

何もかも簡単に割り切ることはできない。複雑でデリケートな問題が横たわっている。ここにきて、ますます「こうだ」と言い切れない現実を感じつつある自分がいる。ただ、そんななかでも確実に言えるのは、原稿を書き進めていく過程で、自分の何かが変わったということだ。私自身の価値観に変化があった。とすれば、この原稿を通して、もしかしたら同じような体験や気づきを、次の世代を担う人たちにも与えることができるかもしれない。それは、きっと、私にさまざまなことを惜しげもなく教えてくださった方々が、役割として私に託したことでもあるのだろう。エカシやフチたち。教えをいただいた方々、貴重な記録を残してくださった方々、そうした数多くの方々がいたからこそ、本稿をここまでまとめることができた。心から感謝しつつ筆を置きたい。

たくさんの方々との出会いがあり、ご教示をいただけたことが本書の出版に結びついた。特にお世話になった団体、アイヌ民族の方々、ならびに研究者や市民運動にかかわる方々の名前を挙げて感謝に代えたい。

アイヌ政策検討市民会議、アイヌ民族博物館、秋月俊幸先生、阿部一司さん、天内重樹さん、石井ポンペさん、石川美香穂さん、植村佳弘さん、石原イツ子さん、石原真衣さん、石原誠さん、伊藤務さん、井上勝生先生、上村英明先生、植村佳弘さん、宇梶静江さん、榎森進先生、大谷洋一さん、大塚和義先生、大野徹人さん、岡田淳子先生、岡田宏明先生、岡田路明さん、小川隆吉さん、小坂田裕子先生、小田博

志野先生、貝沢耕一さん、加藤九祚先生、加藤博文先生、加藤好男さん、萱野茂さん、萱野志朗さん、萱野りえさん、萱野れい子さん、川上淳先生、川上恵さん、川村兼一さん、川村久恵さん、北原次郎太さん、切替英雄先生、釧路アイヌ文化懇話会、葛野辰次郎さん、葛野次雄さん、葛野大喜さん、窪田幸子先生、クライナー・ヨーゼフ先生、計良智子さん、計良光範さん、小泉雅弘さん、郷右近富貴子さん、小坂博宣さん、コタンの会、古原敏弘さん、佐々木利和先生、佐藤隆之さん、清水裕二さん、市立函館博物館、杉原由美子さん、椙田光明さん、杉原京子さん、諏訪良光さん、関根健司さん、関根真紀さん、石純姫先生、高瀬克範先生、竹内渉さん、田澤守さん、田中宏弁護士、谷本一之先生、田端宏先生、多原良子さん、田村すず子先生、知里森舎、富樫利一さん、知里幸恵 銀のしずく記念館、津田命子さん、津曲敏郎先生、手塚薫先生、富樫利一さん、徳田昭子さん、知里幸州生さん、中本ムツ子さん、戸塚美波子さん、土橋芳美さん、戸部千春さん、豊川重雄さん、中川裕人先生、中村斎先生、長谷部一弘さん、根本与三郎さん、野村義一さん、野本崇さん、野本久栄さん、野本正博さん、函館市中央図書館、畠山敏さん、林直光さん、平田剛士さん、平山裕人先生、広瀬健一郎先生、福岡イト子先生、藤野知明さん、北大開示文書研究会、北海道アイヌ協会、本田優子先生、藤村久和さん、前沢卓さん、丸山博先生、村木美幸さん、門別徳司さん、マーク・ウィンチェスター先生、八重清敏さん、矢島国雄先生、山川力さん、山田伸一さん、結城幸司さん、横山孝雄さん、吉田邦彦先生

　また、刊行に向けては、運営会社レディーフォー（Readyfor）のクラウドファンディングを通じて一〇六人の方から一〇五万一千円の資金援助をいただいた。出版費用の約半分を一般市民の方々の

温かいご支援でまかなわせていただいた。お名前（希望された方のみ）を記して感謝に代えたい。

小形はるみさん、伊藤政美さん、髙木幹郎さん、本田優子さん、田中水絵さん、山本牧さん、梯久美子さん、江上壽幸さん、田口温さん、榎本友一さん、三浦祐嗣さん、北海道魚類映画社様、中田実里さん、林英治さん、小笠原み蔵さん、髙橋薫さん、松藤日出男さん、本田良一さん、方波見康雄さん、三枝修さん、伊藤加奈子さん、出口美砂さん、山本悦也さん、伊藤綾子さん、今野恵雄さん、一般社団法人札幌大学ウレシパクラブ様、川崎克さん、嶋田みどりさん、地田哲哉さん、川村湊さん、田中聡さん、小坂勇さん、山本修峰さん、鈴木紀美代さん、柳下文夫さん、江原朱理さん、中原真吾さん、村雲雅志さん、神戸忠勝さん、千葉誠治さん、森田幸教さん、中村一枝さん（順不同）

英語版の執筆に向けては、北大のジェフリー・ゲーマン教授に英文著述の基本を教わり、米国マールボロ大学で環境人類学を研究するレニ・シャルボノ (Leni Charbonneau) さんに監修の労を引き受けていただいた。アイヌ民族の文化を世界に発信したいという思いを共有してくださったゲーマン教授とレニさんに深く感謝する。藤田印刷（釧路）の藤田卓也社長、装幀家・須田照生さんのご理解、ご協力なしにこの出版が成し遂げられなかったことも記しておきたい。

本書を妻の潮と長男直寛、そして北米やシベリアの先住民族に伝わるワタリガラス神話を追う旅の途上で亡くなった星野道夫氏に捧げる。

二〇一九年四月　札幌にて　小坂　洋右

年表：アイヌ民族をめぐる主な出来事

一四五七 コシャマインの戦い。和人勢力に対するアイヌ民族の最初の大規模決起。当初は優勢だったが、アイヌ民族側が敗北して終結。

一六〇四 徳川家康が松前藩の蠣崎（松前）慶広に黒印状を交付。松前藩に蝦夷地（北海道）での交易の独占権を付与。アイヌ民族の自由往来を認めていることから、「居住地である蝦夷地は『国外』との認識がうかがえる」との指摘がある。

一六四三 この頃までに松前藩の家臣が蝦夷地各地に交易の持ち場を与えられ、米を干サケと交換する商場知行制が確立。

一六六九 干サケの交換率が不当に引き下げられたの不満などから静内地方のシャクシャインが決起し、各地のアイヌ民族と同盟。松前藩を脅かすも、和睦の場で殺害される。

一六九八 和人との接触で疱瘡が流行し、多数のアイヌ民族が死亡。

一七一〇年代 松前藩の家臣が和人の商人に諸産物の交易を委ねる場所請負制度が広がる。時代が下るとニシン漁場への強制連行が横行し、アイヌ民族の酷使と人口減少を招く。

一七一一 ロシア帝国の勢力が千島列島東端のシュムシュ島に及び、北千島アイヌを支配下に置く。

一七三三 イシカリでサケ不漁。アイヌ民族の餓死者約二〇〇人を数える。

一七八九 商人飛騨屋による漁場での酷使に耐えかね、国後島と北海道東部メナシ地方のアイヌ民族が決起。七一人の和人が殺害され、制圧した松前藩によって三七人のアイヌ民族が処刑された。

一七九九 幕府が東蝦夷地を直轄。

一八〇七 幕府が西蝦夷地も直轄にし、北海道全域と樺太南部に影響力を及ぼす。

一八二一 幕府が蝦夷地の交易権を松前藩に返還。

194

一八五五 (和暦では一八五四年) 幕府はロシア帝国と日露修好通商条約 (日露通好条約) を結び、択捉島とウルップ島の間に国境を画定する。サハリン (樺太) は画定せず、日露雑居地とした。幕府は蝦夷地を再び直轄にする。

一八六八 明治維新。

一八六九 明治政府が札幌に開拓使を置く。蝦夷地を北海道と改称し、日本の領土に編入する。

一八七一 開拓使がアイヌ民族に入れ墨や男性の耳輪などを禁止し、日本語の習得を打ち出した。同化政策の始まり。

一八七二 開拓使が北海道土地売貸規則、地所規則を制定。七七年に北海道地券発行条例、八六年に北海道土地払下規則、九七年に北海道国有未開地処分法が定められ、大半の土地が国有地、商業資本、和人移住者の農地などに細分化されていった。八六年から一九二二年間の移住者総数は約二〇一万人に達した。

一八七五 明治政府がロシア帝国と樺太千島交換条約を結び、千島列島を領土化。樺太 (サハリン) はロシア領に。政府は樺太のアイヌ民族を宗谷地方、次いで対雁 (ついしかり) (江別市) に強制移住させる。その後、コレラの流行や環境の変化で死者が続出する。

一八七六 北海道猟規則制定でアイヌ民族伝統の毒矢猟禁止。和人の乱獲に加え、七九年には大雪でシカが大量死し、アイヌ民族の飢餓を招く。

一八七八 開拓使がすべての支流でのサケ・マス漁を禁止。シカと並ぶ主食を奪われる。

一八八四 樺太千島交換条約で引かれた新たな国境で、居住地が図らずもロシアとの国境地帯になった北千島アイヌ約一〇〇人に対し、日本政府が色丹島への移住策決行。色丹は資源に恵まれた島と偽って説得を重ねた強制移住だった。環境の変化などで五年ほどで人口が半減。

一八九九 北海道旧土人保護法制定。農業を希望したアイヌ民族に土地を与えることなどを定めたが、

給与地の多くは農耕不適地で、本質は伝統的な生業、文化、コミュニティーを奪う同化政策だった。

一九〇一　旧土人児童教育規程公布。和人とは別の学校、異なる教程での教育を求め、差別とアイヌ語の収奪につながった。

一九二二　知里幸恵、一九歳で死去。翌二三年に『アイヌ神謡集』出版。

一九三一　全道アイヌ青年大会が札幌で開催。

一九三三　日本学術振興会がアイヌ遺骨研究に五年間の予算を付け、北大の研究者が道内、樺太、千島列島のアイヌ墓地から次々遺骨を発掘し持ち帰る。

一九四五　ソ連軍が日本領南サハリン（樺太）と千島列島に侵攻。住んでいた多くのアイヌ民族が和人とともに北海道本島への逃避・移住を余儀なくされる。

一九四六　北海道アイヌ協会設立。六一年に北海道ウタリ協会に改称し、二〇〇九年に北海道アイヌ協会に再び名称変更。

一九七三　旭川アイヌ協議会発足。東京ウタリ会結成。東京ウタリ会はのち解消し、首都圏では関東ウタリ会、レラの会、ペウレ・ウタリの会、東京アイヌ協会の四団体が個別に活動している。

一九八二　札幌市豊平川でサケを迎える伝統儀式アシリチェプノミが一〇〇年ぶりに復活。八七年からは儀式用サケの川での捕獲が特別採捕として認められた。

一九八四　北海道ウタリ協会がアイヌ新法案を総会で採択。アイヌ古式舞踊が国の重要無形民俗文化財に指定。

一九九二　北海道ウタリ協会の野村義一理事長が国際先住民年を翌年に控え、国連総会で演説。

一九九四　二風谷出身の萱野茂氏がアイヌ民族初の国会議員（参議院）になり、アイヌ語で質問。

一九九七　札幌地裁が二風谷ダム裁判で萱野茂氏らの土地の強制収用を違法と判決。アイヌ民族を先住

二〇〇七 国連で先住民族の権利宣言採択。
民族と認定し、憲法一三条(個人の尊重、幸福追求権)、国際人権規約(自由権規約)第二七条に基づく文化享有権も認めた。アイヌ文化振興法が成立。文化や言葉の復興に限定する内容で、道ウタリ協会のアイヌ新法案から大幅に後退。

二〇〇八 衆参両院が「アイヌ民族を先住民族とすることを求める決議」を全会一致で採択。

二〇一六 アイヌ民族有志「コタンの会」が遺骨返還訴訟で北大と和解し、七月に日高・浦河町に一二体が返還される。

二〇一九 政府のアイヌ新法案「アイヌの人々の誇りが尊重される社会を実現するための施策の推進に関する法律(案)」が成立。植民地的支配や同化政策、差別への歴史的認識やそれに対する謝罪、賠償を欠き、国連宣言でうたわれた「先住民族としての権利(先住権)」に基づく政策もないことから、アイヌ民族の団体・個人、アイヌ政策検討市民会議から批判が相次いだ。成立と同時にアイヌ文化振興法は廃止された。

二〇二〇 四月に国立アイヌ民族博物館が白老の民族共生象徴空間内に開設される予定。子孫や地域に返還されなかったアイヌ民族の遺骨が象徴空間内の慰霊施設に集約されることも決まっている。

註

はじめに

(1) アイヌラックルの誕生は物語の序盤であり、そこから暗黒の国の魔神たちとの戦いなどが繰り広げられる。詳しくは、山本多助『カムイ・ユーカラ アイヌ・ラッ・クル伝』を参照。チキサニと疱瘡神との間にアイヌラックルが誕生した、雷神がチキサニとアッニ（オヒョウの木）がいた家を焼いたなど別伝がいくつか存在する。一方で、金田一京助（一八八二～一九七一）の『アイヌの研究』（一九四〇年版）二〇八～二〇九頁には、日高国沙流郡の伝承として、全く別タイプの創世神話が紹介されている。「大むかし、この世がまだ無かった時、森々たる大海の表にただ大雪山の頂だけが水から頭を出していた。国造の神が、その妹神と共に其の頂に降臨し、雲を埋めて陸地を造った。即ち黒雲は巌［岩］と成り、黄雲は土と為り、そして山や川や島々・国々が出来た」。言語学者の知里真志保は『知里真志保著作集 第二巻』一九五～一九六頁で、コタンカラカムイについて考察を加えている。神話学の大林太良は雲が素材となって世界を形作るアイヌ民族の創世神話には、モンゴルの要素が入っているのではないかと指摘した。加えて、米国の「ジェサップ北太平洋調査」（一八九七～一九〇二）から一〇〇年を経た再検証事業「ジェサップⅡ」で、カラスが世界を救ったという、見方によっては創世神話と言えるものがアイヌ民族にもあることが報告された。「天帝が世界を創造したとき、悪魔は天帝の計画、とくに人間に関する計画を挫折させるためにあらんかぎりのことをした。……そこで悪魔は太陽をのみ込むつもりである朝、太陽が昇るずっと前に起きた。しかし、天帝は悪魔の計画を知って、カラスにこの計画の裏をかかせた。太陽が昇りつつあったとき、口を開けてのみ込もうとした悪魔の喉にカラスは飛び降りた。太陽は助けられた」（益子待也「ワタリガラスと太陽」『渡鴉のアーチ』一〇七頁）。

(2) アイヌ民族は、五～一〇世紀に北方から北海道の北部や東部などに渡来したオホーツク文化人からの形質的影響の度合いは縄文人の流れと比べて高くはないとみられている。ただ、オホーツク文化人にも文化的にも受けているとされ、縄文人→続縄文人→擦文人の直系とまでは言えない。オホーツク文化人の影響を形質的にも

198

一部一章

(1) 川森博司『日本昔話の構造と語り手』六九頁。
(2) 中村とも子らは「異類婚姻譚に登場する動物――動物婿と動物嫁の場合」昔話研究所編『子どもと昔話』一〇〇頁で、動物嫁の例外は、沖縄の『熊女房』『えい女房』ぐらいしか見当たらないとしている。また、動物婚のほうが動物嫁より厳しい排除を人間から受けることをめぐって、動物婿は人間と事実上の結婚に至る前に殺されるサブタイプが多いので、動物嫁にくらべると二重に排除されている一面が強いと結論づけている。
(3) アイヌ民族の口承には、神謡(神々の物語)や英雄叙事詩(英雄の物語)、地域によってトゥイタク、ウェペケレ、トゥイタハなどと呼ばれる散文説話がある。神謡を自ら語る神は「自然神」と「人文神(人格神)」に二分され、「自然神」は雷などの自然現象、シマフクロウ、オオウバユリ、カツラの木などの植物神、臼や舟などの物神、疱瘡など病気をもたらす神などさまざま。「人文神」は地域によって名称が変わり、オキクルミ、オキキリムイ、アイヌラックルなどが登場する。ほかに、口承にはなぞなぞや早口言葉、子守歌、即興歌・抒情歌(ヤイサマ、ヤイサマネナ)、まじないの言葉も含まれる。

(3) アイヌ民族の口承伝承には、盗賊の集団(トパットゥミ)やチャシ(砦)をめぐる争いも語られ、交易の高まりとともに富をめぐる抗争が起きたり、狩猟などの領分をめぐりした対立があったりした可能性は否定できない。社会の序列化も同時に一定程度、進んでいたとみられ、それを、交易の拡張期である一五世紀後半からチャシの造成が目立ってくる一六世紀をへて、大規模なシャクシャインの戦い(一六六九年)を鎮圧した和人の支配が強固になる前の一七世紀前半までとみる研究者もいる。とはいえ、アイヌ社会は権力の大幅な拡大や統合をみることなく、江戸前期を迎えている。縄文社会が平和的だったかを巡っては、岡山大の松本直子教授が「日本先史時代の暴力と戦争 遺跡から学ぶ戦争の起源」と題して二〇一六年一〇月一七日付北海道新聞で、縄文人の受傷人骨の比率の少なさから「集団間の戦争があった可能性はきわめて低いことを示している」と述べている。縄文・弥生両社会の特質については松本直子「縄文の思想から弥生の思想へ」『日本思想史講座1――古代』二七~六四頁を参照。

(4) 千歳市の白沢ナベさん（一九〇五〜一九九三）が一九八七年一〇月に語った伝承に中川裕・千葉大教授が訳注を付けた。アイヌ無形民俗文化財記録刊行シリーズ7『オイナ〈神々の物語〉3』二二二〜二三九頁。本書では、この物語に限らずアイヌ口承の引用部分は原文に訳者が付けた補足も参考にしつつ、読みやすさを考えて部分的には筆者が手を入れたり、略したりしている。

(5) 中川裕『アイヌの物語世界』一〇九〜一二二頁。

(6) 根本与三郎エカシ（一九一八〜二〇一三）は釧路管内白糠町出身。酪農に携わる傍ら、クマ撃ちやシカ猟を続けた。「與三郎」の表記もある。狩猟の伝承の聞き書きは藤村久和編集、北海道教育委員会発行『アイヌ民俗技術調査1〈狩猟技術〉』に採録されている。二〇〇二年にアイヌ文化賞を受賞。兄は口承伝承を残した貫塩喜蔵さん。

(7) 火の神はアペフチ、イレスフチ（フチ＝媼、おばあさん）などと呼んで女神とされる地方もあるが、金田一京助（一八八二〜一九七一）は『アイヌの研究』二五九頁で「北部方言地方では（石狩・十勝・天塩・北見・釧路及び樺太）往々火神をuchiと云って男女一対の神のように考えている」と記している。根本エカシからの聞き書きをもとにした前掲『アイヌ民俗技術調査1〈狩猟技術〉』でも、一一一頁に「アペウチカムイ〈abe-uci→huci-kamuy＝火の──姥──神＝火の女神〉」とある一方で、一四八頁には「炉の火の神に捧げるアペウチイナウは、神窓に向かって左側隅で、隅にある杭の少し手前に立てる方をウレシパエカシ〈u-respa-ekasi＝互いに──充分養育する──祖父＝火の神の翁、火の男神〉といい、右側隅はウレシパフチ〈u-respa-huci＝互いに──充分養育する──祖母＝火の神の媼、火の女神〉」とある。また、萱野茂エカシは『萱野茂アイヌ語辞典』の「アペフチカムイ」の項目に「とっても告げ口が好きな者が火の神だというので、狩のために山へ行く場所を火の前で言わないものだよ」という教えをアイヌ語の例文として紹介している。

(8) 前掲『アイヌ民俗技術調査1〈狩猟技術〉』一二一〜一二二頁。

(9) 二重構造モデル（二重構造説）はこんにちまで受け入れられている。文化人類学者・考古学者の小山修三が縄文時代中期、日本列島全体の人口（北海道を除く総数）を約二六万人と推定、縄文時代晩期にはそれが約七万五千人にまで減ったとした考察を下地に置いた上で、埴原和郎は弥生時代、全国の人口は約六〇万人、古墳時代には五四〇万人に増加したと推定。在来人の人口増加率をいくつか変化を持たせて設定しながら渡来人の数を推測し

200

一部二章
(1) 萱野茂『おれの二風谷』一三〇〜一三二頁。萱野茂エカシ（一九二六〜二〇〇六）は、日高管内平取町二風谷に生まれ、アイヌ民具の流出に危機感を覚え、二風谷アイヌ文化資料館の開設に尽力した。一九九四年にアイヌ民族初の国会議員として参院議員になり、アイヌ語で国会質問に立った。『萱野茂のアイヌ神話集成』『萱野茂のアイヌ語辞典』など著書多数。『ウエペケレ集大成』で菊池寛賞と吉川英治文化賞を受賞。二〇〇三年にアイヌ文化賞を受賞。

(2) 姉崎等エカシ（一九二三〜二〇一三）は、胆振管内鵡川村（現・むかわ町）生まれ。三歳の時、母の実家がある千歳に移り、のち猟を覚えた。二〇〇一年に銃を手放すまで六五年間、狩猟を続けた。共著に姉崎等、片山龍峯『クマにあったらどうするか アイヌ民族最後の狩人 姉崎等』（木楽舎）がある。

(3) イナウ（木幣、写真参照）とはヤナギやミズキなどで作る祭具で、人間（アイヌ）の祈りを供物とともに神に送り届ける役目を果たす。イナウそ

イナウ

た。その結果、渡来人は最大に見積もって千年間に約一五〇万人という数字を得た。埴原和郎編『日本人の起源』二一八〜二二二頁に「人口増加率を〇・四パーセントとしても渡来人口は九万四千人余りとなり、これを縄文末期の人口七万五千強と比べると、『渡来者の影響は無視できる程度』どころではないことになる」と記している。遺伝子（DNA）情報を分析し、人類分化の系統樹を作ってきた尾本恵市は、二重構造モデルの基本的枠組みは支持しつつも、埴原が原日本人（縄文人）を南方系アジア人、渡来人を北方系アジア人としたのに対し、原日本人もまた北方系と結論づけている。尾本恵市著『ヒトと文明』を参照。埴原が渡来人の影響を強調するのに対し、尾本は同書で「本土日本人のミトコンドリアDNAのうち大陸由来のDNAの割合はほぼ六五パーセント、縄文系は三五パーセント」と推定される。われわれは想像以上に縄文人の遺伝子を受け継いでいる（宝来聰）」としている。「六五パーセント」の根拠は宝来聰『DNA人類進化学』一〇八〜一〇九頁。

自体が神にとっては喜ばしい贈り物であり、届くことが自分がどれほど敬われているかのあかしでもある。写真は旧アイヌ民族博物館所蔵資料。

(4) 前掲『クマにあったらどうするか』一九九〜二〇〇頁。

(5) 山田孝子は『アイヌの世界観』一一二頁で、アイヌ民族には、人間の土地にシカやサケを下ろす神がそれぞれいて、人間界とその神々を仲介する別の神が狩猟の女神として存在するとの認識があることから「シカ猟やサケ漁は、クマ狩りのような人間とカムイとの交流の場とは考えられない」としている。しかし、更科源蔵の『コタン生物記 Ⅱ 野獣・海獣・魚族篇』二六九〜二八〇頁には、更科自身の調査で、シカを重んじない地方がある一方、生息数の少ない宗谷地方だけはユクカムイ（鹿神）と呼ぶことや、釧路の雪裡ではチメシュ（チメシ）イナウ（削りかけだけのイナウ）で頭を飾して祭壇に収めること、十勝足寄ではユクヌサ（鹿祭壇）があって、オスジカの大きいのにはイナウも酒もたくさんあげたことなどが記されている。ほかに、英雄叙事詩「鹿男の勇者私を助ける」（金成マツ談）では、主人公がシカ神の霊力を頼みとして戦うし、伝承で語られる飢饉の原因に「人間がシカを獲ってもイナウを持たせないから」とのくだりがあって、シカが敬意をもって贈り物（イナウ）を持たせて霊を送り返すイナウを持たせないかもしれないが、一定の神性をシカに見ていたように思える。また、サケは一匹一匹、新しい木の棒イサパキクニで頭を叩いて、霊を神々の国に送り返すほか、最初に遡上するサケに対しては、迎えの儀式アシリチェプノミ（地方によってはカムイチェプノミ）を行うことからのものが儀礼とみなすこともできよう。

(6) アイヌ無形民俗文化財記録刊行シリーズ15『トゥイタク（昔語り）4』五八頁。

(7) 物が宿る魂においては、使う人間とどれだけ密接で、大事にされてきたかも関わってくるようだ。早川昇『アイヌの民俗』一五九〜一六二頁に収録されている鵡川の宇南山野三郎エカシ（一八八〇〜一九五七）が一九五〇年に語った逸話からは、物の魂と、その物を使う人間の魂は「物」のなかで一体化し、使う人の魂はある日、甥があんまり欲しがるので、宇南山エカシはさらに第三者に転売してしまい、自分はそのことで使ってきた猟銃を甥に売ってやった。それで、その猟銃に入っていた魂を取り戻し、ようやく自分は平安を得ることで精神に変調をきたすように売ってやった。逸話の概略を言えば、物の魂と、その物を使う人間の魂が一体化し、

とができた——。原文は次の通り。「甥子の奴、見損ねた奴で、また自分の手からその銃を、全くの他人様へ転売したんだ。その時よ。やっぱり、争われねえもんだな。その甥子じゃなしに、このおらがよ。まるで何んだか何んだかわかってわからねよな気持になってしまって……つまり、ま、ラム・カリ（狂気）ってなもんだったんだな。だが、ま、これもカムィ（神）のお陰だってものだろか、自分で、ウェン・カムィ・オケウェ（悪魔祓い）がどうにかやって退けられてよ。そして、な。知り合いに頼んで、おらのだったその鉄砲を甥御から買って持っててもらって、その鉄砲に入ってたおらの精力、つまりラマチ（魂）を、おらの守り神まで取り戻してもらったけさ。それからが、その守り神への、おらのお詫びだ。随分、ていねえにお詫びしたわけさ。それでともかく、おらは安心しましたね。というのは、もうおらから離れて他人様へ行っていた精力も、おらの守り神様から、また、この身にもどったって言うわけですからな。そうなると、それが、ちょっとお気の毒だったんでしてね。そんな場合、われわれの信仰では、その他人様は、一時的にもせよ、運が下へ向くんでね。事実、また、そうなったようなんでわたるわけよ」。宇南山エカシによると、「物」の魂（霊）は、人の手に物が渡っても取り戻すことができるのみならず、物を贈るとか誰かと交換することがそもそも、物の魂もまた渡し、受け取ることの意味する。しかも、受け取った物の魂には、もしそれが大事に使い込まれたものであれば、渡してくれた相手の精力もまた含まれている。だから、ぞんざいには扱えないということを言っているのである。後段の「カムィ・チェウワンケプ」については、アイヌ語沙流方言辞典に「ceywankep（チェイワンケプ）c(i)-eywanke-p（我々が／される・使う・もの）『使う・もの道具、使うもの」とある。

特別なものさ。ウタリ（同族人）［アイヌ民族の同胞］はそんな解説も加えた。「心を籠めて使って来た道具は、ねれてる道具）って言って、特に大切にして用いたものだよ」品物の交換（ウタサレ）とか言うのは、わわれの言葉で言うラマチの交換だ」「お互いが出し合う品物にゃ、それぞれの人の精力が入ってて、相手の人にわたるわけよ」。宇南山エカシによると、「物」の魂（霊）は、人の手に物が渡っても取り戻すことができるのみならず、物を贈るとか誰かと交換することがそもそも、物の魂もまた渡し、受け取ることの意味する。しかも、受け取った物の魂には、もしそれが大事に使い込まれたものであれば、渡してくれた相手の精力もまた含まれている。だから、ぞんざいには扱えないということを言っているのである。後段の「カムィ・チェウワンケプ」については、アイヌ語沙流方言辞典に「ceywankep（チェイワンケプ）c(i)-eywanke-p（我々が／される・使う・もの）『使う・もの道具、使うもの」とある。

（8）鵡川（胆振管内むかわ町）の三上ツヤさん（一九〇六〜一九七九）が語った物語を藤村久和さんが訳註。アイヌ無形民俗文化財記録刊行シリーズ5『オイナ（神々の物語）2』二二三〜二八四頁。類似の筋立てで、登別の金成ア

（9）江戸時代の狂歌師、戯作者で、北海道南部の和人地での聞き取りをもとに蝦夷地の紀行『東遊記』を著した立松東蒙（平秩東作）（一七二六〜一七八九）は「アイヌは元来一夫一婦にして子供のなき時は、姿を蓄ふるを通例とす」と記述している。夫を亡くした寡婦は自身の親類兄弟の元に戻らずに、そのまま夫方に留まる選択をし、兄弟や有力者が既婚の場合は第二夫人（ポンマッ）となり、有力者の中には何人もの女性を娶った例もあったとされる。また、子どもができない場合に別の女性を迎えて子どもを持つこともあった。アイヌ文化保存対策協議会編『アイヌ民族誌（下）』四四八〜四五一頁参照。

（10）アイヌ民族の作家鳩沢佐美夫は、自伝ともいえる「証しの空文」川村湊編『現代アイヌ文学作品選』一五七〜一五八頁に、祖母と二人きりでオオウバユリ採りなどに出かけた時のことを次のように描写している。「私を木の根方に残して附近の青物採取に出かけた。……私はいつも留守居役である。が祖母からいろいろ注意を受けているので、ぜったいその場を動かなかった。……活動範囲が展がるにしたがって、祖母の戻る時間が長くなって来る。そんなとき私はつい、うとうとしてしまう。すると祖母が来てやさしく起こしてくれた。『こんなところで眠ったらだめだよ。蛇や化物（ばけもの）が出てくるから……』といって、眠るときには、自分の周囲に縄をまわして眠るように、ともいった。何か危害を避ける、お呪（まじな）いらしかった」。

（11）アイヌ無形民俗文化財記録刊行シリーズ3『オイナ〈神々の物語〉1』一二二〜一三七頁。一九八八年八月四日に白沢ナベさんが自宅で中川裕さんに語り、中川さんが訳註。──解体作法に見る動物霊の処理」『日本の狩猟採集文化』一七四〜二〇三頁。

（12）永松敦「九州山間部の狩猟と信仰

（13）金田一京助『アイヌの研究』二二七〜二二九頁。アイヌ伝承に現れたこうした姿勢は、日本人（和人）の自然との向き合い方を映し出す鏡にもなり得る。例えば、地理学者のオギュスタン・ベルクは『風土の日本──自然と文

204

化の通態』(筑摩書房、一九八八年)二三一〜二四三頁で「(日本が)一九六〇年代に地球上でもっとも汚染された国になってしまったとは、いったいどういうことなのだろうか」という問題を提起し、日本人の自然とのかかわり方を掘り下げている。
(14)前掲『オイナ(神々の物語)2』一二七〜一四三頁。一九八八年六月一八日に千歳の白沢ナベさんが自宅で語ったものを中川裕さんが録音し、訳註。
(15)シントコ(写真参照)はアイヌ民族が宝物としてきた大型の漆器。交易で和人から手に入れて家の中に飾った。写真は旧アイヌ民族博物館所蔵資料。
(16)前掲『オイナ(神々の物語)2』一二九頁。本別の沢井トメノ・フチが語った類似の教訓譚がある。「北見の猟師の仕掛け弓の矢が当たったものの、クマは山の奥に逃げてしまった。後を追えなかったのでなかったらクマが獲れたものを」と言って、怒りながらその山に火を付けた。クマはまだ生きている間に山火事になったものだから、やけどを負い、皮膚に膿をもって死んだらしかった。その男も皮膚が溶けて病み、どうしようもなく苦しむようになった。占い師(トゥスクル)に聞くと、そのクマが死んだとおりに、おまえも苦しみ死ぬのだ、もし助けてやっても別の人が同じ苦しみに遭い死ななければならないので、自分の罪は自分で背負いなさいと答えた。その男はそのクマと同じように皮膚が溶けて死んだ」(『アイヌ民俗文化財調査報告書(昭和六一年度)「アイヌ民俗調査6(十勝・網走地方)」』五一頁)。

一部三章
(1)根本与三郎エカシの狩猟方法は前掲『アイヌ民俗技術調査1〈狩猟技術〉』に詳しい。
(2)知里真志保『分類アイヌ語辞典』で「ニヤシコロカムイ」はシマフクロウとされており、前掲『アイヌ民俗技術調査1〈狩猟技術〉』でもシマフクロウとなっている。シマフクロウのアイヌ語呼称はコタンコロカムイ(集落を見守る神)が一般的である。

(3) 恵庭の栃木政吉エカシは穴グマ猟で、クマがなかなか出てこなかった時の体験として、仲間がクマの冬ごもり穴の神さまにお願いしたと回想している。アイヌ民族が、クマだけでなく、クマが冬眠する穴もカムイととらえていたことが分かる。祈った言葉は「この家を治める家の神様、住んで居るのは雌熊か雄熊か分かりませんが、神々の世界で神々様達が相談なさって決められましたように、中に居る熊を静かに神々の元に行かせて下さい」といった内容だったことを栃木エカシは記憶している。『アイヌ無形民俗文化財記録刊行シリーズ4「アイヌのくらしと言葉2」』三四～三五頁。

(4) 八重九郎エカシ(一八九五～一九七八)は『『アイヌ民俗文化財口承文芸シリーズ12 八重九郎の伝承(2)』の「動物名の隠語について」の節で次のように語っている。「これは大切なこと、大切な神様のことですから、平生しゃべらん言葉。そんでそのときによって、言わなきゃならない場合出てくるときしかしゃべらん言葉ではないの。このパセ チロンノプ(pase cironnop「位の重い・狐」熊の隠語か)っていうこと。でまあ、二人も三人も山歩って、晩に帰ってくるっていうと、山歩ったその内容ちゅうかその出来事ちゅうか、その時分にその言葉を使う場面が出てくるの。『パセ チロンノブ アプカシ オカ アン(pase cironnop apkas oka an 位の重い狐の神が歩いた跡がある)。』ってこう言う」(一九頁)。八重エカシはほかに、キツネ(一般にはチロンノプないしチロンヌプ)の姿を見たときには「ケマ コシネ カムイ オマンコラン(oman kor an)(足の軽い神が行っている)」、オオカミ(一般にはホロケウ・カムイ、オロケウ・カムイ)がいる気配がある時には「ヤイチャロイキ カムイ(yaycaroyki kamuy) オカイ コトムアン(自分を養う神がいらっしゃるようだ)」という言い方をするとしている(二〇頁)。

(5) 『アイヌ民俗文化財調査報告書(昭和六〇年度)「アイヌ民俗調査5(釧路・網走地方)』七頁

(6) 宮本イカシマトク・エカシ(一八七六～一九五八)には「宮本エカシマトク」の表記もある。和名は伊之助。犬飼哲夫、門崎允昭『ヒグマ』三三五～三三六頁。一九八七年版には「白老、宮本氏」としか書いていないが、一九九三年版には「宮本伊之助氏」とフルネームで記載がある。

(7) 前掲『ヒグマ』三三二一～三三九頁の「悪熊の処分」の一節で、白老の宮本イカシマトク氏のほかに、十勝・音更については上士幌の浅山時太郎氏、道東の美幌については菊地儀七氏、道南の八雲については椎久年蔵氏(一八八四

〜一九五八)、同じく長万部については司馬力蔵氏(一八八二〜一九五四年)の各古老が語った対処がまとめられている。鵡川については「辺泥（ぺて）五郎氏談」となっているが、辺泥氏(一八七八〜一九五四)は釧路・春採の生まれで、函館の聖公会アイヌ学校で学んだあと、キリスト教布教のため伝道師として鵡川に移り住んだ。前掲『アイヌ民族誌（下）』六二五〜六二六頁にも記載がある。

(8) 前掲『ヒグマ』三三七頁

(9) 砂沢クラ『ク　スクップ　オルシペ　私の一代の話』七五〜八三頁。

(10) アイヌ無形民俗文化財記録刊行シリーズ11『トゥイタク（昔語り）2』五九〜一二一頁。日高管内平取町荷負本村出身の、同町貫気別で暮らした西島テル（モンテケ）さん(一八九六〜一九八八)が語り、藤村久和さんが訳註。

(11) 同様の状況は「キナストゥンクㇽ（アオダイショウ）が人間に惚れる話」にもある。村長の息子に恋したアオダイショウ（女神）が、息子の魂を取って結婚しようとしたが、妻として迎えられた人間の女性がたくさんのヘビ〔女神の仲間たち〕の来襲に怯えつつも息子と一夜を添い遂げたので、そのことが神々に知られ、女神は二人の夢の中に現れて「もう少しで心臓も止まって男〔息子〕は自分の物になるところだったが、おまえは逃げずに状況を見とどけてしまう。カムイ達にこのことを知られた私はチカプサクコタン（鳥のない国）へ追いやられてしまう」と悔しい思いを告げる。『アイヌ民俗文化財調査報告書（昭和五七年度）アイヌ民俗調査2（旭川地方)』八五〜八六頁。

(12) 前掲『クマにあったらどうするか』一七一頁。

(13) 前掲『クマにあったらどうするか』一三頁。

(14) 知里真志保『知里真志保著作集第1巻』一六一頁。

(15) ウィラースレフ、レーン『ソウル・ハンターズ』一七六頁。

(16) 前掲『ソウル・ハンターズ』七七〜八八頁。

(17) 前掲『トゥイタク（昔語り)2』一九三〜二二六頁。登別出身の金成アシリロさんが一九三二年に親類の金成マツさんに語って採録された。訳註は蓮池悦子さん。

(18) ヌサ（写真参照）は、ヌササン、イナウチパという言い方もされる。かつては各自

ヌサ

(19) の家の外にあり、神々を象徴するイナウが何本も並べられ、イオマンテをした家ではクマの頭骨が飾られていた。写真は旧アイヌ民族博物館所蔵資料。

(20) 北海道内では、縄文遺跡でイルカへの儀礼をうかがわせる遺構が見つかるなど動物への信仰、儀礼はかなり古くにさかのぼることは間違いない。イオマンテの起源に関しては、飼いグマ儀礼のルーツをオホーツク文化にみる説がある。一方で、オホーツク文化の遺跡内部にクマの骨塚があり、若い個体が目立つことなどから、飼いグマ儀礼のルーツをオホーツク文化にみる説がある。一方で、オホーツク文化の動物信仰がアイヌ文化には直接はつながっていないとの見方や、子グマ飼育型の霊送りは一八、一九世紀に成立したとの見方もある。詳しくは天野哲也『クマ祭りの起源』などを参照。諸活動におけるアイヌ民族のコミュニティーの連携規模やイオマンテの社会的意味については Watanabe, Hitoshi. *The Ainu Ecosystem: Environment and Group Structure*、並びに渡辺仁「アイヌ文化の成立　民族・歴史・考古諸学の合流点」『考古学雑誌　五八巻一号』に詳しい。

(21) 杉村京子フチ（一九二六〜二〇〇三）は旭川生まれ。白老出身の詩人森竹竹市エカシとの出会いをきっかけに文化伝承に目覚め、母親のキナラブック・フチから手仕事や口承を学んだ。一九九八年にアイヌ文化賞を受賞。妹の杉村フサ・フチも夫の満エカシとともに伝承者として活躍した。京子フチの半生は小坂洋右『アイヌを生きる　文化を継ぐ』を参照。

(22) 杉村キナラブック・フチ（一八八八〜一九七三）は数多くの口承や手仕事を伝承。キナラブクの表記もある。口承は『キナラブック・ユーカラ集』（旭川叢書第三巻、旭川市、一九六九年）『キナラブック口伝アイヌ民話全集』（中川裕校訂、大塚一美編訳、北海道出版企画センター、一九九〇年）などに収録されている。その生涯は小坂洋右『アイヌを生きる　文化を継ぐ』一七七〜一八四頁。

(23) 小坂洋右『アイヌを生きる　文化を継ぐ』一七七〜一八四頁。

(24) 「ニタイサクモシリ　チカプサクモシリ」はアイヌ語で「森のない大地、鳥のいない大地」を意味し、悪い化け物などが追放される淋しい砂漠のような国土と想像されている。「地獄」としてはもう一つ、「じめじめした地下の国」を意味する「テイネポクナシリ」ないし「テイネポクナモシリ」がある。前掲『アイヌ民族誌（下）』四八九〜四九〇頁には「テイネ——」の方は「悪いことをした人ばかりでなく、善神と戦って敗けた魔神［ニッネ・カムイ

一部四章

(1) 『名作浄瑠璃集(上)近代日本文学大系第八巻』四〇一～四六八頁。「蘆屋道満大内鑑」の表記もある。
(2) 折口博士記念古代研究所編纂『折口信夫全集 第二巻 古代研究(民俗学篇1)』二八一～二八二頁。
(3) 折口博士記念古代研究所編纂『折口信夫全集 第三巻 古代研究(民俗学篇2)』三八六～三八七頁。
(4) 柳田國男『柳田國男全集7』二八～二九頁。
(5) 稲田浩二、稲田和子編『日本昔話ハンドブック新版』三二一～三二三頁。
(6) 前掲『柳田國男全集7』二九～三〇頁。
(7) 稲田浩二『アイヌの昔話』三六一頁。
(8) 北海道伊達市の縄文遺跡、北黄金貝塚ではシカの頭骨が並べられ、動物儀礼があった可能性は濃厚である。大島直行は『月と蛇と縄文人』二五八～二五九頁に「北海道にも棲息していない猪、鮫、マムシといった生物が北海道では縄文時代を通じてシンボライズされているのに、アイヌ文化の時代になるとその姿が見えなくなるのです。……山田孝子の研究によれば、アイヌ民族の習俗が和人によって記録され始めた一八世紀以降には、シマフクロウとヒグマ、[シャチも含んだ]鯨、そして蛇が、彼らの世界観の中核に置かれ、シンボライズされています。シマフクロウアイヌ民族は、シマフクロウは空の、ヒグマは山の、そしてシャチは海の支配者だと考えているのです。さらに、蛇については地下の象徴であるとともにコタン(ムラ)の中心をシンボライズするのだといいます」と書いている。ただし、大島は同書二六〇～二六一頁で、詳しくは、山田孝子『アイヌの世界観』第二章「霊魂とカムイ」を参照。続縄文時代に本州「主導」のシンボライズから北海道独自のシンボライズへ移行していく中で、縄文時代には影を潜めていたヒグマとシャチ(鯨)を積極的に選択したとみる一方、和人文化との接触によって、シンボリズムの意味自体が縄文の「再生思考」から、支配＝「強さと優位性の思考」に変質してしまったと考えら

(9) 日本列島で稲作が始まって以来、先述の通り埴原和郎の推定で、千年の間に最少九万四千人、最大で一五〇万人にも及ぶ渡来人が中国大陸から移住してきた。となれば、「人」がずっと一様だったわけでなく、本州以南で文化が変わった背景に外からの文化の移入や形質・遺伝的な変容が大きく影響したことは否めない。一方の北海道でも縄文人の文化・形質を基本部分で受け継いだとはいえ、アイヌ民族は北方から渡来し、五〜一〇世紀にオホーツク海沿岸を中心に住み着いたオホーツク（文化）人の遺伝子も受け継いでいる。それらを踏まえて、集団の交替や、滅ぼし滅ぼされるという決定的な途絶がなく、「条件つき」と言わざるを得ない。が、あえて使ったのは、「あらためての出合い」という表現は「条件つき」と言わざるを得ない。が、あえて使ったのは、一二三〇〇年前に出発点を置いた大づかみの流れがそうであることを踏まえての概括である。

(10) 瀬川拓郎は、そうした葛藤があったことを織り込んだうえで、一般に「砦」と訳される「チャシ」に大量の野生動物が解体された痕跡が残っているとして、「アイヌは商品交換を強く忌避しており、そうであるからこそモノはチャシにおいて無縁化され、商品であって商品ではない『中間的』なものとして、贈与交換を装った商品交換の場に持参されなければならなかったのではないでしょうか」と推測を加えている（瀬川拓郎『アイヌと縄文』二一八頁）。チャシが実際にどのような機能を果たしていたかも含めて、もっと調査を積み上げなければ何とも結論づけられないが、アイヌ民族が交易に際して、内面の葛藤なしに野生の生き物を商品化することはできなかったのではないか、との着眼は無視できない問題提起であろう。

(11) 更科源蔵『アイヌと日本人 伝承による交渉史』二二〇〜二二二頁ならびに近藤泰年『釧路湿原を歩く』三四八〜三四九頁を参照。更科は「昔は熊送りの頭は、皮をつけたまま送ったものである。しかし頭の皮のない熊の皮は、値段が半分以下になるので、毛皮には頭もつけて、皮をとった頭には皮のかわりに、削木幣で飾りつけをして送るのが普通とされ、近年では熊送りの頭は、昔から皮をとって、木幣で飾って送るものとすら思われて、その昔に消えてしまったと思われていた風習を、今日なお断乎として守りつづけている人があるということは、奇蹟に近いといわなければならない」と書いている。

(12) シャクシャインの戦いの要因については平山裕人『シャクシャインの戦い』に、クナシリ・メナシの戦いについ

ては菊池勇夫『十八世紀末のアイヌ蜂起 クナシリ・メナシの戦い』に詳しい。平山は同書で「もし、この決起がなかったら、和人の往来は一七世紀には激化し、ここは早々と和人の地になったかもしれない。それに対し、民族意識に訴え、和人の侵攻を防いだのが、シャクシャインの戦いだった。『アイヌモシリはアイヌのもの』。この形は近代以前まで固く維持されてきた」と総括しており、重要な視点である。これら三つの大きな戦いのほかにも一六世紀前半、ショヤコウジ兄弟が北海道南部で支配を強める和人勢力の蠣崎光広と戦った「ショヤコウジの戦い」や、一七世紀前半、現在の檜山管内せたな町や後志管内島牧村など北海道南部のアイヌ民族が松前藩に対して立ち上がったヘナウケの戦いなど、和人との衝突が起きている。また、ロシア帝国の支配下にあった北千島アイヌは、ロシア人からラッコの毛皮の供出を強圧的に求められたうえに仲間を殺され、略奪にも遭ったことから一七七一年に南千島アイヌとともにウルップ島で決起し、ロシア人を殺害した。これを受けて、ロシア皇帝エカチェリーナ二世は一七七九年、毛皮税の廃止とアイヌ民族の懐柔策に転じた。ただし、その背景には日本との交易関係を樹立するためには地政学的に中間に居住するアイヌ民族を取り込む必要があるとの打算的思惑があった。この経緯は小坂洋右『流亡――日露に追われた北千島アイヌ』八二〜九三頁を参照。

(13)『知床日誌』の記述。榎森進『アイヌ民族の歴史』三六六頁を参照。
(14) 手塚薫「近世におけるアイヌの生活様式の多様性――アイヌ研究の新たな展開」前掲『日本の狩猟採集文化』一〇〇〜一四九頁を参照のこと。
(15) トッカラムをはじめ、祖先たちの苦難は萱野茂『アイヌの碑』の「和人の奴隷だった祖父」三一一〜一四七頁に詳しい。
(16) 松浦武四郎著、更科源蔵・吉田豊共訳『アイヌ人物誌《近世蝦夷人物誌》改題訳』に、トミハセは当時三七歳で、前掲『アイヌ民族の歴史』三六四〜三六五頁にも記述がある。亡くなった父母の墓へ朝に夕に行って何ごとかを語りかけていたと記されている。しかし、アイヌ民族には墓参りの習慣がなく、むしろ墓地に行くことを恐れていた。人は亡くなった後、魂はあの世に行って前世と同じように暮らしていると信じていたから、アイヌ民族の習慣に照らせば、トミハセについての記述には違和感を覚えなくもない。このように武四郎の記述には、注意して読まないといけない部分がある。幕府の雇いとして、松前藩の蝦夷地支配のあり方も含めて報告することを自らに課していたことに加え、道義を重んじる人柄だったがゆえ

に、松前藩を告発、糾弾する姿勢があったことも客観性をやや歪めている可能性がある。ただ、アイヌ民族の酷使や女性に対する非道な行為は、一七八九年に起きたクナシリ・メナシの戦い後の取り調べで、場所請負人側の和人からも虐待があったことを認める証言が得られている（菊池勇夫『十八世紀末のアイヌ蜂起 クナシリ・メナシの戦い』一四一〜一五〇頁）。事実としてあったことは確かである。和人の横暴を和人の側からこれほど詳細に記録した人物は松浦武四郎のほかにおらず、武四郎がいなければ北海道史、日本近世史の見方そのものが変わっていたと思えるほど重要な足跡を残した人物と言える。武四郎の文献を読む際の留意点は『丁巳東西蝦夷山川地理取調日誌（上）』北海道出版企画センター、一九八二年の四五〜四六頁を参照のこと。

（17）海保嶺夫は一九九四年、徳川家康自筆の松前藩への「黒印の制書」の「附」に、現代語にすれば「アイヌ民族のことは、どこへ往来するのも彼らの自由である」と書かれていることを重視。当時、幕府の支配が及ぶ地域では自由な通行、往来は認められていなかったことから、「幕府は蝦夷地を国の外と考えていたことが分かる」などとした。北海道新聞一九九四年五月一八日付を参照。対照的に、榎森進は「黒印状が」アイヌ民族自体の行為のみならず、アイヌ民族の行為のあり方についても直接的な意志表示をしたことを意味しているものと解される」（『アイヌ民族の歴史』一六三頁）とし、支配関係がむしろ強化されていく局面と捉えている。ただし榎森も、黒印状によって蝦夷地の領有が認められたとのスタンスは取っていない。

（18）日露双方が領土化の根拠としてきたのは「国家を作っていなかった民族の土地は、進出した者勝ちで我が物にできる」という「無主の地（テラ・ヌリウス）の論理」である。ロシア帝国が一七一一年に千島列島東端のシュムシュ島に侵入して北千島アイヌを支配下に置いて毛皮税を課し、ロシア名やロシア正教への改宗といった同化政策を採ったものこの論理に基づく。だが、無主の地の論理は、すでに、この国境交渉の六〇年前にドイツの哲学者イマヌエル・カントによって否定されていることも銘記する必要がある。一橋大学の平子友長名誉教授は二〇〇七年の論文「西洋近代思想史の批判的再検討：カント最晩年の政治思想におけるロック批判の脈絡」川越修、植村邦彦、野村真理編『思想史と社会史の弁証法——良知力追悼論集』五〜三〇頁において、狩猟採集民や牧畜遊牧民が先住していた土地を「無主の地」と見なし、国家が外から植民地化する論拠は、英国の哲学者ジョン・ロックや国

際法の父とされるグロティウス、弁証法で有名なヘーゲルの「土地を耕作することは自然法上の義務である」などとする論理を発展させたヴァッテルの「先占理論」で確立したとする。そのうえで、ドイツの哲学者イマヌエル・カントが『永久平和のために』と『人倫の形而上学』を著した意図を次のように説明している。「カントによれば、地球上に生を営むあらゆる人々にはその土地に居住している意図が成立する。ただ、この先占は後からその土地を訪れる人々を直ちに敵としてはならない。それは、何よりも、先占の権利が世界的に承認された状態、文明諸国民が『未開』と名指しされた人々から土地を取り上げることが停止された状態を意味する」。一八世紀にすでにそのような主張がなされていたことに加え、一九九二年にはオーストラリアの連邦最高裁判所が、英国人が領有化する以前、オーストラリア大陸には土地所有者はいなかったとしてそれを覆し、先住民族は土地に対する先住権原を持っていると認める「マボ判決」を下している。このことで「無主の地の論理」は法的に根拠を失った。

(19) 開拓使は一八七六年(明治九年)、アイヌ民族の伝統的な毒矢猟を禁止し、和人も含めてシカ猟を規制する北海道鹿猟規則を施行した。一八八九年(明治二二年)には、シカの生息数が激減したことを理由に北海道庁がアイヌ民族も含めて北海道内のシカ猟を全面禁止にする。シカ激減の背景には皮、角、肉の商品化と、それに伴う和人ハンターの増加、大雪による大量死があり、規制については資源の保全という観点を見逃すことはできない。しかも、全面禁止に至る過程では、アイヌ民族への優遇が全くなかったわけでもない。従って、シカの禁猟をアイヌ民族への同化政策に含めるのは単純すぎるとの見方もあるかもしれない。ただ、アイヌ民族の生活維持より も産業振興を優先したこと、伝統文化への配慮を欠いたこと、困窮するアイヌ民族に対し、シカの代わりとなる食料資源の確保策が取られなかったこと、全面禁猟に当たってアイヌ民族に限ってシカの免許を出すという施策も考えられたはずなのにそれがなされなかったことを勘案すれば、大きな括りでは同化政策と見なせると私は考える。狩猟規制の経過については山田伸一『近代北海道とアイヌ民族 狩猟規制と土地問題』を参照。

一部五章

（1）小川正人『近代アイヌ教育制度史研究』一四九頁に次のように記述されている。「多くの研究が『〔北海道〕旧土人保護法』とともに『〔旧土人児童教育〕規程』の基本的性格も『同化』教育という言葉で説明しようとするのは、たしかにアイヌ語を否定し日本語などを強制した面を捉えてはいるが、実態の把握にとって不十分だろうということである。北海道開拓にさいしての先住民族の抑圧・排除こそがアイヌ語・アイヌ文化の徹底した破壊に始まる『簡易』『卑近』な教育内容・方法・程度をもたらしたのであり、それがアイヌ語・アイヌ文化の徹底した破壊に始まる『簡易』『卑近』な『蔑視』や『別学』原則に反映した、という構造を指摘しておきたい。ここに見られるのはアイヌ民族の排除であって、日本国家の構成員として『同化』するという把握は、実態に照らせば正確ではない」
（2）前掲『近代アイヌ教育制度史研究』二七八頁。ただし、現代語に直している。
（3）中井三好『知里幸恵──十九歳の遺言』二三六～二四一頁。
（4）前掲『知里幸恵──十九歳の遺言』一九三頁。
（5）知里幸恵『銀の滴──知里幸恵遺稿』一六六～一六七頁。
（6）前掲『銀の滴──知里幸恵遺稿』一七七頁。
（7）消滅も含めた札幌市域のコタンの歴史は、加藤好男『19世紀後半のサッポロ・イシカリのアイヌ民族』に詳しい。
（8）前掲『銀の滴──知里幸恵遺稿』一〇八～一〇九頁。引用中の「……」は〈凡例〉にある中略の意味ではなく、原文にそのように記されている。
（9）前掲『銀の滴──知里幸恵遺稿』一〇九～一一〇頁。引用中の「……」は〈凡例〉にある中略の意味ではなく、原文にそのように記されている。

二部一章

（1）横山むつみ「私のなかの歴史　知里幸恵　銀のしずく記念館館長　横山むつみさん　1」『北海道新聞』二〇一五年六月二九日付け夕刊。

(2) 横山むつみ「私のなかの歴史　横山むつみさん　2」『北海道新聞』二〇一五年六月三〇日付け夕刊。
(3) 一万五千年前から一万二千年前までの約三千年間は旧石器時代の細石刃文化を残しつつ、縄文文化の特徴である土器を作っていた過渡期であり、移行期である。それゆえに縄文時代の始まりを一万五千年前ではなく、一万二千年前に置く研究者もいる。
(4) 青野友哉、大島直行「恵山文化と交易」『新北海道の古代2　続縄文　オホーツク文化』一九〜二一頁。
(5) 大島直行は三〇六一本の本州縄文人の調査結果から、その虫歯率を一四・八％と導き出す一方、北海道縄文人の一二八五サンプルから虫歯率を二・一八パーセントと算定した。本州縄文人の虫歯率は大島の率を最大値に、ほか三人の研究者は八・二パーセントから一〇・七パーセントまで幅のある数値を出している。北海道縄文人のわずか二パーセントと比べれば、いずれの数値も非常に高いということでは変わらない。詳しくは大島直行「縄文時代人の虫歯率」小杉康、谷口康浩、西田泰民、水ノ江和同、矢野健一編『縄文時代の考古学10巻　人と社会　人骨情報と社会組織』九一〜九七頁。
(6) 古人骨に残存するタンパク質成分の分析から食生活を推定する手法で、南川雅男は噴火湾沿いの「北黄金貝塚」（伊達市）で縄文前期、食べられていたのは魚介類が三三％、海産大型動物が三〇％、合わせて六割を占め、ほかの四割はほとんどが植物だったと結論づけた。続縄文期も傾向は変わらず、近傍の有珠モシリ遺跡では、福島県の三貫地貝塚（後晩期）で陸上動物が一四％、魚介類が二％と二割に満たず、植物食が八二％と圧倒的だった。前掲『日本の狩猟採集文化』一一七〜一一八頁。
(7) 寺前直人『文明に抗した弥生の人びと』二七七〜二八四頁。
(8) 高瀬克範『弥生文化の北の隣人』二二三〜二三四頁。
(9) 松本直子「日本先史時代の暴力と戦争　遺跡から学ぶ戦争の起源」北海道新聞二〇一六年一〇月一七日付け朝刊。
(10) 山田康弘『人骨出土例にみる縄文の墓制と社会』二八六〜二九三頁を参照。
(11) 小山修三『縄文探検――民族考古学の試み』三四五頁。
(12) 安田喜憲『縄文文明の環境』二七〜三一頁。

(13) クラストル、ピエール『国家に抗する社会』三八頁。
(14) 前掲『国家に抗する社会』三九頁。
(15) 前掲『国家に抗する社会』二五八頁。
(16) アイヌ無形民俗文化財記録刊行シリーズ10『アイヌのくらしと言葉5』一九〜二四頁。
(17) 「ヤユンクルモシリ」ないし「ヤウンクルモシリ」は直訳すれば「陸の人の大地」だが、ここでは中川裕編『アイヌ語千歳方言辞典』の解説に準拠して「北海道」と括弧書きした。中川辞典の「ヤウンクル」の項には「北海道人：文字通りには「陸の人」であり、レプンクル repunkur『海のかなたに住む人々』に対して、「ヤウンクル」の項には「北海道人：自分たちのことをいう呼び名である。しかって、誰がそれを言うかによって意味は変わってくる」とあり、「ヤウンモシリ」の項には「北海道：原義は ya『陸』un『〜に属する』mosir『大地』であり、海の向うにある世界と対比した上での『こちら側の土地』である。したがって、北海道の人間が言えば北海道のことになるし、樺太の人間がいえば樺太のことになる」とある。言語学者の知里真志保は、おおざっぱに陸の民VS沖の民の戦いと捉えられる英雄叙事詩「虎杖丸の曲（クトゥネシリカ）」の構図を、北海道の在来人（陸の民）VS北海道への渡来人＝オホーツク文化人（沖の民）という現実の歴史的対立が下地にあるのではないかと指摘している。
(18) 砂沢友太郎エカシの祖先が暮らしていた小樽では、集落そのものが集団移転という形で消滅させられている。現在の小樽市は明治期、小樽郡と高島郡に分かれていたが、一八八〇年（明治一三年）に小樽郡のアイヌ民族二二戸六七人が隣接する高島郡に移転させられ、その時点で小樽郡ばかりでなく、余市や網走、釧路、静内（現・新ひだか町）、弟子屈などでも行われた。北海道史研究協議会編『北海道史事典』二六八〜二七二頁参照。集団移転は開拓使の「御内命」を受けた郡長の指示で行われたようで、小樽ばかりでなく、余市や網走、釧路、静内（現・新ひだか町）、弟子屈などでも行われた。北海道史研究協議会編『北海道史事典』二六八〜二七二頁参照。集団移転は開拓使の「御内命」を受けた郡長の指示で行われたようで、小樽ばかりでなく、余市や網走、釧路、静内（現・新ひだか町）、弟子屈などでも行われた。北千島アイヌに対してもロシア帝国との間で一八七五年に結んだ樺太千島交換条約に伴い、日本政府が強制移住策を採った。樺太アイヌに関しては、樺太アイヌ史研究会編『対雁の碑』——樺太アイヌ強制移住の歴史』、千島アイヌに関しては小坂洋右『流亡』——日露に追われた北千島アイヌ』を参照。
(19) 萱野茂、田中宏編集代表『アイヌ民族ドン叛乱　二風谷ダム裁判の記録』一三六頁
(20) 『アイヌ民俗文化財調査報告書（平成四年度）「アイヌ民俗調査12（道東地方）」』二七頁

（21）内海﨑一エカシは幼少期からエカシ、フチと生活を共にしてアイヌ民族の暮らし方や文化を習得。一九四六年に北海道ウタリ協会（現・北海道アイヌ協会）静内支部設立時から支部や行事の運営にかかわり、祭司を務めてきた。二〇一一年にアイヌ文化奨励賞を受賞。ヌサを納めた逸話は『アイヌ民俗文化財調査報告書（平成一四年度）「アイヌ生活技術伝承実態調査4」』一六二～一六四頁。
（22）『アイヌ民俗文化財調査報告書（平成一五年度）「アイヌ生活技術伝承実態調査5」』一〇三～一〇八頁
（23）星野道夫『森と氷河と鯨』一二七～一二九頁。
（24）佐々木史郎「トナカイ多頭飼育の生産性」『国立民族学博物館研究報告別冊二〇号』五一七～五四〇頁。

二部二章
（1）前掲『アイヌの碑』（初版）七二頁。捕ったサケを集落の年配者に配り、神々にも食べさせてきたとの記述からは、アイヌ民族が野生の生き物も含めて食べ物を広く分配するという基本姿勢で生きていたことをうかがわせる。筆者も、山菜採りのお供をして、杉村京子フチから「後から来る人やほかの生き物の分を残して採りなさい」と教えられた経験がある。二〇一八～一九年の冬場に千歳アイヌ協会が千歳川上流部で行ったマレクを使った伝統サケ漁でも、魚体の一部をほかの生き物（神々）のために川べりに残し、その発想が今も刻み込まれていることを示した。そもそもシロザケは上流で産卵し、死ぬことで、特に冬場、野生動物やワシ・タカなどを飢えから救い、なおかつ土壌や森に海のミネラルを還元してきた。ところが、明治以降の人工増殖一辺倒の政策は、河口や下流でサケを一括採捕して、上流に上らせず、付随する禁漁政策でアイヌ民族から主食を奪ったばかりでなく、サケの遺伝的多様性や野生サケが持つ適応力、生態系の持続性をも脅かす結果を招いた。人間が資源を独占する発想から脱し、「できる限り自然産卵を併用すべきだ」と主張する専門家の声に耳を傾けるべきであろう。
（2）萱野茂『アイヌの里――二風谷に生きて』七一頁。
（3）萱野茂『妻は借りもの――アイヌ民族の心、いま』一二一頁。
（4）前掲『アイヌの碑』（初版）七七頁。
（5）前掲『近代北海道とアイヌ民族』一六三～二〇五頁。

(6) 前掲『近代北海道とアイヌ民族』一七七～一八五頁。
(7) 山田伸一「札幌県による十勝川流域のサケ禁漁とアイヌ民族」『北海道開拓記念館研究紀要　第37号』二一〇～二一二頁。
(8) 豊川重雄エカシ（一九三一～二〇一五）は石狩出身。漁師の家業を継いだが、サケが捕れなくなって、二〇代半ばに札幌で木彫りを始めた。札幌アイヌ文化協会を設立し、会長に就任。一九九八年にアイヌ文化奨励賞を受賞した。
(9) 結城庄司（一九三八～一九八三）代表は釧路市生まれ。阿寒湖畔のコタン建設に参加したのち、北海道アイヌ協会再建者会議に参加。一九七二年にアイヌ解放同盟を創設し代表となる。アイヌ民族に対する差別的研究を批判し、民族復権の運動を続ける。一七八九年のクナシリ・メナシの戦いの供養祭「ノッカマップ・イチャルパ」の実行委員会初代委員長に就任。著書に『アイヌ宣言』（三一書房）などがある。
(10) 菅豊『川は誰のものか』一〇三～一〇四頁。
(11) 土橋芳美『痛みのペンリウク——囚われのアイヌ人骨』七五～七八頁。
(12) 各地の返還訴訟の全体状況は北大開示文書研究会のホームページに詳細が記されている。人類学研究におけるアイヌ遺骨収集の経緯とその問題点、その後の返還運動については、植木哲也『学問の暴力　アイヌ墓地はなぜあばかれたか』と北大開示文書研究会編『アイヌの遺骨はコタンの土へ——北大に対する遺骨返還請求と先住権』を参照。
(13) アイヌ遺骨返還ガイドラインの策定に向けた基本的考え方は、政府が二〇一三年六月一四日に開いたアイヌ政策推進会議の政策推進作業部会一二回会合で、次のように議事録に残されている。「海外では、民族又は部族に返還する事例が多く見られること、コタンまたはそれに対応する地域のアイヌ関係団体に遺骨を返還することが、アイヌの精神文化を尊重するという観点からは望ましいとも言える。一方、現実問題として、現在、コタンやそれに代わって地域のアイヌの人々すべてを代表する組織など、返還の受け皿となり得る組織が整備されているとは言い難い状況にあることも考慮する必要がある」。この論法が意味するところについて、遺骨返還訴訟を担当してきた市川守弘弁護士は「政府が『アイヌコタン（集落）や返還の受け皿となるアイヌの集団は存在しない』との認識

218

でいることを示している」と指摘する。その上で、返還・再埋葬に取り組む十勝地方の浦幌アイヌ協会の事例を「かつての小コタンがまとまって構成されている集団で、かつてのこれらコタンの有する遺骨管理権を一つの団体として主張している集団なのであるから、アイヌコタンと考えることができる」としている。先の作業部会の見解に対しては筆者も誤認があると考える。受け皿組織は「整備されていない」のではなく、政府の政策によって「その多くが崩壊させられた」のであり、その責任について触れられていないことにも、歴史認識の欠如を感じる。

(14) 北海道ウタリ協会（現・北海道アイヌ協会）の野村義一元理事長（一九一四〜二〇〇八）は、胆振管内白老村（現・白老町）生まれ。一九六四年から一九九六年まで三二年間、現職。一九九二年には、「世界の先住民の国際年（国際先住民年）」（一九九三年）に先立ってニューヨークの国連本部で行われた記念式典で講演を行った。二〇〇五年にアイヌ文化賞を受賞。

(15) 竹内渉編著『野村義一と北海道ウタリ協会』一八一〜一八二頁。

(16) 前掲『野村義一と北海道ウタリ協会』四九頁。

(17) 金子市議の発言への諸反論は、岡和田晃、マーク・ウィンチェスター編『アイヌ民族否定論に抗する』を参照。

(18) 例えば、アイヌ政策検討市民会議は二〇一九年二月に「日本政府の『アイヌ新法』案の撤回を求める声明」を出した。市民会議には少数民族懇談会会長で「コタンの会」の代表でもある清水裕二さんや、紋別アイヌ協会の畠山敏会長、樺太アイヌ協会の田澤守会長、東京ウタリ会会長や首都圏のアイヌ民族各団体が緩やかに連携する「アイヌウタリ連絡会」代表などを歴任してきた宇梶静江さんらアイヌ民族が参加しており、世話人代表の丸山博・室蘭工大名誉教授をはじめ、北大の吉田邦彦教授、同ジェフリー・ゲーマン教授ら学識者も名を連ねている。詳細は市民会議のインターネットサイト（HP）を参照。同年三月三日に

アイヌ新法案撤回を求めるデモ

(19) は「アイヌによる、アイヌのための法律を——先住権なき政府「アイヌ新法」案を問う」集会とアイヌ新法案の撤回を求めるデモ（写真）が札幌市内で行われ、三月九日にはオーストラリア国立大学のテッサ・モーリス＝スズキ名誉教授の講演を中心に据えた連続講座「世界の先住権の常識で再考するアイヌ政策」（北大開示文書研究会、北大大学院メディア・コミュニケーション研究院共催）も札幌で開かれ、新法案を批判的な立場から検討した。

(20) 台湾の蔡英文総統が二〇一六年、先住民族に謝罪したのは記憶に新しい。二〇〇八年にはオーストラリアのラッド首相、カナダのハーパー首相が相次ぎ国内の先住民族に謝罪した。また、米国の上下両院は一九九三年、先住民族のハワイ王国を転覆させ、米国に併合したことへの謝罪を合同決議し、一九九七年にはノルウェー国王ハラルド五世がサーミ民族に謝罪しており、一九九〇年代以降、少なからぬ国で謝罪がなされている。

国連の先住民族権利宣言は、第二六条で「先住民族は、自らが伝統的に所有し、占有し、またはその他の方法で使用し、もしくは取得してきた土地や領域、資源に対する権利を有する」としている。遺骨を取り戻す権利も第12条に規定されている。

(21) 国連は二〇〇七年の先住民族権利宣言で「先住民族」の定義を定められず、国際機関による明確な定義はない。ただし、先住民問題国際作業グループ（IWGIA）は「先住民族と自認する集団は、定義をするのではなく当該集団が先住民かどうかを自ら決めるべきだ」と主張し、国連特別報告者ホセ・マルチネス・コーボ（José Martinez Cobo）が示した概念が最も一般的だとしている。国際社会の共通認識になっているその要件は①先住性（国家による植民地化の時点で原住していたか、そこから強制移住させられた集団とその子孫）②被支配性（独自の生活様式を享受できない植民地的、もしくは社会的・法的な状況に置かれている集団とその子孫）③歴史の共有（植民地経営当時の原住民との歴史的連続性がある）④自認（自ら先住民と認識する集団とその成員）。先住民と非先住民の間に生まれた者とその子孫も除外されない）の四点である。すなわち、どの集団がより古くにさかのぼってその地にいたかということが問題とされるのではなく、植民地支配を受けた時点でそこに居住していたかどうかが決め手であり、その後、差別や同化政策によって文化や諸権利を奪われていったことがそこに「先住民族」認定の要件となることを意味する。窪田幸子、野林厚志編『「先住民」とはだれか？』を参照。先住民族の定義、本質からいって、歴史認識抜きの認定がありえないことはこのことから明らかである。海外の有識者の発言に関しては、

本章の註(18)で触れた連続講座で、テッサ・モーリス＝スズキ氏が「先住権が全く盛り込まれておらず、国際的には奇妙な法案」と断じている。二〇一九年三月二三日付け、北海道新聞「各自核論」を参照。
(22) 八重清次郎エカシ（一九二四〜二〇〇九）は音別（現在は釧路市）の生まれで、白糠で育てられたのち、釧路市の春採コタンに移り住んだ。二〇〇一年にアイヌ文化賞受賞。『コタン伝統の灯を守る』の中で、自身を「私はアイヌである」とし、「私を育ててくれたアイヌの恩は忘れない。その為にはアイヌ民族の伝承文化を伝えることに一生懸命になることだと考え、『アイヌ文化を残そう』と一軒一軒一人一人にお願いに歩きました」と記している。松本成美『八重清次郎小伝』『久摺第一〇集』でもその生涯が紹介されている。
(23) 『コタン伝統の灯を守る』一〜五頁。
(24) 詳しくは石純姫著『朝鮮人とアイヌ民族の歴史的つながり』を参照。多数の聞き取りをもとに戦時中の朝鮮人とアイヌ民族のかかわりを実証している。

二部三章
(1) カピウはアイヌ語で「カモメ」、アパッポは「花」を意味する。「春」を意味するCD「Paykar（パイカラ）」もリリースされている。
(2) 秋野茂樹論集『イヨマンテ アイヌの霊送り儀礼』八〜九頁。
(3) 前掲『クマにあったらどうするか』七八〜八六頁。
(4) 野本久栄エカシ（一九五一〜二〇一九）は白老出身。千歳に住んで三〇代からアイヌ文化伝承活動を始め、儀式の祭司を務めた。一九九六年に千歳市立末広小学校内にアイヌ民族の伝統家屋（チセ）を建設。小学一年生から六年生まで一貫したアイヌ文化教育のカリキュラム作成に携わり、アイヌ文化を学校で学んでいく環境作りに尽力した。アイヌ語新聞「アイヌ・タイムズ」を発行するアイヌ語ペンクラブの会長も務めた。二〇一三年にアイヌ文化奨励賞受賞。
(5) 『アイヌ民俗文化財調査報告書（平成五年度）「アイヌ民俗調査13（白糠地方）」』九五頁。
(6) 前段のタヌキがクマの巣穴に一緒に暮らしていたという証言は『アイヌ民俗文化財調査報告書（平成四年度）「ア

(7) 八重九郎『八重九郎の伝承(7)』六四～六九頁。
(8) 『アイヌ民俗文化財調査報告書(平成六年度)「アイヌ民俗調査14(補足調査1)」』八～九頁。
(9) 前掲『クマにあったらどうするか』一五八～一六三頁。
(10) 根本エカシの言葉は前掲『アイヌ民俗技術調査1〈狩猟技術〉』五六～五七頁。エゾフクロウに関しては知里真志保の『分類アイヌ語辞典』の動物編一九七頁。
(11) マーゴリス、ジョナサン編集『先住民は今 二つの世界に生きる』四～六頁 ウィルマ・マンキラーさんのタイトルは「21世紀の先住民」。日本語テキストは原文"Being Indigenous in the 21st Century"から筆者訳。
(12) このメールを交わした時点では分からなかったが、ヤーガン族のクリスティーナ・カルデロンさんは二〇一〇年に他界していた。

イヌ民俗調査12(道東地方)」の渕瀬一雄氏証言(四四頁)。後段のタヌキの授乳は同書三三頁。

〈参考文献〉

〔日本語文献〕

アイヌ文化保存対策協議会編集『アイヌ民族誌(上、下)』第一法規出版、一九六九年

アイヌ民族博物館『イヨマンテ—クマの霊送り—報告書』一九九〇年

――『イヨマンテ—熊の霊送り—報告書2』一九九一年

『アイヌ民俗文化財調査報告書(昭和六〇年度)「アイヌ民俗調査5(釧路・網走地方)」』北海道教育委員会、一九八六年

『アイヌ民俗文化財調査報告書(昭和六一年度)「アイヌ民俗調査6(十勝・網走地方)」』北海道教育委員会、一九八七年

『アイヌ民俗文化財調査報告書(昭和五七年度)「アイヌ民俗調査1(旭川地方)」』北海道教育委員会、一九八三年

『アイヌ民俗文化財調査報告書(昭和五七年度)「アイヌ民俗調査2(旭川地方)」』北海道教育委員会、一九八三年

『アイヌ民俗文化財調査報告書(平成四年度)「アイヌ民俗調査12(道東地方)」』北海道教育委員会、一九九三年

『アイヌ民俗文化財調査報告書(平成五年度)「アイヌ民俗調査13(白糠地方)」』北海道教育委員会、一九九四年

『アイヌ民俗文化財調査報告書(平成六年度)「アイヌ民俗調査14(補足調査1)」』北海道教育委員会、一九九五年

『アイヌ民俗文化財調査報告書(平成一四年度)「アイヌ生活技術伝承実態調査4」』北海道教育委員会、二〇〇三年

『アイヌ民俗文化財調査報告書(平成一五年度)「アイヌ生活技術伝承実態調査5」』北海道教育委員会、二〇〇四年

アイヌ無形民俗文化財記録刊行シリーズ1『アイヌ民話』北海道教育委員会、一九八八年

アイヌ無形民俗文化財記録刊行シリーズ3『オイナ(神々の物語)1』北海道文化財保護協会、一九九〇年

アイヌ無形民俗文化財記録刊行シリーズ5『オイナ(神々の物語)2』北海道教育委員会、一九九二年

アイヌ無形民俗文化財記録刊行シリーズ7『オイナ(神々の物語)3』北海道教育委員会、一九九四年

アイヌ無形民俗文化財記録刊行シリーズ9『トゥイタク(昔語り)1』北海道教育委員会、一九九六年

アイヌ無形民俗文化財記録刊行シリーズ11『トゥイタク(昔語り)2』北海道教育委員会、一九九八年

「アイヌ民族共有財産裁判の記録」編集委員会編『百年のチャランケ アイヌ民族共有財産裁判の記録』緑風出版、二〇〇九年

青野友哉、大島直行「恵山文化と交易」野村崇、宇田川洋編『新北海道の古代2 続縄文 オホーツク文化』北海道新聞社、二〇〇三年：一〇～二九頁

秋野茂樹論集『イヨマンテ――アイヌの霊送り儀礼』秋野茂樹論集刊行会、二〇一七年

姉崎等、片山龍峯『クマにあったらどうするか アイヌ民族最後の狩人 姉崎等』木楽舎、二〇〇二年

天野哲也『クマ祭りの起源』雄山閣、二〇〇三年

池谷和信編『狩猟採集民からみた地球環境史 自然・隣人・文明との共生』東京大学出版会、二〇一七年

市川守弘『アイヌの法的地位と国の不正義 遺骨返還問題と〈アメリカインディアン法〉から考える〈アイヌ先住権〉』寿郎社、二〇一九年

稲田浩二『昔話タイプ・インデックス：日本昔話通巻第二八巻』同朋舎出版、一九八八年

――『アイヌの昔話』ちくま学芸文庫、筑摩書房、二〇〇五年

アイヌ民俗文化財口承文芸シリーズⅣ『知里幸恵ノート』北海道教育委員会、一九八五年

アイヌ民俗文化財記録刊行シリーズ15『トゥイタク（昔語り）4』北海道教育委員会、二〇〇二年

アイヌ民俗文化財記録刊行シリーズ13『トゥイタク（昔語り）3』北海道教育委員会、二〇〇〇年

アイヌ民俗文化財記録刊行シリーズ4『アイヌのくらしと言葉2』北海道教育庁生涯学習部文化課編、一九九一年

アイヌ民俗文化財記録刊行シリーズ8『アイヌのくらしと言葉4』北海道教育庁生涯学習部文化課編、一九九五年

アイヌ民俗文化財記録刊行シリーズ10『アイヌのくらしと言葉5』北海道教育庁生涯学習部文化課編、一九九六年

アイヌ民俗文化財記録刊行シリーズ14『アイヌのくらしと言葉7』北海道教育庁生涯学習部文化課編、二〇〇一年

稲田浩二、小澤俊夫責任編集『日本昔話通巻 第一巻 北海道（アイヌ民族）』同朋舎出版、一九八九年
稲田浩二、稲田和子編『日本昔話ハンドブック新版』三省堂、二〇一〇年
犬飼哲夫、門崎允昭『ヒグマ 北海道の自然』北海道新聞社、一九八七年
煎本孝『アイヌの熊祭り』雄山閣、二〇一〇年
ウィラースレフ、レーン著、奥野克巳ほか訳『ソウル・ハンターズ シベリア・ユカギールのアニミズムの人類学』亜紀書房、二〇一八年
植木哲也『学問の暴力 アイヌ墓地はなぜあばかれたか』春風社、二〇一七年
宇梶静江『すべてを明日の糧として 今こそ、アイヌの知恵と勇気を』清流出版、二〇一一年
宇田川洋『アイヌ文化成立史』北海道出版企画センター、一九八八年
──『イオマンテの考古学』東京大学出版会、一九八九年
──『アイヌ伝承と砦（チャシ）』北方新書007、北海道出版企画センター、二〇〇五年
榎森進『アイヌ民族の歴史』草風館、二〇〇七年
大島直行「縄文時代人の虫歯率」小杉康、谷口康浩、西田泰民、水ノ江和同、矢野健一編『縄文時代の考古学10巻 人と社会 人骨情報と社会組織』：九一〜九七頁
──『月と蛇と縄文人──シンボリズムとレトリックで読み解く神話的世界観』寿郎社、二〇一四年
小川正人『近代アイヌ教育制度史研究』北海道大学図書刊行会、一九九七年
岡田宏明『文化と環境──エスキモーとインディアン』北海道大学図書刊行会、一九七九年
岡和田晃、マーク・ウィンチェスター編『アイヌ民族否定論に抗する』河出書房新社、二〇一五年
荻原眞子『北方諸民族の世界観──アイヌとアムール・サハリン地域の神話・伝承』草風館、一九九六年
小沢俊夫『世界の民話』中公新書531、中央公論社、一九七九年
尾本恵市『ヒトと文明──狩猟採集民から現代を見る』ちくま新書1227、筑摩書房、二〇一六年
折口博士記念古代研究所編纂『折口信夫全集 第一巻 古代研究（国文学篇）』中公文庫、中央公論社、一九七五年
──『折口信夫全集 第二巻 古代研究（民俗学篇1）』中公文庫、中央公論社、一九七五年

貝沢耕一、丸山博、松名隆、奥野恒久編著『アイヌ民族の復権——先住民族と築く新たな社会』法律文化社、二〇一一年

海保嶺夫『日本北方史の論理』雄山閣、一九七四年

片山龍峯『「アイヌ神謡集」を読みとく』草風館、二〇〇三年

加藤好男『19世紀後半のサッポロ・イシカリのアイヌ民族』サッポロ堂書店、二〇一七年

萱野茂『おれの二風谷』すずさわ書店、一九七五年

萱野茂『炎の馬——アイヌ民話集』すずさわ書店、一九七七年

萱野茂『カムイユカラと昔話』小学館、一九八八年

萱野茂『アイヌの碑』朝日文庫、朝日新聞社、一九九〇年

萱野茂『妻は借りもの——アイヌ民族の心、いま』北海道新聞社、一九九四年

萱野茂『アイヌの里——二風谷に生きて』日本図書センター、二〇〇五年

萱野茂、田中宏編集代表『アイヌ民族ドン叛乱——二風谷ダム裁判の記録』三省堂、一九九九年

樺太アイヌ史研究会編『対雁の碑——樺太アイヌ強制移住の歴史』北海道出版企画センター、一九九二年

川森博司『日本昔話の構造と語り手』大阪大学出版会、二〇〇〇年

菊池勇夫『アイヌ民族と日本人——東アジアのなかの蝦夷地』朝日選書510、朝日新聞社、一九九四年

北原次郎太『アイヌの祭具——イナウの研究』北海道大学出版会、二〇一四年

木村英明、本田優子編『ものが語る歴史シリーズ13 アイヌの熊送りの世界』同成社、二〇〇七年

金田一京助『アイヌ叙事詩——ユーカラ概説』青磁社、一九四三年

金田一京助『アイヌの研究』八洲書房、一九四〇年

―――『アイヌ叙事詩　虎杖丸の曲』青磁社、一九四四年
―――『アイヌ叙事詩ユーカラ集Ⅷ』三省堂、一九六八年

葛野辰次郎著、葛野次雄、竹内渉編『キムスポ』一九九九年

工藤雅樹「古代蝦夷の社会――交易と社会組織」歴史科学協議会編集『歴史評論四三四号』校倉書房、一九八六年：一二三～三五頁

窪田幸子、野林厚志編『先住民』とはだれか？』世界思想社、二〇〇九年

久保寺逸彦編訳『アイヌの神謡』草風館、二〇〇四年

クラストル、ピエール、渡辺公三訳『国家に抗する社会』水声社、一九八七年

倉光秀明（記録）『上川アイヌ――熊まつり』一九五三年ごろ

クライナー、ヨーゼフ編『日本民族の源流を探る――柳田國男「後狩詞記」再考』三弥井書店、二〇一二年

『口承文学2・アイヌ文学　岩波講座　日本文学史　第17巻』岩波書店、一九九七年

小坂洋右『流亡――日露に追われた北千島アイヌ』道新選書二四、北海道新聞社、一九九二年

―――『大地の哲学――アイヌ民族の精神文化に学ぶ』未來社、二〇一五年

、林直光（写真）『アイヌを生きる――文化を継ぐ母キナフチと娘京子の物語』大村書店、一九九四年

小山修三『縄文時代　コンピュータ考古学による復元』中公新書733、中央公論社、一九八四年

―――『縄文探検――民族考古学の試み』中公文庫、中央公論社、一九九八年

近藤泰年『釧路湿原を歩く』福音館書店、一九八八年

佐々木史郎「トナカイ多頭飼育の生産性」松原正毅、小長谷有紀、佐々木史郎編『国立民族学博物館研究報告別冊二〇号　ユーラシア遊牧社会の歴史と現在』国立民族学博物館、一九九九年：五一七～五四〇頁

佐藤孝雄編『シラッチセの民族考古学――漁川源流域におけるヒグマ猟と"送り"儀礼に関する調査・研究』

佐原真、小林達雄『世界史のなかの縄文』新書館、二〇〇一年

佐原真著、金関恕、春成秀爾編『佐原真の仕事4　戦争の考古学』岩波書店、二〇〇五年

六一書房、二〇〇六年

更科源蔵『アイヌと日本人――伝承による交渉史』NHKブックス一一八、日本放送出版協会、一九七〇年
――『コタン生物記Ⅱ野獣・海獣・魚族篇』法政大学出版局、一九七六年
四宅ヤヱ（述）、冨永慶一（採録）『四宅ヤヱの民俗学　韻文編1』『四宅ヤヱの伝承』刊行会、二〇一一年
菅豊『川は誰のものか――人と環境の民俗学』吉川弘文館、二〇〇六年
杉村キナラブック、大塚一美、三好文夫、杉村京子『キナラブック・ユーカラ集』旭川叢書第三巻、旭川市、一九六九年
砂沢クラ『ク　スクップ　オルシペ　私の一代の話』アイヌ民族文化伝承会らぷらん、二〇一二年
瀬川拓郎『アイヌと縄文――もう一つの日本の歴史』筑摩書房、二〇一六年
石純姫『朝鮮人とアイヌ民族の歴史的つながり』寿郎社、二〇一七年
平子友長「西洋近代思想史の批判的再検討――カント最晩年の政治思想におけるロック批判の脈絡」川越修、植村邦彦、野村真理編『思想史と社会史の弁証法――良知力追悼論集』御茶の水書房、二〇〇七年：五～三〇頁
高瀬克規「弥生文化の北の隣人――続縄文文化」藤尾慎一郎編『弥生時代って、どんな時代だったのか？』国立歴史民俗博物館研究叢書1、朝倉書店、二〇一七年：一一四～一三六頁
竹内渉編著『野村義一と北海道ウタリ協会』草風館、二〇〇四年
田口洋美『マタギ――森と狩人の記録』慶友社、一九九四年
谷本一之、井上紘一編『渡鴉のアーチ』（1903―2002）：ジェサップ北太平洋調査を追試検証する』国立民族学博物館、二〇〇九年
知里真志保『知里真志保著作集　第一巻』平凡社、一九七三年
――『知里真志保著作集　第二巻』平凡社、一九七三年
――『知里真志保著作集　第四巻』平凡社、一九七四年
――『知里真志保著作集　別巻1』平凡社、一九七六年
知里幸恵編訳『アイヌ神謡集』岩波書店（岩波文庫）、一九七八年

知里幸恵『銀のしずく――知里幸恵遺稿』草風館、一九九六年

手塚薫「近世におけるアイヌの生活様式の多様性――アイヌ研究の新たな展開」池谷和信、長谷川政美編『日本の狩猟採集文化　野生生物とともに生きる』世界思想社、二〇〇五年：一〇〇〜一四九頁

寺前直人『文明に抗した弥生の人びと』歴史文化ライブラリー四四九、吉川弘文館、二〇一七年

土橋芳美『痛みのペンリウク――囚われのアイヌ人骨』草風館、二〇一七年

冨永慶一採録『四宅ヤエの伝承――歌謡・散文編』四宅ヤエの伝承」刊行会、二〇〇七年

中井三好『知里幸恵――十九歳の遺言』彩流社、一九九一年

中川裕改訂、大塚一美編訳『キナラブック口伝――アイヌ民話全集一　神話編一』北海道出版企画センター、一九九〇年

中川裕『アイヌの物語世界』平凡社ライブラリー190、平凡社、一九九七年

――『語り合うことばの力――カムイたちと生きる世界』岩波書店、二〇一〇年

中沢新一『熊から王へ――カイエ・ソバージュⅡ』講談社選書メチエ239、二〇〇二年

――『対称性人類学――カイエ・ソバージュⅤ』講談社選書メチエ291、二〇〇四年

中村とも子、弓良久美子、間宮史子「異類婚姻譚に登場する動物――動物婿と動物嫁の場合」昔話研究所編『子どもと昔話』、古今社、二〇〇一年：八四〜一〇二頁

永松敦「九州山間部の狩猟と信仰――解体作法に見る動物霊の処理」池谷和信、長谷川政美編『日本の狩猟採集文化　野生生物とともに生きる』世界思想社、二〇〇五年：一七四〜二〇三頁

鳩沢佐美夫「証しの空文」川村湊編『現代アイヌ文学作品選』講談社文芸文庫、二〇一〇年：一五二〜一九六頁

埴原和郎編『日本人と日本文化の形成』朝倉書店、一九九三年

『日本人の起源』朝日選書517、朝日新聞社、一九九四年

早川昇『アイヌの民俗』民俗民芸双書五四、岩崎美術社、一九七〇年

平山裕人『アイヌの歴史　日本の先住民族を理解するための160話』明石書店、二〇一四年

――『アイヌ史を見つめて』北海道出版企画センター、一九九六年

―――『地図でみる　アイヌの歴史――縄文から現代までの1万年史』明石書店、二〇一八年
藤村久和編集、北海道教育委員会発行『アイヌ民俗技術調査1〈狩猟技術〉』平成20年度アイヌ民俗文化財調査報告書、二〇〇九年
藤本英夫『銀のしずく降る降る』新潮選書、新潮社、一九七三年
北大開示文書研究会編『アイヌの遺骨はコタンの土へ――北大に対する遺骨返還請求と先住権』緑風出版、二〇一六年
星野道夫『森と氷河と鯨――ワタリガラスの伝説を求めて』世界文化社、一九九六年
北海道大学アイヌ・先住民研究センター編『アイヌ研究の現在と未来』北海道大学出版会、二〇一〇年
北海道庁『北海道旧土人保護沿革史』一九三四年
本田優子編『伝承から探るアイヌの歴史』札幌大学附属総合研究所、二〇一〇年
前沢卓『前沢卓写真集『アイヌ民族　命の継承』藤田印刷エクセレントブックス、二〇一八年（第二版）
マーゴリス、ジョナサン編集『先住民は今――二つの世界に生きる』米国国務省国際情報プログラム局が編集して米国大使レファレンス資料室が邦訳。二〇一〇年
松浦武四郎著、更科源蔵・吉田豊共訳『アイヌ人物誌（『近世蝦夷人物誌』改題訳）』農山漁村文化協会、一九八一年
松本成美「八重清次郎小伝」『久摺第一〇集』釧路アイヌ文化懇話会、二〇〇三年
松本憲郎「『日本人』の心の深みへ――「縄文的なもの」と「弥生的なもの」を巡る旅」新曜社、二〇一六年
松本直子「縄文の思想から弥生の思想へ」苅部直、黒住真、佐藤弘夫、末木文美士、田尻祐一郎編集委員『日本思想史講座1――古代』ぺりかん社、二〇一二年
丸山隆司『〈アイヌ〉学の誕生――金田一と知里と』彩流社、二〇〇二年
『名作浄瑠璃集（上）』近代日本文学大系第八巻』国民図書、一九二七年
八重九郎『アイヌ民俗文化財口承文芸シリーズ12　八重九郎の伝承（2）』北海道教育委員会、一九九四年
―――『アイヌ民俗文化財口承文芸シリーズ17　八重九郎の伝承（7）』北海道教育委員会、一九九九年
八重清次郎など編『コタン伝統の灯を守る　釧路アイヌ民族文化リムセ保存会　会長八重清次郎』私家版、

一九七六年ごろ

安田喜憲『縄文文明の環境』歴史文化ライブラリー24、吉川弘文館、一九九七年

柳田國男「後狩詞記」『定本 柳田國男集第二七巻』筑摩書房、一九七〇年：一～三九頁

―――『柳田國男全集7』筑摩書房、一九九〇年

山田伸一『近代北海道とアイヌ民族―狩猟規制と土地問題』北海道大学出版会、二〇一一年

―――「札幌県による十勝川流域のサケ禁漁とアイヌ民族」『北海道開拓記念館研究紀要 第37号』北海道開拓記念館、二〇〇九年：二〇一～二二三頁

山田孝子『アイヌの世界観――「ことば」から読む自然と宇宙』講談社選書メチエ24、講談社、一九九四年

山田康弘『人骨出土例にみる縄文の墓制と社会』同成社、二〇〇八年

山本多助『カムイ・ユーカラ――アイヌ・ラッ・クル伝』平凡社ライブラリー26、平凡社、一九九三年

横山むつみ「私のなかの歴史 知里幸恵銀のしずく記念館館長 横山むつみさん」『北海道新聞』二〇一五年六月二九日～七月一一日、夕刊

渡辺仁「アイヌ文化の成立――民族・歴史・考古諸学の合流点」『考古学雑誌 五八巻一号』日本考古学会、一九七二年

〔英語文献〕

Clastres, Pierre. *Society Against the State*. Oxford: Mole Editions Basil Blackwell, 1977.
*Originally published in France as *"La Société contre l'état."* Paris: Les Éditions de Minuit, 1974.

Mankiller, Wilma. "Being Indigenous in the 21st Century." In *Cultural Survival Quarterly Magazine*, March 2009.

Philippi, Donald L. *Songs of Gods, Songs of Humans: The Epic Tradition of the Ainu*. Tokyo, Princeton, N.J.: University of Tokyo Press & Princeton University Press, 1979.

Strong, Sarah M. *Ainu Spirits Singing: The Living World of Chiri Yukie's Ainu Shin'yōshū*. Honolulu, Hawaiʻi:

University of Hawai'i Press, 2011.

Van der Sluys, Cornelia M. I. "Gifts from the Immortal Ancestors: Cosmology and Ideology of Jahai Sharing." In *Hunters and Gatherers in the Modern World: Conflict, Resistance, and Self-Determination*. Edited by Peter P. Schweitzer, Megan Biesele, and Robert K. Hitchcock, 427-454. New York. Oxford: Berghahn Books, 2000.

Watanabe, Hitoshi. *The Ainu Ecosystem: Environment and Group Structure*. Seattle, London: University of Washington Press, 1973.

Willerslev, Rane. *Soul Hunters: Hunting, Animism, and Personhood among the Siberian Yukaghirs*. Berkeley, Los Angeles, London: University of California Press, 2007.

About the Author

KOSAKA Yousuke (Yōsuke) is a Japanese journalist and a senior editorial writer of the Hokkaido Shimbun, a daily newspaper. Born in Sapporo in 1961, he studied linguistics at Hokkaido University and studied journalism at Oxford University. He started his career as a curator of the Ainu Museum in Shiraoi, Hokkaido. He published three books on the Ainu, an Indigenous people of Japan. *Ryūbō: Nichiro ni Owareta Kitachishima Ainu* (Wondering: North Kuril Ainu, who were Expelled by the Japanese and Russian Powers) Sapporo: Hokkaido Shimbun, 1992. *Ainu o Ikiru, Bunka o Tsugu: Haha Kina-Fuci to Musume Kyōko no Monogatari* (I will Live as an Ainu to Hand Down My Culture: A Story of Kina-Fuci and her Daughter Kyōko) Tokyo: Ōmura Shoten,1994. *Daichi no Tetsugaku: Ainu Minzoku no Seishin Bunka ni Manabu* (A Philosophy of the Land: Learning from the Spiritual Culture of the Ainu) Tokyo: Miraisha, 2015. Having tackled the history of the Cold War and the development of the Atomic bomb, he also published *Nihonjin Gari: Beiso Jōhōsen ga Spy ni shita Otoko tachi* (Headhunting Japanese: Men driven to the Intelligence Battle between the Soviet Union and the United States of America) Tokyo: Shinchōsha, 2000. *Hakaisha no Trauma: Genbaku Kagakusha to Pilot no Sūki na Unmei* (Trauma of Demolishers: Checkered Destinies of a Scientist, who Indulged in the Manhattan Project and a Pilot, who was Involved in the Dropping of the Atomic Bomb) Tokyo: Miraisha, 2005. He discusses the future of human beings in *Hito ga Hito o Design suru: Idenshi Kairyō wa Yurusareruka* (Human designs Homo sapiens: Is Genetic Enhancement permissible?) Kyoto: Nakanishiya Shuppan, 2011. Other writings are as follows: *Hoshino Michio: Eien no Manazashi* (Hoshino Michio: Eternal Vision) Tokyo: Yama to Keikokusha, 2006. *Genpatsu wa Yamerareru: Nihon to Doitsu- Sono Rinri to Saisei Kanou Energy eno Michi* (We can Abolish Atomic Power Plants: Japan and Germany-Their Ethics and Ways to Introduce Renewable Energy) Sapporo: Jurōsha, 2013. Revival of Salmon Resources and Restoration of a Traditional Ritual of the Ainu, the Indigenous People of Japan. In: *Indigenous Efflorescence: Beyond Revitalization in Sapmi and Ainu Mosir.* Canberra: Australian National University Press, 2018. 69-78.

Hokkaido Ainu Association, Hokudai kaijibunsho kenkyūkai, Kotan no Kai.

I raised half of publishing cost with crowdfunding on Readyfor. I express gratitude for supporters in putting down names (Without honorifics): Ogata Harumi, Itoh Masami, MIKIO TAKAGI, HONDA Yuko, Tanaka Mizue, Yamamoto Maki, Kumiko Kakehashi, Egami Hisayuki, Atsushi Taguchi, TOMOICHI ENOMOTO, Yuji MIURA, Hokkaido Fish Films, Misato Nakata, Eiji Hayashi, Mikura OGASAWARA, TAKAHASHI KAORU, Mattō Hideo, Honda Ryōichi, YASUO KATABAMI, SAEGUSA OSAMU, ITOU KANAKO, Ideguchi Misa, yamamoto etsuya, Itoh Ayako, Yoshio Konno, Kawasaki Masaru, Shimada Midori, Chida Tetsuya, Kawamura Minato, TANAKA SATOSHI, Kosaka Isamu, yamamoto shuhou, Suzuki Kimiyo, Fumio Yagishita, Akari Ehara, NAKAHARA SHINGO, Murakumo Masashi, KANBE Tadakatsu, Chiba Seiji, Morita Yukinori, Kazue Nakamura, Urespa Club in Sapporo University. (Without honorifics in no particular order)

Without supervision by Jeffry Gayman, a professor of Hokkaido University and Leni Charbonneau from Marlboro College, Vermont, the challenge to publish an English edition alongside a Japanese version would not have been possible. I am also thankful to Fujita Takuya, chairman of Fujita Insatsu, who has managed the publishing activities under Fujita Insatsu Excellent Books in Kushiro and to Suda Shosey, the book designer.

I dedicate this book to my wife, Ushio and to my son Naohiro. Finally, I am immensely grateful to Hoshino Michio, the photographer and essayist who introduced me to the world of wild life and Indigenous peoples in Alaska.

    April 2019 in Sapporo, Japan   Kosaka Yousuke

Acknowledgments

I am especially grateful to the Ainu elders who have taught me various aspects of their knowledge, sense of the world, and oral traditions. Without the support of those below who have been involved in cultural transmission activities, social movements, historical investigations, ethnography, and fighting for the Indigenous rights of the Ainu, I could not have completed this manuscript. Names listed without honorifics in no particular order:

Abe Kazushi, Akizuki Toshiyuki, Amanai Shigeki, Chiri (Yokoyama) Mutsumi, Dobashi Yoshimi, Emori Susumu, Fujimura Hisakazu, Fujino Tomoaki, Fukuoka Itoko, Gōukon Fukiko, Hasebe Kazuhiro, Hatakeyama Satoshi, Hayashi Naomitsu, Hirata Tsuyoshi, Hirayama Hiroto, Hirose Kenichirō, Honda Yūko, Inoue Katsuo, Ishii Ponpe, Ishikawa Mikaho, Ishihara Itsuko, Ishihara Mai, Ishihara Makoto, Itō Tsukasa, Kaizawa Kōichi, Katō Hirofumi, Katō Kyūzō, Katō Yoshio, Kawakami Jun, Kawakami Megumi, Kawamura Ken'ichi, Kawamura Hisae, Kayano Rie, Kayano Reiko, Kayano Shigeru, Kayano Shirō, Kawakami Jun, Keira Mitsunori, Keira Tomoko, Kirikae Hideo, Kitahara Jirōta, Kohara Toshihiro, Koizumi Masahiro, Kosaka Hironobu, Kreiner Josef, Kuzuno Tatsujirō, Kuzuno Tsugio, Kuzuno Daiki, Maesawa Taka, Mark Winchester, Maruyama Hiroshi, Monbetsu Atsushi, Muraki Miyuki, Nakagawa Hiroshi, Nakamoto Mutsuko, Nakamura Itsuki, Nemoto Yosaburō, Nomoto Hisae, Nomoto Masahiro, Nomura Gi'ichi, Nomura Takashi, Oda Hiroshi, Ogawa Ryūkichi, Okada Atsuko, Okada Hiroaki, Okada Michiaki, Ōno Tetsuhito, Ōtani Yōichi, Osakada Yūko, Ōtsuka Kazuyoshi, Sasaki Toshikazu, Sekine Kenji, Sekine Maki, Shimizu Yūji, Sugimura Kyōko, Sugita Mitsuaki, Suwa Yoshimitsu, Suzuki Hideo, Tabata Hiroshi, Tahara Ryōko, Takase Katsunori, Takeuchi Wataru, Tamura Suzuko, Tanimoto Kazuyuki, Tazawa Mamoru, Tobe Chiharu, Toko Shūsei, Tokuda Shōko, Tozuka Miwako, Toyokawa Shigeo, Tsuda Nobuko, Tsumagari Toshirō, Uemura Hideaki, Uemura Yoshihiro, Ukaji Shizue, Yae Kiyotoshi, Yūki Kōji, Yajima Kunio, Yamada Shin'ichi, Yokoyama Takao, Yoshida Kunihiko.

I also am indebted to the Ainu Museum, Chiri-Shinsha, Chiri Yukie Gin'no Shizuku Kinenkan, Hakodate City Museum, Hakodate Main Library, the

English language sources

Clastres, Pierre. *Society Against the State*.Oxford: Mole Editions Basil Blackwell, 1977.
  *Originally published in France as *"La Société contre l'état."* Paris: Les Éditions de Minuit, 1974.
Irimoto, Takashi. *The Ainu Bear Festival*. Sapporo: Hokkaido University Press, 2014.
Mankiller, Wilma. "Being Indigenous in the 21st Century." In *Cultural Survival Quarterly Magazine*, March 2009.
Philippi, Donald L. *Songs of Gods, Songs of Humans: The Epic Tradition of the Ainu*.Tokyo, Princeton, N.J.:University of Tokyo Press & Princeton University Press, 1979.
Strong, Sarah M. *Ainu Spirits Singing: The Living World of Chiri Yukie's Ainu Shin'yōshū*. Honolulu, Hawai: University of Hawai'i Press, 2011.
Van der Sluys, Cornelia M. I. "Gifts from the Immortal Ancestors: Cosmology and Ideology of Jahai Sharing. In *Hunters and Gatherers in the Modern World: Conflict, Resistance, and Self-Determination.* Edited by Peter P. Schweitzer, Megan Biesele, and Robert K. Hitchcock, 427-454. New York. Oxford: Berghahn Books, 2000.
Watanabe, Hitoshi. *The Ainu Ecosystem: Environment and Group Structure.* Seattle, London: University of Washington Press, 1973.
Willerslev, Rane. *Soul Hunters: Hunting, Animism, and Personhood among the Siberian Yukaghirs*. Berkeley, Los Angeles, London: University of California Press, 2007.

———-. *Ainu Denshō to Toride* (Ainu Traditions and Forts). Sapporo: Hokkaidō Shuppan Kikaku Center, 2005.

Yae, Kurō. *Ainu Minzokubunkazai Series 12: Yae Kurō no Denshō 2* (Ainu Folklore and Cultural Assets Series 12: Traditions of Kurō Yae 2). Sapporo: Hokkaidō Kyōiku Iinkai, 1994.

———-. *Ainu Minzokubunkazai Series 17: Yae Kurō no Denshō 7* (Ainu Folklore and Cultural Assets Series 12: Traditions of Kurō Yae 2). Sapporo: Hokkaidō Kyōiku Iinkai, 1999.

Yae, Seijirō. Kotan Dentō no Hi o Mamoru (Preserve Traditions of Ainu Village) privately printed book around 1976.

Yamada, Shin'ichi. "Sapporoken niyoru Tokachigawa Ryūiki no Sake Kinryō to Ainu Minzoku (Prohibition of Salmon Fishing in Tokachi River by Sapporo Prefecture and the Ainu)" In *Hokkaido Kaitakukinenkan Kenkyū Kiyou Volume 37.* Sapporo: Hokkaido Kaitakukinenkan, 2009.

———-. *Kindai Hokkaidō to Ainu Minzoku: Shuryō Kisei to Tochi Mondai* (Hokkaidō in Modern Period and Ainu People: Regulation in Hunting and Problem of Land). Sapporo: Hokkaidō Daigaku Shuppankai, 2011.

Yamada, Takako. *Ainu no Sekaikan* (The World View of the Ainu). Tokyo: Kōdansha, 1994.

Yanagita, Kunio. "Nochi no Kari no Kotoba Ki (Second Record of Words in Hunting)." In *Teihon Yanagita Kunio Shū 27* (Collection of Yanagita Kunio Volume 27), 1-39. Tokyo: Chikuma Shobō, 1970.

———-. *Yanagita Kunio Zenshū 7* (Complete Works of Yanagita Kunio Volume 7). Tokyo: Chikuma Shobō, 1990.

Yasuda, Yoshinori. *Jōmon Bunmei no Kankyō* (Environment in Jōmon Civilization). Tokyo: Yoshikawa Kōbunkan, 1997.

Yamada, Yasuhiro. *Jinkotsu Shutsudo Rei ni Miru Jōmon no Bosei to Shakai* (The Burial System and Society of Jōmon: Examination of Cases in Excavated Human Remains). Tokyo: Dōseisha, 2008.

Yamamoto, Tasuke. *Kamuy Yukar: Aynu Rak Kur den* (Tales of Gods: Story of Aynurakkur). Tokyo: Heibonsha, 1993.

Yokoyama, Mutsumi. "Watashi no Naka no Rekishi (History of my Life=Autobiography=)" *The Hokkaidō Shumbun* (Newspaper, Sapporo). June 29—July 11, 2015.

Tairako, Tomonaga. "Seiyō Kindai Shisōshi no Hihanteki Saikentō: Kant Saiban'nen no Seijisisō ni Okeru (John) Locke Hihan no Myakuraku (Critical Reexamination of Occidental Modern History of Ideas: Context of Kant's Criticism against Locke in Political Thought in his Closing Years)." In *Shisōshi to Shakaishi no Benshōhō: Rachi Chikara Tsuitō Ronshū*. Edited by Osamu Kawagoe, Kunihiko Uemura, and Mari Nomura, 5-30. Tokyo: Ochanomizu Shobō, 2007.

Takase, Katsunori. "Yayoi Bunka no Naka no Kita no Rinjin (Neighbor in the North in Yayoi Culture)." In *Yayoi Jidaitte Don'na Jidai Dattano ka?* (What Kind of Age, Yayoi Period Was?). Edited by Shin'ichirō Fujio, 114-136. Tokyo: Asakura Shoten, 2017.

Takeuchi, Wataru. *Nomura Gi'ichi to Hokkaido Utari Kyōkai* (Nomura Gi'ichi and the Hokkaido Utari Association) Tokyo: Sōfūkan, 2004.

Teramae, Naoto. *Bunmei ni Kōshita Yayoi no Hitobito* (Yayoi People, who Resisted Civilization). Tokyo: Yoshikawa Kōbunkan, 2017.

Tezuka, Kaoru. "Kinsei ni okeru Ainu no Seikatsu Youshiki no Tayousei: Ainu Kenkyū no Aratana Tenkai.(Diversity in the life of Ainu in the Early Modern Period: Evolvement for Ainu Studies)" In *Nihon no Shuryō Saishū Bunka: Yasei Seibutsu to Tomoni Ikiru* (Hunter-gatherer's Culture in Japan: To Live with Wild Life). Edited by Kazunobu Ikeya, and Masumi Hasegawa, 100-149. Kyoto: Sekaishisōsha, 2005.

Tominaga, Keiichi (voice recording). *Shitaku Yae no Denshō: Kayō Sanbun Hen* (Traditions by Shitaku Yae: Part of Songs and Prose). Kushiro: "Shitaku Yae no Denshō" Kankōkai, 2007.

Ueki, Tetsuya. *Gakumon no Bouryoku: Ainu Bochi wa Naze Abakaretaka.* (Violence of Academism: Why Cemeteries of the Ainu were excavated?) Yokohama: Shunpūsha, 2017.

Ukaji, Shizue. *Subete o Asu no Kate Toshite: Ima koso Ainu no Chie to Yūki o* (Every Thing Would be Useful to Live for Tomorrow: It's Time to learn knowledge and courage of the Ainu). Tokyo: Seiryū Shuppan, 2011.

Utagawa, Hiroshi. *Ainu Bunka Seiritsu Shi* (History of Establishing the Ainu Culture). Sapporo: Hokkaidō Shuppan Kikaku Center, 1988.

―――-. *Iomante no Kōkogaku* (Archaeology of *Iomante*). Tokyo: Tokyo Daigaku Shuppankai, 1989.

Shakai Soshiki. Edited by Yasushi Kosugi, Yasuhiro Taniguchi, Yasutomi Nishida, Kazutomo Mizune, and Ken'ichi Yano, 91-97. Tokyo: Dōseisha, 2008.

———. *Tsuki to Hebi to Jōmonjin* (Moon, Snakes, and Jōmon people) Sapporo: Jurōsha, 2014.

Ozawa, Toshio. *Sekai no Minwa* (Folk Tales of the World). Tokyo: Chūōkōronsha, 1979.

Sahara, Makoto, and Tatsuo Kobayashi. *Sekaishi no Nakano Jōmon* (Jōmon in World History). Tokyo: Shin Shokan, 2001.

Sasaki, Shirō. "Tonakai Tatō Shiiku no Seisansei (Productivity of Herding Reindeer in Large Scale)." In *Kokuritsu Minzokugaku Hakubutsukan Kenkyū Hōkoku, Bessatsu* No.20 (Bulletin of the National Museum of Ethnology Special Issue no.20: History and Present of the Eurasian Nomadic Societies) edited by Masatake Matsubara, Yuki Konagaya, and Shirō Sasaki, 517-540. Osaka: Kokuritsu Minzokugaku Hakubutsukan, 1999.

Satō, Takao. *Siratcise no Minzokukōkogaku: Izari Gawa Genryū ni Okeru Higuma Ryō to "Okuri" Girei ni Kansuru Chōsa Kenkyū* (Ethno-Archaeology of Siratcise: A Research and Study of Bear Hunting and a Ritual of "Sending a Soul" along Izari River). Tokyo: Roku Ichi Shobō, 2006.

Segawa, Takurō. *Ainu to Jōmon: Mouhitotsu no Nihon no Rekishi* (Ainu and Jōmon: Another History of Japan). Tokyo: Chikuma Shobō, 2016.

Shitaku, Yae (storyteller), and Keiichi Tominaga (voice recording). *Shitaku Yae no Denshō: Inbun Hen 1* (Traditions by Shitaku Yae: Verse Part 1). Kushiro: "Shitaku Yae no Denshō" Kankōkai, 2011.

Sugimura, Kinarabukku, Kazumi Ōtsuka, Fumio Miyoshi and Kyōko Sugimura. *Kinarabukku Yūkara Shū* (Collection of Yukar told by Kinarabukku). Asahikawa: Asahikawa Shi, 1969.

Soku, Suni. *Chōsenjin to Ainu Minzoku no Rekishiteki Tsunagari* (Historical connection between Korean People and Ainu People) Sapporo: Jurōsha, 2017.

Sunazawa, Kura. *Ku=skup Oruspe: Watashi no Ichidaiki* (Story of My Growth: Autobiography). Tomakomai: Ainu Minzoku Bunka Denshōkai Rapuran, 2012.

Taguchi, Hiromi. *Matagi: Mori to Karyūdo no Kiroku* (Matagi: A Record of Hunters and Forest). Tokyo: Keiyūsha, 1994.

of Ainu education system in modern period). Sapporo: Hokkaidodaigaku Toshokankōkai, 1997.

Ogihara, Shinko. *Hoppō Shominzoku no Sekaikan: Ainu to Amur Sakhalin Chiiki no Shinwa, Denshō* (World View of Northern Peoples: Myth and Traditions of Ainu, Amur, and Sakhalin Regions). Tokyo: Sōfūkan, 1996.

Okada, Hiroaki. *Bunka to Kankyō: Eskimo to Indian* (Culture and Environment: Eskimo and Indian). Sapporo: Hokkaidō Daigaku Toshokankōkai, 1979.

Okawada, Akira, and Mark Winchester., ed. *Ainu Minzoku Hiteiron ni Kōsuru* (Counter-arguments Against Denial of Existence of Ainu People). Tokyo: Kawade Shobō Shinsha, 2015.

Omoto, Kei'ichi. *Hito to Bunmei: Shuryō-saishūmin kara Gendai o Miru* (Human beings and Civilization: A viewpoint from Hunter-gatherers to Modern Society) Tokyo: Chikuma Shobō, 2016.

Orikuchi, Shinobu. *Orikuchi Shinobu Zenshū 1: Kodai Kenkyū "Kokubungaku Hen"* (Complete Works of Orikuchi Shinobu Volume 1: Study of Ancient Times "Part of Japanese Language Studies.") Edited by Orikuchi Hakase Kinen Kodai Kenkyūjo. Tokyo: Chūōkōronsha, 1975.

———. *Orikuchi Shinobu Zenshū 2: Kodai Kenkyū "Minzokugaku Hen 1"* (Complete Works of Orikuchi Shinobu Volume 2: Study of Ancient Times "Ethnology Part 1") Edited by Orikuchi Hakase Kinen Kodai Kenkyūjo. Tokyo: Chūōkōronsha, 1975.

———. *Orikuchi Shinobu Zenshū 3: Kodai Kenkyū "Minzokugaku Hen 2"* (Complete Works of Orikuchi Shinobu Volume 3: Study of Ancient Times "Ethnology Part 2.") Edited by Orikuchi Hakase Kinen Kodai Kenkyūjo. Tokyo: Chūōkōronsha, 1975.

———. *Orikuchi Shinobu Zenshū 15: Minzokugaku Hen 1* (Complete Works of Orikuchi Shinobu Volume 15: Folklore Part 1). Edited by Orikuchi Hakase Kinen Kodai Kenkyūjo). Tokyo: Chūōkōronsha, 1976.

———. *Orikuchi Shinobu Zenshū 16: Minzokugaku Hen 2* (Complete Works of Orikuchi Shinobu Volume 16: Folklore Part 2). Edited by Orikuchi Hakase Kinen Kodai Kenkyūjo. Tokyo: Chūōkōronsha, 1976.

Ōshima, Naoyuki. "Jōmon Jidai no Mushiba Ritsu (Rate of cavities in Jōmon Period)." In *Jōmon Jidai no Kōkogaku 10: Hito to Shakai Jinkotsu Jōhō to*

Matsu'ura, Takeshirō. *Ainu Jinbutsu Shi* (Stories of Ainu Persons). Modern translation by Genzō Sarashina, and Yutaka Yoshida. Tokyo: Nōsangyoson Bunka Kyōkai, 1981.

Meisaku Jōruri Shū Jō: Kindai Nihon Bungaku Taikei 8 (Collection of Masterpieces of Jōruri=Japanese puppet show= Volume 1: Compendium of Modern Japanese Literature Volume 8). Tokyo: Kokumin Tosho, 1927.

Nagamatsu, Atsushi. "Kyūshū Sankanbu no Shuryō to Shinkō: Kaitai Sahō ni miru Doubutsu Rei no Shori (Hunting and Belief in Mountainous Area in Kyūshū: Treatment of Wild Animal's Soul Observed in Manner of Disorganization)" In *Nihon no Shuryō Saishū Bunka: Yasei Seibutsu to Tomoni Ikiru* (Hunter-gatherer's Culture in Japan: To Live with Wild Life). Edited by Kazunobu Ikeya, and Masumi Hasegawa, 174-203. Kyoto: Sekaishisōsha, 2005.

Nakagawa, Hiroshi, and Kazumi Ōtsuka. *Kinarabukku Kōden: Ainu Minwa Zenshū Shinwa Hen* (Oral Traditions by Kinarabukku: Complete Works of Ainu Folktales. Part of Gods' tales). Sapporo: Hokkaidō Shuppan Kikaku Center, 1990.

Nakagawa, Hiroshi. *Ainu no Monogatari Sekai* (World of Stories in the Ainu). Tokyo: Heibonsha, 1997.

———. *Katariau Kotoba no Chikara: Kamuy Tachi to Ikiru Sekai* (Power of Words Exchanging Each Other: A World Living With Gods). Tokyo: Iwanami Shoten, 2010.

Nakai, Miyoshi. *Chiri Yukie: 19sai no Yuigon* (Chiri Yukie: Last Words from 19 Years Young Woman). Tokyo: Sairyūsha, 1991.

Nakamura, Tomoko, Kumiko Yumira and Fumiko Mamiya. "Iruikon'intan ni Tōjō Suru Dōbutsu: Dōbutsu Muko to Dōbutsu Yome no Baai (Animals on Old Tales Concerning Intermarriage Between Humans and Animals: Cases of Animal Grooms and Animal Brides)." In *Kodomo to Mukashi Banashi,* 84-102. Yonago: Kokinsha, 2001.

Nakazawa, Shin'ichi. *Kuma kara Ō e: Cahier Sauvage 2* (From Bear to King: Cahier Sauvage 2). Tokyo: Kōdansha, 2002.

———. *Taishōsei Jinruigaku: Cahier Sauvage 5* (Symmetrical Anthropology: Cahier Sauvage 5). Tokyo: Kōdansha, 2004.

Ogawa, Masahito. *Kindai Ainu Kyōiku Seidoshi Kenkyū* (A study in history

Koyama, Shūzō. *Jōmon Jidai: Computer Kōkogaku Niyoru Fukugen* (Jōmon Period: Restration by Computer Archaeology). Tokyo: Chūōkōronsha, 1984.

――-. *Jōmon Tanken: Minzoku Kōkogaku no Kokoromi* (Exploring Jōmon: A Trial to Ethno-archaeology). Tokyo: Chūōkōronsha, 1998.

Kreiner, Josef., ed. *Nihon Minzoku no Genryū o Saguru: Yanagita Kunio "Nochi no Kari no Kotoda Ki" Saikō* (Investigating Roots of the Japanese People: Reconsideration of "Nochi no Kari no Kotoda Ki" written by Yanagita Kunio). Tokyo: Miyai Shoten, 2012.

Kuzuno, Tatsujirō. *Kimsupo*. Edited by Tsugio Kuzuno, and Wataru Takeuchi. Shizunai: Self-publishing, 1999. * "Kimsupo" means "storage of treasures" in Ainu language.

Kudō, Masaki. "Kodai Ezo no Shakai: Kōeki to Shakai Soshiki (A Society of Ancient Ezo: Trade and Social Organization)." In *Rekishi Hyōron* No. 434. Edited by Rekishi Kagaku Kyōgikai, 13-35. Tokyo: Azekura Shobō, 1986.

Kubodera, Itsuhiko. *Ainu no Shin'yo* (Ainu Gods' Tales). Tokyo: Sōfūkan, 2004.

Kuramitsu, Hideaki. *Kamikawa Ainu Kuma Matsuri* (A Bear Ceremony of Kamikawa Ainu). Asahikawa: Self-publishing, compiled privately around 1953.

Maesawa, Taka. *Maesawa Taka Shashinshū: Ainu Minzoku Inochi no Keishō* (A collection of Maesawa Taka's photographs: The Ainu- Succession of Life) Kushiro: Fujita Insatsu Excellent Books, 2018.

Margolis, Jonathan., ed. *Senjūmin wa Ima: Futatsu no Sekai ni Ikiru* (Indigenous Peoples now: We Live in Two Worlds). Washington D.C.: The State of Department of the United States of America, 2010.

Maruyama, Takashi. *"Ainu"gaku no Tanjō* (The Dawn of "Ainu" Studies). Tokyo: Sairyūsha, 2002.

Matsumoto, Naoko "Jōmon no Shisō kara Yayoi no Shisō e (From thought of Jōmon to that of Yayoi)" In *Nihon Shisōshi Kōza 1―Ancient times*. Edited by Tadashi Karube, Kurozumi Makoto, Satō Hiroo, Sueki Fumihiko, Tajiri Yūichirō, 27-64.Tokyo: Perikansha, 2012.

Matsumoto Shigeyoshi "Yae Seijirō Shōden(Biographical Sketch of Yae Seijirō)" In: *Kusuri* Volume 10. Kushiro: Kushiro Ainu Bunka Konwakai, 2003, 28-37.

Nibutani Dam Saiban no Kiroku (Revolt of the Ainu People: Record of Nibutani Dam Case) Tokyo: Sanseidō, 1999.

Kawamori, Hiroshi. *Nihon Mukashi Banashi no Kōzō to Katarite* (Structure and storytellers of Japanese Old Tales). Osaka: Ōsaka Daigaku Shuppankai, 2000.

Kikuchi, Hayao. *Ainu Minzoku to Nihonjin: Higashi Asia no Naka no Ezochi* (Ainu People and the Japanese: Ezochi in Eastern Asia). Tokyo: Asahi Shimbunsha, 1994. * "Ezochi" means "Hokkaidō" in Feudal Era.

―――-. *Jūhasseiki Matsu no Ainu Hōki: Kunashiri Menashi no Tatakai* (Ainu Uprising in the End of 18th Century: The Battle of Kunashiri Menashi). Sapporo: Sapporodō Shoten, 2010.

Kitahara, Jirōta. *Ainu no Saigu: Inaw no Kenkyū* (Ainu Implements for Ritual: Study on Inaw). Sapporo: Hokkaidō Daigaku Shuppankai, 2014.

Kindaichi, Kyōsuke. *Ainu Jojishi: Yūkara Gaisetsu* (Ainu Epics: A View on Yukar). Kyoto: Seijisha, 1943.

―――-. *Ainu Jojishi, Itadorimaru no Kyoku* (Ainu Epics: A Story of Itadorimaru). Kyoto: Seijisha, 1944.

―――-. *Ainu Jojishi, Yūkara Shū 8* (Ainu Epics: A Collection of Yukar 8). Tokyo: Sanseidō, 1968.

Kondō, Yasutoshi. *Kushiro Shitsugen o Aruku* (Surveying Kushiro Wetland). Tokyo: Fukuinkan Shoten, 1988.

Kosaka, Yousuke. *Ryūbō: Nichiro ni Owareta Kitachishima Ainu* (Wondering: North Kuril Ainu, who were Ejected by Japanese Power and Russian Power). Sapporo: Hokkaidō Shimbunsha, 1992.

―――-. (Photo by Hayashi, Naomitsu) *Ainu o Ikiru, Bunka o Tsugu: Haha Kina-Fuci to Musume Kyōko no Monogatari* (I will live as an Ainu to Hand Down Culture: A Story of Kina-Fuci and her Daughter Kyōko). Tokyo: Ōmura Shoten,1994.

―――-. *Daichi no Tetsugaku: Ainu Minzoku no Seishin Bunka ni Manabu* (A Philosophy of Land: Learning Spiritual Culture of the Ainu). Tokyo: Miraisha, 2015.

Kōshōbungaku 2 Ainu Bungaku: Nihon Bungaku Shi 17 (Oral Traditions 2 Ainu Literary works: History of Japanese Literature Volume 17). Tokyo: Iwanami Shoten, 1997.

Inada, Kōji, and Toshio Ozawa., ed. *Hokkaidō (Ainu Minzoku): Nihon Mukashibanashi Tsūkan 1* (Hokkaido "Ainu People": Series of Japanese Old Tales Volume 1). Kyoto: Dōhōsha Shuppan, 1989.

Inada, Kōji, and Kazuko Inada., ed. *Nihon Mukashibanashi Handbook Shinpan* (Handbook of Japanese Old Tales: New Edition). Tokyo: Sanseidō, 2010.

Inukai, Tetsuo and Masaaki, Kadosaki. *Higuma: Hokkaidō no Shizen* (A Brown Bear: Nature in Hokkaidō). Sapporo: Hokkaido Shimbunsha, 1987.

Irimoto, Takashi. *Ainu no Kumamatsuri* (The Ainu Bear Festival). Tokyo: Yūzankaku, 2010.

Kaizawa, Kōichi, Takashi Matsuna, Tsunehisa Okuno, and Hiroshi Maruyama..*Ainu Minzoku no Fukken: Senjū Minzoku to Kizuku Aratana Shakai* (Restration of Rights of the Ainu People: A New Society Establishing with Indigenous Peoples). Kyoto: Hōritsu Bunka Sha, 2011.

Kaiho, Mineo. *Nihon Hoppō Shi no Ronri* (A Logic of History in Northern Japan). Tokyo: Yūzankaku, 1974

Katayama, Tatsumine. *"Ainu Shin'yōshū" o Yomitoku* (Analyzing Ainu Shin'yōshū=Ainu Gods' Tales=). Tokyo: Sōfūkan, 2003.

Katō, Yoshio. *19seiki Kōhan no Sapporo, Ishikari no Ainu Minzoku* (the Ainu People in Sapporo and Ishikari in the Latter Part of the 19th Century). Sapporo: Sapporodō Shoten, 2017.

Kayano, Shigeru. *Ore no Nibutani* (My hometown Nibutani). Tokyo: Suzusawa Shoten, 1977.

―――-. *Honō no Uma: Ainu Minwa Shū* (A Flaming Horse: Collection of Ainu Folktales). Tokyo: Suzusawa Shoten, 1977.

―――. *Kamuy Yukar to Mukashi Banashi* (Ainu Gods' Tales and Old Tales). Tokyo: Shōgakukan, 1988.

―――. *Ainu no Ishibumi* (Monument of the Ainu). Tokyo: Asahi Shimbunsha, 1990.

―――. *Tsuma wa Karimono: Ainu Minzoku no Kokoro, Ima* (Wife is given: Spirits of Ainu People Now). Sapporo: Hokkaidō Shimbunsha, 1994.

―――. *Ainu no Sato Nibutani ni Ikite* (Living in Nibutani, a Homeland of the Ainu). Tokyo: Nihon Tosho Center, 2005.

Kayano, Shigeru, and Hiroshi Tanaka, ed. *Ainu Minzoku Tun Hanran:*

Kyōiku Iinkai, 1995.

———-. *Ainu no Kurashi to Kotoba 5: Ainu Mukei Minzoku Bunkazai Kiroku Kankō Series 10* (Life and Language of the Ainu 5: Series 10 of Recording and Publishing Ainu Intangible Folk-Cultural Properties). Sapporo: 1996.

———-. *Ainu no Kurashi to Kotoba 7: Ainu Mukei Minzoku Bunkazai Kiroku Kankō Series 14* (Life and Language of the Ainu 5: Series 10 of Recording and Publishing Ainu Intangible Folk-Cultural Properties). Sapporo: 2001.

Hokkaidō Daigaku Ainu Senjūmin Center., ed. *Ainu Kenkyū no Genzai to Mirai* (Present Situation and Future Situation of the Ainu Study). Sapporo: Hokkaidō Daigaku Shuppankai, 2010.

Hokkaidōchō. *Hokkaidō Kyū Dojin Hogo Enkakushi* (Brief History of Former Aboriginal People in Hokkaidō), Sapporo: Hokkaidōchō, 1934.

Hokudai Kaiji Bunsho Kenkyūkai., ed. *Ainu no Ikotsu wa Kotan no Tsuchi e: Hokudai ni Taisuru Ikotsu Henkan Seikyū to Senjūken* (Ainu Remains Should be Returned to Ground of Home Village: A Claim for Restitution of Remains Against Hokkaido University and Indigenous Rights). Tokyo: Ryokufū Shuppan, 2016.

Honda, Yūko., ed. *Denshō kara Saguru Ainu no Rekishi* (History of the Ainu Through Investigating Traditions). Sapporo: Sapporo Daigaku Fuzoku Sōgō Kenkyūjo, 2010.

Hoshino, Michio. *Mori to Hyōga to Kujira: Watarigarasu no Densetsu o Motomete* (Forest, Glacier, and Whale: Seeking for Legends of Raven), Tokyo: Sekaibunkasha, 1996.

Ichikawa, Morihiro. *Ainu no Hōteki chii to Kuni no Fuseigi* (Legal Status of the Ainu and Injustice of the State) Sapporo: Jurōsha, 2019.

Ikeya, Kazunobu. *Shuryō Saishūmin kara Mita Chikyū Kankyōshi: Shizen, Rinjin, Bunmei Tono Kyōsei* (History of Global Environment from View of Hunter-gatherers: Nature, Neighbor, and Coexistence with Civilization). Tokyo: Tokyō Daigaku Shuppankai, 2017.

Inada, Kōji. *Mukashibanashi Type Index: Nihon Mukashibanashi Tsūkan 28* (Old Tales Type Index: Series of Japanese Old Tales Volume 28). Kyoto: Dōhōsha, 1988.

———. *Ainu no Mukashibanashi* (Old Tales of the Ainu). Tokyo: Chikuma Shobō, 2005.

Hokkaidō Kyōiku Iinkai. *Ainu Minwa: Ainu Mukei Minzoku Bunkazai Kiroku Kankō Series 1* (Ainu Folktales: Series 1 of Recording and Publishing Ainu Intangible Folk-Cultural Properties). Sapporo: Hokkaidō Kyōiku Iinkai, 1988.

———-. *Oyna 1: Ainu Mukei Minzoku Bunkazai Kiroku Kankō Series 3* (Stories of Gods 1: Series 3 of Recording and Publishing Ainu Intangible Folk-Cultural Properties). Sapporo: Hokkaidō Kyōiku Iinkai, 1990.

———-. *Oyna 2: Ainu Mukei Minzoku Bunkazai Kiroku Kankō Series 5* (Stories of Gods 2: Series 5 of Recording and Publishing Ainu Intangible Folk-Cultural Properties). Sapporo: Hokkaidō Kyōiku Iinkai, 1992.

———-. *Oyna 3: Ainu Mukei Minzoku Bunkazai Kiroku Kankō Series 7* (Stories of Gods 3: Series 7 of Recording and Publishing Ainu Intangible Folk-Cultural Properties). Sapporo: Hokkaidō Kyōiku Iinkai, 1994.

———-. *Tuytak 1: Ainu Mukei Minzoku Bunkazai Kiroku Kankō Series 9* (Old Tales 1: Series 9 of Recording and Publishing Ainu Intangible Folk-Cultural Properties). Sapporo: Hokkaidō Kyōiku Iinkai, 1996.

———-. *Tuytak 2: Ainu Mukei Minzoku Bunkazai Kiroku Kankō Series 11* (Old Tales 2: Series 11 of Recording and Publishing Ainu Intangible Folk-Cultural Properties). Sapporo: Hokkaidō Kyōiku Iinkai, 1998.

———-. *Tuytak 3: Ainu Mukei Minzoku Bunkazai Kiroku Kankō Series 13* (Old Tales 3: Series 13 of Recording and Publishing Ainu Intangible Folk-Cultural Properties). Sapporo: Hokkaidō Kyōiku Iinkai, 2000.

———-. *Tuytak 4: Ainu Mukei Minzoku Bunkazai Kiroku Kankō Series 15* (Old Tales 4: Series 15 of Recording and Publishing Ainu Intangible Folk-Cultural Properties). Sapporo: Hokkaidō Kyōiku Iinkai, 2002.

———-. *Chiri Yukie Note: Ainu Mukei Minzoku Bunkazai Kōshō Bungei Series 4* (Note of Chiri Yukie: Series 4 of Oral Traditions of Ainu Intangible Folk-Cultural Properties). Sapporo: Hokkaidō Kyōiku Iinkai, 1985.

Hokkaidō Kyōikuchō Shōgai Gakushūbu Bunkaka., ed. *Ainu no Kurashi to Kotoba 2: Ainu Mukei Minzoku Bunkazai Kiroku Kankō Series 4* (Life and Language of the Ainu 4: Series 8 of Recording and Publishing Ainu Intangible Folk-Cultural Properties). Sapporo: Hokkaidō Kyōiku Iinkai, 1991.

———-. *Ainu no Kurashi to Kotoba 4: Ainu Mukei Minzoku Bunkazai Kiroku Kankō Series 8* (Life and Language of the Ainu 4: Series 8 of Recording and Publishing Ainu Intangible Folk-Cultural Properties). Sapporo: Hokkaidō

———. *Chiri Mashiho Chosakushū 4* (Writings of Chiri Mashiho Volume 4). Tokyo: Heibonsha,1974.

———. *Chiri Mashiho Chosakushū Bekkan 1* (Writings of Chiri Mashiho Supplementary Volume 1). Tokyo: Heibonsha, 1976.

Chiri, Yukie., ed. and trans. *Ainu Shin'yōshū* (Ainu Gods' Tales, published in English as a title of *Ainu Spirits Singing*). Tokyo: Iwanami Shoten, 1978.

———. *Gin no Shizuku: Chiri Yukie Ikōshū* (Silver droplet: Collection of Posthumous Manuscripts of Chiri Yukie). Tokyo: Sōfūkan, 1996.

Dobashi, Yoshimi. *Itami no Penriuku: Toraware no Ainu Jinkotsu* (Penriuku in Pain: Captive Ainu Remains). Tokyo: Sōfūkan, 2017.

Emori, Susumu. *Ainu Minzoku no Rekishi* (History of the Ainu People). Tokyo: Sōfūkan, 2007.

Fujimura, Hisakazu., ed. *Heisei 20nendo Ainu Minzoku Bunkazai Chōsa Hōkokusho: Ainu Minzoku Gijutsu Chōsa 1 "Shuryō Gijutsu"* (A Report of Ainu Folk-Cultural Property in 2008: Ainu Folk Techniques Research 1 "Techniques in Hunting"). Sapporo: Hokkaidō Kyōiku Iinkai, 2009.

Fujimoto, Hideo. *Gin no Shizuku Furufuru* (Silver droplet falling, falling). Tokyo: Shinchōsha, 1973.

Hanihara, Kazurō., ed. *Nihonjin to Nihonbunka no Keisei* (Formation of the Japanese and the Japanese Culture) Tokyo: Asakurashoten, 1993.

———. *Nihonjin no Kigen* (Origins of the Japanese). Tokyo: Asahi Shimbunsha, 1994.

Hatozawa, Samio. "Akashi no Kūbun" In *Gendai Ainu Bungaku Sakuhinsen* (Selected Modern Ainu Literary Works) edited by Minato Kawamura, 152-196. Tokyo: Kōdansha, 2010.

Hayakawa, Noboru. *Ainu no Minzoku* (Folklore of the Ainu). Tokyo: Iwasaki Bijutsusha, 1970.

Hirayama, Hiroto. *Ainu no Rekishi: Nihon no Senjūminzoku o Rikai suru Tameno 160wa* (History of the Ainu: 160 Stories for Understanding Indigenous People in Japan). Tokyo: Akashi Shoten, 2014.

———. *Ainu Shi o Mitsumete* (Investigating a History of the Ainu). Sapporo: Hokkaidō Shuppan Kikaku Center, 1996.

———. *Chizu de Miru Ainu no Rekishi* (History of the Ainu by Means of Maps) Tokyo: Akashi Shoten, 2018.

Actual Situation of Life, Techniques and Traditions of the Ainu 3"). Sapporo: Hokkaidō Kyōiku Iinkai, 2002.

Ainu Minzokubunkazai Chōsahoukokusho"Ainu Seikatsu Gijutu Denshō Jittaichōsa 4" (A report on Ainu Folklore and Cultural Assets "Servey on Actual Situation of Life, Techniques and Traditions of the Ainu 4"). Sapporo: Hokkaidō Kyōiku Iinkai, 2003.

Ainu Minzokubunkazai Chōsahoukokusho"Ainu Seikatsu Gijutu Denshō Jittaichōsa 5" (A report on Ainu Folklore and Cultural Assets "Servey on Actual Situation of Life, Techniques and Traditions of the Ainu 5"). Sapporo: Hokkaidō Kyōiku Iinkai, 2004.

"Ainu Minzoku Kyōyū Zaisan Saiban no Kiroku" Kankōkai., ed. *Hyakunen no Caranke: Ainu Minzoku Kyōyū Zaisan Saiban no Kiroku* (Negotiation for One Hundred Years: Record of Trial on Common Property of Ainu People). Tokyo: Ryokufū Shuppan, 2009.

Ainu Minzoku Hakubutsukan. *Iyomante: Kuma no Reiokuri Hōkoku Sho* (Report of Iyomante: A Ritual to Send a Soul of Bear). Shiraoi: Ainu Minzoku Hakubutsukan, 1990.

———. *Iyomante: Kuma no Reiokuri Hōkoku Sho 2* (Report of Iyomante 2: A Ritual to Send a Soul of Bear). Shiraoi: Ainu Minzoku Hakubutsukan, 1991.

Akino, Shigeki. *Iyomante: Ainu no Reiokuri Girei* =collection of his essays= (Iyomante: An Ainu Ritual to Send a Soul). Shiraoi: Akino Shigeki Ronshū Kankōkai, 2017.

Amano, Tetsuya. *Kuma Matsuri no Kigen* (Origin of the Bear Festival). Tokyo: Yūzankaku, 2003.

Anezaki, Hitoshi, and Tatsumine Katayama. *Kuma ni Attara Dōsuruka: Ainu Minzoku Saigo no Karyūdo Anezaki Hitoshi* (How Do You Deal With a Bear at Unexpected Encounter?: The Last Ainu Hunter Anezaki Hitoshi). Tokyo: Kirakusha, 2002.

Aono, Tomoya, and Naoyuki Ōshima. "Esan Bunka to Kōeki (Esan culture and trade)." In *Shin Hokkaidō no Kodai 2 Zoku Jōmon Okhotsk Bunka*, edited by Takashi Nomura and Hiroshi Udagawa, 10-29. Sapporo: Hokkaidō Shimbunsha, 2003.

Chiri, Mashiho. *Chiri Mashiho Chosakushū 1* (Writings of Chiri Mashiho Volume 1). Tokyo: Heibonsha, 1973.

Bibliography

Japanese language sources

Ainu Bunka Hozon Taisaku Kyōgikai., ed. *Ainu Minzoku Shi (Ainu Ethnology).* Tokyo: Daiichi Hōki Shuppan, 1969.

Ainu Minzokubunkazai Chōsahoukokusho"Ainu Minzokuchōsa 1 (Asahikawa Chihō)" (A report on Ainu Folklore and Cultural Assets "Research of Ainu Folklore 1 'Asahikawa area'"). Sapporo: Hokkaidō Kyōiku Iinkai, 1983.

Ainu Minzokubunkazai Chōsahoukokusho"Ainu Minzokuchōsa 2 (Asahikawa Chihō)" (A report on Ainu Folklore and Cultural Assets "Research of Ainu Folklore 2 'Asahikawa area'"). Sapporo: Hokkaidō Kyōiku Iinkai, 1983.

Ainu Minzokubunkazai Chōsahoukokusho "Ainu Minzokuchōsa 5 (Kushiro/ Abashiri Chihō)" (A report on Ainu Folklore and Cultural Assets "Research of Ainu Folklore 5 'Kushiro and Abashiri area'"). Sapporo: Hokkaidō Kyōiku Iinkai, 1986.

Ainu Minzokubunkazai Chōsahoukokusho "Ainu Minzokuchōsa 6 (Tokachi/ Abashiri Chihō)" (A report on Ainu Folklore and Cultural Assets "Research of Ainu Folklore 6 'Tokachi and Abashiri area'"). Sapporo: Hokkaidō Kyōiku Iinkai, 1987.

Ainu Minzokubunkazai Chōsahoukokusho "Ainu Minzokuchōsa 12(Dōtō Chihō)" (A report on Ainu Folklore and Cultural Assets"Research of Ainu Folklore 12 'Eastern Hokkaidō area'"). Sapporo: Hokkaidō Kyōiku Iinkai, 1993.

Ainu Minzokubunkazai Chōsahoukokusho "Ainu Minzokuchōsa 13(Shiranuka Chihō)" (A report on Ainu Folklore and Cultural Assets"Research of Ainu Folklore 13 'Shiranuka area'"). Sapporo: Hokkaidō Kyōiku Iinkai, 1994.

Ainu Minzokubunkazai Chōsahoukokusho"Ainu Minzokuchōsa 14(Hosoku Chōsa 1)" (A report on Ainu Folklore and Cultural Assets "Research of Ainu Folklore 14 'Supplement Investigation 1'"). Sapporo: Hokkaidō Kyōiku Iinkai, 1995.

Ainu Minzokubunkazai Chōsahoukokusho"Ainu Seikatsu Gijutu Denshō Jittaichōsa 3" (A report on Ainu Folklore and Cultural Assets "Servey on

against indigenous populations in the 1980s. "Indigenous communities, peoples and nations are those which, having a historical continuity with pre-invasion and pre-colonial societies that developed on their territories, consider themselves distinct from other sectors of the societies now prevailing in those territories, or parts of them. They form at present non-dominant sectors of society and are determined to preserve, develop and transmit to future generations their ancestral territories, and their ethnic identity, as the basis of their continued existence as peoples, in accordance with their own cultural patterns, social institutions and legal systems."

6 I did not know at that time I sent this mail that Ms. Cristina Calderon had already died in 2010.

7 Ainu Seisaku Kentō Shimin Kaigi (Citizen's Alliance for the Examination of Ainu Policy) issued a proclamation in February 2019 to demand withdrawal of the draft of Ainu new law. Representatives of Ainu bodies like Shimizu Yūji of Kotan no Kai, Hatakeyama Satoshi of the Monbetsu Ainu association, Tazawa Mamoru of the Karafuto Ainu Association, and Ukaji Shizue of former Ainu-Utari-Renrakukai were founding members of the Citizen's Alliance with Maruyama Hiroshi, an emeritus professor of Muroran Institute of Technology, Yoshida Kunihiko, a professor of Hokkaido University, and Jeffry Gayman, a professor of Hokkaido University. See Internet Homepage of the Citizen's Alliance. Public meeting was held on 3rd March with the same purpose in Sapporo, then participants held a protest march against the draft of Ainu new law in the central area of the city (See photo. Photograph by Kosaka Yousuke). A seminar was held on 9th March with a title of "Reconsidering Ainu Policies in light of global common sense concerning the Indigenous rights" also in Sapporo. Tessa Morris-Suzuki, an emeritus professor of Australian National University made a speech presenting a doubtful comment to this draft, which lacks any reference of Indigenous rights.

Sapporo citizens hold demonstration with Ainu people demanding withdrawal of the draft of Ainu new law.

13 *cipsanke* is a ritual to launch a canoe in river. This ritual has been held annually in Nibutani around 20 August.

14 Tokyo Utari kai later dissolved. Now four bodies, Kantō Utari kai, Pewre Utari no kai, Rera no kai, Tokyo Ainu kyōkai are in active.

15 See Okawada, Akira, and Mark Winchester., ed. *Ainu Minzoku Hiteiron ni Kōsuru* (Counter-arguments Against Denial of Existence of Ainu People) (Tokyo: Kawade Shobō Shinsha, 2015)

16 Yae, Seijirō. *Kotan Dentō no Hi o Mamoru* (Preserve Traditions of Ainu Village) (privately printed book around 1976) 1-5. Yae Seijirō-Ekasi (1924-2009)'s biography written by Matsumoto Shigeyoshi is included *Kusuri* Volume 10, 28-37.

17 See Soku, Suni. *Chōsenjin to Ainu Minzoku no Rekishiteki Tsunagari* (Historical connection between Korean People and Ainu People) (Sapporo: Jurōsha, 2017)

Chapter 3 (Part 2)

1 *kapiw* means "sea gull" and *apappo* means "flower" in Ainu language. Their CD album *Paykar*, meaning "spring" is on sale containing the song "Eauwa."

2 In some regions the ritual is called *opunire,* or *opunika.*

3 Nomoto Hisae-Ekasi (1951-2019) was born in Shiraoi and lived in Chitose in the latter half of his life. Having restored *cise*, a traditional Ainu house, on ground of Chitose Suehiro primary school, he has taught pupils about Ainu culture at school. He also officiated various rituals and edited Ainu Times, a newspaper written in Ainu language since 1997.

4 I cited from "*Being Indigenous in the 21st Century*" on website of the Secretary of State, the United States of America. She wrote an introduction on Hurtado, Albert L., ed. *Reflections of American Indian history: honoring the past, building a future* (Norman: University of Oklahoma Press, 2008).

5 In 2007 on adoption of the UN Declaration of the Rights of Indigenous Peoples (UNDRIP), the United Nations could not determine a definition of 'Indigenous people'. Though no official definition exists, the International Working Group for Indigenous Affairs (IWGIA) illustrates that the most common definition is the "working definition" formulated by UN Special Rapporteur, José Martinez Cobo in his study of the Problem of Discrimination

the government further suggested budgetary measures, for example, the construction of local charnel houses. However, repatriation, reburial, and maintenance of facilities needs solidarity, manpower, and financial support from the community. Though not a few Ainu local communities maintain their unity still now, numerous communities have declined or collapsed in these 150 years under assimilation policies. So, in reality, many persons and communities qualified still hesitate over claims of repatriation. If the government would like to realize repatriation in the real sense, it should firstly tackle rehabilitation of each Ainu community by every conceivable means possible. Meanwhile, repatriation of Ainu remains from abroad has been realized. In investigating written records in 1880, the German scientific body, Berlin Association for Anthropology, Ethnology and Prehistory (Berliner Gesellschaft für Anthropologie, Ethnologie und Urgeschichte) founded in 1869, certified one skull from Sapporo Ainu Village as having been stolen from a grave. The association judged the skull should be returned on the basis of the association's ethics code and actually returned it to Japan in 2017. The Australian Government has decided to return Ainu remains obtained through Tokyo University in exchange for Aborigines' remains without condition to get back the remains of Aborigines. At the time of September 2018, Tokyo University had not publicized whether it still retained remains of Aborigines or not and whether it had the intention to repatriate them or not. The Fawler Museum at University of California, Los Angeles (UCLA) has suggested the probability of returning one Ainu remain, too. The United States of America established a federal law, "Native American Graves Protection and Repatriation Act (NAGPRA)" in 1990, which obliges all universities and museums in the country to investigate the remains of native peoples. When academic facilities retain the remains of native people, they should make clear to which tribe the remains belongs and start negotiation with the tribe on the premise of repatriation. As the result of each facility's investigation totally more than 180,000 remains were revealed to correspond for repatriation under this law and of these virtually around 53,000 remains have been repatriated or are under procedure at the end of the year 2015. The cost for investigation, transportation and reburial is generally born by the federal Government. The expenditure since 1994 has reached to around 43,000,000 dollars.

in my childhood and teasing did not cease in school days. I have hated being Ainu till 52-53 years old. Anyone can purchase several fish in paying 10,000 yen (100 dollar) or 15,000 yen. Is there any value, if I would buy fish, *Wajin* caught, at market and let Ainu people eat, offer *kamuy* as offering? Perhaps you cannot understand my feeling.

10 Following Urakawa case, Ainu bodies from place to place have filed suits against Hokkaido University. Thereafter, Hokkaido University agreed with reconciliation with Hatakeyama Satoshi-Ekasi, a chairman of the Monbetsu Ainu association, Urahoro Ainu Association in Tokachi area led by Sashima Masaki-Ekasi and Asahikawa Ainu council (Asahikawa Ainu Kyōgikai) led by Kawamura Ken'ichi-Ekasi. 4 remains were returned to Monbetsu and 77 remains were returned to Urahoro. Asahikawa council got back three remains in June 2018. Ueki Tetsuya described a history of Ainu study in collecting remains under the title of *Gakumon no Bouryoku: Ainu Bochi wa Naze Abakaretaka.* (Violence of Academism: Why Cemeteries of the Ainu were excavated?) in 2017. Ainu repatriation movement is detailed in *Ainu no Ikotsu wa Kotan no Tsuchi e: Hokudai ni Taisuru Ikotsu Henkan Seikyū to Senjūken* (Ainu Remains Should be Returned to Ground of Home Village: A Claim for Restitution of Remains Against Hokkaido University and Indigenous Rights) edited by Hokudai Kaiji Bunsho Kenkyūkai.

11 Due to preparation for the National Ainu People Museum opening in 2020, the Ainu Museum run by local foundation organized by Ainu in Shiraoi was abolished in the end of March 2018. The former Ainu Museum established in 1984 has long kept bears and performed *iomante*, a ritual to send a soul of bear to gods' world for several times. As a curator of the Museum, author had experience to participate in *iomante* twice. In contrast to the former Ainu Museum, the National Ainu People Museum has a policy not to breed bears. So, the Ainu Museum determined to send four bears to Yorkshire Wildlife Park in Great Britain. All four bears landed Great Britain in August 2018 in safe by air transportation and they were released to wide field of 1.6 hectare.

12 The first guideline the Japanese government issued in 2014 restricted claimants of Ainu remains only to direct descendants. In response to successive lawsuits, the government revised the guideline in December, 2018 approving claims by local bodies. It was truly one step ahead and

Hunting and Problem of Land) (Sapporo: Hokkaido Daigaku Shuppankai, 2011), 161-205.

4 Yamada, Shin'ichi. *Kindai Hokkaido to Ainu Minzoku: Shuryō Kisei to Tochi Mondai* (Hokkaido in Modern Period and Ainu People: Regulation in Hunting and Problem of Land), 177-185.

5 Yamada, Shin'ichi. "Sapporoken niyoru Tokachigawa Ryūiki no Sake Kinryō to Ainu Minzoku (Prohibition of Salmon Fishing in Tokachi River by Sapporo Prefecture and the Ainu)" In *Hokkaido Kaitakukinenkan Kenkyū Kiyou Volume 37.*(Sapporo: Hokkaido Kaitakukinenkan, 2009), 210-211.

6 *Asircepnomi* means a ritual for the first fish. In some regions this ritual is called *kamuycepnomi.*

7 Toyokawa Shigeo-Ekasi (1931-2015) was born in Ishikari. His ancestors lived in vanished Kotoni Kotan (village) located near present faculty of agriculture of Hokkaido university in the central of Sapporo. He succeeded to his family business and became a fisherman. However harvest of salmon sharply decreased in Ishikari River. So, he changed his occupation to wood carver. He has officiated *asircepnomi* for years.

8 Yūki Shōji (1938-1983) was born in Kushiro. He participated in establishing an Ainu Kotan (village) at Akankohan (beside Lake Akan). He organized Ainu Kaihō Dōmei (Union for Liberation of the Ainu) in 1972. Heading liberation movement, he has criticized study on the Ainu having discriminative point of view. He organized a committee to perform memorial ritual for victims on the Battle of Kunashiri Menashi (Kunasir Menas) occurred in 1789.

9 Maruyama Hiroshi, emeritus professor of Muroran Institute of Technology, insists the regulation prohibiting Ainu salmon catching in river is unconstitutionality in light of the ruling of Nibutani Dam Case. He points out that the same ground under Article 13 of the Japanese Constitution and Article 27 of International Covenant on Civil and Political Rights (ICCPR) can be adopted. Additional claims of Hatakeyama-Ekasi on 31 August 2018 was as follows: I remember Mr. Kayano Shigeru, a former Diet member from Biratori, said that we had no idea having sold Hokkaido and having rented Hokkaido. You immigrated to Hokkaido one after another and made laws from your selfish reasons. Have you ever inquired us of our opinion? If my act infringes the law you insist, I don't mind I would be arrested. I was bullied

Chihō)" (A report on Ainu Folklore and Cultural Assets 12 "Research of Ainu Folklore 'Eastern Hokkaido area'") (Sapporo: Hokkaido Kyōiku Iinkai, 1993), 27. Description concerning *sisampuri* is directly translated as follows: "My parents let soul return by swearing gods, however, I don't know how to pray for gods in hunting. Around ten aged-*matagi* (hunters) prayed for the universe saying 'We are going to adopt *sisampuri* (A: Japanese way) hereafter.'" Their prayer shows the essence of *kamuynomi* has transformed even trying to introduce way of Japanese. Mr. Fuchise Kazuo was born in Hidaka area in 1920 and migrated to Nukabira, Tokachi area in 1950. It was a record when he hunted the first bear in 19 years old around 1939.

8 Uchiumi Ken'ichi-Ekasi acquired lifestyle and culture of the Ainu in living with grandfather and grandmother in his childhood. He made effort to organize Shizunai branch of the Hokkaido Utari Association (present-day The Hokkaido Ainu Association) in 1946 and officiated regional rituals for a long time. He was awarded Ainu Cultural Encouragement Prize in 2011. His anecdote is recorded in *Ainu Minzokubunkazai Chōsahoukokusho"Ainu Seikatsu Gijutu Denshō Jittaichōsa 4"* (A report on Ainu Folklore and Cultural Assets "Servey on Actual Situation of Life, Techniques and Traditions of the Ainu 4") (Sapporo: Hokkaido Kyōiku Iinkai, 2003), 162-164.

9 Hoshino, Michio. *Mori to Hyōga to Kujira: Watarigarasu no Densetsu o Motomete* (Forest, Glacier, and Whale: Seeking for Legends of Raven) (Tokyo: Sekaibunkasha, 1996), 127-129.

10 Ikeya, Kazunobu. *Shuryō Saishūmin kara Mita Chikyū Kankyōshi: Shizen, Rinjin, Bunmei Tono Kyōsei* (History of Global Environment from View of Hunter-gatherers: Nature, Neighbor, and Coexistence with Civilization) (Tokyo: Tokyō Daigaku Shuppankai, 2017), 1.

Chapter 2 (Part 2)

1 Kayano, Shigeru. *Tsuma wa Karimono: Ainu Minzoku no Kokoro, Ima* (Wife is given: Spirits of Ainu People Now)(Sapporo: Hokkaido Shimbunsha, 1994) 111.

2 Kayano, Shigeru. *Ainu no Ishibumi* (Monument of the Ainu), 79.

3 Yamada, Shin'ichi. *Kindai Hokkaido to Ainu Minzoku: Shuryō Kisei to Tochi Mondai* (Hokkaido in Modern Period and Ainu People: Regulation in

grandmother. Through this experience, Yukie comprehended essence of Ainu culture. On the contrary, I could not have opportunity to learn Ainu language." Watashi no Naka no Rekishi *The Hokkaido Shimbun,* June 30, 2015.

3 The original Ainu word is "Yayunkur Mosir." "*yayunkur*" or "*yaunkur*" directly translated "man of land." Some Ainu people sometimes call Hokkaido as Ainu Mosir (Land of Ainu people) in contrast to Sisam Mosir (Land of Japanese). Nakagawa Hiroshi explained on the entry of "*yaunkur*" in his Chitose dialect Ainu-Japanese dictionary that "Hokkaido people. Literally it means 'man on land' calling themselves in contrast to *repunkur,*'man of offshore.' On the entry of "*yaunmosir,*" Nakagawa added that connotation of this word depends on who says the word. When Hokkaido people say *yaunmosir,* it implies Hokkaido, for people living in Sakhalin, it implies Sakhalin as well. On the other hand, Chiri Mashiho, younger brother of Chiri Yukie, insisted that structure of *yukar*, an heroic epic of Ainu oral traditions, is basically battle between people of land (*yaunkur*) and people of offshore (*repunkur*). He supposed this structure reflects real battle between ancient native people in Hokkaido and so-called Okhotsk people (Okhotsk-culture people) came from oversees probably from north and settled mainly along Okhotsk See coastline during 5th to 10th century.

4 Hokkaido Kyōikuchō Shōgai Gakushūbu Bunkaka., ed. *Ainu no Kurashi to Kotoba 5: Ainu Mukei Minzoku Bunkazai Kiroku Kankō Series 10* (Life and Language of the Ainu 5: Series 10 of Recording and Publishing Ainu Intangible Folk-Cultural Properties) (Sapporo: Hokkaido Kyōiku Iinkai, 1996), 19-24.

5 *nusa* is called *nusasan*, or *inawcipa* in some regions. See photo. Photograph: Collection of former Ainu Museum.

nusa

6 Kayano, Shigeru, and Hiroshi Tanaka, ed. *Ainu Minzoku Tun Hanran: Nibutani Dam Saiban no Kiroku* (Revolt of Ainu People: Record of Nibutani Dam Case) (Tokyo: Sanseidō, 1999) 136.

7 *Ainu Minzokubunkazai Chōsahoukokusho 12 "Ainu Minzokuchōsa (Dōtō*

with poisonous arrow for all kind of animals was totally prohibited allover Hokkaido till 1901. In modern age, number of deer living in Hokkaido declined sharply, because of hunting pressure and heavy snow. Together with prohibition of salmon catching in river, it caused starvation in Ainu communities. The regulations on salmon fishing is illustrated precisely in Part 2 chapter 2.

Chapter 5

1 Ogawa, Masahito. *Kindai Ainu Kyōiku Seidoshi Kenkyū* (A study in history of Ainu education system in modern period) (Sapporo: Hokkaidodaigaku Toshokankōkai, 1997), 278.

2 Nakai, Miyoshi. *Chiri Yukie: 19sai no Yuigon* (Chiri Yukie: Last Words from 19 Years Young Woman) (Tokyo: Sairyūsha, 1991), 236-241.

3 A modern history of villages in Sapporo including process of extinction was described by Katō Yoshio in *9seiki Kōhan no Sapporo, Ishikari no Ainu Minzoku* (Ainu People in Sapporo and Ishikari in the Latter Part of the 19th Century) (Sapporo: Sapporodō Shoten, 2017)

4 Nakai, *Chiri Yukie,* 193.

5 Chiri, Yukie. *Gin no Shizuku: Chiri Yukie Ikōshū* (Silver droplet: Collection of Posthumous Manuscripts of Chiri Yukie) (Tokyo: Sōfūkan, 1996), 166-167.

6 *Jogakusekai* is cultural journal issued monthly from 1901 to 1925 mainly targeted working woman and schoolgirls. It contains mainly novels and information for social life.

7 The original Japanese word is *"uru'oi,"* directly translated "moisture" "dampness."

8 Chiri, Yukie. *Gin no Shizuku: Chiri Yukie Ikōshū* (Silver droplet: Collection of Posthumous Manuscripts of Chiri Yukie), 177.

Part2

Chapter 1

1 Watashi no Naka no Rekishi (History of my Life=Autobiography=) *The Hokkaido Shumbun* (Newspaper, Sapporo), June 29, 2015.

2 Chiri-Yokoyama Mutsumi commented, "Yukie was taught traditions like *yukar* (one genre of Ainu traditions. Heroic epics) by Monasinouku, her

Shakushain's call, Ainu communities from Shiranuka in eastern Hokkaido to Mashike in the middle of Hokkaido united for battle against Matsumae Force. As Ainu force was strong, Matsumae Domain requested reinforcement to Tokugawa Shogunate and other domains. Shakushain was killed by Matsumae soldier at a banquet to make peace offered by Matsumae Domain in Niikappu in October 1669.

8 War of Kunashiri and Menashi: Under abuse and oppression of merchant, Ainu in Kunashiri Island uprose and then Ainu in Menasi area joined. 71 *Wajin* were killed. After Matsumae Domain repressed uprising, Matsumae force executed 37 Ainu.

9 Matsu'ura Takeshirō recorded this description in *Shiretoko Nissi* (Diary in Shiretoko region). A historian, Susumu Emori refers to this episode in *Ainu Minzoku no Rekishi* (History of Ainu People) (Tokyo: Sōfūkan, 2007), 366.

10 Emori, Susumu. *Ainu Minzoku no Rekishi* (History of Ainu People) (Tokyo: Sōfūkan, 2007), 368-372.

11 Having picked up around 100 Ainu people he met in Hokkaido and Sakhalin, Matru'ura Takesirō described *Ainu Jinbutsu Shi* (Stories of Ainu Persons). This is a story Takesirō recorded in this manuscript. Modern Japanese edition is published by Sarashina Genzō, and Yoshida Yutaka.

12 Matsu'ura Takeshirō recorded names of all residents at Nibutani Kotan with age. The name of Tokkaramu can be picked up Takeshirō's *Saru Nisshi* (Diary in Saru area). An anecdote to cut finger and rub poisonous organ of blowfish is not recorded by Takeshirō, but transmitted directly from generation to generation through Kayano-Ekasi's family. Kayano, Shigeru. *Ainu no Ishibumi* (Monument of the Ainu) (Tokyo: Asahi Shimbunsha, 1990), 31-47. Susumu Emori introduced this anecdote in *Ainu Minzoku no Rekishi* (History of Ainu People), 364-365.

13 Hokkaido Colonial Commission prohibited Ainu traditional way of deer hunting using poisonous arrow in 1876 in "Hokkaido Shikaryō Kisoku (Hokkaido regulations for deer hunting)." The regulations restricted number of hunters up to 600 without any incentive both for Ainu and Japanese. Ainu people did not enjoy preferential treatment except for tax free. No record concerning the number of excluded Ainu hunters is left, but surely numerous Ainu must be excluded from deer hunting under number restriction. Hunting

Jōmon People in Hokkaido showed the rate of cavities as 2.18%. Three other researchers also analyzed teeth of Jōmon people in Honshu and achieved result from 8.2% to 10.7%. There was significant difference between Jōmon people in Honshu and those in Hokkaido. For details, see Ōshima, Naoyuki. "Jōmon Jidai no Mushiba Ritsu (Rate of cavities in Jōmon Period)." In *Jōmon Jidai no Kōkogaku Volume10: Hito to Shakai Jinkotsu Jōhō to Shakai Soshiki.* (Tokyo: Dōseisha, 2008), 91-97.

2 Adopting a method to analyze protein remained in bone of ancient people, Minagawa Masao established an analysis technic to determine what kind of food they ate. Under examination of bones excavated in Kita Kogane Kaizuka (shell mound) in Date City, Hokkaido in the early period of Jōmon, Minagawa concluded the composition ratio of residents' food as fish and shellfish 33%, sea mammals 30%. Other 37% were mostly plants. He also investigated bones from Usu Moshiri Iseki ruins near Kita Kogane in Epi-Jōmon period and determined composition ratio as fish and shellfish 37%, sea mammals 27%, plants 34%. Composition ratio was also analyzed in Jōmon ruin cite in Honshu like Sanganji Iseki ruins in Fukushima prefecture in the late and the final stage of Jōmon period. The result was land mammal 14%, fish and shellfish 2%, plants 82%. For more information, see Ikeya, Kazunobu, and Masumi Hasegawa., ed. *Nihon no Shuryō Saishū Bunka: Yasei Seibutsu to Tomoni Ikiru* (Hunter-gatherer's Culture in Japan: To Live with Wild Life), 117-118.

3 Teramae, Naoto. *Bunmei ni Kōshita Yayoi no Hitobito* (Yayoi People, who Resisted Civilization) (Tokyo: Yoshikawa Kōbunkan, 2017), 277-284.

4 Takase, Katsunori. "Yayoi Bunka no Naka no Kita no Rinjin (Neighbor in the North in Yayoi culture). In *Yayoi Jidaitte Don'na Jidai Dattano ka?* (What Kind of Age, Yayoi Period Was?) (Tokyo: Asakura Shoten, 2017), 122-134.

5 See Yamada, Yasuhiro. *Jinkotsu Shutsudo Rei ni Miru Jōmon no Bosei to Shakai* (The Burial System and Society of Jōmon: Examination of Cases in Excavated Human Remains) (Tokyo: Dōseisha, 2008), 286-293.

6 Koshamain's War: An accident that an Ainu was stabbed to death by a Japanese farrier in the southern most in Hokkaido, arose uprising of Ainu people in 1457. Ainu force were finally defeated, however, Japanese power should retreat and then confined in the southern most area.

7 Shakushain's War occurred in June 1669. In response to an Ainu leader

11 Some scholars spell "*iyomante.*"

12 Mounds of bear skulls including cubs have been excavated from dwelling site of Okhotsk-culture people's ruins. Thus, some scholars view that roots of the bear ritual with raised bear derived from Okhotsk-culture from 5th to 10th century. Contrarily, other scholars insist that Okhotsk culture did not directly connect with Ainu culture. There is another view that the bear ritual with raised bear was established in 18-19th century. See Amano, Tetsuya. *Kuma Matsuri no Kigen* (Origin of the Bear Festival) and Irimoto, Takashi. *Ainu no Kumamatsuri* (The Ainu Bear Festival).

13 Sugimura Kyōko-Fuci (1926-2003) was born in Asahikawa. She once left hometown, however, having met Moritake Takeichi-Ekasi, an Ainu poet from Shiraoi, she noticed how important to hand down Ainu culture. Having learnt by her mother Kinarabukku-Fuci, Kyōko-Fuci became one of leading successor of the Ainu culture. See Kosaka, Yousuke. *Ainu o Ikiru, Bunka o Tsugu: Haha Kina-Fuci to Musume Kyōko no Monogatari* (I will live as an Ainu to Hand Down Culture: A Story of Kina-Fuci and her Daughter Kyōko) (Tokyo: Ōmura Shoten,1994).

14 Sugimura Kinarabukku-Fuci (1888-1973) was skillful in hand work like weaving and embroidery. Her various traditions were recorded by her daughter, Kyōko-Fuci and published under the title of *Kinarabukku Yūkara Shū* (Collection of *Yukar* told by Kinarabukku). See Kosaka, Yousuke. *Ainu o Ikiru, Bunka o Tsugu: Haha Kina-Fuci to Musume Kyōko no Monogatari* (I will live as an Ainu to Hand Down Culture: A Story of Kina-Fuci and her Daughter Kyōko) (Tokyo: Ōmura Shoten,1994).

15 A desert-like land, where kindred of bears were exiled, was expressed as "*nitai sak mosir, cikap sak mosir*" in original text. It can be directly translated "a land without forest, a land without birds." Ainu people have imagined this land is a lonely place where evil existences are banished to. There is another hell-like land for Ainu people called "*teine pokna mosir*" or "*teine pokna sir.*" It means "watery underground (below) land."

Chapter 4

1 Having analyzed 3061 teeth of Jōmon people in Honshu, Ōshima Naoyuki concluded the rate of cavities as 14.8%. On the other hand, 1285 teeth of

of den as follows; "God. A god who controls this house. I don't know a bear inside is male or female. As gods in *kamuy mosir* decided after consultation, please let us send this bear to gods' world calmly." This evidence shows that a den has been also regarded as *kamuy*. Hokkaido Kyōikuchō Shōgai Gakushūbu Bunkaka., ed. *Ainu no Kurashi to Kotoba 2: Ainu Mukei Minzoku Bunkazai Kiroku Kankō Series 4* (Life and Language of the Ainu 4: Series 8 of Recording and Publishing Ainu Intangible Folk-Cultural Properties) (Sapporo: Hokkaido Kyōiku Iinkai, 1991) 34-35.

5 Yae Kurō-Ekasi (1895-1978) illustrated special words in hunting in Yae, Kurō. *Ainu Minzokubunkazai Series 12: Yae Kurō no Denshō 2* (Ainu Folklore and Cultural Assets Series 12: Traditions of Yae Kurō 2) (Sapporo: Hokkaido Kyōiku Iinkai, 1994), 19-20.

6 Ainu Minzokubunkazai Chōsahoukokusho *"Ainu Minzokuchōsa 5* (Kushiro/ Abashiri Chihō)" (A report on Ainu Folklore and Cultural Assets "Research of Ainu Folklore 5 'Kushiro and Abashiri area'") (Sapporo: Hokkaido Kyōiku Iinkai, 1986) 7.

7 Inukai, Tetsuo and Masaaki, Kadosaki. *Higuma: Hokkaido no Shizen* (A Brown Bear: Nature in Hokkaido) (Sapporo: Hokkaido Shimbunsha, 1987), 332-339. See also Hozon Taisaku Kyōgikai., ed. *Ainu Minzoku Shi Gekan* (Ainu Ethnology Volume 2), 625-626. Miyamoto Ikasimatoku (Ekasimatoku)-Ekasi (1876-1958) had Japanese name as "Inosuke."

8 The title of the story is *A Sapporo Man who Reclaimed a Female Bear, who Descended to Human Land in Falling Love with a Human.* Hokkaido Kyōiku Iinkai. *Tuytak 2: Ainu Mukei Minzoku Bunkazai Kiroku Kankō Series 11* (Old Tales 2: Series 11 of Recording and Publishing Ainu Intangible Folk-Cultural Properties) (Sapporo: Hokkaido Kyōiku Iinkai, 1998), 193-226. This story was narrated by Nishijima Teru-Fuci (1896-1988) and translated into Japanese by Fujimura Hisakazu. Nishijima-Fuci was born in Biratori.

9 Sunazawa, Kura. *Ku-skup Oruspe: Watashi no Ichidaiki* (Story of My Life: Autobiography) (Tomakomai:Ainu Minzoku Bunka Denshōkai Rapuran, 2012), 75-83.

10 Hokkaido Kyōiku Iinkai. *Tuytak 2*, 193-226. Kan'nari Asiriro-Fuci in Noboribetsu narrated this story in 1932 to her relative, Kan'nari Matsu-Fuci. This story was translated into Japanese by Hasuike Etsuko.

Kankō Series 15 (Old Tales 4: Series 15 of Recording and Publishing Ainu Intangible Folk-Cultural Properties) (Sapporo: Hokkaido Kyōiku Iinkai, 2002), 58.

7 Hokkaido Kyōiku Iinkai, *Oyna 1: Ainu Mukei Minzoku Bunkazai Kiroku Kankō Series 3* (Stories of Gods 1: Series 3 of Recording and Publishing Ainu Intangible Folk-Cultural Properties) (Sapporo: Hokkaido Kyōiku Iinkai, 1990), 121-137. This story was narrated by Shirasawa Nabe-Fuci on 8 August 1988. Nakagawa Hiroshi recorded and translated into Japanese.

Chapter 3

1 To understand an Ainu method of bear hunting by Nemoto Yosaburō-Ekasi more precisely, I recommend to read Fujimura, Hisakazu., ed. *Heisei 20nendo Ainu Minzoku Bunkazai Chōsa Hōkokusho: Ainu Minzoku Gijutsu Chōsa 1 "Shuryō Gijutsu"* (A Report of Ainu Folk-Cultural Properties in 2008: Ainu Folk Technique Research 1 "Technique in Hunting") (Sapporo: Hokkaido Kyōiku Iinkai, 2009).

2 God of fire is normally expressed as an old woman, however in some regions like eastern Hokkaido god of fire is regarded as a pair of an old man and an old woman. Although goddess (a pair gods) of fire is a guardian of family and most familiar spiritual beings, the god is believed to be talkative having close association with other gods. Thus, Ainu hunters left records that they must not consult on hunting or speak out the name of place they were going to go hunting beside fire. Otherwise, gods in mountain would know in advance that hunters is going to appear.

3 According to Chiri Mashiho's *Classification dictionary of Ainu language*, *"niyaskorkamuy"* is Fish Owl (*Bubo blakistoni*). Nemoto-ekasi also told *"niyaskorkamuy"* was fish owl in *Heisei 20nendo Ainu Minzoku Bunkazai Chōsa Hōkokusho; Ainu Minzoku Gijutsu Chōsa 1 'Shuryō Gijutsu'* (A Report of Ainu Folk-cultural properties in 2008; Ainu Folk Technique Research 1 'Technique in Hunting'). Fish Owl has been generally called *"kotankorkamuy* (A god watching Ainu village)" by Ainu people. Nemoto-Ekasi told *"kotankorkamuy"* is ural owl (*Strix uralensis coreensis*).

4 Tochigi Masakichi-Ekasi in Eniwa recalled his experience hunted a bear in a den. The bear persisted to stay in a den, so one of his partners prayed to a god

Suzusawa Shoten, 1977), 130-132. Kayano-Ekasi (1926-2006) was born in Nibutani, Biratori Town. He made effort to establish Nibutani Ainu Bunka Shiryōkan (Nibutani museum on Ainu culture) in his hometown in 1972. Management of this museum is succeeded by his son, Kayano Shirō under the present name of Kayano Shigeru Nibutani Ainu Shiryōkan. Kayano Shigeru became the first member of the House of Councilors as Ainu origin and asked question in Ainu language. He also recorded Ainu oral traditions of his neighbors and published many books on Ainu culture and traditions. He compiled *Kayano Shigeru no Ainu Go Jiten* (Dictionary of Ainu Language).

2 Anezaki Hitoshi-Ekasi (1923-2013) was born in Mukawa. He migrated to Chitose when he was 3 years old and grew up there. He continued hunting for 65 years until 2001. He is coauthor of *Kuma ni Attara Dōsuruka: Ainu Minzoku Saigo no Karyūdo Anezaki Hitoshi* (How Do You Deal With a Bear at Unexpected Encounter: The Last Ainu Hunter Anezaki Hitoshi).

inaw

3 *Inaw* is indispensable ritual implement usually made of willow, table dogwood (*Cornus controversa Hemsley*), or Amur cork-tree (*Phellodendron amurense Rupr,* for high ranking gods like the bear god). *Inaw* plays a role to transmit prayer to gods and are regarded as gifts from humans to gods. It is proud of a god, who is offered many *inaw* from *ainu mosir.* See Kitahara, Jirōta. *Ainu no Saigu: Inaw no Kenkyū* (Ainu Implements for Ritual: Study on Inaw). Sapporo: Hokkaido Daigaku Shuppankai, 2014.

Photograph: Collection of former Ainu Museum.

4 Anezaki, Hitoshi, and Tatsumine Katayama, *Kuma ni Attara Dōsuruka; Ainu Minzoku Saigo no Karyūdo Anezaki Hitoshi* (How Do You Deal With a Bear at Unexpected Encounter? The Last Ainu Hunter Anezaki Hitoshi) (Tokyo: Kirakusha, 2002) 199-200.

5 Hokkaido Kyōiku Iinkai, *Oyna 2: Ainu Mukei Minzoku Bunkazai Kiroku Kankō Series 5* (Stories of Gods 2: Series 5 of Recording and Publishing Ainu Intangible Folk-Cultural Properties) (Sapporo: Hokkaido Kyōiku Iinkai, 1992), 213-284. This story was narrated by Mikami Tsuya-Fuci (1906-1979) and translated into Japanese by Fujimura Hisakazu.

6 Hokkaido Kyōiku Iinkai, *Tuytak 4: Ainu Mukei Minzoku Bunkazai Kiroku*

Kazurō, a physical anthropologist, is widely accepted on the whole still now. His estimation was firstly based on calculation of population in Jōmon period by Koyama Shūzō, an archaeologist. Koyama estimated largest population of Jōmon period except for Hokkaido to be 260,000 at mid-Jōmon. Koyama supposed that number of Jōmon people declined to be 75,000 at the last period. Despite reduction of population at last stage of Jōmon period, population of the Japanese Islands increased in Yayoi period to 600,000 by estimation of Haninara. The population swelled in Kofun Period from 3rd to 6th century up to 5.4 million. Hanihara tried to explain such shift of population with migrants from Chinese Continent. For details, see Hanihara, Kazurō., ed. *Nihonjin no Kigen* (Origins of Japanese) (Tokyo: Asahi Shimbunsha, 1994), 218-222. Basically supporting double structure model, Omoto Kei'ichi, a molecular anthropologist, determined migrants were not Asian from the south, but Asian from the north. Analysis of mitochondrial DNA demonstrates that Japanese have 65% DNA from migrants and 35% from Jōmon people. Contrary to Haninara's view, Omoto stresses influence of Jōmon DNA citing Hōrai Satoshi's view "We succeed DNA of Jōmon people more than we had imagined."

8 *Meisaku Jōruri Shu: Jō: Kindai Nihon Bungaku Taikei 8* (Collection of Masterpieces of Jōruri=Japanese puppet show= Volume 1: Compendium of Modern Japanese Literature Volume 8) (Tokyo: Kokumin Tosho, 1927), 401-486.

9 Orikuchi, Shinobu. *Orikuchi Shinobu Zenshū 2: Kodai Kenkyū (Minzokugaku Hen 1)* (Complete Works of Orikuchi Shinobu Volume 2: Study of Ancient Times (Ethnology Part 1)) (Tokyo: Chūōkōronsha, 1975), 281-282.

10 Orikuchi, Shinobu. *Orikuchi Shinobu Zenshū 3: Kodai Kenkyū "Minzokugaku Hen 2"* (Complete Works of Orikuchi Shinobu Volume 3: Study of Ancient Times "Ethnology Part 2.") Edited by Orikuchi Hakase Kinen Kodai Kenkyūjo. (Tokyo: Chūōkōronsha, 1975), 386-387.

11 Inada, Kōji. *Ainu no Mukashibanashi* (Old Tales of Ainu) (Tokyo: Chikuma Shobō, 2005), 361.

Chapter 2

1   Kayano, Shigeru, *Ore no Nibutani* (My hometown Nibutani) (Tokyo:

Dōbutsu Muko to Dōbutsu Yome no Baai (Animals on Old Tales Concerning Intermarriage Between Humans and Animals; Cases of Animal Grooms and Animal Brides)" that exceptional Japanese old tales to get married with wild animals not transformed into humans were only "*Kuma Nyōbo* (Bear Wife)" and "*Ei Nyōbo* (Ray Wife)" collected in the Okinawa Islands, the southernmost region of Japan.

3 Ainu oral traditions can be roughly classified 1, Tales of gods called "*kamuy yukar,*" "*oyna*" etc. depending on region. The style is verse. 2, Epics (hero's tale) called "*yukar,*" "*sakorpe,*" "*hawki*" depending on region. The style is verse. 3, Tales in style of prose called "*uepeker*" "*tuytak*" etc. depending on region. Among tales of gods characteristics of gods can be classified "gods of nature" and "personified gods." There are various kinds of "gods of nature" such as wild animals, birds, shell, land, lake, trees and natural phenomena like thunder, fire, small pox so on.

4 Hokkaido Kyōiku Iinkai, *Oyna 3: Ainu Mukei Minzoku Bunkazai Kiroku Kankō Series 7* (Stories of Gods 3: Series 7 of Recording and Publishing Ainu Intangible Folk-Cultural Properties) (Sapporo: Hokkaido Kyōiku Iinkai, 1994), 213-239. This tale was narrated by Shirasawa Nabe (1905-1993) in Chitose in October 1987 and translated into Japanese by Nakagawa Hiroshi. As Ainu folk tales have been narrated and handed down within family members or their community, each tale does not have explicit title in Ainu language. Title like *A Daughter Who Married a Cuckoo* here was given by recorders or translator for convenience in translating into Japanese.

5 Nakagawa Hiroshi, *Ainu no Monogatari Sekai* (World of Stories in the Ainu) (Tokyo: Heibonsha, 1997), 109-112.

6 Nemoto Yosaburō (1918-2013) was born in Shiranuka. Working as a dairy farmer, he hunted bears and deer. I performed interviews several times in 2011, but, regrettably he passed away in 2013 at 95 years old. His experience and hunting method is recorded in Fujimura, Hisakazu, ed. *Heisei 20nendo Ainu Minzoku Bunkazai Chōsa Hōkokusho: Ainu Minzoku Gijutsu Chōsa 1 "Shuryō Gijutsu"* (A Report of Ainu Folk-cultural properties in 2008; Ainu Folk Technique Research 1 "Technique in Hunting") (Sapporo: Hokkaido Kyōiku Iinkai, 2009).

7 Double Structure Model (J: Nijūkōzō Model), proposed by Hanihara

NOTES

Introduction

1 Birth of Aynurakkur (Ainurakkur) is just a beginning of this story. This story develops to battle against demons from world of darkness. More detail, see Yamamoto, Tasuke. *Kamuy Yukar: Aynu Rak Kur den* (Tales of Gods: Story of Aynurakkur) (Tokyo: Heibonsha, 1993). Ainu people have handed down another type of creation myth. "Kotankarkamuy (the god to create land) created land from cloud. Black cloud shaped rocks, yellow cloud became soil…" As for factor of cloud in creating land, Ōbayashi Taryō pointed out a probability of influence from Mongolian creation myth.

2 Hokkaido prefectural government started "Ainu Seikatsu Jittai Chōsa (Investigation of life condition for the Ainu) in 1972. Grasped population were about 24,000 in 2006, around 17,000 in 2013 and around 13,000 in 2017. However, census is basically done voluntary inquiry in cooperation with the Hokkaido Ainu Association. Thus it has been pointed out not to reflect actual population. Some guess actual population might be several times or ten times than the number of Hokkaido census in whole country.

3 According to an archeologist, Matsumoto Naoko, death rate of Jōmon people caused by wars was 0.9%, whereas prehistoric death rate of hunter-gatherers in average caused by wars, was 14% by an analysis of an American economist, Samuel Bowles. See Matsumoto, Naoko "Jōmon no Shisō kara Yayoi no Shisō e (From thought of Jōmon to that of Yayoi)" In *Nihon Shisōshi Kōza 1—Ancient times* (Tokyo: Perikansha, 2012) 27-64.

4 Koyama, Shūzō. *Jōmon Tanken: Minzoku Kōkogaku no Kokoromi* (Exploring Jōmon: A Trial to Ethno-archaeology) (Tokyo: Chūōkōronsha, 1998), 345.

5 Yasuda, Yoshinori. *Jōmon Bunmei no Kankyō* (Environment in Jōmon Civilization) (Tokyo: Yoshikawa Kōbunkan, 1997), 27-31.

Chapter 1

1 Kawamori, Hiroshi. *Nihon Mukashi Banashi no Kōzō to Katarite* (Structure and storytellers of Japanese Old Tales). (Osaka: Ōsaka Daigaku Shuppankai, 2000), 69.

2 Nakamura, Tomoko et al.analyzed in*"Iruikon'intan ni Tōjō Suru Dōbutsu;*

Glossary of main words in Ainu language

Ainu: "Ainu" has two meanings. Original meaning is just "Humans" in contrast to kamuy (defined below). It is also used for people's name in contrast to Wajin (J: ethnic Japanese). For example, "We, Ainu perform a ritual to receive the first salmon beside a river, but, Japanese do not have such custom." Sometimes the name of the people is transcribed "Aynu." So, ainu mosir (A: land) originally means human land in contrast to gods' land "kamuy mosir." Now it sometimes used to express the land, where the Ainu people live, i.e. Hokkaido, Sakhalin and the Kuril Islands. "Ainu mosir" is also used to point Hokkaido in a narrow sense as proper noun (place name).

cise: originally it means a house. This word sometimes implies an Ainu traditional house.

ekasi: male respected elder

fuci: female respected elder

inaw (inau): an indispensable ritual implement mainly carved from willow sticks. Ainu believe that inaw transmit their prayer to gods and inaw itself is an offering to gods.

kamuy: gods, deity, spiritual beings. From an animistic point of view, Ainu believe in various gods. Gods normally live in the world of gods (kamuy mosir).

kamuynomi: prayer to gods. Ainu not only pray at rituals, but also at various occasions at gathering, hunting so on.

kotan: an Ainu village

tonoto: unrefined sake (J: rice wine). Tonoto is also indispensable for rituals.

ancestors' remains repatriated from Hokkaido University. They had filed litigation at the Sapporo District Court and achieved reconciliation with Hokkaido University. 12 remains were reburied in Urakawa in July, 2016.

2019 A new Ainu law, "An act to promote policies to realize a society in which pride of Ainu people is respected" is enacted. Ainu Seisaku Kentō Shimin Kaigi (Citizen's Alliance for the Examination of Ainu Policy) and other bodies organized by Ainu people criticize this law as it ignores historical awareness and guarantees of Ainu Indigenous rights.

2020 Opening of the National Ainu Museum is scheduled in Shiraoi. Ainu remains are scheduled to be integrated at a mausoleum in the adjoining area.

dissolves and now four bodies such as the Kantō Utari-kai, Rera-no-kai, Tokyo Ainu Association, and Pewre Utari-no-kai are active.

1982 *Asircepnomi*, an Ainu traditional ritual to receive the first salmon, is restored on the banks of the Toyohira River in Sapporo after an approximately 100 years' hiatus. Since 1986, Hokkaido Prefecture has permitted Ainu to fish for salmon in rivers only as an exceptional measure for the purpose of rituals and the transmission of traditions.

1984 The Hokkaido Utari Association adopts "A Proposal for Legislation Concerning The Ainu People (so-called draft of New Ainu Law)" at annual General Assembly. The government designated Ainu Koshiki Buyō (Ainu traditional dancing) as an Important Intangible Folk-cultural Property.

1992 Nomura Gi'ichi, the Chief Director of the Hokkaido Utari Association, delivers a speech at the General Assembly of the United Nations in New York, celebrating the advent of the International Year of the World's Indigenous Peoples in the next year, 1993.

1994 Kayano Shigeru, a famous Ainu culture-bearer, becomes the first member of Ainu origin of the House of Councilors. He delivers a question in the Diet in the Ainu language.

1997 For the first time in Japanese legislative, executive or judiciary history, the Sapporo District Court recognizes the Ainu as an Indigenous people in its ruling on the Nibutani Dam Construction. It also rules that the compulsory acquisition of land possessed by Kayano Shigeru and Kaizawa Kōichi was illegal on the grounds that the Ainu right to enjoyment of culture (Article 13 of the Japanese Constitution and Article 27 of the International Covenant on Civil and Political Rights (ICCPR)) was violated.

The Act on the Promotion of Ainu Culture is enacted. Because the purpose of the act is restricted to the restoration of the Ainu culture and language, most of the demands from the Draft New Ainu Law submitted by the Hokkaido Utari Association are neglected.

2007 The United Nations adopts the United Nations Declaration on the Rights of Indigenous Peoples.

2008 Both Houses of the Japanese Diet unanimously approve a resolution to recognize the Ainu as an Indigenous People of Japan.

2015 Ainu Elders organize the Kotan-no-kai as a receiving organization for

Japan as a result of the Treaty of Saint Petersburg. Japanese officials attain their object by persuading the approximately 100 Kuril Ainu that Shikotan Island is abundant in natural resources including sea mammals. However, Shikotan Island is poor in their traditional food resources and the Ainu population declines almost half in five years. This occurrence was substantially forced migration.

1899 The Hokkaido Kyūdojin Hogohō (Hokkaido Former Aborigines Protection Act) is enacted. Land is allotted for Ainu who desired to be farmers. However, the lands provided were inappropriate for farming in many cases. This act had essential characteristics of assimilation, depriving the Ainu people of their traditional lifestyle, culture, and their communities.

1901 Hokkaido Prefecture enacts the Former Aborigine Elementary Education Regulation. This stipulated that Ainu pupils learn at Ainu schools, apart from Japanese pupils and under a different curriculum. By prohibiting the Ainu language at school, this education system accelerated discrimination and deprivation of the Ainu's mother tongue.

1923 Ainu Shin'yōshū (In English translation, *Ainu Spirits Singing*), the first publication of Ainu folktales translated into Japanese by Ainu themselves, is published with the original Ainu language text. However, Chiri Yukie, the compiler and translator, dies in the previous year at the age of 19 after completion of the manuscript.

1931 All Hokkaido Ainu youth conference is held in Sapporo.

1933 Japan Society for the Promotion of Science (Nihon Gakujutsu Shinkōkai) funds research on Ainu human remains for five years. Professors of Hokkaido University excavate Ainu cemeteries in various locations in Hokkaido, Sakhalin and the Kuril Islands. The excavated remains form the core 'collection' of around 1000 Ainu remains housed in Hokkaido University.

1945 The Soviet Army invades the Kuril Islands and the southern part of Sakhalin. Ainu residents together with *Wajin* escape and migrate to Hokkaido.

1946 The Hokkaido Ainu Association is established. The name is changed to the Hokkaido Utari Association in 1961, then renamed to the Hokkaido Ainu Association in 2009.

1973 The Asahikawa Ainu Council is established. Ainu people living in the Kanto metropolitan area organize the Tokyo Utari-kai. Later, this body

1799 The Tokugawa shogunate decides to control East-Ezochi directly.

1807 The entire territory of Hokkaido including West-Ezochi and the southern part of Sakhalin comes under direct control of the Tokugawa shogunate.

1822 The Tokugawa shogunate permits the Matsumae Domain to recover control of Hokkaido.

1855 The Shogunate concludes the Treaty of Amity and Commerce with the Russian Empire. The border is fixed between Etorofu Island and Urup Island in the Kuril Islands. The Shogunate deprives the Matsumae Domain of their dominion and puts Hokkaido under direct control again.

1868 Meiji Restoration. The modern period dawns in Japan.

1869 The new Meiji government annexes Hokkaido and establishes the Hokkaido Colonial Commission (Kaitakushi) in Sapporo.

1871 The Hokkaido Colonial Commission introduces an assimilation policy, prohibiting tattooing by Ainu people and the wearing of earrings by Ainu men. The Commission also encourages the learning of the Japanese language.

1872 Proclamation of the Regulations on Land Sales and Leasing in Hokkaido. As a first step, the Hokkaido Colonial Commission adopts a package of land policies granting favorable treatment to the government, industrial capitalists, and Japanese settlers until 1897. The total number of immigrants to Hokkaido in the 36 years since 1886 reaches more than two million.

1875 The Japanese Government concludes the Treaty of Saint Petersburg by which Japan possesses the Kuril Islands and the Russian Empire possesses Sakhalin. The Japanese government forces Sakhalin Ainu to immigrate to Tsuishikari, Ebetsu, close to Sapporo. The change in environment and a pandemic of cholera deprives the lives of Sakhalin Ainu one after another.

1876 The Hokkaido Colonial Commission proclaimed the Hokkaido Deer Hunting Regulations prohibiting Ainu using traditional poisonous arrows. Heavy snow brings about massive fatalities of deer in 1879. These compound factors cause starvation of Ainu people.

1878 The Hokkaido Colonial Commission prohibits the catching salmon and trout in all tributaries of rivers in Hokkaido. Ainu people are deprived of their second staple food, the other being deer.

1884 The Japanese government decides a migration policy for the Kuril Ainu, whose residents became border-dwellers between the Russian Empire and

Chief Events concerning Ainu People since 15th Century

1457 Battle of Koshamain, the first large-scale uprising of the Ainu, occurs in the southernmost region of Hokkaido. Ainu force was suppressed by the Japanese power.

1604 Tokugawa Ieyasu, a founder of the Tokugawa shogunate (Edo shogunate) issues a Kokuinjō (a letter with a black seal) to Kakizaki Yoshihiro, a leader of the Matsumae Domain. The Shogunate granted the Matsumae Domain a monopoly in trade with the Ainu in Hokkaido (called "Ezochi" at the time). As this letter recognized freedom of travel for the Ainu, it has been pointed out that the Shogunate recognized Hokkaido as being outside of Japanese territory.

1643 By this time, the Matsumae Domain's peculiar system of control for Hokkaido of "Akinaiba Chigyōsei," assigning a trading area for each vassal, had been established. The Ainu people mainly obtained rice in exchange for dried salmon.

1669 An Ainu leader, Shakushain, from the Shizunai region, uprises against the Matsumae Domain because of dissatisfaction with unfair exchange rates. Since many other Ainu communities joined the alliance, the Matsumae Domain offers peace. Shakushain is killed at the peace banquet.

1698 Contact with *Wajin* (Ethnic Japanese) brings about a pandemic of smallpox in Ainu communities and causes depopulation.

1710s The Matsumae Domain's vassals tend to leave the management of trading areas to Japanese merchants. This new system, the "Basho-Ukeoi-Seido," later caused forced labour and abuse of Ainu at herring fisheries, which was occasionally accompanied by forced displacement.

1711 The Russian Empire invades Shumushu Island, the easternmost island of the Kuril archipelago, and expands the area under its control in the islands where the Kuril Ainu (North Kuril Ainu) dwell.

1723 Due to a poor catch of salmon, around 200 Ainu in the Ishikari area starve to death.

1789 Ainu in Kunashiri Island and the Menashi region of eastern Hokkaido uprise against oppression by Hidaya, a Japanese merchant, at a fishery. 71 *Wajin* are killed, and after suppression of the uprising, the Matsumae Domain executes 37 Ainu.

allowing for any ambiguity. She recognized that there are many people burdened by the same problems of identity, and that the existence of such "silent people" has been growing. She developed the term "Silent Ainu" to refer to herself and others like her in her research.

Personally, I have encountered not a few "silent people" with various background. One elder woman once disclosed to me that her identity as an Ainu was revealed to her by her neighbors, as her parents and relatives never opened up about being Ainu. In regards to Ainu culture, she has never been taught by her parents and therefore had no desire to learn about it.

Mai's words, "I cannot distinguish fully whether I am Ainu or *Wajin*, Indigenous or non-Indigenous, hunter-gatherer or agricultural" awakened me to the fact that my manuscript lacked an essential angle. Concerning the ambiguity and complexities present in each identity, it is important not to give too much emphasis to common traits or try to classify whole groups of people arbitrarily. Ethnography or other inquisitive pursuits about people and their spiritual cultures should not subscribe too heavily to ideas of fixity. Furthermore, things are always changing in time, including people and their culture.

On the other hand, it is also important to recognize the values that form the heart of lifestyles and worldview. Searching for this core was the guiding principle of this manuscript. In the process of writing, I have discovered many valuable things alongside a tragic history.

Postscript

I sent the manuscript of this book to Ishihara Mai in December 2018 just before publishing. She is a daughter of my old friends, Ishihara Makoto and Itsuko and has just finished her doctoral thesis at Hokkaido University. In her Ph.D work she addressed the identity problems surrounding people with Ainu roots, particularly focusing on her grandmother Tsuyako, her mother Itsuko, as well as herself.

The resultant E-mail from Mai read, "Nature is essentially chaos. Out of fear against the chaos, humans have created a supposed system of classification and order. Humans have in the past held rituals to deal with the chaos. However, these rituals are disappearing since humans are no longer filled with awe of nature. The development of positivist science and technology has resulted in humans losing their ability to correspond with the natural chaos."

I was inspired by her insight, though it was her following message that gave me pause.

"I myself, identifying neither 'Ainu' nor '*Wajin*' am chaos itself. I am off the grid of any perceptible framework. As an individual having roots as an Ainu, I cannot distinguish fully whether I am Ainu or *Wajin*, Indigenous or non-Indigenous, hunter-gatherer or agricultural."

Mai's grandmother, Tsuyako was born in 1925 to Ainu parents. Tsuyako worked hard seeking equal social positioning to *Wajin*. She came to choose a *Wajin* man as her companion in life. As a result, she came to the end of her life indifferent of Ainu culture and language. Many Ainu lived in much the same way in that time of the 20th century. After Mai's mother, Itsuko, herself married a *Wajin* man, she became interested in learning about Ainu culture. In doing so, she realized that she had not acquired anything about her own culture during her life. Isuko ultimately was alienated from other cultural transmission activities upon realizing that she was ignorant of her own culture.

Under these circumstances, growing up Mai developed an awareness that she exists "neither as Ainu or *Wajin*." A question grew inside of her, namely why there is no alternative choice of identity in Japanese society. She felt the demand of Japanese society for one to be explicitly *Wajin* or Ainu, without

People requires historical recognition that the state has controlled the involved peoples through colonial rule and assimilation policies. Moreover, countries which agreed with the United Nations Declaration on the Rights of Indigenous Peoples (UNDRIP), bear a duty to reflect the aspirations of the declaration in domestic policy. Though the Japanese government agreed to the UNDRIP, it ignores Indigenous rights completely in the draft Bill, including the rights to utilize natural resources and to demand repatriation of ancestral remains. This neglect indicates that the Government's recognition of the Ainu as an Indigenous People is just superficial and that substantially, the government persists in its long-standing position not to guarantee any collective rights to the Ainu as a people.

The Diet passed the Bill in April, 2019. Under this 'new law for the Ainu,' many Ainu acquaintances are anxious about being utilized as an "advertising tower" for acquiring a budget for tourism promotion and regional development. [7]

Around the same time, snippets of news gave a shock to persons concerned that the Foundation for Ainu Culture had decided not to approve a subsidy to the Monbetsu Ainu Association led by Hatakeyama Satoshi-Ekasi for holding the 21st event of *kamuycepnomi* in Autumn, 2019. According to Hatakeyama-Ekasi, it was the first time for 20 years' history of yearly Monbetsu *kamuycepnomi*. It also turned out that several groups, which are planning projects to revive or empower Ainu culture, received notification of funding "disapproval" from the Foundation. My acquaintances expressed anxiety to me, "I wonder one might be alienated from official aid if one is involved in the rights restoration movement?" "Would it be a kind of segmentation of Ainu by means of subsidies?"

It is regrettable for me to put down my pen with pessimistic foresight. However, as Ainu people handed down something valuable from generation to generation until today, valuable things must be transmitted to future generations. I desire that this manuscript would serve for Ainu people to regain dignity and self-confidence.

many associates in the world.

Thus, the direction of progress Indigenous Peoples seek for, could have a strong influence on the world. Our future, the fate of future generations, could deeply depend on what requests Indigenous Peoples make. If you can imagine the impact the united voice of Indigenous Peoples could have, there is no reason to despair. As Mankiller described, the sense Indigenous Peoples have for valuing relationships with the land and living things will naturally link to movements seeking to protect nature and to achieve a sustainable society and environment.

"Values" can be replaced with "Virtue" in Ainu society. And "Acquisitiveness" could be reworded, "To live without values." I think losing values is equivalent to losing a brake. If we lose our brakes against limitless modernization, we will someday face an existential emergency.

In February, 2019, the Japanese government announced the draft of a new Ainu law, "to promote policies to realize a society in which pride of the Ainu people is respected." 35 years have passed since the Hokkaido Utari Association (currently the Hokkaido Ainu Association) adopted "A Proposal for Legislation Concerning the Ainu People (so-called draft of New Ainu Law)" at annual general assembly in 1984. Instead of realizing the Association's desire to make law to lessen disparities between *Wajin* and the Ainu, the act adopted in 1997 "The Act on the Promotion of Ainu Culture" concentrated on restoration and promotion of the Ainu culture and Ainu language. This meant that most of the demands from the draft of the Hokkaido Utari Association have been neglected. As far Ainu new law in 2019, though the draft legally defines the Ainu as an Indigenous People for the first time, measures included in the resolution have only discouraged Ainu people once again, because the Bill not only lacks historical awareness, measures for compensation, and an apology for historical injustices, but also makes no guarantees of Indigenous rights. These factors must be two sides of the same coin in terms of the qualification of Indigenous people. It is becoming an international standard that qualification as an Indigenous

Cherokee Nation in North America, stated, "There is enormous diversity among communities of Indigenous Peoples, each of which has its distinct culture, language, history, and unique way of life. Despite these differences, Indigenous Peoples across the globe share some common values derived in part from an understanding that their lives are part of and inseparable from the natural world."

Illustrating in this way that Indigenous Peoples have something important in common, Mankiller called for the global solidarity of Indigenous Peoples. And, with regard to the environmental movement as well, she tried to persuade us from the point of view of Indigenous Peoples.

"Indigenous People are not the only people who understand the interconnectedness of all living things. There are many thousands of people from different ethnic groups who care deeply about the environment and fight every day to protect the earth. The difference is that indigenous peoples have the benefit of being regularly reminded of their responsibilities to the land by stories and ceremonies. They remain close to the land, not only in the way they live, but in their hearts and in the way they view the world. Protecting the environment is not an intellectual exercise; it is a sacred duty."[4]

Her words resonate with me. The most important thing is to have a sense of value and to recognize Indigenous Peoples' relationship with the land, living things and human communities. Surely, both people and nature are vulnerable and have been damaged to a considerable extent. However, they endure still now.

Can you guess the population of Indigenous Peoples in the world? It is estimated in total to be around three hundred million.[5] And, if you are to count members of units of people, there is at least one people in which only one person remains, Cristina Calderon[6] of the Yaghan people. She is the last woman and descendant of a people who reached to the furthest place in human history, Fuego Island, Patagonia, at the southernmost tip of South America. Anyway, when people unite under the category of Indigenous Peoples, the population swells to a size of three hundred million. You have so

with the gods and didn't have an evil mind, they managed to live peacefully. However, finally they were deceived by *Wajin* and continued to decline. I recognize that they were a vulnerable people. I cannot help feeling that that code of conduct which Indigenous Peoples have cherished in modeling nature, cannot cope with the acquisitiveness that lies in the depth of the human mind.

Her mail crushed me. For a while, I could not find the words to reply. I experienced a kind of despair as a result of the perspective which she had thrown directly at me, "The code of conduct which Indigenous Peoples have cherished in modeling nature, cannot cope with the acquisitiveness that lies in the depth of the human mind." It seemed to me quite natural that she, as a member of a people having been assimilated and discriminated against, could not express any hopeful words. Yet, though I sympathized with her stance, her pessimistic view was so overwhelming that I could not find the words to reply. If acquisitiveness is an essence of human beings and the code of conduct and behavior of the majority of peoples are based on acquisitiveness, the world would be hopeless and almost impossible to ameliorate.

It needed time for me to write a reply to her query.

> I apologize to you that my reply is late. Even though not a few Ainu have quit their transactions with the gods, they were driven to do so by external pressure. We have to start with the fact that this situation was not one selected voluntarily by the Ainu people.
>
> You seem to be pessimistic about learning something valuable from the sensitivities of the Ainu people. You also told me that you have no role model nor anything to follow, now that previous generations, nature, and the environment have been lost in this modern age. It is not proper, I think. At the moment when you wrote to me, "People who value nature cannot coexist with people who are willing to conquer nature," you were unconsciously sharing a sense of value with your ancestors who coexisted with wildlife while valuing nature.
>
> Wilma Mankiller, the first woman elected to serve as chief of the

Indigenous Peoples Have a Brotherhood of Three Hundred Million

"I think people who have respect for nature cannot coexist with people who are willing to conquer nature."

I remember a dialogue with Ishikawa Mikaho, an Ainu woman living in Tokyo, whom I guided to *Honryu no siratcise* a few years ago. Having roots on Shibotsu Island close to the Kuril Islands where her grandmother lived, she was born and grew up in Nemuro. I first met her more than 20 years ago when she was 22 years old in Nemuro. While exchanging E-mails, I received an outspoken message from her after the Great East Japan Earthquake on 11 March, 2011.

> I've learned from you before that striving after virtue has been the Ainu code of conduct for life. Numerous old anecdotes tell of cunning merchants who have come in touch with Ainu with contempt. As the Ainu have the ability to estimate people's personalities, even while being scorned, these Ainu could see through the *Wajins*' malicious intentions easily. Do you agree with me? I imagine that Ainu have given up the fight against merchants, since they recognized it was impossible to cope with Japanese brokers. I think people who value nature cannot coexist with people who are willing to conquer nature. I suppose the reason many Ainu have discarded their self-respect was that they could no longer believe in the morals expressed in the Ainu oral traditions. I also speculate that they quit the transactions with the gods. They subsist, but they have thrown away their identity. If even I, as a descendant of the Ainu am to view it so, will it eventually be the death of the Ainu?
>
> Elders belonging to the previous generation, from whom I should have learned, have all passed away now. To whom can I inquire? In addition to the absence of my ancestors, nature and the environment have also been destroyed. Under this situation, after whom, or upon what, should I model my behavior?
>
> Ainu have had rigid confidence. If they correctly associated

me three papers, on which he wrote down the prayers at *siratcise* and said to me, "I entrust *inon'no-itak* (A: words of prayer)' to you. It took a long time for me to make this amount of *inon'no-itak*." Before long, I heard from common acquaintances that he suffered from a disordered health condition and could not officiate over the *kamuynomi* at the *siratcise*. I was surprised to hear that, because he did not look sick at all when I met him.

Honryū no Siratcise has been used for overnight at hunting and for ritual to send soul of bears. (Photograph by Kosaka Yasushi)

A skull of a bear is enshrined at *nusa* at Honryū no Siratcise in Eniwa. (Photograph by Kosaka Yousuke)

On the left side of the ground are remnants of cooking utensils and the *nusa* is formed on the right of the Honryū no Siratcise. Surrounded by *inaw*, a bear skull is enshrined. This basecamp has therefore been used recently by Ainu hunters.

Ainu hunters were skillful in making a temporary shelter. Venturing out from a basecamp, they occasionally overnighted in such shelters, even in the snowy season. Anezaki Hitoshi-Ekasi used to cut down several branches of a pine tree, spread them on both sides of the trunk of a thick fallen tree, and nestled himself under them to sleep. He related, "As I can overnight at makeshift shelter, the only things I have to take to the mountains are hunting gear and salt. Shooting mountain birds like grouse for temporary food, I can stay in the mountains as many days as I want." It is most important to lighten belongings when hunting in order to move nimbly.

Ever since Anezaki-Ekasi and Nemoto Yosaburō-Ekasi passed away in 2013, I have made a habit of visiting *Honryū no Siratcise* at least once a year to put *inaw*, disordered by blizzards during the winter, back to where they should be. Then, I pray briefly to the gods including the bear god enshrined there.

An official ritual to pray to the gods has been held annually at the other *Banjiri no Siratcise* along the same Izari River, officiated by Nomoto Hisae-Ekasi[3] from Chitose together with Japanese hunters.

When I met Nomoto-Ekasi, an old friend of mine, in April 2015, he handed

unprecedented, and so it is doubtful whether the story can come to a finale with a positive relation to nature. The tragic ending of the modern fox was created by Yūki Kōji to reflect such changing circumstances.

Performance of a new drama *Akan Yukar 'Lost Kamuy'* created by Akanko Ainu Theater "Ikor" started in March, 2019 at the Spa town of Akanko Onsen beside Lake Akan. Describing the extermination of wolves, which the Ainu people traditionally worshipped as *kamuy,* under a protective policy for livestock industry by the Meiji government, this drama shows the importance of coexistence with nature. Toko Shūsei, a stage director of Ikor, combines traditional Ainu dance with the motion of the wolf projected by computer graphics technology.

As Yūki Kōji and Toko Shūsei demonstrate, it is just as important to create new stories for the modern era as well as retaining the old traditions. Creating a new story proves the vital and creative capacities of Indigenous Peoples. Likewise, such media allows for opportunities to revive the power of their native language.

Ainu people have lost a great deal historically at the hands of colonialism, and it will take a great effort to reinstill identity, pride, and culture. It is therefore imperative that their efforts for revitalization are carried out with the compensatory support and solidarity by the Japanese government and people.

Siratcise; **Trace of Ainu Hunters**

Slashing through bamboo grass as tall as a person, one finds a *nusa*, an Ainu style altar with *inaw* below the precipice. This place, along with Izari River in Eniwa is called by Ainu hunters as Honryū no Siratcise. "*Siratcise*" means a house made of rock used for a hunting basecamp. It was a convenient place for hunters in the past, primarily because it provides shelter from the wind, snow, and rain. Water could be gathered from Izari River nearby. At least five *siratcise* are known along this river system.

These basecamps are located at the halfway point between Eniwa town and the neighbouring mountain region. When hunters were blessed to receive a bear, they could thus carry the body to one of these basecamps in order to perform the ritual called *hopunire*.[2]

One scene of animation film *The Fox of Shichigorō-stream*
©tane project/Koji Yuki

and featured a dialogue entirely in the Ainu language with both Japanese and English subtitles. Following the format of traditional Ainu tales, the story is narrated in the first person by the god of the fox:

> As humans continued throwing away waste, all living thing disappeared from the polluted stream, where my kindred have lived for a long time. It has become more difficult to look for food for my children here, so I walked into the human town. A mouse ridiculed me, saying, "You are all skin and bones! It must be impossible for you to catch me with your skinny body. Your kindred will die out sooner or later." The mouse himself had become so fat from eating so much human scrap. As a result, I was able to catch him. Though I could find food, I couldn't adapt to the urban environment. I returned to my familiar stream, but there was no room to survive. I have made up my mind to leave my home stream once more.

In many of the Ainu traditions, including those introduced in this manuscript, humans and gods finally restored peaceful relations. Stories which were created in the past, when humans lived harmoniously with nature, came to conclude in harmony with wild animals as well. On the contrary, modern society has created a scale of environmental destruction that is dependent on the organization of the opportunities and systems in place, and it is especially important to consider the environmental conditions that can fully support the cultivation of Ainu culture.

Other languages have seen the endangerment now faced by the Ainu language and have been successful in realizing revitalization. The Maori language, for instance, was estimated in the 1980s to be subject to a rapid extinction. In 1987, however, the government of New Zealand enacted the Maori Language Act designating the mother tongue of the Maori as an official language. It also contributed to the introduction of the *Kōhanga Reo* ("Language Nest") Program. In this program, Maori children have supported immersion in their language and culture from infancy and continuing into their school years. Maori have also developed their own indigenous language pedagogy called *Te Ataarangi*, which has been instrumental in elevating the status of Maori language. Likewise, the Sami people of northern Europe have seen success in reviving their languages from the near brink of extinction with similar methodologies. Like New Zealand, these measures were carried out with support and solidarity from the government and their passing of pertinent language acts.

Some language instructors have adopted the measures of these other languages to suit the Ainu. Sekine Kenji, a teacher at the Nibutani Ainu language course, visited New Zealand with his wife, Maki in order to learn the *Te Ataarangi* method and integrate it into his own classrooms.

Kayano Shirō, son of Kayano Shigeru-Ekasi, is a contributing writer to the newspaper *The Ainu Times*, and has written articles in Ainu language multiple times a year since 1997. He also sponsors FM Pipaus, a mini FM radio station in Nibutani which features programs in the Ainu language. These individual efforts are instrumental to the success of the revitalization movement, though as was demonstrated in the cases above, support from the prefectural and federal Japanese governments is also required to ensure the vitality of the Ainu language.

Yūki Kōji, a son of Yūki Shōji, wrote a modern story of the gods titled *Shichigorō-sawa no Kitsune* (J: The Fox of Shichigorō-stream). His story was adapted into an animation film and screened at the Sapporo International Short Film Festival in 2015. It was the first movie based on a tale of the gods,

Young and upcoming Ainu talent is supported today by several platforms. Each year since 1997, for example, there has been an Ainu language speech contest called Itak An Ro (A: "Let's Speak!"). The event provides particular motivation for young Ainu including children to learn their language. The event also has a competition for adults, which consists of two categories: oral traditions and speech.

Furthermore, the Foundation for Research and Promotion of Ainu Culture (present-day the Foundation for Ainu Culture) initiated a training program in 2008 with the goal of developing the cultural skills of heirs of Ainu culture and encouraging the performing arts. Motivated young Ainu who take part in the program rigorously learn traditional handcraft, language, performance, and ritual manners for three years under the instruction of curators and staff from the Ainu Museum in Shiraoi.

Sapporo University has also established the Urespa Scholarship in 2010 to financially support young Ainu students. Supported students are taken into the school's Urespa club, which focuses on semiweekly culture and language courses and various Ainu rituals and festivals in diverse locations.

An Endangered Language

UNESCO, having recognized the precarious situation of the Ainu language, classified it as "critically endangered" in 2009. It is currently estimated that small number of Ainu people are able to speak their language, and Ainu language in daily and family life has practically disappeared. The history of assimilationist and prohibitionist policies regarding Ainu language and culture were undoubtedly the driving force of this trend. Despite the Act for the Promotion and Protection of Ainu Culture having been enacted in 1997, the number of Ainu speakers has not noticeably increased in the years since.

On the other hand, a large amount of written and audio records of Ainu traditions have been accumulated. Such documents are open to any person, and therefore the circumstances surrounding the access to studying the Ainu language and worldview have been enhanced. Many young people, motivated and supported by the above programs, particularly aspire to cultivate the Ainu language as a mother tongue once more. Future revitalization efforts are

This song has been performed by the sister duo, Kapiw & Apappo[1] consisting of Toko Emi and Gō'ukon Fukiko from Lake Akan in Kushiro. In the song, the mother singing is the *eauwa*, a duck who expresses her difficulties in rearing her children. The song was recited as the final piece in a concert in Kushio held in August 2011 six months after the Great East Japan Earthquake accompanied destructive tsunami. Kushiro was also damaged by tsunami and horrible scenery still remained in actuality and peoples' minds.

Resonant within the song is the life stories of the women forming the musical duo, who were the subjects of a documentary film titled: *Kapiw and Apappo: A Story of Ainu Sisters* by Satō Takayuki. The duo formed in the aftermath of the 2011 earthquake when Emi, who had been living with her children in the Tokyo area, fled to Lake Akan out of fears of the radioactive pollution resulting from the nuclear accident at Fukushima. Once Emi returned to Lake Akan, where she herself had grown up, she and Fukiko created Kapiw & Apappo. The above song was featured in the finale of the film, embodying the stories of struggle and action to be taken by mothers looking after their children. The premiere of the film was accompanied by a Kapiw & Apappo concert in April 2017, both of which were sold out. Such success, demand, and high praise of Ainu-based music and film would have surely been inconceivable in years prior.

Kapiw & Apappo is just one of a host of Ainu artistic endeavors that have received much acclaim. Other Ainu musicians, such as MAREWREW (Ainu language for butterfly) and the Ainu Art Project led by Yūki Kōji have reconfigured traditional Ainu art and have brought much esteem in the process. Other well-known groups include Imeruat (Ainu language for lightning) and the internationally-acclaimed OKI DUB AINU BAND, both of which through their progressive and creative performances, have challenged the stagnated notions of Ainu culture.

Modern Ainu culture has likewise breached international boundaries. In March 2017, an Ainu performance-based event called *Ainu Meet Somalian* attracted a significant audience. The performers were Ainu of the younger generation, who shared songs, oral traditions, dance, and traditional instruments such as the *mukkur* in an effort to raise relief funds for Somali people struck by famine.

Part2 Chapter3

Ainu Culture Lives On

Despite the immense difficulties the Ainu have faced historically, they have still handed down songs, stories, dances, and rituals that live on and grow through the present time.

ee ei eauwa	ee ei eauwa
ee ei eauwa	ee ei eauwa
nempak po e-kor ya?	How many children do you have?
re po ku-kor ne.	I have three children.
nekon e-iki wa e-ipere?	How do you provide food for your children?
ku-ikka wa ku-ipere.	I steal food to feed them.
ee ei eauwa	ee ei eauwa
ee ei eauwa	ee ei eauwa
nekon e-iki wa e-imire?	How do you provide clothes for your children?
ku-ikka wa ku-imire.	I steal clothes to dress them.

Concert of Kapiw & Apappo at a cafe "This Is" in Kushiro in August 2011.
Gō'ukon Fukiko (right) and Toko Emi ©2016 office+studio T.P.S

with a promise to receive 50 yen for an annual salary.[16]

Despite the 12 year-old boy's determination to earn money for curing his adoptive mother by himself, Iso Toshi died within a year after he started working as an apprentice.

Anecdotes also showing the considerateness of Ainu people during World War II have been collected from place to place. A considerable number of Korean workers who ran away from harsh labour in the coal mines and the mining industry sought respite in houses having a thatched roof. Thatched roofs were symbolic of the housing style of the Ainu, who were ready to help them in hiding or escaping from the authorities. Testimonies of such hidden rescue operations were published in 2017.[17]

Such cases should be memorized by *Wajin*, because this kind of generosity seems to be uncommon in the rearing of children of those who belonged to the majority and stood on the side of discrimination.

of houses where Ainu families lived.

Yae Seijirō-Ekasi's real father and mother were one of such families, in which *Wajin* parents decided to put out their three children to Ainu families in 1924 when Seijirō-Ekasi was a new-born baby. Declaring himself as an Ainu, Seijirō-Ekasi officiated Ainu rituals in the Kushiro area in the latter half of his life. He recorded the details in his autobiography issued around 1976 when he was in his 50s.

> My real parents are from Aomori Prefecture. I don't know why, but they returned to Aomori Prefecture leaving three children behind. I was taken over by Iso Toshi, an Ainu woman in Shiranuka. I've heard that my adoptive mother chewed rice which she then fed me every day. Owing to this woman, I was able to grow up and become independent.
>
> In my childhood, people were plagued by shortages of food. So, I imagine how much pain she took to raise me. One day, she told me with tears that she was refused to buy milk for me because of the reason that she was Ainu. Being unable to understand this kind of situation, I went to town to buy milk with my adoptive mother when I was eight years old. We were told again, "I don't sell to Ainu." I asked myself the question why Ainu were discriminated against so severely. Nonetheless, I was happy living with a woman having a good personality.
>
> I started going to the Shiranuka Primary School when I was eight. There were 80 pupils and most of them were Ainu. We made good friends, but children of *Wajin* ambushed me on my way back home and bullied me. The school was 6 kilometers away from my home. I was thrown into a river and my textbooks and notebooks became useless. Sometimes I could not get to the school. I asked my mother why I had been bullied. She replied, "Because you are Ainu. You must not be defeated by bullying and must keep going to the school." I cannot forget those sad days. My adoptive mother fell sick when I was 12 years old. As she didn't have any money to purchase medicines, I started working as an apprentice in the Tokachi area

Shizue-Fuci, now living in the Tokyo metropolitan area. Originally born in Urakawa, Ukaji-Fuci had moved to Tokyo in her 20s, where, through the readers' column of a newspaper, she called upon fellow Ainu living in the Metropolitan area to join in solidarity. Her action triggered the formation of the Tokyo Utari-kai (An association of Ainu living around the Tokyo metropolitan area).[14] In 2014, not only Ainu people, but also citizens and intellectuals followed her action in criticizing Kaneko's highly discriminatory utterance. Though these unified efforts could not bring Kaneko to withdraw his utterance, he was defeated in the next Sapporo City Assembly election. Many Sapporo citizens thus demonstrated their intolerance for discrimination.[15]

Especially, those who take sides with ethnic discrimination should know the following anecdote about Ainu people adopting children left behind by *Wajin* parents.

Ever since the Meiji Restoration in 1868, a large number of *Wajin* have migrated to Hokkaido. Many of them could not withstand the severe circumstances and returned to their homeland, leaving their children behind in Hokkaido. In many cases, the families who undertook the role of taking care of these children were Ainu. The characteristic behavior of Ainu people not to desert abandoned children was well-known, even to newcomers. In the case that it was unavoidable for homesteaders to leave their children behind, they used to rely on their Ainu acquaintances or just left their babies in front

Yae Seijirō-Ekasi prays at Furusato Matsuri (Village Festival) in Shiranuka in 2002 (Photograph by Ōishi Yoshikatsu)

In one respect, Kayano-Ekasi and Kaizawa were able to claim the illegality of the compulsory acquisition of land which was carried out by the Hokkaido Expropriation Committee. Furthermore, they demonstrated the cultural significance of the Saru River to the local Ainu, referencing the importance of rituals like *cipsanke*[13] which occurred on the river. The latter claim was supported by a right to enjoy culture, which was formulated in line with Article 13 of the Japanese Constitution and Article 27 of International Covenant on Civil and Political Rights (ICCPR).

The District Court ruled in favor Kayano-Ekasi and Kaizawa, stating that the compulsory acquisition of their land under the construction of the dam was illegal on the basis of Article 13 of the Japanese Constitution and Article 27 of the ICCPR. It is notable that the ruling resulted in the first time an official entity in Japan articulated the Ainu as an Indigenous people. These principles were reinforced in 2007 with Japan's vote in favor of the United Nations Declaration on the Rights of Indigenous Peoples. However, despite the Nibutani dam having been ruled as an illegal project, the construction had finished by the time the court case was concluded, and the dam was permitted to continue its operation.

"As Ainu People do not Desert Abandoned Children…"

The Ainu elders' struggle for acquiring Indigenous rights have proceeded gradually, however, their activities still cannot succeed in eradicating discrimination and prejudice. Hate speech and salient racism still manifest in Japanese society.

For instance, in summer, 2014, Kaneko Yasuyuki, a member of the Sapporo City Assembly, tweeted, "The Ainu people do not exist anymore." In responding to an interview by the Hokkaido Shimbun, a daily newspaper, Kaneko argued, "They (The Ainu) enjoy favorable treatment as a minority. It is wrong to favor them because of their being a minority. They are the same Japanese." Kaneko not only insisted that the Ainu people do not exist, but also fortified his stance that spending budget specifically on the Ainu was irrelevant and inappropriate.

One of the persons who cried out against Kaneko's utterance was Ukaji

the Rights of Indigenous Peoples has been cited in the protests against the Shiraoi plans to declare that the consolidated memorial storage infringes on the rights of the Ainu people.[12]

The Nibutani Dam Case as a Significant Ruling for Ainu People

Perhaps the most notable legal battle for the Ainu people is that surrounding the events of the construction of the Nibutani Dam, in the Nibutani district of Biratori, which has the densest population of Ainu anywhere. The process of constructing the dam was originally tied to the development of Tomatō, the East-Tomakomai industrial area, though the purpose of the dam changed throughout the planning process from taking water for industrial use to multi purpose including flood control, irrigation and hydroelectric power. Following protest by local residents in other communities, the Government ultimately settled to construct the dam on the Saru River in Nibutani. Development included the expropriation of land by Nibutani residents, which was met by protest from Kayano Shigeru-Ekasi and another local Ainu leader, Kaizawa Tadashi (later succeeded by his son, Kōichi). Kayano-Ekasi and Kaizawa Kōichi filed a lawsuit in 1993 which would become a hallmark case for the Ainu and their rights in Japan.

Kayano Shigeru-Ekasi (center) and Kaizawa Kōichi (right) at press conference after ruling of Nibutani Dam case. Left side is Tanaka Hiroshi, a lawyer spoke for plaintiff. (Photograph provided by Kayano Reiko)

Sakhalin and the Kuril Islands. As a result, the University has been the main recipient of protests and legal action by Ainu activists. Ogawa Ryūkichi-Ekasi and Jōnoguchi Yuri-Fuci are two such activists, who initiated negotiations on the repatriation of Ainu remains beginning in 2011. They repeatedly requested to meet with the president of Hokkaido University, only to be met with continuous postponements.

They filed a lawsuit against Hokkaido University at the Sapporo District Court in September 2012. The Japanese government issued the first guideline for repatriation of Ainu remains two years later in 2014. This guideline seemed to work against the plaintiffs, because it restricted claimants of Ainu remains only to direct descendants. Nevertheless, researchers of Hokkaido University had not recorded the names of each remains except for several rare cases. This meant that the chance for applications was eliminated from the start for most eligible persons. Consequently, based on this guideline, not only most of the descendants, but also members of the local Ainu community could not collectively apply for repatriation of their ancestors' remains. As the Ainu burial and memorial services have traditionally been performed as a community unit, Ogawa-Ekasi and Jōnoguchi-Fuci demanded the remains be returned to the entire local community and this point became a focus of this case.

With this logic, plaintiffs were met with a measure of success as the University was required to return the remains of 12 Ainu ancestors in March 2016. The remains were finally reburied in their homeland of Urakawa in July 2016. The Urakawa case thereafter inspired new lawsuits to arise in several places throughout Hokkaido.[10]

In infrastructural and tourism-based marketing strategies associated with the 2020 Tokyo Olympic and Paralympic Games, the Japanese government is carrying out projects in Hokkaido affecting the Ainu community. One such project is the construction of the National Ainu museum in the town of Shiraoi.[11] By 2020, the government has planned to build one large mausoleum in the complex, which would consolidate all of the Ainu remains being held throughout the country. This move on the part of the government has likewise been met with protest by Ainu communities who have been calling for the return of remains to their native villages. The United Nations Declaration on

Ainu Ancestors Held in Research Institutions

Many Ainu elders have rallied around another central movement regarding the repatriation of ancestral remains, a large number of which still remain in the possession of research institutions around Japan. Researchers desired to determine "From which race did Ainu people stem, Caucasoid or Mongoloid?" The supposed race of the Ainu has long been a research topic amongst physical anthropologists and anatomists, with inquiries dating back to the colonial era of the 19th century. Researchers in both Japan and abroad have been eager to collect the remains of Ainu individuals to pursue their investigations. Often, Ainu cemeteries were excavated without free, prior, and informed consent on behalf of local Ainu residents. At the time of writing, there are approximately 1600 remains still held within several institutions, including Hokkaido University, Tokyo University, Kyoto University, in addition to thirteen museums.

Reburial of Ainu remains got back from Hokkaido University at Kineusu cemetery in Urakawa on 17 July 2016. (Photograph by Hirata Tsuyoshi)

Hokkaido University remains as the largest incubator of the remains amongst all of the known institutions having around 1000 remains, presumably due to its location in Ainu territory and proximity to other Ainu areas such as

Throughout the ordeal, he recalled the abuses felt by his community as a result of fisheries labour in the feudal era and the Japanese settlement in the area, detailing the deprivation brought unto the Monbetsu Ainu. "There was an Ainu Kotan consisting of 17-18 houses around here. It was *Wajin* who disrupted our community. Having learned about the Ainu past, I know that we had an unforgettable history. Our ancestors, especially young men, were transported away for forced labour with a fate to never come back home. Women were sexually abused and they were compelled to drink a kind of medicine for abortion when they became pregnant. Only old men and old women were left in the villages. Regardless of gender, our ancestors were treated like slaves. It was a story my ancestors only back just three or four generations ago experienced. When I think about this kind of history, I can not help feeling vexation against *Wajin*. Your ancestors deprived us of land, of livelihood. We were robbed of everything. Our ancestors have lived here by catching salmon. Is there anything wrong with recreating such a life of our ancestors? Now the Japanese Government certified Ainu as an Indigenous people and I am one of them, an Indigenous man of the world. So, I have a right of self-determination authorized worldwide. I do so on the basis of this right. What you do now is a regression against the trends of the world."[9]

In the provocation, Hatakeyama-Ekasi mentioned that he would not oppose his arrest, presumably to bring light to the archaic policies to which his fishing activities are subject. He voiced his stance that the Japanese laws were incredibly one-sided and functioned to limit the Ainu from engaging in their traditional ways of living.

He also insisted, "If you respect laws, why don't you revise the law. More than ten years have passed since the United Nations adopted the Declaration on the Rights of Indigenous Peoples. Moreover the United Nations' Committee on the Elimination of Racial Discrimination recently put forth a recommendation to the Japanese government on the status of the Ainu people. You should reflect on them."

Ultimately, he was prevented from lowering his canoe into the river. The Monbetsu Ainu Association, thus, was forced to perform the ritual with fish voluntarily offered by a Japanese angler, which had been caught legally from the ocean nearby.

These limitations have continued up to the present day. Additionally, fishing requires a process of approval from the prefectural government, by way of an application in which the individual must include their name, intended location and time of fishing, and anticipated number of fish to be caught. However, these barriers to freely fish have been met with protest as they are seen to infringe upon the Ainu's rights as Indigenous Peoples to engage and manage the resources in their native territories.

One such protest was demonstrated by Hatakeyama Satoshi-Ekasi, an Ainu elder and chairman of the Monbetsu Ainu Association in northern Hokkaido. In August 2018, Hatakeyama-Ekasi set out with his handmade dugout canoe, intending to catch salmon in the Mobetsu River for the ritual to receive the first salmon. Hatakeyama-Ekasi deliberately avoided taking the measures to obtain prior permission for fishing. As he attempted to load his canoe into the river, he was stopped by a dozen policemen who obstructed his entrance into the river. The policemen insisted that he follow the legal protocol and apply for permission, though Hatakeyama-Ekasi persisted in his resistance.

Hatakeyama Satoshi-Ekasi (center) is obstructed salmon fishing for ritual by policemen at Mobetsu River in 2018. (Photograph by Kosaka Yousuke)

allowance of the group to catch salmon. The stipulation was phrased by the government as "special catching" and only allowed the Ainu to catch salmon in relation to rituals and succession of traditional technique. A formal measure of the stipulation was adopted in 1987. The success of the restoration of *asircepnomi* in Sapporo sparked other movements elsewhere, including in the communities of Chitose, Asahikawa, and Shiraoi (among others). Toyokawa-Ekasi envisioned a future where salmon fishing would be permitted to the Ainu for subsistence and consumption grounded on the rights of Indigenous people. However, the government has persisted in its limitations to salmon fishing as being strictly tied to Ainu ritual activities.

Kuzuno Tatsujirō-Ekasi prays to gods at *asircepnomi* in Sapporo on 15 September 1993. (Photograph by Kosaka Yousuke)

Restoration of Ritual to Receive the First Salmon

In the Ainu language, salmon is referred to *sipe, siepe* translating to "primary food," or *kamuycep*, "the fish gifted by the gods." Clearly, salmon is a central component to Ainu culture and subsistence. In the early 1980s, a movement to restore the traditional rituals surrounding the return of salmon upstream gained momentum. The ritual, called *asircepnomi*,[6] faded as a result of the prohibitive measures and regulations of the Meiji colonial policy. In 1982 however, the first *asircepnomi* was held at the Toyohira River, a tributary of Ishikari River in Sapporo in over 100 years.

Toyokawa Shigeo-Ekasi fishes salmon for *asircepnomi* in 1987
(Reprinted from *Asircepnomi 30 nen no Ayumi*)

The propagator of the revival was the Sapporo Ainu Culture Association and included the core members of Toyokawa Shigeo-Ekasi[7] and Yūki Shōji,[8] then a representative of the Union for Liberation of the Ainu. Toyokawa-Ekasi's ancestors stemmed from Kotoni Kotan along Kotoni River system, one of four villages in central Sapporo which disappeared as a result of the historic fishing bans.

In the initial stages of their restoration movement, the Sapporo Ainu Culture Association was not permitted to actually catch salmon in the river but rather had to purchase salmon from a market. However, Toyokawa-Ekasi persistently negotiated with the Hokkaido prefectural government, resulting the eventual

crisis of existence.

In 1882, Uchimura Kanzō was dispatched to the Chitose River region by the Sapporo Prefectural Government, the successor to the Hokkaido Colonial Commission, with the task of considering effective countermeasures against salmon poaching. Having investigated the real situation of the Ainu under the new regulation, however, Uchimura bravely proposed, from a humanitarian perspective, that the authorities generously overlook the activities of the Ainu poachers.

He advised, "If the government enhanced monitoring of poachers, this policy would cause starvation to death of the Ainu."[4] Moreover, he appealed that what the government should prioritize was protection of the spawning grounds in the upper reaches of the Chitose River, while making the Ainu catch salmon downriver, at a location which would not endanger the spawning grounds. Colleagues of his division who were for encouraging industry made an effort to realize his proposal; however, those in high places were averse to changing established policy. Probably, the bigoted atmosphere of the upper officers made him feel alienated; Uchimura left the office of Sapporo prefecture.

Additionally, massive fatalities of deer caused by heavy snow did harm to the life of the Ainu people, especially in the Tokachi area. Having received word of their plight, Sapporo Prefecture dispatched Togano Yonakichi there in 1884 to survey actual conditions. Togano reported, "The severest period was the last winter. According to Ainu, more than 10 persons died. I could not determine whether death was caused by starvation or not. In order to stave off hunger, they boiled bare deer bones and sipped the hot water. After they had eaten all remaining scraps of deer skin and salmon skin, they searched for shellfish in frozen ponds and collected mistletoe on trees to eat."[5]

Although Togano carefully avoided pinpointing the reason for death as shortage of food, under these circumstances it is difficult to assume other causes than starvation. Nevertheless, the government did not slacken the prohibition policy nor the monitoring of poachers. Consequently, this policy provoked some Ainu into poaching for a living. The arrest of Kayano-Ekasi's father was an extension of those lines.

Kayano-Ekasi suggested that his father was just one of many men who were arrested at the helm of Japanese policy, in which traditional activities of the Ainu were conflated with theft. Such a mindset reflects the Japanese impression that they had come to own the land of Hokkaido. As Kayano pointedly wrote, however, "It is our common understanding that we have neither sold nor rented Ainu Mosir to the country of Japan."[2]

"This Policy Would Cause Starvation to Death of the Ainu"

The first regulation on catching salmon in Hokkaido rivers was issued in 1876 by the Hokkaido Colonial Commission, prohibiting night fishing and the *tes* net system of lining stakes across a river to make the salmon linger below. Despite the fact that particular groups of persons were not specified in the regulation, this policy would unavoidably have caused serious damage to the Ainu lifestyle because these had been Ainu traditional styles of fishing.

In the decision-making process leading up to implementation, the Sapporo head office of the Hokkaido Colonial Commission indicated reluctance, insisting, "The Ainu of Chitose County live in a mountainous region, so will be difficult for them to subside other than through the fishing of salmon." In contrast to this suggestion by the head office that the regulation would be too severe on native residents, the Tokyo office, which wielded actual authority, adhered to a prohibition policy and replied, "When one takes gains and losses into account totally, damage for the minority can be ignored. It may be possible to induce them to be farmers."[3] This stance of the Tokyo office to convert hunter-gatherers to farmers and to ignore the wellbeing of the minority is nothing other than assimilationism.

Two years later, in 1878, the Colonial Commission strengthened the regulation to prohibit harvesting of salmon and trout in all river tributaries in Hokkaido. Only trawling in main streams and estuaries were permitted, an amendment which can be regarded as an incentive to commercial fishermen and Japanese settlers having the resources to secure fishing nets and manpower. On the contrary, for most Ainu, who lived along secondary waterways such as the Chitose River and the Kotoni River, tributaries of the main Ishikari River in central Hokkaido, the new regulations brought about a

Part 2 Chapter 2

Struggles Towards the Future

As Indigenous Peoples in diverse areas may share commonalities of culture on a basis of hunter-gathering lifestyles and in some regions reindeer herding or fishing-based lifestyles, they too share the burdens of human rights violations on behalf of states that do not fully recognize their rights as Indigenous inhabitants in their territories.

Kayano Shigeru-Ekasi, referenced in the second and fifth chapters of part1, profoundly captured the detriment brought to the Ainu communities by the settlement of the *Wajin*, persisting through his childhood in the 20th century. In his memoir, he detailed the picture of his father crying, despite having lost one of his eyes. This resulted from the intrusion of the police into his household and the subsequent arrest of his father. His father was arrested on a count of fishing salmon, which the Japanese authorities charged as a 'theft' of the fish.[1]

Fishing was an activity perpetually risked by his father despite the strict regulations and legal consequences. His father would distribute the fish for elders of the village and likewise caught fish ceremoniously for the gods. However, salmon fishing in river had been prohibited by the government and thus once his activities were revealed they amounted to arrest.

An exhausted salmon in upper reach of Chitose River in January. (Photograph by Kosaka Yousuke)

In fact, such stories populate lands around the world and are maintained today by Indigenous communities, many of whom still stress the importance of human relationships with the creatures and phenomena surrounding them. The fact that such stories occur so frequently across globe, from Eurasia to the Americas and Southeast Asia, points to a shared common heritage in a hunter-gatherer lifestyle.

In the span of all human history, hunting and gathering practices account for 99% of lifestyle activity over time.[10] For the vast majority of our shared human existence, peoples around the world have engaged in lifestyles embodying an ecological mindset.

We now live in an age when ecological and human security is being compromised as a result of the extraction and exploitation of nature and its resources. Such trends plaguing the modern era are in direct contrast to the balanced relationship with nature emphasized by Indigenous communities, often through their stories. It is perhaps imperative for humankind to reshift our gaze towards the values that have been cultivated out of thousands of years of common relation to nature. We can do so by welcoming the stories of the Ainu and other Indigenous communities, and paying heed to their insightful guidance.

Alaska Peninsula. During our five-week stay in the wilderness, wild animals such as brown bear, fox, seals, ermines, porcupines, and caribou (reindeer) occasionally appeared. We supposed the first appearance of humans in this place dates back to around 2200 BCE. Living in the wilderness, we could vividly imagine the environments and life of hunter-gatherers settled here more than 4,000 years ago.

Excavation at the Hot Spring ruins in Alaska Peninsula in 1984.
(Photograph by Kosaka Yousuke)

approaching the village of bears. She reckoned that her brother must have been searching for her, taking along his dog and neighbors. Upon realizing the imminent arrival of the humans, the bears held a village meeting. They ruled it necessary to eject the woman and her family in order to evade conflict with the approaching humans. Her family fled to a cave, where they were to be found by the woman's brother the next day. Before they were caught, her husband whispered to her:

"I will soon die. You shall return to the human village and establish a clan of bears to bridge our worlds together."

The following morning, her husband went out of the cave and was killed by men. The young woman was thus returned to the village where she was born. The children she bore with the bear could not forget their home in the woods, and eventually they left the human village. The young woman remarried sometime later with a human and bore more children. She and her descendants have become the clan of the bear.[9]

The Tlingit tale clearly resembles the themes of human and non-human relationships so prominent in the Ainu stories. In 1984, while participating in an archaeological and cultural anthropological expedition to Alaska organized by specialists from Hokkaido University and Meiji University, I found similar flora and fauna to those of Hokkaido around the Hot Spring ruins in the

A porcupine walking around Hot Spring ruins in Alaska Peninsula.
(Photograph by Kosaka Yousuke)

not have an elder male to perform the prayer service, and so they had to ask another local elder to come to their *nusa*. The elder ultimately decided that it was becoming too difficult to perform *kamuynomi* and ruled that the *nusa* should be closed. By invalidating the *nusa*, the elder claimed, they would avoid the detriment that would come with allowing it to decay without proper care.[8]

The story of Uchiumi-Ekasi is one of many that catalogs the devastation faced by many Ainu communities driven to abandon their ritualistic activity as a direct result of the pressures of assimilation. Relationships with the spiritual world were increasingly severed as it became more difficult to maintain the necessary resources and practices to engage with the gods. Central tenants of Ainu culture, such as prayer and hunting, were essential to maintaining a certain worldview. When many Ainu were faced with disruptions to their places and customs, their traditions ultimately were compromised.

Traditions Shared Across Continents

The values central to traditional Ainu ways of living find counterparts in communities around the world. Common themes of human and non-human relationships and engaged attunement to the environment live on in the stories and beliefs of many people. One such Tlingit folktale, hailing from modern-day Alaska, bears stark similarities to the stories of the Ainu explored in this plot:

One day in autumn, a young woman stepped into the forest to collect berries. On her walk, she slipped on the dung left by a bear. She cursed such bad luck brought to her by a bear. A male bear who wandered nearby became angry upon hearing her words. The bear captured the young woman and took her to live in his village deep in the woods.

The young woman, after living in the world of bears, came to have a great affinity for the animals. She ultimately married the bear who brought her to the village. Together, they had two babies.

One day, she heard the familiar barking of a dog, seeming

names, it means, actual existing place names are 6 or 7 times more than the number listed in Takeshirō's record. A researcher, Akiba Minoru, found 8,000 Ainu place names, when he tallied all of the place names in Takeshirō's diaries. So, in actuality, there exist around 48,000 place names in total all over Hokkaido. What is the significance of this? Referring to Hokkaido as Ainu Mosir, the Ainu people have lived in comfort on our own land. Numerous Ainu place names are evidence (of our presence). I still believe Hokkaido is the land of the Ainu people.[6]

Clearly, environmental knowledge is richly inscribed into the local landscape and a familiarity with the land has been essential to social, ecological, and spiritual orientation. To be separated from the *kotan*, from these places of deeply embedded knowledge, is to be disassociated from the primary locus of cosmic order. Even for those Ainu who were able to stay within their native *kotan*, the assimilative pressure of the Japanese has gradually transformed the character of potency of daily ritual, and in many cases these practices have become obsolete.

Fuchise Kazuo is one Ainu who can recall the detrimental effects of assimilation policy on his spirituality and custom. Born in Hidaka area in 1920, he was resettled in Nukabira in the Tokachi area. At age 19, he had hunted his first bear. He stated that his parents were able to return the soul of a bear by calling the names of the gods. By the time he caught his own bear, however, he did not know how to properly pray to the gods. In that moment, the older hunters in the group gathered and shared a prayer stating that they would thereafter adopt a way more reminiscent of *sisampuri* (A: the Japanese style) to pray to the Universe instead of praying to gods.[7]

Prayers traditionally occurred inside and outside the home. The goddess, or two gods of fire would have prayers devoted inside while other gods would be communicated to through a *nusa* located outside. It was the case for many families, however, that some decided to discontinue such practices as they declined between generations.

Uchiumi Ken'ichi-Ekasi is one elder who recalls the end of ritual practice amongst his family in Shizunai (present-day Shin-Hidaka). His family did

to settle at Husko Kotan where Sunazawa-Ekasi was born.

One must consider the effect such migration must have on peoples indigenous to a land. For the Ainu, the *kotan* was not only the setting for daily life, but also the unit of ritual and social order. As residents were driven out of *kotan*, the rituals and ceremonies endemic to the Ainu lifestyle faced decline. With these trends also came a decline in a shared sense of place, as the *kotan* and surrounding area were steeped with meaning and cultural significance. The topography of an Ainu person's native place was constituted by elements stemming from generations of traditional knowledge and ritual. Traditionally elders would worship the *kamuy* at *nusa* (A: altar)[5] placed outside of each home with certain number of *inaw*.

Near *kotan* are *cinomisir*, sites where *kamuy* would communicate potential danger to villagers. The places refer to as *iwor* are the areas in which wild plants would be gathered and animals hunted. Other place names hold significant meanings, and could indicate the occurrence of specific activities and the knowledge embedded in that site. Notable examples include the *ican*, or spawning spots for salmon; the *oyaus*, the places to lay nets; *mem*, or spring locales; *wensir* or *weysir* indicate cliffs that are too steep for pathways; and *harusnai* have been fields particularly abundant with wild plants.

I remember Kayano Shigeru-Ekasi stressing, in his statement against compulsory acquisition of his property by the Hokkaido Expropriation Committee in 1988, how important it was for the Ainu to live by maintaining a keen connection to the land. Kayano-Ekashi, recounting all Ainu place names existing on both sides of the Saru River in the Nibutani region, including the area scheduled to be submerged by the Nibutani Dam, summarized that there were 72 Ainu place names on both banks.

> The reason why Ainu have named each location precisely is clear. Because we have been hunter-gatherers, when we succeeded in hunting a deer or bear, we sometimes have made our family carry the meat from the mountain. In such cases, if we cannot point to the place, our family members cannot retrieve the meat.
>
> Matsu'ura Takeshirō recorded 10 Ainu place names here in Nibutani 130 years ago. Now, if I can enumerate more than 70 place

Sustaining Relationships Between Humans, Non-Humans, and the Land

> Our land, Hokkaido,[3]
> our Ishikari River, going up the middle of the land,
> I am a man, from Sorachi,
> in the midstream of our Ishikari River
> I am Tomo-Ainu, a long time resident of Sorachi.
>
> Upstream on the Ishikari River lives my elder brother, Kansatoku-*Nispa* (A: honorific title to respected, wealthy man).
> Many *sisam* are working in the garden, the garden belonging to the god of water and beside the great god of the mountain.
> In all of his work, my elder brother maintains his fitness and health.
> We ourselves are from this place, we are not outsiders.
> Please allow us to live a healthy life here as we pursue our works.
> Please allow our children to grow up without any trouble.
>
> Divine mountain! Together with the god of water, the god of the mountain, and the god of land! With the goddess of fire who cherishes us so! We offer you our *tonoto* and send this message.[4]

The above is a prayer by Sunazawa Tomotarō-Ekasi, the husband of Sunazawa Kura-Fuci mentioned in chapter three, recorded at *kamuynomi* (A: prayer to gods) near Asahikawa in 1964. In the prayer, he alluded to the contemporary situation of Hokkaido, in which the *sisam* have established new communities as a result of a profit-driven labour force.

Sunazawa-Ekasi grew up in the Husko Kotan in Uryu and saw the end of his life in Ashibetsu. His ancestors hailed from Otaru but were ultimately driven to Uryu by the Japanese. Following the establishment of a coal mine, however, his family was obliged to relocate to Takikawa. Upon resettlement there, a Japanese prison labour camp associated with railway construction was established, causing his family to move once more. Finally, the family came

Chiri Mutsumi (right) and her husband Yokoyama Takao stand with wooden statue of Chiri Yukie. (Photograph by Kosaka Yousuke)

aspires to give other Ainu inspiration and motivation for living out their lives with their genuine identity.

Mutsumi was well versed in the burdens facing many Ainu people. Born in 1948, her adolescence was colored by the same oppressions as many Ainu. Her parents and grandparents were hesitant to use the Ainu language at home, instead opting to learn Japanese under the pressure of the overwhelming majority society. Despite suppressing their culture, Mutsumi was still victim to heavy discrimination and bullying as a result of her Ainu identity.[2]

Mutsumi and Chiri Yukie both lived with the pressures of discrimination and oppression, but nevertheless ultimately pursued projects to realize the culture of their people. Like her great aunt, Mutsumi was also plagued with disease in the final years of her life. Though diagnosed with cancer, Mutsumi continued to work tirelessly as the director of the memorial museum, which is run as a non-profit organization. Mutsumi passed away in September 2016, six years after the opening of the museum. Like Yukie, her final years were spent devoted to the transmission of Ainu culture.

Part 2

A 10,000 Year Journey

Chapter 1

The Spirits Still Sing Today

In the Part 1, the difference of perceived distance to wild life between Ainu people and Japanese is revealed throughout the comparison of folktales. In contrast to Japanese folk tales, Ainu folk tales maintain a close relationship between humans and wildlife through to the end. Difference of livelihood, Ainu as traditional hunter-gatherers and the Japanese as rice cultivators, is in part constituted by the differences in practice contributing to worldview. Historical interaction between the two people groups dates back to at least the 15th century, however gradually the oppression and abuse of the Ainu was brought by the *Wajin*. Beginning in 1869, the Japanese reinforced control and exploitation to the Ainu systematically through governmental institutions. Facing deprivation of her language and culture, Chiri Yukie, a 19 year old Ainu girl, strived to write down the tales of Ainu gods in order to transmit them to future generations.

Though Chiri Yukie died in 1922, she once again attracted public attention on 19 September 2010 with the opening of a memorial museum in her name in her birthplace at Noboribetsu. The Chiri Yukie Silver Droplet Memorial Museum was established by her niece, Chiri-Yokoyama Mutsumi, alongside other esteemed devotees of the famed *Ainu Shin'yōshū*.

Mutsumi founded the memorial museum in order to celebrate her great-aunt's work and share her life story. Upon opening the museum, Mutsumi recalled that even though Chiri Yukie was burdened by prejudice, she still maintained her pride to live as an Ainu. "Though Yukie was annoyed by prejudice, she wrote in diary, 'I am Ainu. I am satisfied with being an Ainu. If I were a *sisam,* I would not be a warm person.' She declared to live as an Ainu in that hard times for the Ainu people. Thus, we have to transmit her biography."[1] The museum perpetuates Yukie's legacy and spirit in this way. It strive to bring hope back to her people.

Yukie finished proofreading of Ainu Shin'yōshū before her evening meal on 18 September 1922. Though she was elated with the conclusion of the project, she looked pale and unwell. Kindaichi was anxious that she had overworked herself, but Yukie assured him she had merely caught a cold. She made plans to attend the Nezu Shrine festival the following day with Kindaichi's son, Haruhiko.

That evening around eight o'clock, however, Yukie fell having succumbed to a pain in her chest. A doctor arrived to the scene, calling for Yukie to be given an injection. However, Yukie rejected such a measure as she saw it as a last resort. Soon, Yukie was met with cardiac failure. Her death was pronounced at eleven o'clock that night.

The final tragedy of Yukie's life was that she did not live to see her book published the following year in 1923.

Okamura Chiaki was an editor of *Ainu Shin'yōshū*. Through these intimate diary entries, one can become familiarized with the inner attitudes held by Yukie. Despite the narratives around her stating that she should hide or be ashamed of her Ainu identity, Yukie expressed her gratitude for the ways in which her life as an Ainu shaped her character. She wrote, "If I were a *sisam*, I would not be a warm person," expressing her doubt of the Japanese mentality to have empathy or sympathy for those in less fortunate circumstances. Because she and her people had endured hardship under discrimination and persecutions, she had been able to cultivate sympathy towards the weak. Diary entries such as these suggest her pride of the Ainu people, whose disadvantages only brought them an enhanced richness through compassion.

Though Yukie was aware of the declining situation of the Ainu, she also recognized that it was the Japanese who had lost something valuable. The Ainu way of life was vibrant, colored by regular performance of oral traditions and the dancing and singing that accompanied daily life. In the Ainu world, the surrounding landscapes were alive with the gods who offered their protection to the humans. The Ainu people shared what they hunted equally, and mutual aid has traditionally been an important factor of their social life. Though elements of their world view were becoming increasingly suppressed, such values were still intrinsic to Ainu lifestyle. In contrast, as Chiri Yukie saw it, the Japanese had lost such customs and sensitivities long ago.

Her diary also indicated her sentiments towards her supporters in Tokyo, namely Okamura Chiaki and Kindaichi Kyōsuke. Her reflections suggest that she sees the Japanese of being incapable of understanding the full extent of the dismal circumstances facing the Ainu. Yukie wrote in ways that expressed her alienation from others living around her.

The hardships she endured throughout the process of publishing her work- the burden of her cardiac disorder, the death of her dear friend- only worked to strengthen her identity as an Ainu. Much of the distress brought to her was a factor of the shameful policies on the side of the Japanese government, which deprived her Indigenous people of their own culture, language, traditional livelihoods, and ways of being. Ainu disadvantages were rooted in the inequalities perpetuated by the Japanese, but nonetheless her work would

be the result from this ordeal.

It is time of the test for us, the Ainu, too. We are passing through the most correct way of God's decree. We should not cut corners. If we dare cut corners relying solely on our intuition, we cannot avoid tumbling down a deep ravine.

Ah, ah, what a great trial! What we regard as our treasures will be robbed from all of us at some point in time.

They say, Yasuko in Asahikawa died at last. What she had got in the end, pulled around dark back street of life! In case she would linger on, she had to return to house of evil embrace.

"Death! Do me a favor, receive me!" so she wished. And then, as she desired, she died in disease. How can I hear the news without tears! Though, I have made every effort to stay calm, I cannot help my final derangement.[5]

Another diary entry dated two weeks later on 12 July 1922 reads:

I hear Ms. Okamura Chiaki worries about me, telling that when I am in Tokyo, if I keep silent, no one will recognize me as an Ainu. My contribution to the *Jogakusekai*[6] manuscript might oust me as an Ainu, which might be cause for contempt.

I have never concerned myself with what she thinks. I am an Ainu. I am an Ainu from top to toe. Nothing about me resembles a *sisam* (A: ethnic Japanese)?! Even though, I have named myself a "*sisam*" of words, I am still an Ainu. There is no significance to that. It is meaningless to be a *sisam* through lips....Is it important to be a *sisam*? As you are an Ainu, it doesn't mean you are not human. We are all humans. I am satisfied with being an Ainu. If I were a *sisam,* I would not be a warm[7] person and I would be an ignorant person living without even knowing the existence of Ainu and other miserable people. I have experienced pain and have lived full of tears. I am receiving a harsh whip in God's trial. I am receiving a whip of love. I am obliged to God for grace.[8]

them again.

The opening story to Ainu Shin'yōshū is reflective of Yukie's desire to see the well-being of her people. The protagonist of this story is the famed fish owl god who watches over the Ainu village. In the story, the god created a shower of treasures like droplets of gold and silver over a family which, although appearing to be impoverished, is actually descended from an honorable and prosperous lineage. This story is the source of Yukie's famous prose, "silver droplets falling, falling all around." Embedded within Yukie's most well-known words, then, is the hope for her people; although facing disparity in the present, the Ainu will once again revive the honor and richness they have previously known.

Death from Misfortune

While Yukie stayed at Kindaichi Kyōsuke's home in Tokyo for finishing Ainu Shin'yōshū, she heard the news of death of her close friend Yasuko, an Ainu from Asahikawa. Yasuko grew up in poverty and was sold into a brothel as a teenager. While there, she was infected with a disease, which she disclosed to Yukie in a letter. She further informed Yukie that her family still was indebted to the brothel, and so she would have to return to work as a prostitute once recovered. In her writing to Yukie, Yasuko expressed her uncertainty over which circumstance to pray for, either to remain ill and not having to work or to be healed. After receiving Yasuko's sorrowful letter, Yukie was informed of the death of her friend.[4] The news of Yasuko's death, the result of what Yukie regarded physical and mental torture, resulted in severe shock for the young girl residing in Tokyo.

Yukie recorded her indignation in a diary entry dated 29 June 1922.

> It would be sin trying to resist destiny, trying to defy power of nature. You are just a human. It may be too silly for a small, very tiny human attempting to resist God, having absolute and infinite power. Why God must inflict upon us this suffering? Ordeal! Trial!! I must train my body with flame in mind. Wash my body with tears of hot-blood gushing like fountain. Something brilliant thing must

thematic similarities with Japanese folklore is illustrative of her intention to make her culture understood by her audience.

Furthermore, Yukie was influenced greatly by Christianity as missionaries had a profound presence on Hokkaido, even within Ainu communities. Following her aunt who became a missionary herself, Yukie embraced the doctrines of the religion. Her selection of stories may have likewise been influenced by this spirituality, as many of the themes steeped in the contrast of good and evil are reminiscent of popular Christian teachings. Yukie found herself with a great responsibility to share and represent her culture through stories, and was able to effectively do so by carefully sharing her world across cultural differences.

Someday We Would Match Japanese

> In the past surely our happy ancestors never imagined for a moment that this, our homeland, would in the future be reduced to the kind of miserable state at hand.
>
> Time flows ceaselessly and the world goes on progressing endlessly. If sometime two or three strong ones should emerge from among those of us who now expose for all to see the ugliness resulting from our defeat in the arena of fierce competition, then the day will soon come when we will keep pace with the advancing world. That is our earnest hope, and what we pray for day and night…(translated by Sarah M.Strong)

This excerpt found in the introduction of *Ainu Shin'yōshū* suggests Yukie's awareness of her own role as a representative for her culture. She stresses the unitary ambitious held by her people, by which it is not she alone but the collective Ainu voice that aspires to achieve equal footing with the rest of the world. Disadvantage and privation were faced by the entire community, though through the emergence of a few distinguished individuals, the entirety of the Ainu people could once again recover their dignity. By speaking in the plural on behalf of all Ainu, her objective is not to evoke shame for the Japanese but rather to instill hope in her people that prosperity will come to

and communicate the strife the Japanese were bringing to her homeland.

Already by her teenage years, Yukie had witnessed widespread devastation to her homeland and the Ainu way of life. By the 1910s, all four of the Ainu villages located in central Sapporo (the modern day capital of Hokkaido prefecture) had already disappeared. Since 1878, the Meiji government had prohibited villagers to catch salmon in all tributaries of the Ishikari River including in Sapporo. The villagers had depended on salmon, and thus being deprived of their essential staple food, the original inhabitants of Sapporo area eventually dispersed to the estuary of the Ishikari River or to the inland city of Asahikawa, 150 kilometers upriver from their home. Around the remnants of the four villages, the Kotoni railway station, the Sapporo railway station, the Hokkaido University campus, and Odori Park came to be constructed.[3] In spite of the large scale displacement of villages like those in Sapporo, Yukie still retained a humble tone to her Japanese readership, telling them of the joy it would bring to her and her ancestors if they could read and acknowledge the Ainu stories.

Through the introduction to her writing, Yukie clearly attempted to subtly navigate the dilemma of addressing the ethnic Japanese. In composing the rest of the Ainu Shin'yōshū, Yukie chose 13 tales of the gods out of the varied and numerous Ainu oral traditions at her disposal. Once again, Yukie's awareness of the social conditions are reflected in her strategic curation of the stories found her in her book. Despite the wide cultural differences between the Ainu and the Japanese, it seems that Yukie deliberately selected stories that could easily be understood by both peoples.

Amongst her collected stories are those that feature themes and characters well-known to the Ainu. Several of the stories in *Ainu Shin'yōshū* feature Okikirmuy, a famed personified god who has interactions with other deities such as the god of the fox, the frog, or the god of hare. There are common themes throughout these selected stories, many embodying the principle of "what goes around comes around." Villains or mischievous gods are featured throughout tales and ultimately come to justice as a consequence of malicious actions. These themes are easily relatable to common Japanese folktales, which often similarly communicate the rewards of virtuous behavior and punitive outcomes for bad behavior. Yukie's curation of stories on a basis of

Yukie regarded Hokkaido as the "world of freedom in the past" and yearned for a life like her ancestors stating, "they must have been happy people." By relegating her people's sense of happiness to the past, the reader gets the impression that Ainu people in the present are now met with unhappiness in their deprivation of freedom. Yukie described her ancestors life in vivid detail, reflecting on the boundless hunting and fishing practices that were available to them. Yukie's opening remarks introduced the stark contrast of life between the Ainu of the past and the difficulties they faced in her present time. Yukie was an outstanding literary talent, and was able to weave together beautifully poetic depictions in order to convey the miserable conditions faced by her people.

A Humble Mediator Between Worlds

It is perhaps a curious fact as to why Yukie provided her introduction only in Japanese. With her abilities, she surely could have written her thoughts in Japanese and in the Ainu language. Furthermore, all of the chapters in her collection were written in both Japanese and Ainu. However, in the latter part of her introduction, she hints at her reasoning for this decision with an appeal to her readership: "If the many of you who know us could kindly read them, I, together with the ancestors of my people, would consider it a source of supreme happiness, of boundless joy" (translated by Sarah M. Strong).

Yukie was undoubtedly aware that her audience would have been primarily ethnic Japanese. Given the pressures of assimilation, the plenary power of the government, and the authoritarian attitudes to which the Ainu were subject, Yukie had to maintain a strong degree of reserve with her audience. When describing the condition of her homeland, Yukie wrote, "this land has undergone rapid change as development goes on, progressively turning mountains and fields to villages, villages to towns..." Notably, her remarks lack a subject and maintains a certain passivity when writing of the displacement of her people. In context, however, it is clear that the unacknowledged actors perpetrating the changes to her society are the Japanese and the Japanese government. Despite her young age, Yukie was able to artfully subvert the constraints put upon her in the context of assimilation

"Hokkaido was Our Ancestors' World of Freedom"

Despite a heart condition making her rather sickly and fragile, Yukie had great talent and was attuned to the social conditions surrounding the Ainu. She approached her project with a sense of imminence and worried that the valuable tales and knowledge of her Ainu language would be lost if not recorded promptly.

In addition to the tales of the gods, she wrote an introduction in Japanese expressing her own views and emotions about her people.

> In the past this spacious Hokkaido was our ancestors' world of freedom. Living with ease and pleasure in the manner of innocent babes in the embrace of beautiful, vast nature, they were truly the beloved children of nature. Oh what happy people they must have been!
>
> Inland in winter to push through the deep snow blanketing the fields and forests and, without a thought for the cold congealing heaven and earth, to cross mountain after mountain to hunt bear; on the sea in summer, to float small, leaf-shaped boats upon green waves swept by cool breezes and, with the song of the white gulls for company, to fish the whole day long; in spring when blossoms open, bathed in gentle sunlight and accompanied in song by the ceaseless chirping of birds, to gather butterbur and pick mugwort; in red-leaved fall, after pushing through the pampas grass, its plumes marshaled by the autumn gales, with the evening salmon-fishing fires extinguished, to dream beneath the round moon as outside the deer call to their mates in the valley—ah, what a pleasant life that must be! A realm of peace! But that is now a thing of the past; the dream was ruptured decades ago. This land has undergone rapid change as development goes on, progressively turning mountains and fields to villages, villages to towns…(translated by Sarah M. Strong)

People revitalized Countries
Countries declined again
Why and until when God continues tormenting us in struggle

A people, once had a large population,
has reduced to 15,000 to 16,000,
in small number
on the island of the north ocean
exists in confined places[2]

The writer of this poem was an Ainu young woman, Chiri Yukie, who published a collection of folktales about the Ainu gods' called *Ainu Shin'yōshū*, translated into English as *Ainu Spirits Singing* by Sarah M. Strong, who has published an informative book on the life and stories of Yukie by the same name. One of Yukie's phrases reading, "Silver droplets falling, falling all around" remains well known in Japan, even 97 years after her death at 19 years old.

Yukie was born in Noboribetsu in 1903 in height of enforcement of the Act and regulations towards the Ainu people. Despite the pressures of assimilation all around her, she had two teachers of Ainu language and oral traditions. Her aunt, Kan'nari Matsu and her grandmother, Monasinouku, were native speakers of Ainu. Yukie went to live with the women in Asahikawa when she was six years old and was obtained their knowledge of Ainu language and traditions. Because Yukie was required to speak Japanese at school, she became bilingual, which was something of a rarity in the time period.

One day when Yukie was 15 years old, her household was visited by Dr. Kindaichi Kyōsuke, a linguist specialized in the Ainu language. Much to his amazement, Kindaichi discovered that Yukie had an unbelievable ability to memorize long epic narratives in the Ainu language. He recommended that she join him in his home in Tokyo so that they could record the stories together. From then on, all of her energy was spent writing out the stories of the gods in the Ainu language. Remarkably, her recordings were made with the Roman alphabet and were translated into Japanese by herself in 1922.

Chiri Yukie (left) and her aunt Kan'nari Matsu (Owned by Sasaki Yutaka and deposited to Chiri Yukie Gin no Shizuku Kinenkan, provided by Chiri Shinsha)

language. A survey conducted in the 1920s concluded, "Most Ainu do not use the Ainu language and younger people hardly know it."[1]

As the assimilationist policies cast their shadows over the future of Ainu culture and language, some individuals emerged to restore the traditions threatened by the legislation of Japanization.

> When I look back at history for thousands of years
> Countries perished

Chapter 5

"Ainu Spirits Singing": A Gift from a 19 Year Old Girl

In feudal Edo period, the Matsumae Domain issued policy prohibiting the Ainu from learning to read or write in Japanese for the purpose of keeping their societal status low. In other words, the local feudal government attempted to maintain control by suppressing the abilities and opportunities available to the local population. It was in the interest of the Matsumae to keep the Indigenous population different from the settling Japanese to maintain a certain power balance. After 1855, the Edo Shogunate replaced the Matsumae Domain as the direct authority controlling Hokkaido. In contrast to the Matsumae Domain, the Shogunate introduced different policies reflective of an assimilationist stance, or the Japanization of the Ainu. Instruction was issued to change names for Ainu families, and enforced costumes and hairstyles in Japanese fashion. However, a large number of Ainu evaded or actively resisted the enforcement of these new policies.

In the modern age beginning in 1868, the Meiji government perpetuated these assimilationist policies especially with respect to language and culture in order to deprive the Ainu of their mother tongue and their traditional manners. Using Ainu language in schools or in public office was out of the question. The severity of discrimination by the Japanese towards the Ainu accelerated the Japanization process. The effects of widespread discrimination often permeated into the home of Ainu families, where language and culture were not passed between generations out of fear. By 1900, parents and elder generations were generally found to hesitate to speak the Ainu language at home, and elders became passive about performing oral traditions as they had before.

Assimilationist policies were promoted gradually through legislation. A significant piece of legislation, The Hokkaido Former Aborigines Protection Act (Hokkaido kyū-dojin hogohō), was passed in 1899. It had the specific objective to place Ainu people within the agricultural sector. In 1901, further regulations to education (Kyū-dojin jidou kyōiku kitei) were introduced which required all instruction and educational resources to be in the Japanese

Matsumoto Jūrō

Uchimura Kanzō

imposed in 1876, forced the Sakhalin Ainu into agricultural labour. After his protests did not successfully intervene in the relocation measures, Matsumoto Jūrō resigned from the Colonial Commission.

Similar resignations were made in protest of the policies put forth by the Commission. Uchimura Kanzō, officer of the Sapporo Prefectural government (1882-1886), resigned after his concerns about the detrimental effects for the Ainu as a result of fishing regulations being ignored.

Despite such conscionable objections to colonial policy made by select Japanese officials, assimilationist and oppressive policies for the Ainu continued. The Hokkaido Colonial Commission together with succeeding Sapporo prefecture of government extended its alterations to traditional ways of living on Hokkaido, such as by implementing further measures to ban subsistence practices such as hunting and fishing.[13] As a result of such policies, the Ainu were deprived of their livelihoods and were placed in disadvantaged positions in relation to the Japanese now settled in their land. At the same time, the Government promoted development of new industries such as livestock production, commercial fisheries, and canning of salmon and deer meat.

result, the overseer assumed had become diseased and permitted his return home.[12]

Tokkaramu's struggle to return home resulted in a notable lineage in the Saru river's valley. His grandson is Kayano Shigeru-Ekasi, who would become the first Ainu member in the House of Councilors in the Japanese National Diet. Kayano-Ekasi made remarkable strides to preserve and promote his Ainu culture, from making the first speech in the Ainu language to the Diet and developing Ainu resources in his hometown of Nibutani. He is revered for having recorded folktales from Ainu elders, embarking on extensive ethnographic collections of Ainu material culture, compiling an Ainu-Japanese dictionary, and establishing a language school.

Takeshirō's writings captured the state of the Ainu as Hokkaido was in the midst of an epochal transition. In 1855, the Edo Shogunate demoted the status of the Matsumae Domain and placed the extent of Hokkaido (in addition to the southern part of Sakhalin) under its own direct administrative control. Given the geographical distance of Hokkaido to Edo, however, much of the local power continued to lie with the upper-class merchants in control of the industries.

Having achieved well-regard for his work throughout his expeditions of Hokkaido, Takeshirō was appointed by the Meiji government to serve as an advisor in the Kaitakushi (1869-1882), the Hokkaido Colonial Commission in 1869. Having extensively documented the torment and social injustice the merchants had wrought upon Ainu communities, Takeshirō took his new post with the objective of dismantling the power held by the exploitative merchants.

After only six months with the position, however, Takeshirō resigned from his post when it became apparent that the new Government would still remain dependent on the profit harnessed by the merchants and their hold on the fishing industry. The monopolies rampant in the fishing industry would ultimately not be formally abolished until eight years later in 1876.

Other officials in the Colonial Commission shared a degree of Takeshirō's sympathy for the Ainu. One such official was Matsumoto Jūrō, who was vocal about his opposition to the forced displacement of the Sakhalin Ainu to the area of Tsuishikari near modern day Sapporo. The migration campaign,

on eating the roots of wild plants before she came to Yaekoere's hut in the mountains.[11]

A Young Ainu Boy Driven into Forced Labour

Takeshirō's expeditions likewise took him to the Saru River region, another area devastated by the forced labour campaigns. Many inhabitants of the area were driven to fisheries in Akkeshi, 350 kilometers away from their villages along the coastline.

The story of a young boy of 12 years, Tokkaramu, tells of the harsh circumstances resulting from the campaigns. Along with his father and mother, Tokkaramu was forced to move away from his home in the Saru river's valley for Akkeshi. While his parents were relegated to fishing work, Tokkaramu was isolated from them by being resigned to a post in the fishery kitchen. The three family members left behind five other children, with ages ranging from 5 to 14, to fend for themselves.

Eager to escape from hard work and return home to support his siblings, Tokkaramu deliberately cut off his forefinger on his left hand. He reckoned he would be seen as unfit for kitchen work if he was short a finger. In spite of his mutilation, his overseer did not permit his return home and insisted he continue work. Tokkaramu devised another plan, this time rubbing the poisonous organ of a blowfish on his body. When his skin turned yellow as a

Kayano Shigeru-Ekasi records Ainu song by Kaizawa Toroshino-Fuci in 1966. (Reprinted from *Tsuma wa Karimono*)

The following story is featured in Takeshirō's biographical collections and is illustrative of the dismal conditions faced by Ainu in the wake of Japanese settlement.

> An old woman, Yaekoere once knew a happy life in the village of Ican, in Fukagwa. Her two daughters had married and between them they gave Yaekoere five grandchildren. Her older daughter, Peratorka, came to be subject to the lust of a Japanese guard named Toramatsu. As a result, Toramatsu ordered Peratorka's husband to work at a distant fishery. Peratorka was then forced to join Toramatsu at his own fishing post. Yaekoere's younger daughter and her husband faced a similar fate and were taken away to a fishery. They did not return for over ten years. One after another, Yaekoere's grandchildren were forced into labour either in the mountains or at different fisheries. Ultimately, Yaekoere was left alone with no one to care for her. Eventually, Yaekoere made the decision to leave Ican and retreat to a self-made shelter in the mountains in 1857. She disappeared from her home village, leaving only with an axe and a single pot.
>
> Another woman named Yaeresikare came from the Kabato Kotan, located downstream from Ican Kotan along the Ishikari River. There she lived with her husband, Irimo, an Ainu man. A Japanese guard ordered Irimo to leave Kabato for a fishery far away in Otaru. The guard then forced Yaeresikare to become his mistress. The guard had syphilis and infected Yaeresikare. As a result of her disease, she was abandoned by the guard and left without any support. Her body steadily declined and she came to lose her nose as a result of the disease. She tried to commit suicide by drowning herself in the river, but local villagers intervened in her attempt and took her to live with Yaekoere in the mountains.
>
> The women were later joined by another named Hisirue. Hisirue was 71 years old and came from Uryu Kotan. She had been cared for by her two sons, though like so many Ainu men they were drafted into the fisheries and taken from home. Hisirue had to depend solely

profound impact on the Ainu population. In 1807, there were an estimated 26,000 Ainu in Hokkaido. By 1854, this number had decreased to 18,000,[10] an overall decrease of 30%.

While he was compiling his geographical surveys and developing family registers in the region, Takeshirō attempted to reveal the misconduct and abuse by collecting the biographies of nearly 100 Ainu people. His compilation included the stories everyday Ainu folk alongside well-known figures so as to demonstrate the severity of the oppression faced by the communities. Takeshirō requested for his biographical work to be published in 1857. His extensive geographical and ethnographic records on Hokkaido and Sakhalin produced numerous volumes, but his depictions of the disparities of the Ainu people were denied publication. These works only surfaced after his death in 1912.

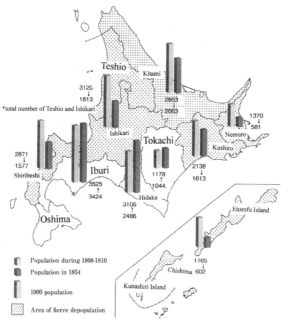

Shift of Ainu population in the first half of the 19th century.
(Reprinted from Hirayama, Hiroto. *Chizu de Miru Ainu no Rekishi*)

Matsu'ura Takeshirō: Japanese Witness of Ainu Abuse

A Japanese explorer, Matsu'ura Takeshirō (1818-1888) was a cartographer who came to Hokkaido six times to conduct geographical surveys. In his travels, he recorded the extremities of life faced by the Ainu from region to region. His writings tell of an old woman from Shari, who depicted the harsh conditions faced by all members of the community in her region. In Shari and the neighboring Abashiri area, young women (from 16 to 17 years old) were taken to Kunashiri Island to act as mistresses for the Japanese men settled there. The young men of the area likewise fared hardship. Many of them were forced into labour campaigns and never returned home. Many of these men ended their lives alone.[9] Though some Ainu were able to maintain autonomy and prosperity through trade and strategically moving to remote settlements, the disparities as described by Takeshirō were commonplace amongst the majority of Ainu. Widespread oppression and poverty were commonplace under the control of the Matsumae and Edo Shogunate's direct control period (1799-1822, 1855-1868).

Matsu'ura Takeshirō (Provided by Matsu'ura Takeshirō Memorial Museum)

With forced labour campaigns increasingly removing men from their traditional villages, only aged-women, the elderly, children, or otherwise unable persons were left in the *kotan*. The limited opportunities in the *kotan* thus made it less likely for prosperity to reach the villages. Furthermore, as the proportion of Japanese settlers increased on Hokkaido, there was an influx of infectious disease such as smallpox, syphilis, and measles. These epidemics did not have a presence previously on Hokkaido, and so the Ainu were left particularly vulnerable. The social divisions being caused by the labour campaigns resulted in an increase of unmarried Ainu men, which only reduced the birth rate amongst the Ainu. The Japanese also forced abortions amongst their Ainu mistresses. Such effects of Japanese settlement had a

falcon feathers used for arrows and even live hawks to be used for falconry in Honshu.

In the Edo period, the Japanese presence on Hokkaido was enhanced by the establishment of the Matsumae Domain on the southern tracts of the island. The Matsumae had been granted exclusive rights by the Edo Shogunate to regulate commerce and trade with the Ainu. The Matsumae would receive Ainu goods such as dried salmon in exchange for the Japanese commodity of rice. Thus, for a time all of the trade between the Ainu and Japanese was mediated through the Matsumae Domain. The Domain increased their influence by establishing trading points throughout the island, effectively dividing Hokkaido into regions based on commercial activity.

Over time, the exchange rate of goods became increasingly unfavorable towards the Ainu. The rise of such inequalities subsequently resulted in turbulence, notably culminating in the large-scale uprising in 1669, known as Shakushain's War.[7] Shakushain, an Ainu leader, unified numerous communities to fight against the exploitative practices instigated by the Matsumae. The defeat of Shakushain came with his murder at a banquet for supposed reconciliation, at the invitation of the Matsumae Domain.

Though Matsumae assigned divided regions to its vassals, gradually, the wealthy merchant class in Honshu came to preside over these regions. Further exploitation of the Ainu and the resources in Hokkaido strengthened as an increase in agricultural production in Japan drove up the demand for fertilizer. The Matsumae promoted the development of herring fisheries, from which fish-based fertilizers could be produced. Many Ainu, having already been deprived of resources in earlier trade-based inequalities, were forced into the fishing industry. Many villagers were forcibly displaced by Japanese forces in the process. The displacements and deprivations felt by the Ainu led to further uprisings, War of Kunashiri and Menashi,[8] notably in the eastern part of Hokkaido and Kunashiri Island in 1789. This conflict once again resulted in Ainu defeat at the hands of the Matsumae forces.

stage of the Jōmon period. It indicates that the disparity was somehow solved. This phenomenon was as true in other ruins from the same stage. This shift suggests that Jōmon society had a kind of mechanism to restrict, or eliminate, disparity.[5]

When viewed in the long term, it can be said that the Jōmon people maintained a sustainable society and did not create a 'country' in the Japanese Islands. Thereafter, from the Yayoi people who introduced rice cultivation to Japan, emerged a country characterized by power, wealth and disparity. Thus, in terms of maintaining a sustainable society, the probable 'choice' Epi-Jōmon people made not to introduce rice cultivation 2300 years ago would be comprehensible. In contrast, however, during the Ainu Culture period starting in the 13th century, two expanding powers, the Japanese and the Russians, encroached upon Ainu Mosir, the land of the Ainu people. The first tragedy brought about by Japanese power was in 1457, while Russian invasion of the Kuril Islands happened in 1711. Knowing the tragic destiny of the Ainu people controlled by Japanese power and Russian power, I cannot help but wondering whether the 'choice' of the Epi-Jōmon people not to accept the new wave was a good one or a bad one.

The First Ainu Uprising in 1457

The people who came to settle in Hokkaido dynamically maintained the sense of a hunter-gatherer lifestyle with probably origins stemming from the Jōmon period. By the 15th century, however, interactions with the *Wajin* began to increase. The expansion of Japanese power into Ainu territory resulted in the first large-scale conflict between the cultures in 1457. In this battle of Koshamain,[6] the Ainu maintained strong forces, consistently taking and compromising Japanese-built fortifications built on the southern part of Hokkaido. Ultimately, though, the Japanese regained strength and came to defeat the Ainu, thus securing their presence on the island.

Contact with the Japanese thus increased in frequency, and trade between the Ainu and *Wajin* prospered. From their southern neighbors, the Ainu would obtain knives, axes, pots, and lacquered wares. They would likewise export sought-after goods such as bear products (primarily gallbladder and fur),

beginning of the Epi-Jōmon period, emphasized the symbolizing of wild animals coincides with this supposition. An earthenware with a handle of a bear-like wild animal and spoons with grips shaped in the form of bears or sea mammals have been excavated from Esan Kaizuka. They prove that the Epi-Jōmon people continuously maintained a close connection with nature even after the Jōmon culture.

Recent research indicates that Yayoi culture accompanying rice cultivation did not expand homogeneously like the dropping of a pebble into a pond, even in Honshu. One archaeologist points out that an adroit mechanism to restrain communities from concentrating power and creating hierarchies seems to have been adopted in the southern part of the Kinki region.[3] There is also evidence that in the northern part of Honshu, people at one time in the middle of the Yayoi period abandoned cultivation and returned to the hunter-gathering life once again.[4]

Focusing on these cases suggesting a kind of resistance against agriculture, I cannot dispose the presumption that the Jōmon people in Hokkaido dared to persist with hunting, and not to choose an innovated lifestyle. Speaking a little more daringly, I contend that, having been inspired by contact with agricultural society, the Epi-Jōmon people might even have strengthened their self-consciousness as hunter-gatherers.

The history of Japan tells that people in the Kofun period, the successor of the Yayoi period, constructed above-ground giant tombs since 250 CE, 550 years after the introduction of rice cultivation. This indicates that agriculture brought about an accumulation of wealth accompanied by economic disparity. Persons of power emerged and in the process of gaining fortune and power, communities probably repeated wars against each other.

In reality, even the Jōmon society could not block the advent of hierarchy caused by economic disparity. For example, two types of tombs were discovered through excavation of the Karimba 3 ruins formed 3,000 years ago in the late Jōmon period in Eniwa in central Hokkaido. One type of tomb had precious lacquered ornaments and the other did not have any ornaments. However, unlike the Yayoi society, social disparities in the Jōmon period did not produce "countries," characterized by persons in positions of power. In addition, funerary goods have not been excavated from these ruins in the last

at two percent on average, whereas that of Honshu Jōmon people runs at ten percent.[1] Specialists concluded that people in Hokkaido depended on fish such as salmon and cod, shellfish, sea mammals like seals and whales, and land mammals such as deer containing rich protein. On the other hand, Jōmon people in Honshu ate mainly nuts like acorns, chestnuts and walnuts, containing an abundance of starch.[2]

I suppose nuts could be easily replaced by rice without hesitation, because it required time and labour to remove the astringent taste from acorns. I also guess that people in Hokkaido did not feel like reducing their intake of various "traditional" foods obtained through the rich resources of the forests, seas and rivers. In other words, they did not appreciate the superiority of rice to replace the natural foods they could fish, hunt and collect in the area surrounding their village.

Now, we have seen that hunter-gatherers have placed a particular value on nature and that in their lives they have regarded association with wildlife as important. It is possible to presume that there might have been leaders or elders in Hokkaido, who foresaw that they would lose something important in exchange for the introduction of rice cultivation. The loss might be not only their close associations with wildlife, but also their intimate routines like prayer to the gods, various rituals, performance of oral traditions, dancing and singing. Later on, people in Honshu, indeed, experienced a loss of these kinds of activities in the long term.

The evidence that relics excavated from the Esan Kaizuka (J: shell mound), a representative ruin at Cape Esan in southernmost Hokkaido from the

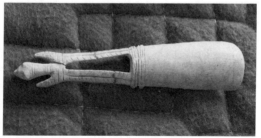

Spoon with bear like grip excavated from Esan shell mound.
(Collection of Hakodate City Museum)

Chapter 4

Historical Interactions Between Ainu and the Japanese

Having examined the difference between Japanese folk tales and Ainu folk tales, it has been revealed that the difference in lifestyle between agricultural people and hunter-gatherers forms disparate world views. The crucial turning point which brought about a shift in lifestyle in the Japanese Islands was the introduction of rice cultivation 2300 years ago. As mentioned before, rice farming techniques did not cross north of the Tsugaru Strait separating Hokkaido from Honshu. As residents on both sides of the Straits had had close contact and had enjoyed a common culture in the Jōmon period, the period preceding the Yayoi, people living in the southernmost regions of Hokkaido would unquestionably have obtained information on rice cultivation without delay. Amidst such a situation, the presumed reason for the new agricultural wave not reaching Hokkaido has been tended to be explained ambiguously by the reasoning that the Hokkaido climate was too cold for rice farming. At the same time, the Hokkaido Epi-Jōmon people, who thus did not have the benefit of innovative agricultural techniques, have historically been regarded as backward.

However, recent achievements in archaeology suggest another probability, that the Epi-Jōmon people 2300 years ago selected to remain as hunter-gatherers.

Epi-Jōmon Culture: Succession of a Sustainable Society

Archaeological surveys indicate zero evidence that Epi-Jōmon people attempted rice cultivation in Hokkaido, even in the southernmost area, a finding which reveals Epi-Jōmon people's stubborn attitude not to accept rice cultivation. In addition, physical comparison of human remains between Hokkaido Jōmon people and Jōmon people in other places makes clear that eating habits in Hokkaido were completely different from other places. For example, rate of incidence of cavities in Hokkaido Jōmon people remains

such traditions associated with hunting could state that they function to clear remorse on the part of the hunter. On the other hand, further understanding of the Ainu worldview may build connections between the essential spirit of a hunter-gathering people and their traditions.

story of the bear goddess and the killer whale god, and illuminates the central importance of man's mediatory function between the gods.

The narrator's actions to return the souls of the bear cubs to *kamuy mosir* through ritual quells the anger the killer whales felt towards the bears. Though not explicit in the story, it is understood that the killer whales are also grateful to the humans for returning their children. The human narrator likewise acts to solve detrimental problems for the bears. Humans, through their mediation, are thus awarded the gratitude of both sides in the conflict.

In the story, bear kin are exiled to a desert-like lonesome land without birds or trees.[15] In spite of their disadvantages, they can survive because of the offerings of humans, who send them food in prayer and ritual. The survival of bears in their exile is dependent upon human action.

The relationship is mutual, however, as the female bear promised to protect the family of the human narrator and indeed honored her pledge. The side of humans therefore is blessed by the guardianship of the bears. The mutual and reciprocal relationship between the bears and Ainu is established as the result of an active intervention on the part of the humans.

The story ends with the human narrator advising his own children to do their part in maintaining the mutual relationship between themselves and the kindred of bear. He reminds them of the bear goddess's guardianship, and credits his children's birth to her protection. His story serves as a will to his children, to ensure that succeeding generations will uphold the reciprocal care between humans and bears. Consequently, humans confirm their close connections with wild animals on a basis of such a reciprocal relationship.

As mentioned before, Ainu have regarded success in hunting not by individual skill, but by the belief that the object of the hunt has received their arrow or bullet as a measure of their merit. In the act of hunting, the gods choose a man and give him meat and fur as gifts as appreciation. Humans must also express their gratitude and appreciation in order to continue to receive such gifts, and the Ainu sense of morality is reflected in these principles. In the case that a hunter is attacked by a bear, he must consider if he is upholding these principles by the manner in which he is hunting. Even if it is clear that the hunter in question is clear of any fault, it does not necessarily follow that the bear has malicious intent. One interpretation of

raccoon dogs, turtles, and the ceremony for the domesticated bear. Bear ceremonies are commonly found throughout the Eurasian continent, though the customs for domesticated bears are strictly unique to Hokkaido, Sakhalin, and some areas along the Amur River region (in modern day Russia).

The Ainu traditionally take live cubs during hunting expeditions at dens in the early spring. As mentioned before, a female bear will give birth to cubs during the hibernation period in the den, so the cubs are gathered at the same time that the mother bear is hunted. After the mother bear's soul is sent back to *kamuy mosir* (either at the site of her death or back in the village), one of villagers will take the cubs back home to be incorporated into his family. The cubs will be cared for by the wife of the family, who will treat the cub like her own children, supplying breast milk and food. The cub typically resided in a cage next to the house. After two years of rearing the cub, the family will invite villagers and guests from other villages for the bear ceremony, usually in winter.

Sugimura Kinarabukku-Fuci cuddles a bear cub in her arms. (Photograph provided by Sugimura Kyōko-Fuci)

Once the soul of the bear is released into the *kamuy mosir*, it will relay to the rest of the gods how friendly the humans were and how they supplied the bear with many offerings. This message provides the gods with confidence that *ainu mosir* is a hospitable and welcoming place, and thus the gods are willing to leave *kamuy mosir* without hesitation for the realm of humans.

Sugimura Kyōko-Fuci[13] from Asahikawa belonged to the generation which reared bear cubs and let their souls return to *kamuy mosir* through *iomante*. Showing a photograph of her mother, Sugimura Kinarabukku-Fuci,[14] cuddling a cub in her arms, Kyōko-Fuci recalled the *iomante* held in February, 1977 and said, "I felt relieved when kisara (the name of the cub she reared) accepted an arrow. I was moved to tears with gladness." This anecdote proves that Ainu people traditionally have believed in the real existence of *kamuy mosir*.

Understanding *iomante* can enhance the meaning of folk tales such as the

that it is not the goddess who has the intention to kill the narrator. There is some other force which has manipulated the goddess and influenced her reprehensible behavior. Listeners of this story are steeped in anticipation for the moment when the mastermind of the goddess' actions will be revealed. By the end of the story, however, there is still uncertainty as to what drove the goddess to act in such a manner. This is an important part of the craft of Ainu oral narrative. Had the force behind the goddess's violent urge been revealed, then it would follow that there was a clear purpose prompting her to assail the narrator. If this were the case, the tension between the gods of the bear and the god of the killer whale would have been lost. An underlying intent of the story is to suggest that the bear goddess may also be a victim and that her actions may be unexplainable. Despite not knowing what drove her violent confrontation to a human man, the listeners are left with nothing but sympathy for the goddess.

The story also reinforces the Ainu view of life that soul and body exist as separate entities. This is particularly evident in the moment the human narrator releases the souls of the cubs to the son of the killer whale god. His methods for sending their souls to *kamuy mosir* are implied to be constituted by killing them, so that their souls may return to the domain of their father. Even though the killer whale god has great power, it is evident that he cannot release the souls of the cubs by himself as long as they are living in domain of humans. It is therefore necessary to have the mediatory assistance of humans, so that the gods can ultimately receive souls from the human realm.

The Day to Release the Bear's Soul to the World of Gods

The Ainu people are famed for their bear ceremony, or *iomante*,[11] which takes place after they have raised a bear cub for approximately two years at home. The above story may allude to the bear ceremony as it tells of the man's domestication of the bear cubs. Just as the man killed the cubs to release their souls, the purpose of the bear ceremony is to send the souls of the cubs to *kamuy mosir*.[12]

Iomante refers to any ritual in which the soul of an honorable god is sent back to *kamuy mosir*. This includes ceremonies for the fish owl, the fox,

return to the place where my father and mother live, with plenty of dumplings, *inaw*, and *sake*. But the killer whale god was angry with me." She told me of how the killer whale god spoke to her, stating that he came to admire her as the beautiful daughter of a bear god residing at the eastern end of the mountain. But he was ashamed of her mind, a mind he said was terrible and of ill-nature. He declared that she should no longer be his wife. He claimed that character of her kindred is not adequate to protect a human village. The killer whale god sought to exile all of the children of the bear god, to a desert-like land void of birds and forest. Furthermore, the son of the killer whale god was seeking to reclaim the two children she bore to him.

She told me she knew how deeply I had come to love her children, but it is true that the killer whale god has immense power. She asked me to send the souls of her children back to *kamuy mosir* by whatever means possible. They will then enter *kamuy mosir* and be received by the son of the killer whale god and raised with love. She said she will watch the cubs grow up from a distance.

I did what the bear goddess asked of me and I sent the souls of her cubs to *kamuy mosir*. I felt pity for the mountain gods who were subject to the strict orders of the killer whale god. I now respect the bear goddess more than ever in prayer. Now, you, my children have grown and assist me voluntarily. I have led a fortunate life and have had an amiable wife and dutiful children.

I've now told you, my children, how the daughter of a god living at the eastern end of a mountain had a temptation to kill me, yet she immediately repented and has since become my guardian. Thanks to the bear goddess, you were born. You must worship these mountain gods who are now settled on a land without birds or forest. I leave my advice for you, and I will die naturally with great happiness.

Although the main character is attacked by a bear at the beginning of this oral tale, listeners would be gradually come to know that the female bear does not have wicked mind. The poignancy of this story comes when it is revealed in respect to the human and animal relationships. This story is known as *A Bear God Digs a Den and Gives Birth to Cubs*.[10] In this tale, the leader of the village Uraspet is attacked by a female bear, though as a result of the incident he came to act as a mediator between the bear and her husband *repunkamuy*, or the god of the killer whale. This tale is told by the leader of Uraspet village to his children:

> One morning, I was surprised to find the entrance of a bear's den in my backyard. When I went back outside, this time with my bow and arrow in tow, a female bear rushed out and ran after me. I am rather swift and have hearty endurance, and so the bear finally died due to her fatigue. I carried the body of the bear back to my hunting hut and spoke to it:
>
> "What made you angry enough to run after me? I will listen to you in my dreams tonight to judge whether I shall enshrine you with respect or neglect your being."
>
> In my dream, a young woman emerged beside me. She introduced herself as the daughter of a bear god living at the eastern end of a mountain. She told about her relationship with her husband, the son of the god of the killer whale and how she came to be pregnant by him. "One day" she told me, "I suddenly felt like killing you out of anger. You have a famed reputation for your ability in running and your courage surpassing humans. Being so close to your house gave me a sudden stomach ache. I decided to dig a den behind your house and there I bore two babies. But I could not resist my sudden impulse to kill you. Which god manipulated me to commit such sinful behavior? Now I truly regret what I did from the bottom of my heart. Will you do me a favor and undertake a role to mediate with the gods for me? I will permit your return after this matter has been settled."
>
> Following the bear goddess' entreaty, I enshrined the goddess to let her soul go back to *kamuy mosir* and looked after her two cubs. Then, one night in my dream, the woman sat beside me again and confessed, "Owing to your generosity and gracious behavior, I could

taken a human out of good nature, the body would be treated with reverence and *inaw* would be offered in order to send its soul back to *kamuy mosir*. However, in such an instance, the Ainu would also remind the spirit of the bear to apologize to the gods of *kamuy mosir* for having taken the life of a human, the beings they are supposed to protect.

On the contrary, if a bear killed a human solely out of ill-nature, the corpse would be cut into pieces and left on a decayed tree or stump to prevent it from reviving. The body would not receive *inaw*.

In the event that a man was merely injured in a confrontation with a bear and his resulting wounds successfully healed, *inaw* would be sent to the *kamuy mosir* in honor of the bear's spirit as an expression of gratitude. Like other elements of hunting practice, though, the practices associated with victims of a bear attack vary from region to region.

The autobiography of Sunazawa Kura-Fuci, born in Asahikawa, illustrates the sentiments surrounding bear-human conflict. Kura-Fuci lost her own father in an incident with a bear when she was in her third year of primary school. In her region, it is customary to bury a bear under the human it had killed. Before being placed into the ground, the bear would have all of its claws and teeth removed. The bear which killed her father was subject to this custom.

Sometime later, Kura-Fuci's uncles had shot a bear in a hunting expedition and upon inspecting the bear's body, they saw that it had no claws or teeth. They concluded that this bear was reincarnate of the one who killed their brother. The uncles returned from their hunt crying with grief. However, one of the uncles had a dream in which the bear stood by him apologizing, "It was my fault to kill a human. I will never repeat such a thing, please forgive. If you carve me an *inaw* and let me return to *kamuy mosir,* I will forever protect you and ensure that you receive prey." The men believed this revelation and allowed the soul of the bear to return again to *kamuy mosir*.[9]

Man Mediates the Troubled Relationship Between Bears and Killer Whales

There is a complex folktale detailing the essence of the Ainu's inner world

Pase translates to "highly-ranked" and *cironnop* or *cironnup* refers generally to "animals we kill." In different contexts, *cironnup* directly refers to fox. The Ainu language thus has immense versatility and special words have been used in the hunting context which are not employed in daily life.

Teshi Toyoji-Ekasi, from Kussharo Kotan in Teshikaga, described the reverence one must hold for the bear when hunting, "Since the bear is a god, one must show decent courtesy and not shoot it while it is sleeping. It must be woken up with some words beforehand."[6] Anezaki-Ekasi, recalling his own hunting days, echoed this sentiment. He would not immediately pull the trigger on his gun when confronted by the bear, even if the bear was just a few meters away. Instead, he would wait until the bear would recover from its temper and find calm. At that moment he would shoot the bear. Both Teshi-Ekasi and Anezaki-Ekasi are illustrative of the reverent manner the Ainu must have when hunting the bear, their esteemed god.

To be Attacked is to Be Loved by a Bear

Hunters carry out a lifestyle following prey, though on occasion the object of a hunt may resist in order to evade death. This manifests in the animal attacking back. Such an occurrence has happened for Ainu hunters, even those well informed about animal behavior. To the Ainu, then, what does it mean to be attacked by a bear?

Miyamoto Ikasimatoku-Ekasi, a leader of Shiraoi and a revered hunter, illuminated the answer to this question by stating that a man killed in a hunt was one "loved by the bear." The Ainu believed the victim of a bear attack would be taken to *kamuy mosir* by the bear god.[7] This belief resonates within an oral tale from Biratori, telling of an attack of a hunter by a female bear god. As the story progresses, it is revealed that her attack arose from her affection for the man.[8]

Ainu hunters would thoroughly examine the body of a bear attacked humans to determine the reasoning on the side of the bear. They considered all possibilities, including self-defense on the side of the bear. Experienced examiners would be able to conclude the nature of the bear, whether it had violent or peaceful inclinations. If the bear at question was determined to have

Bears do not commence hibernation immediately; rather it is a gradual process and bears will go in and out of the dens repeatedly in preparation for winter. As its more intense hibernation period approaches, hunters could often spot tracks of dirt left by the bear walking on snow. The Ainu recognized the bear's knowledge and knew that bears would enclose themselves in the den just prior to the arrival of heavy snowfall. In the hibernation period, hunters believed they could identify an occupied den by tiny frost formed at the den's opening, thought to be created by the sleeping bear's breath.

Nemoto-Ekasi recalls a time his hunting group reached the den of a sleeping bear, a few weeks after the bear holed up for winter. The first step of their operation was to place a material in front of the den, such as a rucksack, clothing, or cloth. In case the bear emerged from the den before the other preparations were finished, the bear would go after the decoy material instead of the humans. The next step was to take a cut tree trunk, around three meters in length, and place it in front of the den entrance. This would hinder an attempt by the bear to jump out.

Sometimes when the hunters were working the bear would send a loud roar from inside. Nemoto-Ekasi said the bear's shriek would be enough to give one goose-bumps. Sometimes the bear would take a long time before emerging from the den. Then, a distinguished hunter would sit in front of the den cross-legged and pray to the bear (its *kamuy* spirit).[4] In these moments, he would send prayers echoing the sentiment that the bear would soon faultlessly be sent to the gods' world. The prayer tried to persuade the bear to come out with ease of mind.

There is great regional variation in regard to rules and beliefs associated with hunting. In some instances, sexual intercourse is prohibited before the hunting expedition. In the field, hunters must not call out to their partners by name and they must not respond if they are summoned by name by their own partner. It is forbidden to speak of the deceased in the times around the hunt. In some regions, Ainu avoid mentioning the snake and eagle, which the bear dislikes. Yae Kurō-Ekasi[5] recalled the hunting beliefs in the region of Tsurui, in eastern Hokkaido. There, if one stumbles upon the tracks of *kimunkamuy* (A: god of the bear), use of its name as such should be avoided. Instead, the hunter will state that he "found the place where *pase cironnop* has walked."

Chapter 3

As We are Deprived of Life...

The previous chapter illustrated the ideas and views towards nature the Ainu people hold, influenced by their lives as hunter-gatherers. To reiterate, hunting is not a practice in expounding skill or toughness, but rather an act to maintain a relationship between humans and gods. It is one practice in which humans justify their blessings brought to them by the gods by maintaining a certain behavior.

Ainu hunting techniques have been diverse and traditionally vary with the season. In early winter and early spring, hibernating bears would have been caught in their dens. Cubs would have been taken specifically in the spring as female bears give birth to their cubs in the hibernation period. The bear cub would then be reared for around two years at the home before having its soul sent to the domain of gods by way of ritual. In summertime, the Ainu would often use a sophisticated trap consisting of a poisoned arrow which would be triggered by a tripwire along the bear's path. Once the Meiji government established authority in Hokkaido, however, this type of trap was prohibited. This led to the last bear hunters of the Ainu, men like Nemoto Yosaburō-Ekasi and Anezaki Hitoshi-Ekasi to adopt the use of guns for their hunting tours.

Nemoto-Ekasi tells of his hunting tours, which consisted of four or five men and would typically last from December to January.[1] Each hunting trip was initiated with a prayer to gods of fire[2] and *niyaskorkamuy*,[3] the fish owl god. Together, these gods help hunting expeditions and so it is necessary for the Ainu to offer their prayers.

A hunting tour would commence with a survey around den sites in autumn, which were known be utilized by bears in the previous winter season. The hunters would examine each den and estimate the likelihood of a bear coming to hibernate in the location for the coming season. Knowledge of the bear's patterns and customs were necessary to make these judgements. For example, if the bear had not maintained the grass stored in the den used as its bedding and left it relatively untidy, then the hunters could assume the bear would not return to occupy that den site.

There I could not revive myself no matter how hard I tried. After my body decayed enough to be covered with maggots, I finally revived back into a small blue dove.

In the story of the blue dove, the Ainu demonstrate their awareness of the Japanese ontology in which souls cannot be released from the body upon death.

The relationship between the Ainu and wildlife, as it is incorporated within their broader ontology, may be summarized through a consideration of the dynamics between souls and physical bodies. Given the centrality of hunting to their culture and livelihood, the necessary respect for wildlife is encapsulated by the perceived essence of a wild animal, comprised of its godly status and a trans-corporeal soul. The delicate regard that must be given to animals as godly beings translates to practices which prohibit meaningless taking of life. Such ill-regard would surely have dire consequences for humans.

In the case that a hunted bear could not be carried down to a hunting camp or back to the village, Ainu hunters would carve a special stick called *newsarkamuy* from a nearby tree which would act as a god to talk to on the mountain. This stick would be erected on the spot to hold a conversation with the god of bear, so that the mind of the god would not be alone when the hunters descended. Such a custom is illustrative of the Ainu worldview towards the souls of wild animals.

Ainu Tradition Tells "The Japanese do not Have Power to Revive"

In a conception that supposes the integration of soul and body, death is more finite and mere termination. The same conception is extended to the killing of an animal; once the animal dies, its life is over. A familiarity with this type of ontology can enhance an understanding of the Japanese worldview, in which the body and souls do not exist separately. For example, in the tale *The Monkey Tried to Get Married with a Young Woman,* the happy ending results in the death of the monkey. As the monkey drowns, so too does its soul die. If this were not the case, in the Japanese world view the soul of the monkey would come back to haunt the family of the young woman. Understanding such a conceptualization is central to understanding this story.

In fact, the Ainu recognized the fact that the Japanese did not distinguish between the soul and the physical body. They demonstrated their understanding of the Japanese conceptualization the folktale titled *Why a Blue Dove Became Smaller*.[7] The tale begins with a scene in which a blue dove leaves the Ainu land for the land of *Wajin* to see a lord, called a *Tonosama*. The blue dove narrates;

On my way to the *Wajin* land, the god Samayunkur persuaded me not to visit that place. He tried to convince me to be his guest instead, saying, "the *Wajin* enshrine gods with strips made from paper, and so their gods do not revive into another life. I will worship you properly by carving you an *inaw* so that you may reincarnate." I ignored Samayunkur's advice and flew to the land of the *Wajin*. When I was there, I received an arrow shot by a *Wajin*.

rather as an activity to confirm the relationship between humans and the gods.

It may not seem intuitive at first that a being such as a *kamuy* returns home when it is killed by humans. This however is a central difference between the ontologies of hunter-gathering peoples and agricultural peoples.

Hunter-gatherers commonly regarded the soul as an entity which can exist separate from the physical body. The meat of an animal is seen as a gift from the god, and so the soul can continue to live on even after the death of the corporeal.

An Iskar Boy who was Carried off by a Mountain Witch[5] is a typical Ainu folk tale reflective of this concept. A woman went out to collect wild lily bulbs with her son. She laid him down in a specific place in the grass to come find her little boy later. Having been absorbed in her collecting, she did not notice that her son was taken from where she had left him. She searched and searched for him but ultimately gave up and returned home. With immense anxiety and turmoil over the loss of her child, she could not eat anything and finally died. After her soul was resigned to the afterlife, she could finally detect the place where her son was taken in his kidnapping and instructed him the route to come back home.

A common motif in Ainu traditional stories features a god looking down on his or her own dead body from a vantage point that is located between the ears of the body. These scenes are often evoked during rituals to send souls of *kamuy* back to *kamuy mosir*.

> When I recover consciousness, there is an extended body of a mountainous bear (a body of himself) and I sat between ears of the bear. Honorable chief of Uraspet worshipped (in front of the body) with two young men behind him.[6]

Souls of humans can likewise be expressed in this way, sitting between the ears as they observe their own funeral.

To the Ainu, it is an intuitive notion that the soul and body exist separately and the soul can exist beyond the time of the corpus. This theme is central to the oral traditions and such an expression is taken as a natural component of life.

"I have the sentiment that I am blessed not only when I receive bears but also when hunting small animals. Though I did not place *inaw*[3] as an offering, I made a habit out of offering grains of rice to small animals to show my reverence to them. Hunters are destined to take lives, so we are not inspired by a notion of success or competition in our hunting. Nevertheless, even those hunters who use rifles and profit off of the animals must maintain a sense of gratitude. In the event that you summon a bear, the bear will not be pleased by a superficial invitation. Indeed, this is true for humans. We have a story of a bear who wishes to be summoned by good-natured humans. These represent the Ainu way of thinking to keep a clean and moral mind in everyday life."[4]

Sense of Ainu: A Soul can be Separated from a Body

Anezaki-Ekasi's words represent an easily understood reverence for wildlife, though he may use unfamiliar language to talk about his interactions with animals. For example, when Anezaki-Ekasi speaks of "summoning a bear," he is referring to an event in which he killed a bear. This notion is central to the Ainu worldview and their relationship to animals as hunters, and will be elaborated upon below.

The gods spend their daily life in the domain of *kamuy* (*kamuy mosir*), and occasionally some of the gods of wild animals descend onto the world of humans (*ainu mosir*). When they do so, the gods take with them gifts for the humans, such as fur and meat. When a *kamuy* finds a hunter deserving of their presence, the *kamuy* will receive an arrow or bullet from the hunter as a means of accepting an invitation.

The Ainu hunter thus invites the *kamuy* to his home. A hunter or group of hunters will provide a feast to express their thanks to the gods with prayers and offerings. Just as the humans receive gifts from the gods, they too send the gods back to their homeland of *kamuy mosir* with gifts to take back. The relationship between the *kamuy* and the Ainu hunters is thus reciprocal in its nature.

Hunting then is not registered as an activity of competition or valor, but

interruption in the gods' area.

Just as Ainu demonstrate humility in entering a mountain area, one regarded as a garden of the gods, they too must feel an increased burden when they hunt bears, deer and even other smaller animals. The act of taking the life of wild animals must be regarded with serious weight. With special regards to the bear, as one of the most significant gods to the Ainu people, this creature must be considered with utmost respect.

Nemoto Yosaburō-Ekasi, referred to in the previous chapter, has elaborated on the attitudes held in the act of hunting.

"Animals we hunt should not be the targets of our stress, nor should they be sought out to grant us honor in competitive games. We likewise should not view them as something harmful or something to be exterminated for the sake of not entering our human communities. My uncle, Reiki Takushirō, taught me the following phrase: 'As animals are given to us by the gods, so we must share them with all members of our community. We must be grateful to them for living.' This means that we must not capture more than we need. When you shoot an animal, you must take care to make sure they do not suffer. It would be beyond any conception of our ancestors to sell the bear's meat for the sake of making money."

These thoughts were echoed by another notable Ainu bear hunter, Anezaki Hitoshi-Ekasi[2] from Chitose.

Anezaki Hitoshi-Ekasi hunts in mountain covered with snow.
(Photograph provided by Watanabe Sayuri)

Chapter 2

Because We Have to Deprive Life...

Entering the mountains on their regular expedition to cut trees for charcoal, an Ainu son and father were stopped by the sight of an axe and a saw laying before their coal pit. Surely they had put the tools away the day before-why were the tools laying out now? They immediately saw tracks on the snow, indicating the presence of a fox sometime before. Clearly the fox was responsible for disordering their tools for the mountain work.

It is common in many places to curse such animal mischief as that carried out by the fox. Contrary to this, however, the father instead collected twigs to make a fire and sat cross-legged on the ground. He started praying to the gods.

"Ainu ne yakka kamuy ne yakka urespa ne manup..."

He prayed, "We have no choice but to step into the mountain. I have to raise my children and must obtain money as a human. I know I intrude in your homes and gardens. It brings me great pain. I suppose you gods must raise your children as we do. Unless I work on the mountain, my children will starve. Dear gods, please consider my position and forgive my human act."[1]

The father's attitude as expressed in his prayer indicates a lack of propensity to blame animals like the fox. Rather than becoming angry at some perceived mischief on behalf of the fox, the father instead asked for forgiveness, understanding, and mercy from the gods as he entered the space to carry out his work and support his family.

This is a true story as described by the famed Ainu storyteller, Kayano Shigeru-Ekasi in his book *My Homeland Nibutani*.

Kayano-Ekasi recalls this story as occurring sometime between 1941 and 1944 during World War II. Referred as *kemakosnekamuy* (a god with swift feet), the fox has been revered as a respectable god by the Ainu. The reverent response to the presence of the fox by Kayano's father is thus natural in this context. Furthermore, more than simply acknowledging the presence of the fox, Kayano's father asked for understanding and forgiveness in respect to his

the Yayoi period these same animals were generally regarded as harmful. The development of performing arts in the 7th to 8th centuries included the theatrical depiction of animals such as deer, though in these productions the animal characters would commonly apologize for their harmful actions towards human beings.[10] Cultural trends such as these influenced a shift in general public attitudes which came to favor the extermination of certain species.

Comparing Ainu traditions and Japanese old tales, Inada Koji, a specialist on old tales, concluded the following:

> In the past, people living in Honshu, Shikoku, and Kyushu had tales similar to the old tales of Ainu and people in the Ryukyu Islands have handed these down even to today. However, tales in Honshu, Shikoku and Kyushu have developed independently. As a result, the old style of tales remains only in both ends of the Japanese Islands. In terms of origins and time of change, the shift in Honshu, Shikoku and Kyushu occurred at the beginning of rice cultivation. On the other hand, traditions of Ainu and Ryukyu Islands retain structure of hunter-gatherers' period ascending to Jōmon period.[11]

To fully understand the current state of the Ainu people and to work towards positive relations with the majority Japanese, it is important to understand the historical imbalances and injustices to which they have been subject. Much of the inequality and exploitation faced by the Ainu stems from their cultural differences from the contemporary majority, which is largely characterized from their different traditional practices and engagement with a hunter-gatherer lifestyle. The suppression of their traditional lifestyle and thus their worldview has created the foundation for their state today. By beginning to understand the values and ontology of the traditional Ainu, one may begin to formulate intercultural understanding and equality between the different cultures now living on Hokkaido.

could not stay with her human family any longer and left. Following her departure, Abeno-Yasuna would walk into the forest and call for his wife, begging her to talk with her son. Upon these calls, the fox appeared to Abeno-Yasuna in the shape of Kuzunoha. Despite Yasuna's plea for her to take care of her son, she morphed back into a fox, leaving him with the parting sentiment: "It is not only humans, but indeed all living things which are reluctant to leave their families. Despite the pain of abandoning love and leaving my child, alas, I was found out to be a fox. If I maintain my contact with humankind, I will surely be alienated from my family of foxes. I cannot bear these circumstances. It is so painful for me, but I must say goodbye. Goodbye my son, my dearest son."

Like the stories detailed previously, this story concludes with the separation of man from his animal counterpart. In contrast with tales like *The Grateful Crane*, this story differs in that, through Abeno-Yasuna, it demonstrates the desire of a human to live with the animal. Moreover, the son of Yasuna and Kuzunoha, a half-blooded fox-human, is unambiguously regarded as the offspring of Yasuna.

In his studies of folklore, Orikuchi Shinobu has made arguments for the etymological origins of the Japanese word for fox (*kitsune*) through a tale which originated at the latest in the Heian period (794-1185) and bears similar themes to the story of Abeno-Yasuna above. The tale tells of a man who encountered a beautiful woman on his way home and invited her to come back with him. They eventually married and had a child, though one day his wife likewise revealed her identity as a fox. The man did not desire to live separately, and every night would call out to his wife, "Kitsutsu Neyo! (return home and share bed with me!)."[9] These storylines have common themes for humans desiring to maintain their relationships with animals even once their identity has been revealed.

Over time, settled agricultural societal structure came to be more dominant in the Japanese Islands and the practices influenced by a hunter-gathering lifestyle began to subside. In the Jōmon period, it was known that people had great reverence for animals such as deer and wild boars. In contrast, after

A Hunter-gatherer Spirit Lost

To approach the problem of why the Japanese discriminated against the Ainu so fiercely, it is important to consider the changes of culture brought to the Japanese as they moved away from hunter-gatherer lifestyles. As agricultural lifestyle prevailed in Japanese society, hunter-gatherers like Ainu people were regarded primitive and undeveloped. However, it is important to know that the Japanese seemingly succeeded the Jōmon hunter-gatherers' culture to some extent after the Yayoi period even as they mixed with migrants from the Eurasian continent.

The boundaries between such cultural epochs are not rigid, and the deeply sedimented beliefs cultivated by the Jōmon-era people for over 10,000 years pervaded into the new forms of life that came alongside settled agriculture. Probably, the abundant oral traditions and spiritualities developed by Jōmon culture would have coevolved alongside the new social structures of the Yayoi period. Esteemed folklorists such as Yanagita Kunio and Orikuchi Shinobu have demonstrated the persistence of the centrality of wild animals in the daily social and spiritual life of peoples well into subsequent eras of the Yayoi period. However, over time attitudes towards wild animals and non-human nature began to shift, as indicated by the Japanese folktales that commonly conclude with the exclusion of wildlife from human communities.

There is a Japanese story called *Ashiyadōman-ōuchikagami*,[8] featured heavily in Kabuki dramas of the Edo period (1603-1868).

> It tells of a young man called Abeno-Yasuna, who saved the life of a white-fox in the forest. Following the rescue, a young woman came to visit him. She claimed she was the younger sister of his fiancee Aoi, who had committed suicide sometime before. This woman, Kuzunoha, was a mirror image of her late older sister, and she and Abeno-Yasuna eventually married and had a baby boy.
>
> When their son was five years old, another woman came to visit Abeno-Yasuna, also claiming to be Kuzunoha. In the confrontation, Yasuna's wife confessed to be the white-fox that he had saved in the forest. Once her true identity surfaced, she concluded that she

Age	Period in Japan	Period in Hokkaido	
500BCE	Jōmon period (15,000-2,300 years ago)		
BCE / CE	Yayoi period (2300 years ago- 3rd century CE)	Zoku-Jōmon period (Epi-Jōmon period) (2300 years ago- 7th century CE)	
500CE	Kofun period (3rd-7th century)	Satsumon period (7th-13th century)	Okhotsk culture period (5th-10th century)
1000CE	Nara period(710-)		
	Heian period(794-)		
1500CE	Kamakura period(1185-)	Ainu culture period (13th century-)	
	Muromachi period(1338-)		
	Edo period(1603-) (Tokugawa period)		
	Modern era(1868-)		

Chronological Table of Japan (except for Hokkaido) and Hokkaido

restrictions, a large number of the Ainu were forced into positions in which they had to give up hunting and participate in agricultural initiatives. Because they could not engage with traditional means of subsistence and were excluded from benefiting in the developmental efforts being carried out in Hokkaido, many of the Ainu faced economic disparities and faced extreme poverty. Despite this, however, many Ainu were able to protect their traditional values stemming from their hunter-gatherer background.

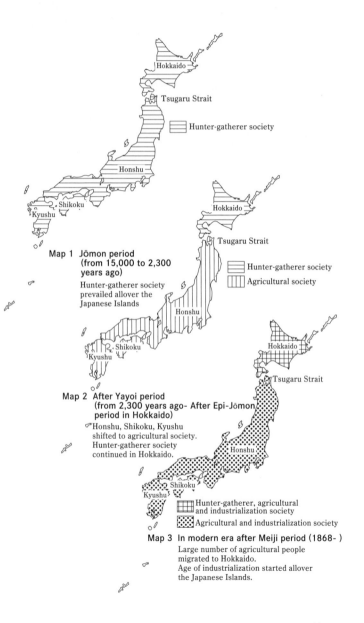

settlers from the Eurasian continent. These migrants first began to mix with native Jōmon people in the northern areas of Kyushu and southern regions of Honshu; soon, the new culture and lifestyles began to spread further in the Japanese archipelago.

Hanihara's estimates place the number of migrants in the first thousand years since the Yayoi period to be between 94 thousand to 1.5 million. Given the relatively small population of the Jōmon people, the new settlers undoubtedly had a large impact on the culture and lifestyles across the archipelago.

Following the widespread societal shift from predominantly hunting, gathering, and fishing lifestyles to rice-based cultivation, cultural values and attitudes were gradually changed to reflect the new agriculture-based priorities. An exception to this shift was Hokkaido, as new practices towards rice cultivation did not breach the Tsugaru Straits, which separates Hokkaido from the largest island of Honshu. Therefore the people living in Hokkaido were able to develop hunter-gatherer techniques further while more southern cultures converted to agricultural practices. The Tsugaru Strait in other words acted as a cultural border between the predominantly agricultural world and the predominantly hunter-gatherer world.

During Ainu culture period, the *Wajin* began crossing the straits northwards, eventually gaining a foothold in the southern part of Hokkaido.

As trade increased between the Ainu and the *Wajin*, the former were subject to exploitative trade practices. Then, the *Wajin* subjected the Ainu into forced labour campaigns, such as into the logging and fisheries industries, which further challenged their abilities to maintain traditional subsistence activities. In the period before the Meiji Restoration in 1868, they were pulled into the Japanese feudalistic system as it expanded into Hokkaido.

The 1868 victory of the Meiji Government against the preceding feudalistic regimes heightened the degree to which the Ainu were exploited and discriminated against. The new government annexed Hokkaido into Japan and established assimilation policies towards the Ainu. At the same time, the government promoted to settle down Japanese migrants from all over the Japanese Islands (Map3). These policies placed restrictions on the Ainu speaking their own language or engaging in traditional activities. Under these

"I've heard one Japanese boasting that he has hunted 50 bears individually, but we, Ainu take bears in order to share them with members of the *kotan* (A: Ainu village), so we used to hunt just two or three bears yearly for the whole village in the period when I was engaged in hunting."

According to Nemoto-Ekasi, the leader of group made a fire after they hunted a bear and the leader prayed to gods of fire asking for his prayer to be transmitted to the bear god. "We are going to carry you to our village and send you on grandly to *kamuy mosir*."

Nemoto-Ekasi's view toward wildlife does not differ from the world view suggested in Ainu oral traditions. His words provide convincing evidence that traditional worldview are reflected in traditional practices.

Today, most Ainu live in modern Japanese society in a manner different than that of their ancestors. Their lifestyles are largely similar to majority Japanese. The number of independent hunters has steadily decreased. However, this does not mean they have lost the way of thinking that was cultivated by the hunter-gatherer lifestyle over generations. Speaking with Ainu people today, one can notice their attunement and attention to nature, especially with wildlife. There is common disdain towards environmental destruction. Thus, despite changes in Ainu lifestyle in recent generations, the attitudes and beliefs towards the environment fostered over time still remain today.

Cultural Conflict Between Agricultural People and Hunter-gatherers

These three maps chronicle the historical shifts in lifestyle and Japanese dynasties on the Japanese archipelago over thousands of years.

Jōmon culture refers to a culture of hunter-gatherers dating back to 15,000-12,000 years ago and existed on the extent of the modern day Japanese archipelago (Map1). The Jōmon period lasted around ten thousand years. The Yayoi period, the age of agriculture, followed around 2300 years ago except for Hokkaido (Map2). Japanese physical anthropologist Hanihara Kazurō suggests the "double structure model,"[7] which theorizes that the end of the Jōmon period was characterized by the introduction of rice cultivation from

that I, too, will die soon. Before too long, I shall make my ascent into *kamuy mosir*.

I will leave a will for you, my children, not to leave gifts for me and my ancestors, and instead to pray to the *kamuy*. In this way, I will be able to receive any of the offerings you will make.

With this will, I will leave the human world.[5]

This story ends here, with the woman awaiting her final ascent into *kamuy mosir* to join *kimunkamuy*. In addition to rejoining her *kamuy* husband, she will also reunite with her son in the realm of *kamuy*. This story outlines that familial "relatives" can and do live between the two domains and they are expected to take on the role of connecting the two worlds together. The woman herself acted as an intermediary by having children in both worlds, both by the *kamuy* and by her human husband. As the story unfolds, the relationship between the two worlds becomes firmer and the borders between them are blurred.

Ainu Menfolk, the Gods, and the Bear Hunt

Nemoto Yosaburō-Ekasi.
(Photograph by Kosaka Yousuke)

The words of Ainu elder Nemoto Yosaburō-Ekasi[6] from Shiranuka, eastern Hokkaido introduces the relationship between the Ainu spiritual culture and its reflection in traditional practices.

Nemoto-Ekasi was regarded as one of the last bear hunters having practiced Ainu traditional style. According to him, the bear is a respectable god deserving of worship.

He insisted that when you successfully hunt a bear, you should treat it with reverence and praying to the spirit of the bear is indispensable. Nemoto-Ekasi maintains the principle that one should not boast of one's accomplishments, or compete with others.

After some time I became pregnant and I gave birth to a handsome boy. Our life together with my mother was all the more comfortable and wealthy, as the god would give me a gift each time we met. Eventually, I also gave birth to a beautiful daughter.

One day, during one of our meetings, the *kamuy* had a different tone. He told me, "Please listen carefully. I am destined to marry a woman in *kamuy mosir*. She is not as charming as you, and indeed it is only you I am attracted to. My father ordered me to get married to a *kamuy* woman once he found out about our companionship together. If I do not marry this woman, my father will banish me from *kamuy mosir* and send me to hell. Now, it will be much more difficult for us to meet as we have before. I am sure that a good young man will find you and our children will easily come to be attached to him. You will get along with him greatly and have more children with him.

I imagine that my new wife in *kamuy mosir* will be eager to have a child. Sooner or later, I will take our son with me to *kamuy mosir*. My parents will be relieved and then they will have to respect you as the mother of my son. Following this, I will come for you and take you to *kamuy mosir* as well. However, I don't wish for you to leave your mother before her death. I will arrange it so that she will ascend to heaven before you die."

In spite of what he had to say, I was angry with his words. However, I had no means to resist this fate. It was not long after we parted that a young man holding a quiver came to visit me, just as *kamuy* said. We had a good life together. He was good at hunting, liked my children, and they came to call him "father."

One day he took my son hunting and my son disappeared. I believed that my son was taken to *kamuy mosir* on this day. My mother and my new husband, however, did not even seem to be aware of my son's disappearance.

My new husband and I now have several children together. My oldest daughter has found a partner to live with. My mother died when our grandchildren were born. Since she has passed, I am sure

In part, the different cultural lifestyles and associated values could account for these different patterns in storytelling. One could argue that a hunter-gatherer lifestyle would yield more intimacy with the natural world, while settled agricultural communities are more restrictive to what lies beyond the immediate human barriers.

The centrality of the human and non-human relationships to the Ainu can be observed in another oral tale about the marriage of the bear god to a human. In the Ainu language, the bear god is normally called *kimunkamuy* (god of mountain), though given the centrality of the bear to Ainu spirituality, this deity is often simply referred to as *kamuy*.

The narrator of the following story is a young human woman who lives with her mother. Her mother was a hard worker which brought them a life of prosperity and comfort. The young woman herself was able to become incredibly skilled at fishing.

> One day when I was hauling my bounty of fish ashore from the river, I heard a sound which led me to believe something serious was about to happen. Amidst the roots of a tree I saw a huge fine-furred bear about to make his descent towards the riverbank where I stood. Suddenly, he changed into a young man wearing a fine black garment. He greeted me and said, "I am the son of a mountain god. I haven't been able to find any beautiful women in *kamuy mosir*. When I looked down upon *ainu mosir*, I saw the most charming lady here. It was you."
>
> I told him that it could hardly have been enjoyable for him to meet such a miserable woman as myself. But with this he replied:
>
> "It does not matter how you look. It is your mind which attracts me."
>
> We talked for a long while. Then I returned home, where I distributed my abundance of fish to impoverished elderly women. I felt that I would like to meet the man again before too long. Indeed we did meet and we would sleep together. He would give me many gifts to bring home. When my mother asked me where I would get such gifts, I could not conceal our encounter.

higher and higher until he was gone.

The fluttering of my husband's wings sounded like words to me. In his parting words, he told me, "Don't cry. If you love me, you must cover your head with six scarves. You may take off the coverings one by one, for each passing year. After six years, a handsome young man will visit you. You will get married to him and together you will have your first child, a baby boy. Bring up this boy as if he were my son. The second and third babies you will bear shall be brought up as the children of the young man. Eventually, you will come to have an obscure disease and die. I will then receive your soul and we will live a genuine married life in the land of the *kamuy*."

Just as he had predicted, I came to marry a young man and we had three children. As time passed, I came to recognize that I was dying. Therefore, I spoke to my three children:

I feel I am dying now and will leave you all soon. When I depart from this world, I will marry the cuckoo *kamuy*. I want each of you to know my life story.

This story can be read in contrast to the Japanese tale *The Grateful Crane*. Recall that the woman in that story was forced to leave the old man and his wife following her identification as a crane. Notably, the circumstances that lead to the crane's departure were not of her own fault; indeed, it was the Japanese old man who violated his promise when he peered into her room. Nevertheless, it is conveyed in the story that the crane chose to leave voluntarily.

When the above Ainu tale is considered, the tale centers around the young human woman having faith in her non-human husband. The story ends as the woman is dying and will move onto the next realm to have her true marriage with the cuckoo *kamuy*. An interpretation of the notable differences in thematic patterns between Ainu and Japanese storytelling, demonstrated with the two examples above, is that the Japanese folklore contains messages which promote barriers to wildlife. In contrast, the Ainu tales demonstrate a much more porous membrane between the domains of human and non-human.

pick it up for me." When the monkey approached the river to pick it up, she pushed the monkey into the water. The monkey drowned to its death as the jar filled with water. She returned home and lived a happy life.[1]

This story comes to an end with the killing of the monkey who was to marry the old man's daughter. Just as was the case in *The Grateful Crane*, wildlife comes to be excluded from human affairs.

The Mukashibanashi Type Index, a comprehensive classification of old Japanese folk tales, shows that most Japanese tales of intermarriage between human and nonhuman creatures follow a pattern in which a groom from the outside is killed and a bride from the outside returns to her place of origin. There are very rarely happy endings to these sorts of stories.[2]

In Contrast to the Japanese, Ainu Folktales Tend to Have Happy Endings

When looking into the oral traditions of Ainu,[3] a completely different worldview in regard to wildlife emerges. A tale *The Daughter Who Married a Cuckoo*[4] demonstrates this point.

The first part of the story tells of a human family being attacked by bandits. The father of the family binds his newborn baby to the eaves of his house and prays for gods to protect her. Though her parents are ultimately killed in the ensuing struggle, the daughter is rescued and brought up by the cuckoo *kamuy* (god). Once the girl is grown, she marries the cuckoo *kamuy*.

According to Ainu traditional belief, *kamuy* primarily live in *kamuy mosir* (A: the domain of gods) and cannot stay on *ainu mosir* (A: human domain) perpetually. The Cuckoo thus received messages from gods urging him to return home. What follows is the remainder of the epic, as told by the daughter in the story. An essential feature of Ainu oral literature is reciting the stories in the first-person perspective of the characters with which the story is concerned. Throughout this book, this tradition will be upheld:

One day, his shape shifted back into his cuckoo form and flew

the wild animal, they feel the need to put distance between them. This story shows that Japanese society regards such way of living as the norm.

Here we see that there is a tacit agreement and the characteristics of Japanese society come into view. Wild animals will occasionally visit the settlements of humans, but humans will ultimately not allow the animals to settle alongside them.

Agricultural people like the traditional Japanese may be said to have a tendency to adhere to notions of land possession. "Possession," in this sense means to differentiate between what is "that which I own" and "that which lies outside of what I own," which has facilitated delineations between insiders and outsiders. In particular, wildlife tends to dwell on the outskirts of the village and occasionally consumes farm products. The more wild animals harm farms, the more people strengthen their defenses, not only practically but also psychologically. Thus, people began keeping their distance from wildlife. One reading of the Japanese view toward nature is reflected clearly in the story *The Grateful Crane*.

There is also a more explicit old Japanese tale that can help us to understand the Japanese view toward nature. It is a story *Saru no Mukoiri* (J: A Monkey Tried to Get Married to a Young Woman).

> An old man who had three daughters had great difficulty cultivating his field.
>
> When the old man was cultivating his patch, suddenly a monkey appeared. He asked the monkey to help him saying, "If you assist me, I will give you the hand of my daughter in marriage." In response to his promise, the monkey assisted the old man. The next morning, the old man begged the eldest daughter to be the monkey's partner in life. His efforts were made in vain as the first daughter refused. The second daughter also turned down her father's request. The youngest did not refuse his request and asked her father, "present me a silver hair ornament and a big jar." She let the monkey carry the jar for her and chose a route which took them alongside the deepest part of a river. She washed her hands in the river and spoke to the monkey, "I dropped my hair ornament in the stream, please

Part 1: An Invitation to the Tales of Spiritual Beings

Chapter 1

The Place of Wildlife in Ainu and Japanese Folk Tales

In order to understand an ontology influenced by a hunter-gatherer lifestyle, it is first helpful to consider the worldview of agricultural peoples. In investigating this worldview, folk tales provide a good source of analysis as they provide a direct link into the lives of those who told them. A good example may be the well-known old Japanese folktale *Tsuru no Ongaeshi* (J: The Grateful Crane).

> Once upon a time, an old man found a crane caught in a trap. In a moment of mercy, the old man decided to save the crane. A few days later, a beautiful young woman visited the old man and his wife saying, "I am going to weave a piece of textile. Don't look into the room in which I am weaving." The young woman then shut herself in a room for a long while. Three days later, she handed a gorgeous textile piece to the old man that was more beautiful than he had ever seen before. The textile was valued at a high price and made the old couple very happy. The next time the woman was weaving, however, the old man yielded to temptation and decided to peep into the room. Peeking into the room in secret, he saw the crane he had saved a few days before, and it was weaving by pulling out its own feathers. The young woman, having been ousted as the crane, could no longer stay with the old couple. She parted from the couple by saying "I will never forget your mercy." She transformed into her proper shape and left them for the sky.

This story is so prevalent that Japanese hardly ever inquire as to why the crane needed to leave the old couple. This implies a presupposition that wild animals cannot live with humans, as was the case with the crane when its true identity surfaced. At the moment human families find out the identity of

I associate these acts with the rituals of the Potlatch (party) practiced by Indians in Northwest Coast of America."[4]

Another archeologist, Yasuda Yoshinori, provides a clear point.

"The principles of Jōmon were founded upon egalitarianism. They did not introduce the mechanisms of hierarchical society. They had mechanisms and systems to avoid agriculture, which ultimately did bring about economical disparities and hierarchy. To maintain their principle of egalitarianism, they have developed nonproductive activities like making large number of earthenwares and clay figures, constructing stone circles, and performing rituals with giant trees. They mainly spent energy in intellectual and artistic activities."[5]

These features, forming the historic basis of Ainu culture, have led to its sustainability over time.

I am convinced that the way of thinking specific to hunter-gatherers cultivated, in other words, "a philosophy of nature" that provides us with a compound way of seeing the world; one that offers us hints toward finding out a way to escape the deadlock of postmodern society.

*

This manuscript is consisted of two parts. The first part, "An Invitation to the Tales of Spiritual Beings," the difference of spiritual culture between the Ainu and the Japanese is illustrated through comparison of folk tales and relationships with nature. Readers should observe the grounds for cultural difference by way of consideration of the lifestyles of traditional hunter-gatherers and rice cultivating peoples. The second part, "A 10,000 Year Journey," outstanding Ainu people devoting themselves to restoring their culture and Indigenous rights in the modern era are described.

maintain strong elements of their culture and world views.

Traditional culture, such as a variety of performing arts, wood carving, weaving and embroidery, selecting useful wild plants, cooking native dishes, to name a few, have been handed down by a considerable number of Ainu people, maintaining the spirit of their ancestors. These traditions will be elaborated upon in subsequent chapters.

The essence of traditional Ainu activities has been conveyed by Ukaji Sizue-Fuci, an Ainu artist who revitalizes old clothing to create new patchwork embodying the stories and tales of her culture: "Humans cannot be considered as having a unique existence on the earth. If we destroy nature, we will not be able to live any longer. The Ainu strongly value this concept. Every morning and evening, I say the following reminder to myself 'Owing to a god of river, owing to a god of soil, owing to a god of sky, I live.'"

A description of the natural environment of Hokkaido is essential to understanding the Ainu culture. Mass quantities of snowfall grace the island in winter. In the coldest months, temperatures often fall -20℃ to -30℃ (-4°F to -22°F). This severe climate is also home to creatures such as the fox, deer, raccoon dogs, hares, brown bears, white-tailed eagles, sea eagles, sea lions, and sea otters (though the latter has seen a significant population decrease recently).

Archaeological research suggests that the Ainu culture can be traced to the Jōmon culture, which lasted over 10,000 years (approximately from 15,000 to 2300 years ago) by settled hunter-gatherers. Such a widespread and largely homogenous culture has rarely persisted for such a long term in all of human history. In their investigations of graves and associated burial accessories, some archaeologists suppose that Jōmon society had a certain social mechanisms to equalize economic disparities. Those who specialize in studying human remains subject to injury in war have concluded that Jōmon communities were relatively peaceful and engaged in fewer conflicts than other hunter-gatherer communities living at the same time.[3]

As he stood on the largest Jōmon ruins called San'naimaruyama in Aomori Prefecture, Koyama Shūzō, a cultural anthropologist, described that "valuable goods like jade products were thrown away lavishly on the mound. It also looked as though undamaged earthenwares were deliberately destroyed.

the northern part of Japanese Archipelago. According to census data from Hokkaido prefectural government, as of 2017 the population of the Ainu in Hokkaido is estimated at 13,118.[2] However, accurate figures of the Ainu cannot be determined, as many people with probably Ainu ancestry will not reveal their identity from fear of discrimination. These figures also do not factor the population of Ainu living outside of Hokkaido, which would increase the total figure substantially. Historically there have also been Ainu populations in the northern part of Honshu, in the southern part of Sakhalin Island, the Kuril Islands, and the easternmost settlements were found in the southern part of Kamchatka Peninsula.

In addition to hunting, fishery, and gathering, they have been engaged in trade both with Japanese and with Indigenous peoples in Sakhalin, China, and maritime areas of Eurasia. They exported many goods valued in this international market, such as salmon, furs, and tail-feathers of eagles to name a few. Additionally, they also practiced small-scale agriculture.

Furthermore, many of their oral traditions have been recorded and handed down. A great number of oral literatures have also been transposed into writing both in Ainu language and in Japanese. Despite widespread language loss as a result of Japanese colonization and assimilation policies, these recordings have in part allowed for their world views to be maintained.

Thirdly, the great brown bear, native to Hokkaido, is of utmost importance to the Ainu. On one hand, the brown bear has been revered spiritually as an important god and powerful being in Ainu Mosir. On the other hand, the bear has also been central to maintaining certain practices and attitudes towards subsistence.

An imperative part of Ainu history was the acquisition of their lands and subsequent colonization by the Japanese people. By the turn of the 20th century, Japan had effectively carried out its colonial aims over Hokkaido. The Ainu on Sakhalin and the Kuril Islands were subject to consistent power struggles between Japan and Imperial Russia, with the latter group being placed formally under the Russian Empire since 1711 (while many of the Sakhalin Ainu have faced forced relocation to Tsuishikari, inland of Hokkaido in 1876). Despite the harsh geopolitical conditions and subsequent discriminations to which the Ainu were subject, they have been able to

agriculture on earth.

This episode in *the Kojiki* can be analyzed as follows: the emergence of abundance of food progressed into a certain overproduction and vulgarity, and the natural grace of plant life was ordered into cultivation.

In contrast then, how might mythical world of the Ainu be read —a world in which thunder gave birth to a new life in the act of burning down a tree? In the forest fire produced by thunder, the forest was burnt and death reigned in its place. However, as the birth of Cikisani's baby demonstrates, new life will follow such destruction with time. Thus, when one examines an environment with a long-range perspective, powers like thunder and fire can cause transition and reproduction of life, like the forest. Therefore, the Ainu myth can be interpreted as telling of the natural cycles of life.

When one only compares these two origin stories, it seems there is difference in a way of thinking between Ainu- having lived as hunter-gatherers- and *Wajin* (J: the ethnic Japanese) who have long depended on rice cultivation. With this perspective, history on the Japanese Archipelago, especially when including Hokkaido (the traditional territory of the Ainu, referred to as *Ainu Mosir*) could be grasped as a friction between two spiritual worlds.

Generally, it is said that hunter-gatherers give weight the virtues of equality, fair distribution, and value individual ability. In contrast, agricultural society, especially rice growing people are said to consider collectivism and cooperation as important, and such communalization can lead to tendencies to exclude outsiders. Can such characteristics be applied to Ainu and Japanese societies?

Before analyzing this case further, one crucial point should be addressed: hunting to some may seem to be a rather cruel act, because it deprives wild animals of their lives. However, for many hunter-gatherers it is imperative to maintain a careful regard and respect for the lives of wild animals and live in ways conscious of their connections and implications towards nature, land, and environment. Traditionally, these are core values to the Ainu people.

A few general statements regarding the Ainu and their culture will be made to provide the reader with some preliminary context.

First of all, they are an Indigenous people in modern-day Japan living in

The Ainu and the Japanese:
Different ground gives life to different spirits

Introduction

In ancient times, death was required for new life to come into being.

> There is a story that tells of a long time ago when this earth and its humans did not exist. High gods of the celestial world assembled and decided to dispatch some competent gods among them down below to create land, animals and plants. As the land grew, so too did places of doom and misfortune. In response to emerging evils, the gods erected a robust Cikisani (A: elm tree) on a hill, upon which an owl would engage in a nightly watch. Cikisani, herself princess goddess, was so beautiful that the god of thunder fell in love with her. In his love for her, Cikisani was enveloped in flames and her beautiful shape disappeared forever from the earth. However, from her flames a baby came to the land. He was Aynurakkur, meaning "Humanoid god."[1]

Fire and wood are endowed with life as the originators of human beings- this is the creation story maintained by the Ainu since time immemorial. The Ainu are the Indigenous people living primarily in Hokkaido, the northernmost large island of modern-day Japan.

As a counterpart, the Japanese creation story is conveyed in the historical recording of *the Kojiki*. *The Kojiki* tells of the deity Susanoo, who was offered a variety of delicious foods by the goddess and princess Ohogetsuhime. Susanoo was curious about how Ohogetsuhime could produce such abundant and delicious food. He spied upon Ohogetsuhime and saw she was producing food from her mouth, nose and buttocks. Susanoo became angry, thinking he was offered unclean food by the princess. In his anger, he killed Ohogetsuhime. What came out from Ohogetsuhime's dead body was silkworms, rice, millet, small beans, wheat, and soybeans. Another deity, Kamimusuhi collected the seeds of these crops. These were thus the origins of

NOTE TO THE READER

In order for readers to grasp essence of the Ainu culture, concise explanations are put at the beginning of Japanese edition together with photos and English explanation.

Following traditional practice, I have written Japanese names including Ainu having Japanese names with the family name preceding the given name. Additionally, following Ainu practice, I have indicated respectable male Ainu elders with the term *Ekasi,* endemic to the Ainu language. The female counterpart to this honorific term, *Fuci*, is also used.

Specifically, the *c* symbol denotes a [ch] sound, as in chair or chisel.

The Ainu language was largely standardized in the formations of dictionaries spearheaded by Kayano Shigeru-Ekasi, Nakagawa Hiroshi, and Tamura Suzuko. Ainu and Japanese language terms are listed first in the original language and then followed by an English translation in parentheses, with an "A" to denote words of Ainu language origin and a "J" to note those of Japanese origin. Throughout the book, the ethnic Japanese are sometimes referred to as *Wajin* instead of Japanese or *Nihonjin* (J). There is a glossary of frequently used Ainu words in the appendix of this book.

Part 2: A 10,000 Year Journey —— (62)

Chapter 1 The Spirits Still Sing Today —— (62)
Sustaining Relationships Between Humans, Non-Humans, and the Land (64)
Traditions Shared Across Continents —— (67)

Chapter 2 Struggles Towards the Future —— (71)
"This Policy Would Cause Starvation to Death of the Ainu" —— (72)
Restoration of Ritual to Receive the First Salmon —— (74)
Ainu Ancestors Held in Research Institutions —— (78)
The Nibutani Dam Case as a Significant Ruling for Ainu People —— (80)
"As Ainu People do not Desert Abandoned Children…" —— (81)

Chapter 3 Ainu Culture Lives On —— (85)
An Endangered Language —— (87)
Siratcise; Trace of Ainu Hunters —— (90)
Indigenous Peoples Have a Brotherhood of Three Hundred Million (93)

Postscript —— (98)
Chronology : Chief Events concerning Ainu People since 15th century —— (100)
Glossary of main words in Ainu language —— (105)
Notes —— (106)
Bibliography —— (123)
Acknowledgments —— (137)
About the author —— (139)
**Map of Hokkaido, the Japanese Islands and North Pacific coastal areas
(on endpaper inside cover, showing approximate historical resident area
of the Ainu and locations of main museums exhibiting culture, history and
lifestyle of the Ainu)**

The Ainu and the Japanese:
Different Ground Gives Life to Different Spirits

KOSAKA Yousuke

CONTENTS

NOTE TO THE READER (3)

Introduction (5)

Part 1: An Invitation to the Tales of Spiritual Beings (10)

Chapter 1 The Place of Wildlife in Ainu and Japanese Folk Tales (10)
In Contrast to the Japanese, Ainu Folktales Tend to Have Happy Endings(12)
Ainu Menfolk, the Gods, and the Bear Hunt (16)
Cultural Conflict Between Agricultural People and Hunter-gatherers (17)
A Hunter-gatherer Spirit Lost (21)

Chapter 2 Because We Have to Deprive Life… (24)
Sense of Ainu: A Soul can be Separated from a Body (26)
Ainu Tradition Tells "The Japanese do not Have Power to Revive" (28)

Chapter 3 As We are Deprived of Life… (30)
To be Attacked is to be Loved by a Bear (32)
Man Mediates the Troubled Relationship Between Bears and Killer Whales(33)
The Day to Release the Bear's Soul to the World of Gods (36)

Chapter 4 Historical Interactions Between Ainu and the Japanese (40)
Epi-Jōmon Culture: Succession of a Sustainable Society (40)
The First Ainu Uprising in 1457 (43)
Matsu'ura Takeshirō: Japanese Witness of Ainu Abuse (45)
A Young Boy Driven into Forced Labour (48)

Chapter 5 "Ainu Spirits Singing": A Gift from a 19 Year Old Girl (51)
"Hokkaido was Our Ancestors' World of Freedom" (54)
A Humble Mediator Between Worlds (55)
Someday We Would Match Japanese (57)
Death from Misfortune (58)

著者略歴

小坂 洋右（こさか・ようすけ）

　1961年札幌市生まれ。北海道大学卒業。英国オックスフォード大学ロイター・ファウンデーション・ジャーナリスト・プログラム修了。アイヌ民族博物館学芸員などを経て北海道新聞記者に。論説委員などを歴任して現在、編集委員。アイヌ民族にかかわる著書に『流亡——日露に追われた北千島アイヌ』（北海道新聞社）、『アイヌを生きる　文化を継ぐ——母キナフチと娘京子の物語』（大村書店）、『大地の哲学　アイヌ民族の精神文化に学ぶ』（未來社）。ほかに『日本人狩り——米ソ情報戦がスパイにした男たち』（新潮社）、『星野道夫　永遠のまなざし』（山と渓谷社）、『破壊者のトラウマ——原爆科学者とパイロットの数奇な運命』（未來社）、『人がヒトをデザインする——遺伝子改良は許されるか』（ナカニシヤ出版）、『〈ルポ〉原発はやめられる——日本とドイツ　その倫理と再生可能エネルギーへの道』（寿郎社）などがある。日本語訳に『アイヌ民族文献目録〈欧文編〉』（ノルベルト・R・アダミ編著、サッポロ堂書店）など。分担執筆に Revival of Salmon Resources and Restoration of a Traditional Ritual of the Ainu, the Indigenous People in Japan. In: *Indigenous Efflorescence: Beyond Revitalization in Sapmi and Ainu Mosir*. Canberra: Australian National University Press, 2018. 69-78. 北海道新聞の北海道庁公費乱用取材班として新聞協会賞、日本ジャーナリスト会議（ＪＣＪ）奨励賞を受賞。『〈ルポ〉原発はやめられる』で第27回地方出版文化功労賞奨励賞を受賞。

アイヌ、日本人、その世界
The Ainu and the Japanese :
Different Ground Gives Life to Different Spirits

2019年5月31日　第1刷発行
2019年7月31日　第2刷発行

著　者　小坂 洋右　KOSAKA Yousuke
発行人　藤田 卓也　Fujita Takuya
発行所　藤田印刷エクセレントブックス
　　　　〒085-0042　北海道釧路市若草町3－1
　　　　　　　　　　TEL　0154-22-4165
　　　　　　　　　　FAX　0154-22-2546

印　刷　藤田印刷株式会社
製　本　石田製本株式会社
装　丁　須田 照生

©Kosaka Yousuke 2019, Printed in Japan
ISBN 978-4-86538-096-5 C0039

＊造本には十分注意しておりますが、印刷、製本など製造上の不備がございましたら「藤田印刷エクセレントブックス（0154-22-4165）」へご連絡ください
＊本書の一部または全部の無断転載を禁じます
＊定価はカバーに表示してあります

藤田印刷エクセレントブックス

〒085-0042　釧路市若草町3番1号　TEL0154-22-4165　FAX0154-22-2546

義経伝説の近世的展開
——その批判的検討

蝦夷渡り伝説は史実ではないと退けていただくだけでは、歴史学は何の力にもならない。史実は平安末期・鎌倉初期のこととはいえ、江戸時代に生成されて広まったという点において、その解明は近世史研究が行うべきことがらである。

(本書「はしがき」より)

菊池勇夫 著　2016年10月発売　四六判縦・256頁　定価1,700円＋税

ひろがる北方研究の地平線
中川裕先生還暦記念論文集

中川裕先生還暦論文集刊行委員会　編

人気漫画「ゴールデンカムイ」。アイヌ語監修を担当した中川裕先生の教え子たちによる還暦記念論文集！

2017年6月　B5判　巻頭口絵4頁＋本文200頁　定価2,037円＋税

前沢 卓 写真集　アイヌ民族 命の継承

この写真集が100年後の世界に生きる人達へ、より多くのことを伝えてくれるように心から願っている。（前沢卓 あとがきより）

2018年3月発売　A4縦・228頁　定価3,200円＋税

アイヌの神々の物語
四宅ヤエ媼伝承　　藤村久和・若月亨[訳・註]

ヤエ媼が聞かせてくれた15のユーカラ——永い年月を語り継がれた物語は、アイヌ民族の文化や歴史を学び理解を深める上で大きな影響を与えてくれます。初版はA4判（非売品）で発刊しましたが、この度アイヌ語辞典として携帯に便利なA5判（342頁）で再販・販売します。「アイヌの神々の物語」の世界にぜひ触れてみてください!!

2018年6月発売　第2版　A5縦・342頁　定価1,200円＋税

父からの伝言　　ムックリ演奏CD附属

果たして私は父や母の良き理解者であったと言えるだろうか、と今も時々自問を続ける毎日です。でも唯一父から受け継いだムックリ制作と演奏だけは今なお続けております。私の生き甲斐でもあるムックリ演奏CDを付帯したのは、アイヌ民族の文化伝承である民族音楽を歴史に残したい一念からです。
本書がアイヌ民族理解の一助になることを願ってやみません。

本書「あとがき」より

鈴木紀美代 著　2019年4月発売　A5変型版　定価1,500円＋税